Mastering Hidden Costs and Socio-Economic Performance

A volume in
Research in Management Consulting
Anthony F. Buono, *Series Editor*

Mastering Hidden Costs and Socio-Economic Performance

Henri Savall

and

Véronique Zardet

Harvard-L'Expansion
Strategic Management Award,
Paris

INFORMATION AGE PUBLISHING, INC.
Charlotte, NC • www.infoagepub.com

Library of Congress Cataloging-in-Publication Data

Mastering hidden costs and socio-economic performance / edited by Anthony F. Buono, Henri Savall, and Vironique Zardet.
 p. cm. – (Research in management consulting)
 Rev. translation of: Mantriser les co{ts cachis / Henri Savall, Vironique Zardet. c1987.
 Includes bibliographical references.
 ISBN 978-1-59311-907-2 (pbk.) – ISBN 978-1-59311-908-9 (hardcover)
1. Cost control. 2. Performance–Measurement. 3. Business consultants.
I. Buono, Anthony F. II. Savall, Henri. III. Zardet, Vironique. IV. Savall, Henri. Mantriser les co{ts cachis.
 HD47.3.M374 2008
 658.15'52–dc22

                   2008008111

Printed in the United States of America

CONTENTS

▪ PART I ▪

HIDDEN COSTS REDUCTION
AND SOCIO-ECONOMIC PERFORMANCE

▪ PART II ▪

SETTING UP SOCIO-ECONOMIC MANAGEMENT

▪ PART III ▪

TWO TOOLS FOR THE CUSTOMIZED MANAGEMENT OF THE ENTERPRISE

▪ PART IV ▪

CONCLUSION

PREFACE

This volume is a first for the Research in Management Consulting series. As research and theory building in management consulting have grown rapidly during the past several years, the series is dedicated to capturing the latest thinking from applied scholars and scholarly practitioners in this field. Complexity and uncertainty in today's fast-paced business world have prompted a growing number of organizations—profit and not-for-profit alike—to seek guidance in their concomitant change efforts. External and internal consultants and change agents have become increasingly visible in most, if not all, organizational change initiatives. Individual consultants and consulting firms have become increasingly involved in not only providing organizational clients with advice and new ideas but in implementing those ideas and solutions as well. While the series will continue to seek out and explore emerging trends, innovative perspectives, and new insights into the world of management consulting, it is also useful to look back—especially in different countries and cultures—to recapture and revisit past frameworks, intervention models and contributions.

This volume is a translation and modest updating of Henri Savall and Véronique Zardet's original work on mastering "hidden costs," initially published in French by Economica in 1987. I first met Henri Savall and Véronique Zardet in the mid-1990s, through our association with the Management Consulting (MC) Division of the Academy of Management. My first exposure to the Socio-Economic Institute of Firms and Organizations (ISEOR) and their integrated approach to organizational intervention and diagnosis began through our collaboration during a series of Professional Development Workshops on consulting skills for the MC Division. Working with them and other members of the ISEOR team—Marc Bonnet, Rickie Moore, Michel Peron, and Georges Trépo

Mastering Hidden Costs and Socio-Economic Performance, pages vii–ix
Copyright © 2008 by Information Age Publishing
All rights of reproduction in any form reserved.

(HEC)—I became increasingly intrigued by their integrative, dual focus on the qualitative and quantitative dimensions of organizational
life, and the extended role of consultants as "intervener-researchers."
After working together over the next several years, Savall, ISEOR's found-
ing director and a professor at University Jean Moulin Lyon 3, invited me
to study at ISEOR headquarters in Ecully, France during an upcoming sab-
batical. I quickly accepted the offer and was able to immerse myself in the
"SEAM" approach to organizational analysis, working closely with Savall,
Zardet, Bonnet and a host of other ISEOR intervener-researchers. Our 2007
co-edited volume, *Socio-Economic Intervention in Organizations* (Information
Age Publishing, 2007), was one result of that extended stay.

Over the years, our ongoing collaboration led to numerous opportunities for exchange and broader exposure to the socio-economic model and
its place in the organization development field. During one of our con-
versations, we discussed the possibility of disseminating Savall and Zardet's
early work to a wider audience. Their innovative framework, which is based
on their experiences in French and European enterprises, has significant
potential for our thinking about organizational diagnosis and intervention.
French enterprises have traditionally been grounded in conflict, much
more so than in other countries such as Japan and the United States, where
seemingly stronger consensus about organizational goals and objectives
provides the foundation for more cooperation and collaborative practices.
As Savall has argued, "consensus and collaborative practices in [French]
organizations must be constructed and reinforced on a daily basis through
management actions that focus on individuals who are neither an indistinguishable part of the masses nor entirely independent and self-sufficient."
If socio-economic intervention can be effective in such conflict-based environments, think of the possibilities in initially more cooperative ventures.

Savall and Zardet's work focuses on the ramifications of this reality, as
dysfunctions—the difference between planned and emergent activities and
functions—lead to a series of costs that are "hidden" from an organization's formal information systems (e.g., income statements, balance sheets,
budgets). As their insightful work underscores, as organizations begin to
accumulate dysfunction upon dysfunction, they inadvertently undermine
their performance and create excessive operation costs, with lower productivity and less efficiency than they could achieve. As you will discover in this
volume, a unique aspect of such "hidden costs" is that they are collectively
produced. In essence, no single individual is responsible for a particular
cost. At the same time, however, each individual is jointly accountable with
other organizational members for the creation of these hidden costs. These
problems cannot be reduced through the action of any individual, yet if
a single individual is missing from the improvement action, hidden costs
typically subsist. Based on their extensive work over more than a quarter of

a century, Savall and Zardet illustrate how these issues and concerns can be effectively dealt with. The frameworks, tools and ways of thinking about organizations, people and management in this volume—the socio-economic approach to organizational diagnosis and intervention—hold great promise for our attempts to create truly integrative approaches to management and organizational improvement efforts.

—**Anthony F. Buono**
Waltham, Massachusetts

ACKNOWLEDGMENTS

Since the first edition of this book, socio-economic theory of organizations and socio-economic methods of management have gained their letters of nobility both in national and international spheres. The most noteworthy marks of recognition our works have received include the Rossi Award Medal discerned by the Academy of Moral and Political Sciences (Institut de France, Paris) in 2001, the ILO (International Labor Organization, Geneva) publication of our work in English, French and Spanish in 2000 (co-authored by our colleague Marc Bonnet), and the special issue of the Journal of Organizational Change Management (United States) in March 2003 entirely dedicated to ISEOR's work. Finally, the American Academy of Management (Management Consulting Division and Research Methodology Division) entrusted the ISEOR with the organization of its first colloquium located outside North America. In a field largely dominated by Anglo-Saxon managerial thought, these events constituted unmistakable recognition of the innovative, original and robust character of the research the ISEOR has conducted for thirty three years. The last major step was the publication of the book co-edited with Anthony Buono, published by Information Ager Publishing in the United States in 2007, entitled Socio-Economic Intervention in Organizations.

Our work dedicated to the socio-economic analysis of organizations began in 1973, and was marked by the publication of *Enrichir le travail humain [Job enrichment, an economic evaluation]* (Savall, 1974, 1975). While this journey began as an individual effort, it was greatly expanded by the creation of the *Institut de Socio-Economie des Entreprises et des Organisations* (ISEOR) in 1975. The ISEOR, directed since its creation by Henri Savall, experienced relatively rapid growth—today its team is composed of more

Mastering Hidden Costs and Socio-Economic Performance, pages xi–xv
Copyright © 2008 by Information Age Publishing
All rights of reproduction in any form reserved.

than 125 active researchers, making it one of the most important center of management research in France.

This book was written with a view to disseminating the research findings that have resulted from more than thirty years of progressive accumulation. Thus, the volume is based on numerous pilot-actions representing a wide variety of both activity sectors and research issues and themes. We are therefore particularly appreciative to the enterprises and organizations that have become partners with ISEOR, often for periods of several years, in order to experiment new modes of management. Their executives, managers, supervisors, workers and employees, and personnel representatives have always accepted the constraints that a demanding and rigorous exterior intervention constitutes. Our thanks go especially to M.A. Lanselle, Social Affairs Director of the Péchiney Groupe, and J.M. Doublet, Secretary General of the National Foundation for Business Management Education (FNEGE), for the support they expressed by contributing the preface and foreword to the book's first edition in 1987.

The enterprises and organizations that have been our partners over the past eight years, including small- and medium-sized enterprises such as Gelpat and Gifa, large group enterprises including Aubert and Duval (ERAMET), Casino (Serca), Flammarion, the Chambers of Commerce of Bordeaux and Morbihan, the CETIM Technical Study Center, the General Council of the Loire, the Urban Community of Bordeaux, the Direction of Labor, Employment and Professional Training of Rhône-Alpes, and the URSSAF of Lyon, In the hospital and public health domain: the ARIMC, the Haie Vive, the hospitals of the Croix Rousse and Édouard Herriot of Lyon. Organizations in other countries include Belgium (the Clinique Saint-Pierre, Horivert Multi Small Businesses (CEQUAL), the FOREM, TEC-Hainaut, Clinique Notre-Dame de Tournai, Mutualités Chrétiennes), Morocco (RESO-RSIG, OFPPT), and Mexico (the small- and medium-sized industries of Picorey, El Retorno, Impulsora Textil, (Mérida), Grupo Mensajería, Aguacates Periban, Paulina Hotel, Integración Automotriz, (NABIS-CO), Golden Gate (COMPITE), Muebles Vizcaya, Maderas Nueva Vizcaya, INFOSID, Víctor Vela, Cremería Wallander, Alejandro Wallander, AGN Aviation, Editora Productora, Hotel Santa Cruz, Lavandería Moderna, Botanas Hebi, Super Servicio Arrieta, Tornillos Aguila, DISA Construcciones, Kaf KOALA), and two ministries of Yucatán State Government : Oficialía Mayor and Instituto para Equidad de Géneros; in Switzerland: Schilliger, Clinique La Lignière.

A number of companies have been central players in our intervention research, including: Brioche Pasquier, Belin, the Bresson Company, Fortech (Usinor), the Bourges Technical Center (DGA), Industrial Arms and Surveillance Services, Giat Industries, The Poste, France Telecom, Lenôtre, the Banque Populaire Provençale and Corse, ITS, Metallurgy Manufacturing of

Tournus, Logirem, Antenne 2, Bresson and Rande, Grasset, and the Algoe Firm. We would also like to thank the enterprises of the groups: Péchiney, Rhône-Poulenc, Thomson, BSN-Gervais-Danone, Renault, the Banques Populaires bank, Citicorp, GMF, the Caisses d'Epargne bank, CTT (Postal and Telecommunications of Portugal), Dickson-Constant, and Technord (Belgium). In addition, Générale de Protection (Protection One), Ninkasi, Institut Paul BOCUSE, the North-Isère Workshops, the Cercle de la Librairie, the National Center for Territorial Public Administration and its delegations in the Alps, the Saint Etienne Regional Hospital Center, the Civic Hospices of Lyon, the Massues Center, Les Amis de l'Atelier, MAS André Berge, the Hospital of Morges (Switzerland), and the City Government of Amiens and Saint-André-la-Côte;

Since 1988, socio-economic management has been set up in nearly 500 notary public offices (all small enterprises with from 1 to 55 employees), at the request of the Higher Council of Notary Public Offices and in partnership with the Regional Council of the Appeal Courts of Chambéry and Riom and the County Governments of Belfort-Haut-Saône, Haute-Vienne, Ille-et-Vilaine, Tarn-et-Garonne, Deux-Sèvres and other numerous regions of France. The National Foundation for Business Management Education (FNEGE) who has regularly extended their aid to us through scholarships and research programs since the creation of the ISEOR in 1975. Jean-Marie Doublet and Jean-Claude Cuzzi, in the capacity of Secretary General, have both played particularly active roles in the development of research conducted by the ISEOR. The Ministry of Industry and Research has sponsored our initiatives since 1980. The Order of Public Accountants, for their special support and the confidence they have shown us for nearly twenty-five years, both the Higher Council and the Regional Council of Rhône-Alpes, of Île de France, of Aquitaine, as well as BDO Gendrot Consultants and In Extenso (Deloitte & Touch), Groupe Uni Expert, Rostan Dyen, CCI-Conseils, the Comec Group, and many others, including Construction, Urban and Literacy Planning authorities, who have regularly contributed exceptional support.

Maurice Bernadet, Philippe Lucas, Michel Cusin and Bruno Gelas, the successive presidents of the University Lumière Lyon 2 as well as Dean Paul Rousset, founder of the University Lumière Institute of Technology, have all actively supported our work and the development of the innovative academic programs we have created. We also express our deep gratitude to Roger Delay-Termoz, Deputy Director of the Graduate Business School Group of Lyon until 1994, whose loyal support was so vital to developing the ISEOR.

Finally, it should be remembered that this book is the fruit of intense teamwork, on the part of researchers who, through their direct action inside enterprises, through their academic work (theses, research papers) and through their publications, have contributed to developing the socio-economic theory and analysis based on the scientific experimental procedure. Our thanks go particularly to the present intervention-research team: Marc Bonnet, Isabelle Barth, Vincent Cristallini, Olivier Voyant, Laurent Cappelletti, Miguel Delattre, Nathalie Krief, Emmanuel Beck, Philippe Benollet, Florence Noguera, Karine Rymeyko, interveners in charge of research; Nouria Harbi, Michel Grivel, Georges Aublé, Jeannette Rencoret, Djamel Khouatra, Frantz Datry, Julien Henriot, Françoise Goter, Sébastien Payre, Renaud Petit, Emmanuelle Rey, Floriane Bouyoud, Elodie Brigeot, Samia Khenniche, Messaouda Larayedh, Sofiane Seghier, Simone Khamx-ay, the team's intervener-researchers; Michelle Bonnard, Raymonde Bro-card, Cécile Ennajem, Delphine Fauré, Nadège Joly, Bertrand Marmond, Irène Pérani, Cendrine Portejoie, Paméla Vihel, members of administrative and management services. We also extend our thanks to our colleagues Jean-Pierre Algoud and Isabelle Géniaux who have joined our teacher-researcher team.

Many young researchers and PhD students, having passed several years of their career at the ISEOR, today have responsibilities as teacher-researchers. Among them we particularly thank, in France: University professors Thierry Nobre and Jean-Michel Plane, associate professors Sandra Bertézène (Annecy); Marie-Christine Chalus (Lyon 1), Caroline Faure (Toulon), Manuel Garcia (Saint-Etienne), Stéphane Leymarie (Metz), Pascal Moulette, Melchior Salgado (Lyon 1), Evelyne Tillet (Clermont-Ferrand), Odile Uzan (Paris) and professors from Business Schools and other Academic institutions: Stephan Bourcieu, Rodolphe Ocler, Pascal Colin, Patrick Haim and the regretted Philippe Pétiau. Abroad, in Tunisia, Radouane Bensalem, Mansour Mrabet, Hatem Kammoun, Raouf Bouguerra, Sami Boussofara, Mohamed Triki; in Brazil, Marcelo Lima; in Morocco, Abdel Majid Aman and Mustapha Lahlali; in Burundi, Gervais Nkanagu and Hercule Yamu-rémie; in Angola, Kiamvu Tamo; in Mexico, Martha Fernandez, Lourdes Brindis, Brenda Briones, Gerardo González, Claudia González, Mario Ibarra, Griselda Martínez, Laura Peñalva, Silvia Pomar, Hilda Ramírez, Victor Sánchez and the regretted Oscar Enriquez; in Switzerland, Eric Davoine and Chantal Thouverez; in the United States, Mark Hillon.

Regarding our "adventure" in the United States (operation baptized *Lafayette 2000* and then *Lafayette 2010*), our gratitude is addressed first to the members of our French team, Marc Bonnet and Michel Péron, assisted by Monique Péron, Rickie Moore, Jacques-Henri Coste and Georges Trépo (HEC). Our action in the United States and the presentation of the ISEOR's work at the annual conventions of the Academy of Management (AOM) since 1998 (San Diego, Chicago, Toronto, Washington, Denver, Seattle, New Orleans, Hawaii, Atlanta and Philadelphia) could not been carried out so rapidly and efficiently without the support of Marilyn Harris, Guilan

Wang and Randy Hayes (Michigan), Tony Buono (Massachusetts, past chair of the Management Consulting Division, AOM), David Boje (New Mexico and past chair of the Research Methods Division, AOM) and Grace-Anne Rosile, as well as Terri Scandura and Herman Aguinis (Florida and Colorado, past chair of the Research Methods Division, AOM).

At the ILO, we are indebted to Pierre Trémeau, M. Maertens, M. Retournard, M. Henriques and Pierre Hidalgo for their constant support in promoting socio-economic management among member countries of the International Labor Organization. Last, but not least, we thank Gilles Guyot and Guy Lavorel, successive presidents of the University Jean Moulin Lyon 3, as well as our incumbent President Hugues Fulchiron for opening the doors of the University and its Institute of Business Administration (IAE) to welcome our team of 15 professors and associate professors from the ISEOR and EUGINOV (Ecole Universitaire de Gestion Innovante) having requested their transfer from the University Lumière, thus permitting us to pursue our creative action in favor of innovative management research and education, in view of intensified national and international development.

We would also like to express our recognition to the CEOs and directors of the 1200 businesses, organizations and institutions (such as Serge, Louis-Marie and Pascal Pasquier, Henri Talaszka, Michel Foucard, Jean-Pierre Méan, Jean Caghassi and Bernard Richerme) that have granted us their confidence, as well as to the managers and personnel in 34 countries, with which we have co-produced the concepts, tools and methods that have come to be called *socio-economic management* of enterprises and organizations. Special thanks to Michel Péron (University of Paris-Sorbonne Nouvelle), a specialist of Anglo-Saxon civilization who played an essential role in the breakthrough of ISEOR research in the United States and whose help was most valuable for the final editing of ISEOR publications in English.

—**Henri Savall**, Director of ISEOR
Véronique Zardet, Co-Director of ISEOR
University Professor of Management Sciences
Laureates of the Academy of Moral and Political Sciences
(Institut de France)

REFERENCE

Savall, H. (1974, 1975). *Enrichir le travail humain: l'évaluation économique* [Job Enrichment, an economic evaluation]. Paris: Dunod.

INTRODUCTION

When this book was initially published in 1987, the emergency was saving businesses and jobs. Most business strategies were quite alarming, based on downsizing, labor shedding, and cuts and withdrawal, in a word based on defensiveness. Today, while the context may have changed in an era of globalization and hyper-competition, such defensive strategies are still all too commonplace. Such strategic helplessness may result from errors in strategic analysis and misunderstandings of the underlying sources of economic performance.

An enterprise is a strategic vehicle of sorts, one that has lost too much momentum from internal and external hemorrhage caused by the multiple dysfunctions that occur on a daily basis. Since 1976, we at the Socio-Economic Institute of Firms and Organizations (ISEOR) have been working on the development of a method of change management—referred to as socio-economic management, precisely because it consists of simultaneously improving the enterprise's economic and social performance.

Many firms, from a wide range of business sectors, have implemented innovative actions to reduce their dysfunctions and hidden costs. From among these actions, one approach has proved to be particularly fruitful. It consists of enhancing the development of actual *human potential,* instead of accumulating fleeting competencies, so striking is the difference between the potential skills individuals possess and the jobs they are actually entrusted with.

As soon as one considers reducing hidden cost, one is confronted with the question of reallocating the economic resources and human potential thus recovered. The most favorable strategic situation is, of course, that of growth, for it allows the enterprise to increase both its economic and social performance. Employment does not decline, it can even increase if growth

Mastering Hidden Costs and Socio-Economic Performance, pages xvii–xxvi
Copyright © 2008 by Information Age Publishing
All rights of reproduction in any form reserved.

is sufficiently strong and enduring, while employment conditions improve, qualitatively and financially speaking.

At the other extreme is a firm in a saturated market, in the phase of maturity or even decline. In this case, the pursuit of economic performance entails lowering employment, if one is not careful, and then lowering the hourly volume of activity, by recovering hours through hidden cost reduction. However, in recent years, business practices have been observed that resolutely aim at maintaining consistent levels of employment. Companies seek to improve or restore economic performance through the reduction of external costs, and not through the reduction of wage costs.

Strategies other than those involving downsizing are also possible. For example, adopting a persevering rhythm of small-dosed, yet constant hidden cost reduction efforts offers the double advantage of avoiding brutal employment reductions and affording time for the firm to work out new strategic scenarios of development through new markets, new products and new services.

The socio-economic management tools we have developed in numerous businesses and organizations allow reconsidering the firm's organization and services every six months, in view of the coming quarter(s), through priority action plan preparations. This makes it possible to perform light, small-scale redesigns to ensure progress, through successive modifications of job content, making the most of every individual's potential while preparing them for technological and professional development and allowing everyone time to progressively adapt their professional behavior.

It is thus a question of resisting strategies that attempt to maximize immediate and short-term economic results, in order to allocate part of the enterprise's human resources to ~~potential creation~~ activities, that is, commercial development activities, as well as technological and socio-organizational innovations that produce economic performance one or two years further on. We therefore advocate strategies of active, incisive development that stop the lowering of salaries by pursuing dynamic, incentive-based policies. Thanks to a number of firms having succeeded in this, we have been able to prove that salary hikes finance themselves through hidden cost reductions, and that this is precisely the indispensable condition in a firm implementing long-term economic improvement strategy. Indeed, employees sustain their acceptance of efficient change processes when a reward is offered them, other than the qualitative, psychological advantages engendered by the change.

Improvement of the firm's competitiveness, profitability and/or economic and social efficiency can no longer be obtained merely by accumulating financial, technological and human resources, or working hours. Social and cultural evolution in daily living environments and in working environments has made coercive management styles increasingly inoperative. Employees are protected in the business environment by legislation, by government social and economic intervention, and by public opinion and pressure groups. They no longer accept to work under any conditions, or to obey any organizational "game" rules. As relatively well-respected citizens and consumers, employees want to be professional producers who are valued and taken into consideration in their organizations.

When this rule of professional consideration is not taken into account, the enterprise accumulates dysfunction upon dysfunction, counter-performance, excessive operation costs, and insufficient productivity or efficiency. These are *hidden costs*. What is unique about hidden costs is that they are collectively produced; no single individual, in particular, is responsible for a particular cost. Inversely, each individual actor is jointly liable with other individuals for the production of these hidden costs. These hidden costs cannot be reduced through the action of one single individual, yet if one single individual is missing from the improvement action, hidden costs subsist. Therefore, it is futile to seek solutions for improving the firm's efficiency by asking one volunteer or group of volunteers to say what is good for the enterprise as a whole (as found, for example, in quality circles). The firm's performance results from an efficient combination of the behaviors of *all* company actors. Improvement must stem from a coordinated series of actions throughout the firm. Pilot experiments have shown that this approach is feasible, efficient and preferable to other approaches, as confirmed by those who have adopted it. Indeed, the framework presented in this volume offers a synchronized plan of action, admittedly demanding, yet intelligible for company actors. Our experience has shown that they accept these demands because they perceive the professional rewards they offer, through personal growth in their skills and competencies, which traditional organization demands they leave behind when they get to work in the morning.

This synchronization, of course, is very demanding for all actors: for the CEO, whose management style and work methods are examined; for top management who often must furnish the same effort and accept taking intensified initiatives and responsibilities; for intermediate managers who must also furnish comparable effort as well as developing their pedagogical function towards the group for which they are responsible; and for supervisors who must keep up with corresponding evolutions if they are to avoid being eliminated by the increasing levels of competency among workers and employees.

The overall elevation of competency levels among *all* company actors is the fruitful, yet difficult, path to rebuilding businesses and organizations, no longer guided nor protected by nearly century-old Fayol-Taylor doctrine. This is why only a personal, contractual approach to management, coordinating a decentralized network of intelligent actors, who are conscious of their power and their limits, can create the foundation for competitiveness, profitability and company efficiency, as well as to ensure the quality of its products.

The legitimacy, or the *raison d'être*, of an individual effort toward greater professional rigor, toward enhancing everyone's professionalism, resides in the group effort of all the actors who compose the organization. The individual who, in a *personalized management* company, refuses to play the game of community interest—in a community he or she has chosen to work in—can hardly maintain a place in that organization. Can other actors, regardless of their position in the power structure, tolerate such deviance in the face of intense economic competition? When faced with this question, with this problem, all businesses and organizations are alike. All must find an answer, be they family-owned SME's, business partnerships among friends, large national firms, government agencies, hospitals, city governments or other public administrations.

World economic crisis has the merit, perhaps, of recalling the ancient but sound principle of economic efficiency, founded on the respect of resources too rare to accommodate the insatiable human appetite, always hungering for new satisfactions, for "progress." What was striking about the 1980s in France was the appearance of a generalized consensus on the refusal to waste resources, a widespread, spontaneous accord occurring in all social groups and affinity networks. This was a new phenomenon, opening hopeful perspectives on the modernization of French management. The socio-economic management approach we conceived thirty three years ago, and which we have unceasingly constructed and perfected through real-life experimentation in real businesses, and not through utopian reverie, is *one* possible response to the challenge firms and organizations are continuing to face. Coming out of numerous research projects, both basic and applied, carried out in France with French actors, socio-economic management claimed its own identity, without excluding other contributions (foreign countries of reference), emancipating itself from the vice of imitation, importation, translation and modestly seeking its own legitimacy in the economic feasibility of its experimentation in France's socio-cultural environment. Our present day efforts focus on expanding this influence to a wider English and Spanish speaking world. Contrary to Anglo-Saxon management—notably American or Japanese approaches—socio-economic management does not presuppose peace and social consensus. Rather it constructs them, with a state of conflict as its startingpoint, recognized as such and not eluded.

AN OVERALL APPROACH TO EFFECTIVENESS AND EFFICIENCY

Product quality first appeared in socio-economic analysis in 1974 as a hidden cost indicator. A cost is said to be hidden when it does not explicitly appear on the company information system, such as the budget, financial accounting and cost accounting, or in usual ledgers and logbooks. Our method of hidden cost analysis in an organization includes five socio-economic indicators: absenteeism, industrial injuries, staff turnover, product quality (goods and services) and direct productivity (product quantity).

The first experimentation by ISEOR on quality-related hidden costs began in 1976 and was followed by numerous in-depth research projects on quality in industrial firms, for-profit service companies and public service agencies, of different sizes and in various locations in France. This experimentation led to the formalization of a diagnostic method, a piloting method for quality improvement actions, and an evaluation method for the results of such actions. The concepts, ideas and findings presented in this book are based on experimental research carried out by nearly 450 intervener-researchers over 33 years and representing 1,000,000 hours of research work of which almost 650,000 hours were spent in the field, inside businesses, organizations, factories, offices and workshops.

Innovative Socio-Economic Management

Innovative socio-economic management, created and experimented by ISEOR, is a mode of management that closely associates the social aspect of a firm with its economic performance. It includes overall management methods founded on the firm's human development as the principle factor of short-, medium- and long-term efficiency. Socio-economic management of organizations is based on a theoretical construction called socio-economic analysis and set up in businesses and organization through an intervention method referred to as *socio-economic intervention* (see Figure I.1).

An enterprise is considered to be a complex entity where five types of structures (physical, technological, organizational, demographic and mental) interact with five types of human behavior (individual, activity group, categorical, affinity group and collective). This constant and complex interaction creates a pulse of activity, which constitutes the enterprise's operation. However, one can observe certain abnormalities, disturbances and discrepancies between the desired operation and the actual operation. These gaps are *dysfunctions* that can be classified into six categories: working conditions, work organization, time management, communication-coordination-cooperation, integrated training and strategic implementation. These six families constitute both explicative variables of dysfunctions and domains of solutions for the dysfunctions identified during the diagnostic of the enterprise. As illustrated in Figure I.2, these dysfunctions generate hidden costs that affect the firm's performance.

Socio-Economic Diagnostic of Organizations

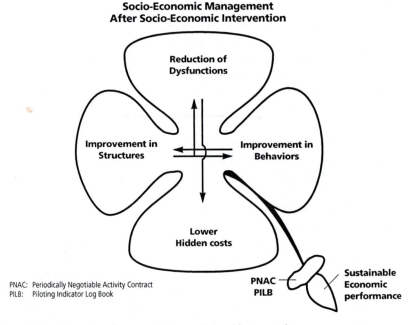

Dysfunctions
- Working conditions
- Work organization
- Communication-coordination-cooperation
- Time management
- Job training
- Implementation of the strategy

Structures
- Physical
- Technical
- Organizational
- Demographic
- Mindsets

Behaviors
- Individual behaviors
- Business departments
- Socio-profesional categories
- Affinity group
- Organization taken as a whole

Hidden costs
- Absenteeism
- Industrial accidents
- Personnel rotation
- Poor product or service quality
- Direct productivity losses

Atrophied
SIOFHIS

SIOFHIS:
Humanly integrated and stimulating operational and functional information system

Atrophied Economic performance

Socio-Economic Management After Socio-Economic Intervention

Reduction of Dysfunctions

Improvement in Structures

Improvement in Behaviors

Lower Hidden costs

PNAC: Periodically Negotiable Activity Contract
PILB: Piloting Indicator Log Book

PNAC PILB

Sustainable Economic performance

Figure I.1   The socio-economic diagnostic and intervention.

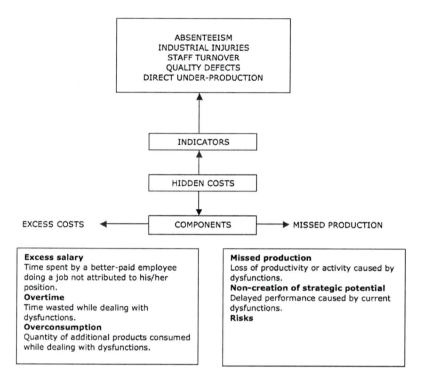

Figure I.2 Hidden costs and performance.

Dysfunctions engender costs for the firm, which are usually "hidden." These hidden costs affect the firm's economic performance and they are made up of six components. The first three constitute overhead the firm could avoid, or at least reduce, if its dysfunction level was lowered. These overhead-related costs include *excess salary* (or compensation paid without work in exchange, e.g., in certain cases of absence), *overtime* or time wasted (paid time spent correcting dysfunctions instead of performing saleable production), and *overconsumption* (e.g., energy consumption, raw materials or supplies consumption levels that would be lower if the firm had fewer dysfunctions to correct). The fourth component of hidden costs is particular in nature, for it doesn't represent a tangible cost, but rather a "non-product" or a *loss of production sales* (i.e., occasions missed to make or sell a product, opportunity costs). In the same way, the fifth component represents the value of investments, especially immaterial investments, that the firm could have made or self-financed, that is, the opportunity cost of *non-creation of strategic potential.* The sixth component designates the *risks* the firm faces caused by certain dysfunctions or due to the overall level of general dysfunction.

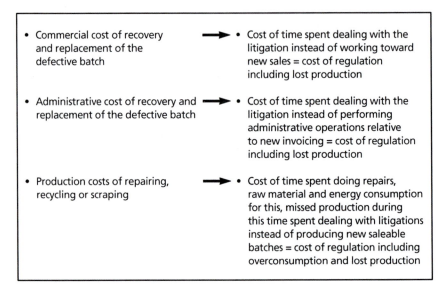

Figure I.3   Quality defects and non-quality hidden costs.

Figure I.3 applies this schema to the case of quality defects, such as those found in a defective batch of merchandise, with the non-quality costs illustrated in the right-hand column. These non-quality hidden costs diminish the potential economic performance of the firm, which would have been greater if the firm had been able to avoid these quality dysfunctions.

Socio-economic theory can be summarized with the aid of the two schemas. Research in socio-economic management, tested inside organizations, has shown that only an overall approach to the enterprise is capable of a) explaining the levels and mechanisms of economic performance and b) inspiring sustainable improvement actions for this economic performance.

The Double Image of Quality

Our conception of *socio-economic strategy* distinguishes two relevant environments for company strategy: the *external environment* (the marketing territory) and the *internal environment* (the usual territory of personnel management and operations management). In reality, socio-economic strategy strives to reconnect these two environments by extending a marketing approach to the internal environment.

There are two definitions and two levels of quality evaluation: *external quality*, judged by the consumer in the external environment, and *internal quality*, judged by the producers of quality, within the enterprise. The two do not necessarily coincide, for some companies can only attain high external quality at the price of controlling and regulating very expensive dysfunctions. This is what happens when a firm succeeds in attaining a good external image for its product due to severe and costly controls, even when the staff is aware that time and resources must be invested in detecting quality defects before delivering the products to clients. ISEOR's diagnostics have shown that the *internal image* of quality in this case is "poor" to "bad," even though the *external image* is satisfactory, even very satisfactory, but at an *exorbitant manufacturing cost.*

Product Quality and Company Efficiency

The comparative analysis of the firm's external environment and its internal environment reveals a certain discrepancy between production modes and the evolution demanded by consumers. Several indicators permit tracing the evolution of these exigencies:

- Increased demand for external quality, expressed by the consumer in direct or oblique manner through increased competition among firms regarding quality criteria;
- Increased demand for rapid market response, reduced delivery delays and greater product differentiation, provoking shorter series that seriously undermine the classical rules of launching and organizing production and generally disturb optimal cost calculations;
- Increased price competition for an equivalent degree of quality; and
- The imperative to reduce the company's financial charge, leading to reduced levels of inventories, credits and storage expenses.

These considerations alone are enough to show the fuzzy boundary between the concept of quality and the concept of efficiency. Our experience in enterprises has shown that there is continuity between *product quality* and *operation quality*, grouped together in the concept of *overall internal efficiency* of the firm (see Figure I.4). This conclusion argues in favor of two axioms:

- Anchoring the notion of quality in that of efficiency: In socio-economic analysis, the two indicators "quality" and "direct productivity" are tightly embedded and constitute what we shall call the overall effectiveness or integral quality of the firm.
- Promoting a considerable evolution in production conditions, in order to adapt to the external environment (notably consumer demands) and the internal environment (personnel-producer demands for quality).

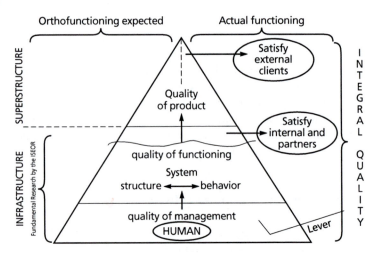

Figure I.4   Integral quality.

Our research and experimentation have shown us that quality and efficiency improvement actions should be part of the company's overall strategy and be decided and steered from the very highest level of the enterprise, that is, by the top managers themselves. Indeed, the stakes of socio-economic development actions are two-fold: a) conquering, re-conquering or defending market shares and b) releasing new profitability and self-financing margins within the firm. Despite the interest of specialized quality approaches, which most often are conducted by internal specialists (e.g., heads of quality control, technical directors, production managers), our experience has demonstrated that the effectiveness of these approaches and these company specialists depend more on the *strategic positioning of quality and efficiency improvement actions*, meaning at the very level of executive direction.

· PART I ·

HIDDEN COSTS REDUCTION AND SOCIO-ECONOMIC PERFORMANCE

An operational method of hidden cost calculation was created, refined and implemented in various enterprises by the ISEOR. This method was developed out of the observation that accounting information systems do not bring to light certain costs, which are nonetheless sustained by enterprises. Existing information systems simply do not allow either surveying or a fortiori reducing these costs. It has become customary to refer to these costs, which are not brought to light, "hidden costs." These costs, however, do exist.

The first "evidence" that these costs exist is the intuition that business executives share about them. As an example, an electronics industry official realized—after having invested 15 million Euros in technological improvements—that the firm's efficiency and profitability had not improved. In other words, the earnings expected from the technological improvements were absorbed, literally "swallowed up" by additional costs the firm could neither identify nor master. Such intuition is also triggered by rough estimates of organizational problems. An enterprise with a very high rate of absenteeism, for instance, can empirically deduct that this absenteeism is very expensive, but without knowing how much it is actually costing the firm.

A second type of evidence that attests to the existence of unidentified costs is provided by enterprises that, after having implemented innovation

Mastering Hidden Costs and Socio-Economic Performance, pages 1–6
Copyright © 2008 by Information Age Publishing

1

actions, succeed in operating at lower costs. Thus, it appears that such focused actions can make it possible to reduce certain operating costs.

Finally, a third type of proof is of a more theoretical nature. The study of macro- and micro-economic analyses reveal a "residue," a portion of the enterprise's profits or losses that cannot be explained by quantities of capital and labor, which constitute the variables notably emphasized in the so-called production function economic models. In other words, the explicative model chosen does not hold up to facts, indicated by the "residue" which remains inexplicable in this type of theory.[1]

ISEOR has based more than thirty years of work on these observations, developing and implementing business change strategies that are planned and then *evaluated* by businesses themselves (Savall, 1975). In order to achieve this, the ISEOR devoted a first work phase to constructing an operational method of hidden cost calculation, in order to equip its research center with relevant tools for evaluating technological and organizational innovation strategies (see Savall, 1979). This first work phase produced two results: a) a methodological "product," the operational method of hidden cost calculation; and b) a substantive "product," the amount of hidden costs calculated by applying the Hidden Cost Calculation Method in different types of enterprises. These results on hidden costs thus constituted basic data offering multiple applications, both for researchers as well as private business practitioners or public decision-makers.

This section presents a) the nature and origins of hidden costs and their stakes, which reside in the search for pockets of under-efficiency in enterprises, b) an operational method of hidden cost calculation, and finally c) the findings of hidden cost assessment in different enterprises.

THE STAKES OF HIDDEN COSTS: SEARCHING FOR THE ENTERPRISE'S POCKETS OF UNDER-EFFICIENCY

Why is it that enterprises do not calculate their hidden costs, since they intuitively know they exist. In our opinion, there are two main reasons: the lack of adequate measurement tools and the existence of socio-organizational resistance.

Adequate Measurement Tools

The method we developed for detecting hidden costs has made it possible for us to observe the inadequacy of existing management tools, notably accounting information systems. These tools are poorly adapted, first of all, because hidden costs are *diffused and dispersed* throughout the entire enterprise. They are generated by all actors' activities, in all workshops, offices and departments. However, information systems are often not conceived to measure phenomena to the smallest unit in the enterprise—the individual. Information systems are usually limited to collecting information at the level of work units and departments, minimally containing several dozen people.

Accounting information systems are also based on nomenclature that does not include the essential hidden cost categories. General accounting assesses costs by their nature (e.g., personnel costs) and object (e.g., production department, x product), while hidden cost calculation proceeds through what could be called *"agent" or "actor" accounting*. It calculates cost generated by the productive activity of an agent, regardless of object and nature.[2]

Socio-Organizational Resistance

The absence of measurement tools is a cause of technical order, which results from causes of a higher order. Hidden costs, by their very diffused and dispersed nature, question the professional behavior of all individuals in the enterprise—shopfloor workers, office workers, supervisors, intermediary staff, executive management, top management, shareholders, personnel representatives and so forth. One can thus observe a sort of "tacit" complicity, often unconscious, among the different sectors of the enterprise, in maintaining hidden costs. Why calculate hidden costs if there is not a will to master them?

As with any voluntary action, hidden cost reduction action requires liberating time and developing decision-making energy, then applying those decisions and ensuring they are respected by all company actors. This resistance is complicated by the fact that such decisions often involve major stakes, both for the enterprise itself as well as at the macro-economic level. Thus, hidden cost evaluation might lead to the conclusion that one third of the personnel is occupied with unproductive or "parasitic" activities, caused by the current level of dysfunctions. These dysfunctions, however, are susceptible to socio-organizational innovations. The problem can thus be posed in terms of reducing the number of employees to eliminate parasitic tasks, in the case where the enterprise cannot envisage in the short-term a commercial recovery matching its current production capacity. Hidden costs are not hidden by accident. However, their calculation can be of great interest.

Hidden Cost Calculation

Detecting and calculating hidden costs enable a thorough examination of the enterprise's efficiency level, or more precisely, explaining the differences between desired efficiency and actual efficiency, or between two units of the same enterprise or two enterprises of the same group or in the same business sector. Explaining hidden costs essentially serves the objective of *transforming enterprises*. Hidden costs, once detected, make it possible to engage in a process of seeking out solutions for greater efficiency. The *short-term* objective is to *increase the enterprise's profitability*, or in the case of public agencies, to better balance and respect their budget. In the *long-term*, the economic stakes are the *enterprise's survival* and its *development* through improving its effectiveness and competitiveness.

Thus, in the first phase, hidden costs address the micro-economic stakes of the enterprise's efficiency; these stakes continue into the second stage, included in the macro-economic scope, since the enterprise's competitiveness is one of the levers of France's national economic policy. In sum, hidden cost evaluation is twofold. First, *a posteriori* evaluation of actions (following evaluation), to incite company actors to continue perfecting the process that had improved organizational effectiveness. Second, *a priori* evaluation of actions, before the evaluation, provides a decision-aid tool for the enterprise's executive management. In this case, current hidden costs are evaluated, enabling a prognostic on the degree of their possible compression. This makes it possible to estimate whether sufficient revenues would be available to partially or totally finance the additional investments costs envisaged.

We utilize both in our research "construction sites": the diagnostic of a unit includes hidden cost evaluation prior to elaborating the operating improvement project (see Chapter 6). The process ends with an evaluation of implemented actions, including the comparative calculation of hidden costs between the diagnostic phase and the evaluation phase (see Chapter 10).

THE RECEPTIVITY OF FRENCH ENTERPRISE TO HIDDEN COSTS

After 1973, when Savall began research on hidden costs, French society was hit with a long and profound economic crisis that meant diminished energetic and financial resources. Thus, the last two decades have been characterized by the necessity to "do better" with stagnating or diminishing resources. This tendency spread at different rates according to various business sectors, which explains the differences of receptivity to hidden costs between 1973 and the present.

Between 1973 and 1978 only *certain industrial enterprises* were seriously concerned with seeking resources through internal efficiency. The service sector was still growing fast, and public services were fed by their external environment, the public authorities. This explains why the hidden cost evaluation method was designed and implemented exclusively in the industrial sector until 1978. From 1978 on, other business sectors manifested interest in their hidden costs, beginning with the lucrative service sector, especially banks and financial establishments. The year 1982 was also marked by a net shift toward accrued interest in internal efficiency research. Indeed, a constraining national economic policy toward businesses began in 1982: frozen salaries, compressed public resources, and encouragement to develop internal efficiency. The ISEOR's fields of experimentation were suddenly and massively multiplied by demands from lucrative service sector enterprises (telecommunication service societies, public housing management) and public organizations such as hospitals, social and educational institutions, mayors' offices, and so forth. This strong economic constraint has never relented, and socio-economic management turned to the strategic consolidation of large and even very large public organizations (accompanying them during privatization, for example).

The necessity to better manage the resources of *all* organizations has never been denied since, but socio-economic management also demonstrated in recent years its capacity to lead enterprises toward economic redeployment, without losing sight of the social component. Thus, in addition to the fields of experimentation cited above, ISEOR has conducted successful interventions in domains as varied as liberal professions, cultural enterprises, chambers of commerce, and sports clubs. Research on hidden costs is inscribed in the context of economic and social development. The evaluation method and the hidden cost results presented here emerge from experimental "sites" in a wide variety of business sectors.

NOTES

1. Among the critics of the production function model, François Perroux' courses at the *Collège de France* can be cited (Collège de France directory 1965–1966) on the evaluation of analytical and statistical work on production functions and the interest of production functions that recognize the existence of the learning process (K. Arrow). See also the criticism of A. Bienaymé, in *La croissance des entreprises*, vol. 1, "*Analyse dynamique des fonctions de la firme* [A Dynamic Analysis of the Functions of the Firm], Bordas, 1971, pp. 39–41.
2. Such assessments do not rule out articulating hidden cost measurement in classic accounting systems. It is with this goal that the ISEOR participated (in 1984) in preparing the 39th National Conference of the Order of Expert Accounts and Certified Public Accounts entitled, "Accounting and Perspectives: accounting answers to new information needs." The second section of this work, entitled "The reduction of hidden costs," is based on the work of H. Savall and the ISEOR (see Savall & Zardet, 1992).

REFERENCES

Savall, H. (1974, 1975). *Enrichir le travail humain* [Enriching Human Work]. Paris: Dunod

Savall, H. (1979). *Reconstruire l'entreprise : analyse socio-économique des conditions de travail* [Reconstructing the Enterprise : Socio-Economic Analysis and Working Conditions]. Paris: Dunod, 1979.

Savall, H., & Zardet, V. (1992). *Le nouveau contrôle de gestion: Méthode des coûts-performances cachés* [New management control: The hidden cost-performance method]. Paris: Eyrolles.

CHAPTER 1

THE ORIGIN
OF HIDDEN COSTS

Research work carried out by ISEOR in the mid-1970s revealed the links between dysfunctions, hidden costs and the enterprise's economic performance. Enterprises that implemented our method of assessing hidden costs were able to subsequently plan rationally for their reduction. This social demand influenced ISEOR researchers to conduct in-depth analysis of hidden cost sources and origins, which in turn led to constructing, through experimentation, a method of socio-economic analysis. It was at this stage that the "fundamental hypothesis" of socio-economic analysis, which will be discussed in this chapter, was formulated.

The chapter is divided into two sections. The first part is devoted to the analysis of the underlying causes of hidden costs—*structures* and the *behaviors* of company actors. The second part presents the general characteristics of the *socio-economic method of enterprise analysis*, through the introduction of its three essential tools: dysfunction analysis, hidden cost assessment and study of training-job adjustment.

Mastering Hidden Costs and Socio-Economic Performance, pages 7–25
Copyright © 2008 by Information Age Publishing

7

THE ENTERPRISE: A COMPLEX AGGREGATE
OF STRUCTURES AND BEHAVIORS

How is it possible to account for dysfunctions and the hidden costs they generate? If we refer to existing doctrines in social sciences, two major currents dominate: the structuralist approach and the behavioralist approach. Simply stated, structuralism affirms the predominance of structure over behavior and explains the results obtained by organizations by the deterministic relationship of structure over behavior. From this perspective, only the modification of structure is likely to inflect the results of productive organizations (i.e., Structures → Behaviors → Results).

The study of dysfunctions in enterprises, however, shows that, in a given unit, thus within identical structures, individuals adopt differentiated productive behaviors, which result in different individual performances, whether this is a matter of absenteeism, direct productivity or quality. This clinical analysis shows the importance of the behavioral factor. Thus, the *behavioralist current* considers human behavior as the principal factor for explaining levels of attained results. In this theory, determinism is shifted to the relation of Behavior → Results. Management modes inspired by the behavioralist current mainly utilize "psychological manipulation" techniques under the guise of such "noble" notions as responsibility, motivation, and professional conscientiousness, that is, they resorted surreptitiously to coercive principles borrowed from certain morality or value systems.

ISEOR studies on the actual functioning of enterprises once again contradicted this determinism. Indeed, the same individual confronted with different work structures is capable of behaving professionally in very different ways; hence the need to keep the importance of structures in mind. Based on this criticism, we constructed an explicative theory of dysfunctions, recognizing two driving forces in enterprise operation: structures and behaviors *interacting with one another*. This explicative hypothesis, which is referred to as the *fundamental hypothesis*, is schematically expressed in Figure 1.1.

This fundamental hypothesis suggests that every enterprise and every work unit should be conceptualized as a set of structures interacting with a set of human behaviors, the sum of which drives economic activity. This activity can be segmented into two groups: *orthofunction*, which is the functioning sought, expected and/or desired by actors; and *dysfunction*, which is the variance be-

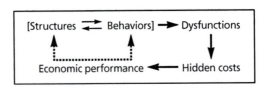

Figure 1.1   The fundamental hypothesis.

tween actual functioning and orthofunctioning. This explicative hypothesis further calls for two important remarks. First, the concept of structures is envisaged in the wider perspective compared with the classic acception in management literature. Second, it also leads to practical consequences: if one is to improve the level of the enterprise's economic performance, it is necessary to conduct *synchronized actions* both on structures and human behaviors.

DYSFUNCTIONS: STRUCTURAL AND BEHAVIORAL INDICATORS

Hidden cost assessments, carried out since 1973, have shown that the five indicators of dysfunction, summarized in Table 1.1, are simultaneously in-

TABLE 1.1 Dysfunction Indicators

Dysfunction indicators	Structures	Individual and collective behavior
Absenteeism	Interest of the work relationship with colleagues working hours	Human causes: • individual perception of collective norms "got to be there at work" • individual need to be psychologically regulated outside the workplace • perception of fairness at the abusive absenteeism practices of certain employees
Work accidents	"Technical" causes: material, occupational accident prevention, security information and training	Accidental human causes or attributable to various reflexes, both individual and collective, with respect to security
Personnel turnover	The enterprise's capacity to attract, motivate and retain personnel	Human instability: evasion behavior or refusal of conditions imposed by professional work (limit: positive aspects of mobility)
Non-quality	"Technical" causes: control organization, remuneration modes, definition of production objectives, training and information system	Human causes: attention, dexterity, professionalism, degree of perfectionism
Direct productivity variance	• material, technological • remuneration mode • work methods and procedures • training and operational information systems	Human causes: • professional agility • rapidity of reflex action • concentration • capacity to adjust to unforeseeable events

dicators of structures and behaviors. Interaction between structures and behaviors, however, is not symmetrical. Structures are relatively permanent elements of the organization and characterized by their stability and their forcefulness. In terms of their stability:

- Their principal attributes' capacity endures over time;
- Their principal attributes' capacity *slowly, progressively* and *autonomously evolves;* and
- They have a high level of social (both individual and collective, more or less conscious), material and financial *energy expenditure* necessary to achieve faster development.

Structures thus carry degree of *inertia*, not only with respect to actors, but also with respect to time. Who has not experienced difficulties relative to the implementation of a new organization chart?

The second major characteristic of structures is their *forcefulness*, i.e., their capacity to influence human behavior. This property is identifiable through relatively constant elements of behavior (apparently complex and multi-form), produced through a relatively asymmetrical interactive bond:

$$\text{Structures} \Longrightarrow \text{Behavior}$$

The "*structuring*" effect consists in the fact that certain (*structural*) elements exert a conditioning influence on human behavior. For example, payment by piecework constitutes a structural element because it leads to behavior that does not heed product quality.

Structures

The set of elements in the organization that exhibit the two properties of persistence and cogency, typical of structures, can be classified into five categories (see Table 1.2) illustrating the different categories of structure: physical, technological, organizational, demographic and mental structures.

Physical Structures

These can be identified directly by their particular characteristics of space, volume, and physical atmosphere, or indirectly by certain indicators of their impacts, such as certain physiological nuisances (e.g., noise, heat, excessive physical fatigue, mental stress, illnesses, accidents). The efficiency of human activity is connected to physical structures, among other factors.

Technological Structures

These include different types of equipment classified according to specific criteria, such as their degree of complexity or sophistication (simple,

TABLE 1.2 Principal Elements of an Organization's Structure

Physical	Technological	Organizational	Demographic	Mental
1. Physical space	1. State of use and upkeep, recent or old equipment	1. Organization chart	1. Adjustments in the number of employees	1. Executive management style
2. Office and workspace configuration	2. Sophistication, complexity, degree of automation	2. Sociogram	2. Age pyramid and population structure	2. "Company ethic" (organizational culture)
3. Nuisances:	3. Adaptability of equipment to the activity's requirements	3. Work division	3. Instances of representation and coordination	3. Micro-climates
• noise	4. Incidence on training-job adjustment	4. Operating methods	4. Employment basin	4. Dominant socio-cultural conceptions (professional ideologies)
• heat	5. Nuisances in connection with materials	5. Work hours and rhythms	5. Initial training structures	
• toxic conditions		6. Procedures	6. On-going training	
• lighting		7. Communication-coordination-cooperation system	7. Qualification structures	
		8. Operational and functional information system	8. Professional and promotional channels	
			9. Recruitment policy	

Note: This grid is not exhaustive; it is notably susceptible to being adapted in function of organizations.

mechanical, automated) and/or their economic value. For example, heavy equipment constitutes an economic stake in itself, and tends to be highly controlled by the organization. At the opposite extreme, "light" tools are mainly seen as accessories to human work. These structures can also be analyzed through certain objective effects they exert on human behavior, such as the degree of "human dependence on the machine," or other ergonomic constraints such as high frequency repetitive gestures or activity devoid of stimulation (e.g., surveying an automated process requiring little human initiative).

Organizational Structures

These factors result from the division of labor in the enterprise and functional relationships (in the etymological sense) among different units and individuals. The distribution of major functions, tasks and responsibilities has an incidence on the content of the work, and consequently, on the adjustment of the employee's training (e.g., potential competency from initial and on-going training, professional experience) and that person's job. The degree of adjustment has significant effects on the degree of interest in the work.

The nature and quality of work relationships further constitute structural elements, both in terms of operational communication (i.e., circuits of information indispensable for performing the task) and in terms of the emotional dimension of work relations. These relational structures explain the existence of a propensity for tension and conflict, and include tension-regulation procedures. Furthermore, it is noteworthy that organizational structures largely find their justification in socio-cultural factors, stemming from conceptions inherited from the organization's history, rather than in application of scientific laws on the functioning of human organizations, which are of the same nature as those that explain the functioning of the physical universe.

Demographic Structures

These structures can be defined as the characteristics of the working population in terms of professional, hierarchical position, age, seniority, gender and education categories (initial, on-going and professional experience). They can also be examined through certain impacts they exert on human behavior, such as unsatisfied professional ambitions or a lack of know-how and competency.

Mental Structures

These include elements that durably characterize the organization's mindset, whether they are management styles imposed by executives, dominant conceptions that influence management decisions, or the state of mind and work atmosphere prevailing among personnel.

Limits of the Differentiation Between Structures

It should be underscored that, in all rigor, these different structures are closely interrelated. For example, technological choices can be tied to certain conceptions of decision makers (mental structures), in the same way that the configuration of office space can influence work organization. Yet, despite the limits of differentiation between the multiple structures, it is useful to adopt a classification of structures in function of their nature in order to facilitate analysis of the organization's operation. Also, from a more paradigmatic viewpoint, hierarchical classification of structural problems facilitates defining priorities for action. Nevertheless, it remains important that the interrelations among different structures be fully perceived in the last phase of the analysis, especially during the implementation of the solutions destined to remedy the observed dysfunctions.

Behavior

Behavior is actually the *observed* human action that has an incidence on the physical and social environment. Behavior is distinguished from attitude, which constitutes potential behavior or relatively permanent personality traits. Attitudes are translated into observable behavior when confronted with events. In this sense, attitudes constitute elements of individual psychological structure. Behavior is downstream from structure-sets, including attitudes, and is characterized by its *conjunctural* and relatively *instable* nature. The same individual, for example, can follow five behavior rationales (or logics) depending on the situations in which he or she is placed and on the nature of the problems that person is faced with:

- *Individual logic* refers to personality as well as the professional and extra-professional characteristics (especially family) of the individual that lead him or her to behave in a relatively autonomous manner.
- *Group activity logic* in which the individual's behavior is conditioned by the fact that he or she belongs to a certain department, workshop or agency. For example, one may adopt production-personnel behavior when faced with sales personnel, or behave like a head-office agent as opposed to a branch-office member.
- *Categorical logic* that reflects one's belonging to a given professional category and conditions the person's behavior. One acts like a supervisor when faced with certain types of problems that affect the

professional category as a whole (e.g., questioning one's authority or style of command). The category may be hierarchical, in the sense of an organization chart, or in a professional sense (e.g., engineer/non-engineer; doctor/nurse/administrative personnel-service personnel, in a hospital; "artists"/administrative personnel in a television studio; sales personnel/administrative personnel within the same bank agency).

- *Affinity group logic* in which the individual's behavior is explained by membership in an affinity group, either inside or outside the enterprise. This affinity can stem from academic backgrounds (e.g., in certain industries, one can observe strong solidarity among managers from the same graduate schools), or from shared moral, religious or political convictions, or from trade-union affiliation.
- *Collective logic* which is captured when all company employees behave as though they were literally "one single person." This behavior rationale is rare, and one typically encounters it when serious events threaten the survival or development of the enterprise or establishment (e.g., risk of closing down the unit, a new law perceived as a threat to the company).

Behavior results from four main factors: a) the individual's characteristics, b) the structural characteristics of the individual's environment (professional and extra-professional), c) the individual's personal chronobiology,[1] and d) the environment's conjunctural phenomena. Just as with structures, different behavior rationales can interact. Still, this classification is useful for practical application to the analysis of dysfunction causes and solutions. It is also useful in the adaptation of intervention strategy to each firm or unit.

The Boundary between Structure and Behavior

Certain behaviors seem relatively permanent in the first analysis, lending them properties close to those of structure, especially in terms of their relative stability and influence on other behaviors. In an organization, such relatively stable behavior eventually becomes genuine mental structure. Thus, in order to clarify our analysis, we classify the constant portion of human behavior under structure, whereas the more conjunctural portion, more susceptible to fluctuation, and which actually constitutes an exterior sign of interaction between the organization and individuals, constitutes behavior *stricto sensu.*

Relatively stable behaviors—in essence elements of mental structure—can be linked to the probable existence of genuine behavioral algorithms, susceptible to being distinguished by a certain precision of behavior. These behavioral algorithms show the external signs of instability and, consequently, are in function of a conjunction of relatively haphazard or uncertain events. The feasibility of such a distinction, however, does nothing to resolve the problems involved in defining boundaries: enduring individual or collective behaviors can progressively acquire all the fundamental properties of structures and insidiously slide from the behavior pole to that of structures.

From a descriptive point of view, such an evolution of behaviors would be considered as the appearance of a new structure inflecting actors' playing rules. From a more analytical point of view, the conversion of certain behaviors into structures creates a collective referential, from notions such as precedent, jurisprudence, usual customs and practices of units, which acquire the status of rules. Such conversion results from the collective recognition of a practice that becomes relatively stable. The transformation cycle of behavior into structure is of systemic nature and results from the alternation of asymmetrical relations between structures and behaviors:

$$S \rightleftarrows B \rightleftarrows S \quad \text{-----------}$$
$$t_0 \qquad\qquad t_1 \qquad\qquad t_2 \qquad \text{-----------}$$

This cycle applies, in the first case, to previously-mentioned transformation phenomenon of certain behaviors into mental structures (mS), when certain common, daily behavior has progressively become instituted:

$$mS \rightleftarrows B \rightleftarrows mS'$$

The more widespread second case leads to a renewal of decision-making theory (decision theory), which we are developing with ISEOR's experimental research work. In this case, the behavior pole includes a particular category of behavior that is qualified as decisions. Hence, the structure set (pS: physical; tS: technological; oS: organizational; dS: demographic; mS: mental) impacts the entire structure set thus inflected:

$$
\begin{pmatrix} p \\ t \\ o \\ d \\ m \\ t_0 \end{pmatrix} \xrightarrow{\ S\ }
\begin{pmatrix} op\ d \\ ad\ d \\ ma\ d \\ st\ d \\ \\ t_1 \end{pmatrix} \xleftarrow{\ }
\begin{pmatrix} p \\ t \\ o \\ d \\ m \\ t_2 \end{pmatrix} S'
$$

with: op d = operational decisions
with: ad d = administrative decisions
with: ma d = management decisions
with: st d = strategic decisions

Analysis of this relation (Structure ⬌ Behavior) has made it possible to underscore the *double responsibility*, individual and collective, of individuals in the creation of hidden costs. Indeed, we have noted that individual responsibility in the creation of dysfunctions (e.g., evasion-of-work behavior, "slowdown" on the part of an employee) does exist, but that it is much rarer than collective responsibility. A sort of solidarity exists in the creation of dysfunctions and especially in setting up regulations. We sometime employ the expression of "unconscious actor complicity" to indicate the fact that dysfunctions, especially when they are recurrent, are rarely the responsibility of one single individual, contrary to a certain dominant ideology that stems from the theories and practices of classic Fayol-Taylorist management.

The practical consequences of these results are that, if one is to take action on hidden costs, this implies action on individual behavior and especially collective behavior, and on mental structures. In sum, hidden costs result from the *permanent* and *complex interaction* between company structures and human behaviors, which create both orthofunctions and dysfunctions.

If the deep-seated origin of hidden costs is to be found in these complex connections between two groups of variables, another level of observation is possible. Indeed, interactions between structure and behavior manifest themselves in a certain number of "territories" or domains of the organization's operation. There are six of these domains: working conditions, work organization, communication-coordination-cooperation, time management, integrated training, and strategic implementation. These six domains, explained in detail in the following chapter, constitute the classification grid utilized for taking stock of dysfunctions and for seeking solutions. This nomenclature of dysfunction and action domains is indispensable for conducting hidden cost reduction actions. It corresponds to the fourth group of variables composing the socio-economic analysis model, represented schematically by a four-leaf clover (see Figure 1.2). This model gave rise to the creation of basic tools for the socio-economic analysis of organizations.

BASIC TOOLS OF THE SOCIO-ECONOMIC ANALYSIS METHOD

The Socio-Economic method was conceived and developed for the analysis of the relationship:

[Structures → Behaviors] Dysfunctions → Hidden Costs.

It includes three basic tools: dysfunction analysis, hidden cost assessment, and training-job adjustment (competency grids).

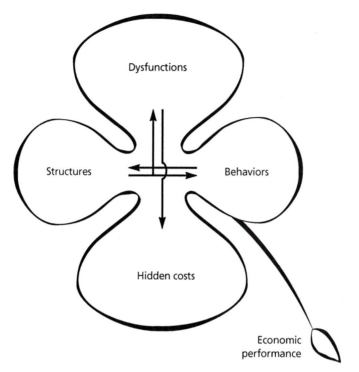

Figure 1.2 The socio-economic four-leaf clover.

Dysfunction Analysis

The basic methodological option is to analyze *only dysfunctions,* without referring to the strong points in company operations at the stage of preliminary analysis (the diagnostic).

Dysfunction analysis is thus the analysis of the operation of the organization, very similar to a study of their weak points (which has been a classic focus). The meaning of the term diagnostic, as we understand it, is much closer to the medical acception (action devised to determine the ailment) than to that currently utilized in management (strong and weak point analysis). At first, this methodological orientation causes reactions of rejection or passiveness among actors, comparable to a "cultural shock." But these initial reactions are actively engaged in the following phase of researching solutions for dysfunction reduction.

Dysfunction analysis groups together a set of concrete methods with a three-fold objective: a) descriptive study of dysfunctions, b) descriptive study of dysfunction regulations, and c) analysis of dysfunction causes, in terms of structure and behavior.

Chronologically, it is carried out in three phases:

III		I		II
Causes	←	Dysfunctions	→	Effects (Regulations)

The first two phases (inventory of dysfunctions and of their effects) are carried out essentially in the field-object of the analysis. The third phase is born of a different approach, predominantly explicative, which constitutes the "expert opinion" of the researcher-interveners. This opinion requires critical distance from the opinions of actors. It is founded both on tangible data (collected by means of interviews, direct observation and document analysis) and the intangible *non-dit* (unvoiced comments). The expert opinion consists of identifying the major dysfunctions and causes, classified hierarchically in function of their degree of impact on dysfunctions.

Hidden Cost Assessment

This tool of the socio-economic analysis method is an extension of the dysfunction analysis, since its objective is to assess the cost of regulations. It is a *fundamental tool of the method* in that it enables creating *new information* expressed in monetary form, which produces a particular impact on company actors. In fact, when ISEOR has applied the socio-economic analysis method without assessing hidden costs, we observed significantly different reactions, in the sense that the impact or "cultural shock" was lessened.

Training-Job Adjustment and Competency Grids

The analysis of training-job adjustment in a unit is a tool intended to be both descriptive and explicative of certain dysfunctions. Regarding the causes of dysfunctions, training-job adjustment is a cross-sectional analysis of technological, organizational, demographic and, in certain cases, mental structures. Training-job adjustment analysis aims to explain certain dysfunctions according to the following logic.

A *job* is defined by its capacity to absorb, mobilize and develop the professional competency of individuals. *Training* is defined as the set of competencies acquired during initial training, on-going professional training (retraining and updating), and finally through the individual's professional experience. *Professional experience* includes all professional situations in an individual's history that create knowledge, techniques and methods of work. Thus, professional experience contributes to modifying the mental structures of individuals.

The *job sphere* (J) designates jobs that have been codified by the enterprise or unit. Jobs require a certain number of competencies necessary to perform the tasks confided to individuals. Finally, the *training sphere* (T) represents the set of combined competencies possessed by all individuals in the unit. It seems reasonable to associate individuals' potential competencies with their current competencies, i.e., those competencies that could become real without having to invest too much energy.

In training-job adjustment analysis (see Figure 1.3), three zones are identified:

- Zone A, zone of training-job adjustment that represents the competencies required and available. Zone A is a source of efficiency that nourishes orthofunctioning.
- Zone B, *first zone of inadequate adjustment* or discrepancy that represents those competencies possessed by individuals, but not utilized or mobilized by the jobs. Zone B is often a source of frustration and demotivation; it thus potentially breeds dysfunctions.
- Zone C, *second zone of inadequate adjustment* that represents those competencies required for the full achievement of the job, but not possessed by individuals. Zone C is fundamental, for it is a source of the enterprise's inefficiency and under-quality. It plays a crucial role in explaining *poorly-assumed tasks*: an individual is asked to implement competencies that he or she has not developed, either through a lack of initial training nor on-going training or through prior professional experience.

In order to measure training-job adjustment, we have created a visualization grid for competencies available in the unit—the *competency grid* (see Figure 1.4). This table, which is drawn up and filled out by the immediate supervisor (or with that person's assistant), includes: a) the individuals who make up the studied unit (rows), and b) the operations carried out by the unit (columns) classified into two zones—current job content (technical operations, management operations, relationship operations) and the evolution of jobs (i.e., new operations to be accomplished). This zone is largely

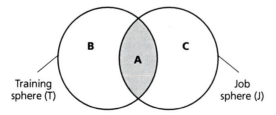

Figure 1.3 Training-job adjustment schema.

Activities — In the organization at the start of the period

Actors

Activity	P1	P2	P3	P4	P5	P6	P7
Particular existing know-how							
Observations							
Food in-shop sampling	◪	◪	◪				
Decision-making capacity	■	■	◪				
Spanish	—	—	■				
English	—	—	■				
Typing	◪	◪	□				
Development-management							
Time management	◪	□	□				
Scheduling	◪	□	□				
Personnel management	■	□	□				
Shop decoration	◪	□	◪				
3C meetings	□	□	□				
Establish equipment estimates	◪	□	—				
Establish cocktail estimates	◪	□	—				
Management	◪	○	○				
Training practice	□	□	□				
Conduct meetings	◪	□	□				
Management analysis & follow-up	□	□	□				
Participation 3C meetings	◪	◪	◪				
Control and follow up of shop product	◪	◪	◪				
Operations / Security-management							
Control of delivery receipts	■	■	◪				
Relations with the hierarchy	■	■	■				
Inter-service relations	◪	◪	□				
Shop reception control	■	■	◪				
Quality control	◪	◪	◪				
Preparation of orders	■	■	◪				
Respect hygiene, security & procedures	■	■	◪				
Additional sales	■	■	□				
Bacteriological analysis and follow up	□	□	□				
Control of orders shop/clients	■	■	◪				
Product management all shelves	■	◪	□				
Shelf displays	◪	◪	◪				
Reception quality	■	■	◪				
Cash register management	■	■	◪				
Taking orders over telephone	◪	◪	◪				
Taking orders in person	◪	◪	◪				
Knowledge of products	◪	■	□				
Entering data	◪	◪	□				
Advising customers	■	◪	◪				
Answering the telephone							

Legend: ■ Current practices mastered; ◪ Occasional practices or not entirely mastered; □ Knowledge of principles without practice; — Neither theoretical knowledge nor practice; ○ To be created.

Figure 1.4 Competency Grid: Sales team in a catering company.

open (columns without headings) to permit tracking the evolutions of jobs, driven by either technological innovations, product innovations or socio-organizational innovations.

The underlying goal is to assess the competency level of each person with respect to the operations identified according to a four-level scale:

1. ■ symbolizes an employee with good theoretical knowledge and efficient, regular practice of the operation.
2. ◪ symbolizes an employee with good theoretical knowledge and occasional practice of the operation. Personnel with regular practice of the operation, but whose theoretical knowledge is *limited to basic principles* are included at this level.
3. ☐ symbolizes an employee with basic knowledge of theoretical principles, but with no practice of the operation.
4. (empty cell) symbolizes an employee with no theoretical knowledge and no practice of the operation.

This scale reflects our conception of *competency*. Competency for a particular operation or set of tasks is available when the employee has theoretical knowledge of the operation and has actually practiced it. This theoretical knowledge can be acquired through initial or on-going training.

Combining these factors seemed useful to us, insomuch as we have observed that theoretical knowledge degenerates in the absence of practice and, conversely, exclusively practical knowledge is vulnerable to unanticipated changes in processes, procedures, task scheduling, modification of product lines and models, and so forth. The competency grids, once filled-out, visually displays the state of competencies that are available in a given unit by degrees of blackened squares. It is a *descriptive* tool in that: a) reading across the rows permits measuring the *degree of individual multitasking capacity* for each individual, which reveals that person's training-job adjustment, and b) reading down the columns permits measuring the *degree of vulnerability of the group to unanticipated events* such as absences and work overload.

The competency grid in Figure 1.4 shows the vulnerability of certain tasks such as "advising clients" or "bacteriological analysis and follow-up controlling." This table also shows that the optimal evolution of jobs would imply prior training actions, due to the current lack of competencies. Failure to do so could trigger dysfunctions, which is the case for management training as shown on this company's competency grid.

The competency grid has proven itself to be an extremely useful tool, while remaining very simple to employ for a multitude of applications: competency diagnostics, training program design, competency growth assessments, strategic potential diagnostics in the event of changes in products, technologies, markets and company organization. It is an apparently simple instrument, both in terms of drawing up the table, as well as its application to management decision making. In reality, its use in real-life situations has repeatedly demonstrated that caution is indispensable to its utilization and that a minimum climate of trust is necessary *a priori*. Drawing up a competency grid requires courage, rigor and confidence on the part of intermediary supervisory staff:

- *Courage* to carry out estimates of the personnel's real competencies as close as possible to observed reality, without indulgence. For example, accepting to recognize and indicate through symbols on the competency grid, the fact that one employee is more competent than another, even though the latter might have a higher salary.
- *Rigor* in "measuring" personnel competencies in a very detailed manner, proceeding analytically, operation by operation, and not by an approximate, subjective overall assessment. Rigor, declared and practiced, is a factor in restoring confidence;
- *Confidence* on the part of the personnel assessed by this tool toward their immediate manager that the assessment is be done rigorously and fairly, that the results will not be utilized for destructive purposes (e.g., choosing which employees to dismiss). The intent is for constructive purposes, such as developing personal competencies and reducing the unit's vulnerability; and
- *Confidence* in the *capacity of individuals to evolve*, in the possibility for each one to find a personal advancement track, usually inside the enterprise, or to better negotiate outside the enterprise when the person's projects are completed or circumstances compel the individual to do so.

This tool does not become truly meaningful until actors are willing to trust one another and accept the need to develop their competencies. This commitment requires confidence on three levels. First, there must be confidence on the part of the department head who accepts to train a collaborator. Second, there must be confidence on the part of the team leader who entrusts a new task to the collaborator, enabling that person to implement and consolidate the newly acquired competency. Finally, there must be confidence on the part of the collaborator in his or her own capacity to learn and assume a new activity, thus improving competencies and professional behavior. The legitimacy of this *a priori* confidence is then "verified" (or invalidated) through competency grid updates.

Integrated Training

Integrated training is based on five principles. First, competencies are acquired through various modes of training and are observable in the practice of activity operations. Second, training stresses dysfunction regulation and prevention, and not exclusively orthofunctioning. Third, the various modes of competency acquisition are initial training, on-going professional training, apprenticeships or conceptualized professional experience, conscious and transmittable. These three modes of competency acquisition are indispensable and inseparable. Fourth, an operation is always carried out in co-operation, involving two or more employees. Finally, training is primarily dispensed within a micro-space, for every operator is a trainer, often without being aware of it. It is a question of lending visibility to this "*de facto* integrated training*,*" not recognized and badly managed, thanks to the internal training plan.

Integrated Training Stages
The first step is a diagnostic of competencies, carried out employing the competency grid.

This diagnostic determines the unit's personnel training needs, which are initially examined with reference to the objectives of competency evolution for the chosen period. As illustrated in Figure 1.5, based on this assessment an internal training plan can be created. The next phase is to distinguish *collective training needs* and the composition of training groups by levels (e.g., all rated personnel) and *individual training needs* and the choice

---

Competency-Evolution Objectives under the Heading of the Multiskilled Versatility Objective

- End-of-year objective: complete multiskilled versatility for reception (production + claims) and multiskilled management: knowledge of all files in one of the two activities, production or claims, and knowledge of the less complex files (approximately 70%) in the other activity.

- Competency evolution objectives thus implied:

Reception Production	Reception Claims	Management Production	Management Claims
P7 (Sep.–Oct.) P6 (Nov.–Dec.)	P5 (Sep.–Oct.)	P7 (Sep.–Oct.) P6 (Nov.–Dec.)	P3 (Nov.–Dec.) P2 (Nov.–Dec.) P5 (Nov.–Dec.)

Figure 1.5 Training plan assessment.

of the internal trainer (e.g., P4 trains P1 and P3). Successful training is fully achieved when the acquired competencies are implemented.

The *structure-behavioral* theory of business operation, by stressing *diachronic interactions* (i.e. implying a time lapse) and *asymmetric interactions* (the predominant influence sometime results from structure, sometimes from behavior), leads to a conception of interactions as highly interwoven between structure and behavior, whose boundaries are ambivalent (either mental structure or behavior, depending on the point of view adopted). Beyond the scientific interest for such conceptualization, this theory leads to practical applications in the domain of *transformation actions of the organization's operation,* actions motivated sometimes by social policy considerations (e.g., social development, improvement of work-life conditions, qualification improvement, improvement of professional affiliates within the organization), sometimes by economic objectives (e.g., improving efficiency, the productivity-quality couple), or by actions accompanying the introduction of technological innovations.

The praxeological recommendations this theory provides can be summed up in a general principle, largely experimented in different ISEOR research sites inside businesses and public service agencies: *Organizational improvement actions are efficient when they originate in a project that was drawn up in participative fashion and which provides for simultaneous actions on structure, in the broad sense, and on human behavior.* These actions cannot be carried out by tackling one explicative element after another. Indeed, structures and behaviors produce dysfunctions in different domains simultaneously. These domains of dysfunction constitute the operational contact points where sustainable hidden cost reduction solutions can be researched.

This principle is verified both by the relative or complete failure of mono-centric actions addressing only structures or only behaviors and *a contrario* by the success of bi-centric actions of structuro-behavioral nature.

ENHANCING ORGANIZATIONAL PERFORMANCE THROUGH SOCIO-ECONOMIC INTERVENTION

Socio-economic theory, created by Henri Savall and elaborated and experimented with by the ISEOR research team, is based on the premise that improvement of the enterprise's effectiveness and efficiency requires a new and integrated approach to business problems. Major-function approaches have proved their limits and their inefficiency in environments that have become particularly turbulent and complex.

This approach and its underlying theory are not limited to wishful thinking – it proposes an operational procedure with a view to approaching the enterprise globally. This approach, referred to as the socio-economic intervention method, was constructed and verified in numerous enterprises and organizations, from a broad range of business sectors, of different sizes, different legal status and very diverse economic situations.

NOTE

1. Chronobiology studies the biological rhythms of the human being with respect to time periods of the day, month and year. This analogy is borrowed from Reinhberg (1974, p. 128).

REFERENCE

Reinhberg, A. (1974). *Des rythmes biologiques à la chronobiologie* [From biological rhythms to chronobiology]. Paris: Gauthier Villars.

CHAPTER 2

EVALUATING HIDDEN COSTS

Hidden costs are those costs that are not detected by the company information system, including budgets, profit and loss account, general accounting,
analytical accounting, piloting logbooks (Savall, 1979). In symmetrical fashion, the term visible cost designates all cost categories that appear on the
company information system. A cost is considered visible when it displays
three characteristics: a dedicated denomination (e.g., personnel costs), a
measurement (e.g., sum of salaries and fringe benefits) and a system of surveillance. For example, salaries and wages are examined every month and
limitation objectives are set.

Hidden costs are characterized by their strong capacity to explain the
quality (or lack thereof) of the organization's operation. Visible costs can
measure amounts and variance, but do not have the power to analyze overall causes. On the contrary, hidden costs are phenomenological in nature.
For example, high hidden costs linked to absenteeism provide insight into
the extent to which the enterprise's operation has been negatively impacted and the costs associated with the regulations set in place to compensate
for those absences.

The expression "hidden costs" actually refers to hidden cost-performance, in that the reduction of a cost constitutes a performance, and the
reduction of a performance amounts to a cost. One can see this as an extension of the two strictly comparable notions of cost and performance,
which are defined in reference to a zero origin, while hidden costs and
performances are situated as continuums of one another. Indeed, perfor-

Mastering Hidden Costs and Socio-Economic Performance, pages 27–66
Copyright © 2008 by Information Age Publishing

27

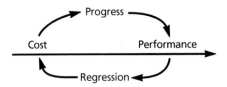

Figure 2.1   Hidden costs and performance.

mance can be considered either as cost decrease or as product increase as illustrated in Figure 2.1.

DYSFUNCTIONS AND HIDDEN COSTS

The socio-economic theory of organizations stresses the importance of the enterprise's quality of operation, otherwise stated, the capacity of productive organizations to implement their resources, measured in terms of quantity and quality, material and physical, and monetary and human. This perspective makes it possible to shed light on the multitude of dysfunctions—which represent problems and difficulties—that constantly disturb the life of the enterprise. Such dysfunctions prevent the enterprise from fully attaining its objectives and efficiently exploiting its material and human resources. The result is wasted resources.

The economic consequences of these dysfunctions should be evaluated—especially since dysfunctions can be corrected through regulation, that is, the way in which enterprises react to detected problems (dysfunctions). Regulations can require time investment, result in production losses and over-consumption of raw materials, external services, financial expenses, salaries and/or waste.

The Components of Hidden Costs

Hidden costs are the monetary translation of regulation activities (i.e., dysfunctions → regulations → hidden costs). This link was modeled on two axes. First, the basic dysfunctions, which are concrete disturbances or abnormal operations, have been grouped together into five indicators that are considered as families of dysfunctions: absenteeism, work accidents, personnel turnover, quality defects, and direct productivity variance or non-production (missed production). Second, regulation of dysfunctions, which are grouped together into two types of activities: human activities and product consumption (goods or services). This classification of regulations is then applied to hidden cost evaluation, which involves six components. The quantity of product consumption is financially evaluated based on the actual price supported by the enterprise, referred to as overconsumption. Human regulation activities are expressed in time units (e.g., hours, minutes) and translated into monetary value (Euros, dollars). Human time is valuated in reference to the hourly contribution to the variable cost margin, regarding overtime and non-production (missed production). Overtime refers to regulation activities (e.g., making telephone calls, training temporary staff), whereas non-production (missed production), which is also a measure of human time, indicates an absence of activity, or work stoppage, caused by dysfunctions (e.g., machine breakdown, stock depletion, work accidents).

Human time is valorized in terms of the variance between salaries when the activity is performed by a person holding a position that is better remunerated than the position of the person that should have performed the job; these components are called excess salary. Under the heading of non-creation of potential, the cost of immaterial investment actions is calculated in terms of the human time that the enterprise could not dispose of, over a given period, because actors were preoccupied with dysfunction regulations and were thus unable to free sufficient time for certain long-term activities (i.e., implementation of strategic objectives neglected during the period taken into consideration). Delay in immaterial investment can readily compromise profitability, and even threaten the enterprise's survival—it is therefore truly a hidden cost. Only the first four components have direct impact on the current profit and loss statement, while the non-creation of potential's main influence is on future profit and loss statements. The last hidden costs component pulls together the risks provoked by the dysfunctions.

In sum, the hidden cost evaluation model entails associating each of the six components of hidden costs incurred by regulations that are set up by the enterprise to the five indicators of dysfunction. Figure 2.2 presents an illustration of hidden cost evaluation broken down according to its components, with an application in Figure 2.3. As these Figures indicate, hidden costs are divided into two categories: a) hidden costs incorporated into visible costs, and b) hidden costs that are not included in visible costs. Hidden costs incorporated into visible costs include costs diluted into different cost lines of existing information systems. They are referred to as "hidden" because they are diluted and not identified as specific lines. Thus, the cost of absenteeism includes remuneration of temporary staff hired to stand in for the absent personnel, an expenditure found in the line "personnel outside the enterprise" in the profit and loss statement. Hidden costs included in visible costs represent actual costs for the enterprise and are inscribed as debits in the profit and loss statement.

Indicators	Components						
	Over-salary (1)	Surtemps (excess time) (2)	Over-consumption (3)	Non-production (missed production) (4)	Non-creation of potential (5)	Total hidden costs (1)+(2)+(3)+(4)+(5)	Risks*
Absenteeism						Hidden costs linked to absenteeism	
Work accidents						Hidden costs linked to work accidents	
Personnel turnover						Hidden costs linked to personnel turnover	
Quality of products						Hidden costs linked to product quality	
Direct productivity variance						Hidden costs liked to direct productivity variance	
Total	Excess salary engendered by the 5 indicators	Overtime (excess time) engendered by the 5 indicators	Over-consumption engendered by the 5 indicators	Non-production (missed production) engendered by the 5 indicators	Non-creation of potential engendered by the 5 indicators	Total hidden costs	Risks engendered by the 5 indicators
Economic concepts	Historical costs			Opportunity costs			
Accounting concepts	Over-expenditure			Non-production (missed production)			

Figure 2.2 General model of hidden cost calculation.
Source: Excerpted from H. Savall, *Coûts cachés et analyse socio-économique des organisations* [Hidden Costs and Socio-Economic Analysis of Organizations], *Encyclopedia of Management, Economica*, June 1989, p. 40.

* Risks are indicated as a reminder, without quantification. They represent a source of counter-performance assimilated into hidden costs, insofar as they provoke restrained performances. This is the case when the perception of risks impedes taking decisions or undertaking activities that would improve either profitability for the period, or creation of potential.

Indicators	Qualitative Evaluation	Quantitative Evaluation	Financial Evaluation					
			Over-salary	Sur-temps (excess time)	Over-consumption	Non-production (missed production)	Non-creation of potential	Total
Absenteeism and work accidents	High absenteeism during packaging period	5.8% on the average including						
		2.3% complete compensation for absences	53,000	11,400		46,300		110,700
		3.5% uncompensated absences		17,600		70,600		88,200
Personnel turnover	Little personnel turnover	N/E*	N/E					N/E
Non-quality	Bread crumbs for 1.5% of average production	About 75 tons/year			74,400			74,400
	Dough discarded at the GEFRA or after kneading at 0.4%	About 21 tons/year			33,800			33,800
	Unsold products taken back	1% of products				82,600		82,600
	Commercial damage	N/E						N/E
Direct productivity variance	Overweight frequent with most articles	An average of 1% over-weight or about 50 tons/year			80,300			80,300
	Manufacturing fluctuation including non-production (missed production) enumerated in the accounting scheme	Hypothesis of 4% discrepancy on the average compared to "optimal" productivity				192,900		192,900
Total	Certain costs are not evaluated or are under-estimated		53,000	29,000	188,500	392,400	N/E	662 900 (under estimated)

Figure 2.3 Hidden costs evaluation of manufacturing operation: An agri-food firm (in Euros).
a Not evaluated, given the time allotted to the study

Hidden costs not included in visible costs include absence of production resulting from dysfunctions, that is, paid time not contributing to a product or a semi-product (e.g., absence of personnel responsible for a workstation or a function; quality defects requiring repair time for articles already manufactured, which reduces saleable production over the given period). This category of costs is thus financial performance reduction (products) anticipated in provisional sales. Thus, it concerns virtual or opportunity costs, which correspond to under-activity, a failure to attain the earning that is actually possible. This category of costs is taken into consideration based on the postulate that the portion of production thus lost could have been sold if non-production (missed production) time were reduced or eliminated.

In the perspective of a general accounting system that would make hidden costs evident, a simple example of a profit and loss statement is presented below. Assuming a visible costs total of 800, a visible products total of 900, and a hidden costs total of 300 (of which, 100 is hidden costs incorporated into visible costs and, 200 is hidden costs not included in visible costs), the following is a Profit and Loss Statement displayed according to typical accounting methods:

Visible costs	800	Visible products	900
Earnings	100		
Total	900		900

A Profit and Loss Statement displayed according to accounting that revealed hidden costs, in contrast, would present the following:

Visible costs	800	Visible products	900
(including incorporated hidden costs:	100)		
Hidden costs not incorporated (non-production (missed production))	200	Non-production (missed production) (virtual products)	200
Earnings	100		
Total	1100		1100

This second display clearly illustrates the difference in the nature of the two categories of hidden costs. Hidden costs included in visible costs (100) are actual expenditures, and, as such, they put a strain on the debit side of the profit and loss statement. Hidden costs that are not included in visible costs (200) represent virtual products that put a strain on the credit side of the profit and loss statement.

A Practical Approach to Hidden Cost Evaluation: The SOF Method

We have provided a detailed introduction to the method of hidden cost evaluation in a previous book (Savall, 1979), applied to each one of the five dysfunction indicators. The discussion in this section is thus limited to outlining the principle characteristics and methodological innovations associated with the SOF method.

The SOF method is broken down into three stages or modules—a social module (S), an organizational module (O), and a financial module (F)—the objectives of which are summarized in Table 2.1.

As an example, in the data processing department of a bank (Zardet, 1985), the SOF method applied to the quality defects indicator provided the following results. The social module had:

- Quality defects and data processing errors that due to the centralization of data processing impacted the entire bank (450 persons).
- Errors and incidents from several sources, which are often related to one another, including technical causes (computer programs, file capacity), human causes (i.e., manipulation errors) and organizational and demographical causes (e.g., lack of integrated personnel training, lack of competency).

Incidents that occurred during data processing were classified in the following typology: abnormal program stoppage (33%), manipulation error (7%), abnormal job control language (internal program link written by the computer systems design and production department : 13%), file exceeding capacity (23%), and "others" (24%).

The organizational module analyzed every type of incident from the perspective of the regulations set up to correct it. For example, the incident "file

TABLE 2.1   Basic Objectives of the SOF Method

Module	Objective
Social	• Detect the elementary dysfunctions (inventory of dysfunctions). • Explain the multiple causes of dysfunctions connections. • [Structures ↔ Behavior] → Dysfunctions
Organizational	• Explain the modes of dysfunction regulation: study of effects. • Compile an inventory of the economic incidence of regulations: quantity of time, consumption, production "losses."
Financial	• Study the price and unit cost of regulation components. • Evaluate in monetary units the economic incidence of regulations.

exceeding capacity" was regulated according to the schema presented in Figure 2.4. This incident occurred 12 times in two months, or 72 times per year.

Finally, in the financial module the hourly cost, evaluated by the contribution to the margin on variable costs, amounted to 43 euros. Hidden costs connected to "files exceeding capacity" incidents came to approximately 4,640 euros (1.5h × 72 × 43€), knowing that the incidence on clientele was not financially evaluated. These hidden costs are thus under-estimated, especially since such incidents can cause commercial harm, in terms of lost clientele.

The sum of all hidden costs linked to quality defects (incidents) in the data processing department was estimated at 9,580€. This represents 1,440€ per department employee per year, keeping in mind that certain major repercussions could not be financially evaluated, such as the repercussions on delayed processing for the other departments of the bank, incidence on the clientele, commercial damage, and financial effects on the firm (e.g., calculation errors of bank charges).

Data Collection Techniques and Datasets

For each one of the three modules, mutually-enhancing data collection techniques should be utilized to produce qualitative, quantitative and financial forms of information (see Table 2.2). In ISEOR's work, different collection techniques have been utilized in an attempt to increase the quality of collected information, especially in terms of its reliability and its precision, by combining for each module at least two, if not all three, collec-

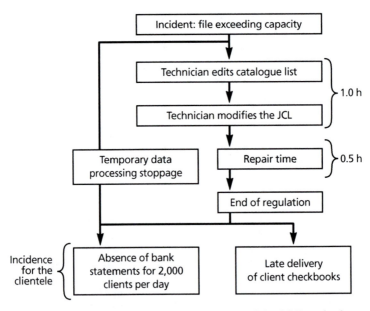

Figure 2.4   Illustrative organizational module of the SOF method.

TABLE 2.2 Data Collection Techniques

Module	Data collection techniques		Forms of information obtained		
	Major	Minor	Qualitative	Quantitative	Financial
Social	• Interviews • Documents	• Direct observation	Yes	Yes	No
Organizational	• Direct observation • Interviews	• Documents	Yes	Yes	No
Financial	• Documents	• Interviews	Yes	Yes	Yes

tion techniques: interviews, direct observation and analysis of documents. Another characteristic of the qQFi method (Qualitative, Quantitative and Financial), conceived and developed by ISEOR, is the constant effort, in the course of the diagnostic, to express each hidden cost in the most accurate financial terms possible, compared with its transitional expressions (qualitative and quantitative).

These combinations make it possible to cross-examine information collected by different data collection techniques. Indeed, the numerous diagnostics performed by ISEOR have shown that even cooperative actors can forget to point out certain phenomena, or have a biased perception of them, when compared to observable reality. As an example, one of ISEOR's intervener-researchers noticed a pile of rejected products in a corner of a workshop in a textile firm. None of the personnel interviewed (workers, supervisors, managers) had mentioned that phenomenon. Exploring the pile of rejects, the intervener-researcher learned from the supervisor that that dysfunction was so anchored in daily routine that no one had thought to point it out (see Petiau, 1983).

The results obtained from the application of these three modules—the social, organizational and financial—are presented in three complementary forms:

- Qualitative information permits identifying phenomena relative to actors' perception, which could not be measured quantitatively.
- Quantitative information permits measuring the quantity of phenomena, such as the absenteeism rate, number of work accidents, and number of hours spent repairing defects. Within this context, such quantitative information is distinct from financial information.
- Financial information represents the expression of dysfunction regulations in monetary terms, for example, the costs incurred by absenteeism amount to 1,900€ per person per year.

It should be pointed out, however, that the objective of a socio-economic diagnostic is to "maximize" financial information, even if it is the combined sum of qualitative, quantitative and financial information that makes up the diagnostic. Indeed, the socio-economic method entails uncovering financial resource deposits allotted to the regulation of dysfunctions, a portion of which, our experience has shown, can be mobilized for activities that create economic value.

Fields of Application for the SOF Method

If the SOF method was specifically conceived for evaluating the hidden costs pertaining to each of one of the dysfunction indicators, we have also applied it to numerous other objects such as a single indicator, the entire group of five indicators,[2] and one elementary dysfunction or a domain of dysfunctions. Thus, hidden costs linked to time management dysfunctions could be evaluated, for example, in a construction and public works company. In all cases, care should be taken not to undertake a double accounting of hidden costs. For example, quality defects generated by absences should be counted only once. They should be entered either under the absenteeism indicator or the quality defects indicator.

In general, ISEOR's evaluations have mainly addressed the entire group of indicators, given that the objective pursued is an evaluation of the overall amount of hidden costs, which constitute a potential efficiency reserve for the company, referred to as hidden cost-performance deposits. If this deposit is not "mined," it remains a hidden cost deposit. If, however, one succeeds in mining this deposit, thus recovering part of it toward the creation of new economic value (more products or better products, goods or services), the deposit is referred to as hidden cost-performance, the recovered portion of which constitutes a veritable performance potential.

It should also be pointed out that strong links exist between the indicators of absenteeism, personnel turnover, work accidents, product quality and direct productivity variance (Savall, 1978). Depending on the enterprise, hidden costs can crystallize around either absenteeism or personnel turnover. It is also known that good direct productivity is often achieved to the detriment of high hidden costs for quality defects. Thus, evaluating only one indicator incurs the risk of distorting the diagnostic.

The SOF method has been applied in different sectors of activity, including industries, service companies and public utilities. ISEOR's nearly thirty years of application suggests that this method is applicable to literally every sector of activity, whatever its legal status, its size, and its objective. The only application particularity, in function of the sector of activity, concerns the direct productivity discrepancy indicator. In those industries that manufacture countable products per time unit, hidden costs represent the discrepancy between theoretical quantities and actual quantities of products, which are defined themselves in terms of production norms or allotted time. For example, in a workshop mounting and controlling television tubes, the norm of reference was 75 tubes per person per day. Since the actual average number was 69.6 per person per day, the direct productivity discrepancy was evaluated at 5.4 tubes per person per day, considered as non-production (missed production). In all other enterprises, whether processing industries or service sector organizations, hidden costs linked to direct productivity variance are represented by the entire portion of real activity judged abnormal by the actors. In this case, an inventory is taken of all time spent on unproductive or under-productive activities, such as searching for a lost document, waiting for someone to begin working, and so forth.

Finally, the hidden cost evaluation can be more or less in-depth according to the time-budget allotted to the diagnostic and the degree of precision desired. The first evaluations performed by the ISEOR (between 1974 and 1977), required roughly six months for a full-time researcher to cover one indicator.[3] In 1985, a complete hidden costs evaluation of a workshop with a hundred employees demanded two weeks for an intervener-researcher. Over time, ISEOR has also adapted the original method of hidden cost evaluation to create a quick method of evaluation applicable to small- and medium-sized enterprises (SMEs). With this approach, a researcher can perform a hidden cost evaluation for a SME from fifty to three hundred employees with five days of fieldwork, plus five days of laboratory processing and write-up of the diagnostic report (see Bonnet & Domeur, 1984; Savall & Bonnet, 1985). This rapid method of evaluation supposes the modification of data collection techniques: direct observation is delegated to the enterprise, with methodological support provided by the researcher. It also supposes a stricter selection of researched information. For example, for hidden costs linked to non-quality, only major types of defects and repairs are selected, either based on their frequency or the seriousness of their impact, as corroborated by the unitary cost calculation for these defaults and repairs.

Common Principles for Hidden Cost Calculation

Based on ISEOR's intervention research, there are five hypotheses that are common to all types of hidden cost calculations: isoproductivity of work time, indirect labor productivity, rational resource allocation, the economic value of human work time and charging direct labor to fixed expenditures.

Isoproductivity of Work Time

The first hypothesis is that each unit of work time, regardless of the day or week and the individual involved, comes out to an average and constant production. In order to be able to add up human time, this hypothesis is necessary, even though it does not reflect reality. It should be underscored, however, that the model of hidden cost evaluation takes into account part of the productivity variables in the direct productivity indicator.

Indirect Labor Productivity

The second methodological hypothesis is that calculating time spent on regulations implies all categories of actors, both for direct and indirect labor. The study of dysfunctions has shown that the production process involves not only so-called direct labor (workers, employees directly involved in production), but also supervisory and managerial staff, in activities that involve scheduling, division of work, coordination of operations among different groups of individuals, choices of dysfunction regulations and participation in those regulations. Socio-economic analysis thus rejects the classic dichotomy between direct and indirect labor, a segmentation that is viewed as unrealistic when considering the operational and functional solidarity between those two categories of labor.

Calculating Unitary Price

Calculating unitary prices of product consumption does not pose any particular problems. However, when products come from internal company services, an option should be taken on the level of internal transfer prices. The evaluation of work time hidden costs is based on three main methodological options: rational allotment of resources, economic value of human work time and classifying direct labor with fixed expenditures.

The rational allotment of resources supposes that a company's equipment and staff levels are rationally determined in function of the production and activity levels anticipated for a given period. Fixed expenditures for that period, in connection with equipment and staff, are thus determined in view of performing a "standard" level of production or activity.

Hence, when actual production or activity levels are below that standard, the under-activity is the source of a cost corresponding to a fraction of fixed expenditures. For this reason, non-production (missed production) time, notably caused by absenteeism, is evaluated at a unitary price that includes fixed expenditures. This methodological option amounts to considering that the non-production (missed production) can be attributed to the dysfunction analyzed.

In practicing this method of calculation, dysfunctions are evaluated in reference to a base of zero-dysfunctions, which amounts to compiling all non-production time. This time is thus only partially compressible. This calculation option implies considering that the reference level of activity fixed by the enterprise corresponds to an activity level without dysfunctions, which is a simplification of reality, since it is inconceivable that an enterprise can do away with all of its dysfunctions. The interest of a zero reference point is that it is fixed.

The time dedicated to regulations poses an evaluation problem. There are two possible methods of examining the economic value of human work time. First, one can incorporate into the cost of human work time a contribution to fixed expenditures, referred to as structural expenditures, notably including general expenses, in accordance with the reasoning noted above. Structural expenditures are engaged in order to attain the standard level of productivity, therefore all time not assigned to production contributes to an under-utilization or waste of structural expenditures. Second, one can consider that organizational members, through their activity at work, pursue the objective of contributing to the achievement of the company's economic and financial results, especially the business operating profits. Work time is thus evaluated in terms of its contribution to the company's gross margin on variable costs.

Both methods have been applied to hidden cost evaluations. The second method appears indispensable in all cases where the enterprise has development opportunities. In the other cases, it would appear advisable, as a general principle, to apply the contribution to structural expenditures approach. An example of this method of calculation is illustrated in Table 2.3.

Observations of personnel management practices and evolutions in labor legislation show that direct labor costs, formerly considered as variable expenditures in function of the company's activity level, should be considered as fixed expenditures. With the exception of certain personnel categories (e.g., salaried employees with limited, short-term contracts), an enterprise cannot rapidly vary the number of its employees, unless it engages considerable direct and indirect layoff costs. Currently, one could consider that an average delay of one year is necessary to diminish personnel expenditures. Consequently, direct labor should be included in fixed expenditures when estimating the financial value of human work (see Table 2.3 for an example of this method of calculation).

Knowing How to Interpret Hidden Cost Results

There are three points to consider with respect to hidden cost evaluation: a) the incomplete nature of the financial evaluation, b) financial

TABLE 2.3   Attributing Direct Labor to Fixed Expenditures

Principle	Example 1984—Agri-food SME (240 employees)
Earnings	14,500,000€
minus	
variable expenditures depending on the level of activity (personnel expenditures excluded)	– 9,700,000€
equals	
Gross margin on variable costs (MVC)	4,800,000€
Hourly contribution to margin on variable costs	Hourly contribution to margin on variable costs

$$= \frac{MVC}{number\ of\ anticipated\ hours}$$

$$= \frac{4,8000,000}{204,000\ h} = 23.5$$

The 204,000 hours break down as follows:
69,000 h manufacturing personnel
96,000 h packaging personnel
11,000 h supervisory personnel
20,000 h maintenance personnel
8,000 h management personnel

amounts made available to the enterprise by lowering hidden costs, and c) the zero reference base for hidden cost evaluation.

Under-Estimation of Hidden Costs

Socio-economic evaluation of dysfunctions is generally under-estimated for three reasons. First, the financial elements of the evaluation are incomplete and certain economic incidences of dysfunctions are evaluated on only a quantitative or qualitative basis. Such is the case when, for example, in a fast evaluation one cannot take into account the incidence of machine manipulation errors on wear-and-tear and the equipment breakdown rate. Second, the time spent by indirect labor, supervision and management in regulating dysfunctions is under-estimated. For example, one day spent by a supervisor giving instructions for mending defects is time taken away for other, potentially more efficient activities. Finally, certain missed opportunities linked to dysfunctions that exist within the enterprise are difficult to evaluate financially. This is the case with commercial damage provoked by overly long delays and insufficient quality.

Despite these problems, one should not renounce, ahead of time, attempts to evaluate these cost components. As an illustration, in an optical enterprise, a rather precise evaluation of commercial damage was made through interviews with head salespersons (Bonnet & Felder, 1984).

TABLE 2.4   Evaluation of Commercial Damage in an Optical Store

Economic effects of dysfunctions	Qualitative data	Quantitative data	Financial data
Loss of sales caused by delays in series and samples deliveries		1 month average delay causing 15% loss of sales on the average	394,000€
Loss in price caused by uncertainty about quality and delivery		Estimated loss of 10% on prices	960,000€
Loss of orders	Contacts not followed up Dissatisfied clients Impossibility of creating new designs, etc.	Not evaluated[a]	Not evaluated[a]
Total	Loss of orders not taken into account		1,354,000€

[a] Not evaluated given the time allocated to the study

As the analysis in Table 2.4 indicates, the total costs came to more than 1,300,000€, or roughly 12,300€ per person per year. Commercial damage represented 65 percent of total hidden costs evaluated in this company.

Surplus Made Available by Lowering Hidden Costs

Hidden costs include a non-production (missed production) component that does not appear in the cost total inscribed in the company's profit and loss statement. Loss of margin on variable costs linked to time lost in mending defects or to personnel absences are some examples. Three cases can be envisaged:

1. If the market is not saturated and can absorb the equivalent of the non-production (missed production) suffered by the enterprise, the enterprise loses the margin on variable costs in terms of earnings not achieved.
2. If the market is completely saturated and cannot absorb the over-production obtained through reduction of dysfunctions, the improved economic performance could consist of reallocating the recovered time to taking action on other dysfunctions.
3. In the context of alternate work arrangements, the reduction of hidden costs could permit a substantial reengineering of production time.

The same reasoning applies when reallocation of recovered time permits launching new products that are welcomed by the market and produce a margin on variable costs. This illustrates the interest of taking into account the complete cost in calculating under-activity. Indeed, considering only the marginal cost leads to impoverishing the field of analysis, by envisaging only the case of production unable to evolve in nature of activity or increase in quantity. The narrowness of the analysis, induced by employing marginal cost or direct-costing, has been responsible for numerous management errors based on erroneous estimations of variable cost, particularly under-estimation of provisional costs.

Evaluating Absolute Hidden Costs

Hidden costs represent absolute costs. This premise means that one is evaluating in monetary units the entire group of hidden costs provoked by the dysfunctions that an organization is subjected to, without predicting what portion of it is compressible. There are three reasons for this. First, various hidden cost evaluations have shown that hidden costs linked to a dysfunction indicator are not proportionate to the frequency of the observed phenomenon. Thus, hidden costs linked to 8 percent absenteeism are usually proportionately inferior to those linked to 15 percent absenteeism. Indeed, beyond a certain threshold, the disturbances created by absenteeism increase more than proportionately. Thus, it is not possible, strictly speaking, to calculate hidden costs attributed to only a fraction of the dysfunctional phenomenon analyzed, because they obey a non-linear function that is difficult to determine.

Second, another method could entail evaluating hidden costs linked to dysfunction defined as discrepancies between observed operating performance and anticipated, or "standard," operating performance established by the organization. Yet, such a method would suppose that the organization had clearly defined its standards in terms of "admissible" absenteeism rates, "optimal" personnel turnover rates, "acceptable" rates of quality defects, and so forth. Such clarification of objectives and standards concerning socio-economic indicators is rarely performed in firms. Thus, calculation based on standards appears difficult to apply.

Third, the last reason for evaluating absolute hidden costs is related to the difficulty in fixing realistic thresholds of compressibility for hidden costs. If all managers and researchers agreed that no absenteeism was an unrealistic hypothesis, opinions would still vary greatly regarding the optimal level of compressibility. Should absenteeism be at 4 percent, 6 percent or 10 percent? Hidden costs are thus calculated on a zero base, which implies that they should be considered as partially compressible costs.

In conclusion, a deposit of hidden costs is only partially exploitable. The difficulty is that the compressible portion of hidden costs cannot be determined a priori. However, the accumulation of cases in the ISEOR database already permits us to formulate prudent, yet useful prognostics for certain types of activities and enterprises. These have often proved more reliable than the usual projections based on findings established according to classic methods. For some years, the findings on the compression of hidden costs we have accumulated have permitted us to extract several general conclusions on the degree of compressibility of hidden costs and the conditions of success (see Savall & Zardet, 1992).

RESULTS OF HIDDEN COST EVALUATIONS

Table 2.5 and Table 2.6 present illustrations of hidden costs evaluated in different sectors of activity. In order to facilitate the comparisons, all hidden costs have been actualized to Euros and have been adjusted to the number of employees in the studied unit. The table displays the amplitude of hidden costs: between 8,300€ and 577,000€ per person per year in the five examples chosen. In comparison with gross minimum wage in 1989,[4] as an illustration, these hidden costs represent between 74 percent and 515 percent of annual minimum wage. This assessment provides an overall idea of the economic stakes involved in hidden cost reduction, the importance of which is clear when compared to labor management negotiation where the stakes are sometime a half-point salary increase.

These results, however, also bring into focus the distribution of hidden cost among the five indicators, which is extremely varied depending on the case. Generally speaking three indicators appear more frequently: absenteeism, non-quality, and, to a lesser degree, variance in direct production. Thus, absenteeism can represent as much as 73 percent of total hidden costs (bank), non-quality costs can attain as much as 87 percent of hidden costs in a semi-industrial glassworks plant.

Hidden Costs Linked to Absenteeism

The amount of hidden costs linked to absenteeism depends on three principal factors: a) the absenteeism rate (i.e., the frequency of absences in proportion to the number of anticipated hours); b) the motive for absences, in connection with the compensation determined by internal company agreements or by the activity branch concerned; and c) cost of regulation

TABLE 2.5 Hidden Cost Results per Person per Year in Five Units (Euros)

Sector of Activity	Metallurgy	Glassworks	Appliance Metalwork	Bank	Electronics
Unit involved in the evaluation	Machining workshop	Pressing and firing workshop	Assembly line	Branch office	Television tube assemblage and control workshop
Number of employees in the unit	35	111	390	22	67
Total hidden costs per person per year	22,200	47,700	15,300	8,300	57,700
Absenteeism	2,600	5,800	4,900	6,000	7,900
Work accidents	1,700	500	500		500
Personnel turnover	200	Not evaluated[a]	300	600	Taken into account in direct productivity variance
Non-quality	10,300	41,400	9,200	1,700	47,700
Direct productivity variance	7,400	Not evaluated[b]	400		4,600

[a] Not evaluated because personnel turnover was nil for the period.
[b] Not evaluated given the time allotted to the financial evaluation of this study.

TABLE 2.6 Hidden Cost Results per Person per Year in the Service Sector (Euros)

Sector of Activity	Assurances	Telecommunication service	Telecommunication Service	Mayor's office	Bank
Unit involved in the evaluation	Personnel reception and management office	Accounting department	Technical service department	Election organization service	Branch office
Number of employees in the unit	16	6	12	11	12
Total hidden costs per person per year	8,200	13,800[a]	11,000[a]	10,400	6,600
Absenteeism Work accidents	1,700	5,100[a]	1,500[a]	1,900	1,700
Personnel turnover	100[a]	4,200	700	Not evaluated[b]	2,500
Non-quality	6,400	4,500	2,500	8,500	2,400
Direct productivity variance					

[a] The total only takes into account the absenteeism partially compressible through socio-economic actions.
[b] Not evaluated given the time allotted to the financial evaluation of the unit.

modes set up to deal with absences at workstations (e.g., over-manning, temporary workers).

The absenteeism rate is calculated in the following way (the number of days anticipated excludes holidays and paid vacation):

$$\frac{\text{number of hours or days of absence}}{\text{number of hours or days anticipated over a given period}}$$

This rate can be calculated over a short period of two weeks to one month, but one should, in this case, make sure that the rate that is calculated is close to the annual rate.

The absenteeism rate is distributed according to absence motives. These represent the motives evoked by the absent employees, which consequently may only partially account for the profound reasons for absences, often more complicated. The motives for absences, presented in Table 2.7, are grouped together into three categories corresponding to three different rationales: a) absenteeism partially compressible through actions of socio-economic innovation, b) absenteeism representative of the enterprise's internal social climate, and c) absenteeism incompressible through actions of socio-economic innovation, of external origin.

The distribution of absenteeism rates among these three categories provides an abundance of information. Looking at Table 2.7, the overall ab-

TABLE 2.7 Absenteeism and Hidden Costs[a]

	Case 1 Bank	Case 2 Chemicals	Case 3 Telecommunication services
Unit studied	Data processing department	Automated production workshop	Accounting department
Overall annual absenteeism	9.0%	11.0%	7.8%
Partially compressible absenteeism	5.5%	5.0%	7.8%
Absenteeism representative of internal social climate	2.1%	0.6%	0.0%
Absenteeism of external origin	1.4%	5.4%	0.0%

[a] The amount of hidden costs linked to absenteeism depends on three principal factors:
1) the absenteeism rate (i.e., the frequency of absences in proportion to the number of anticipated hours)

senteeism rate is higher in Case 1 than in Case 3 (9% and 7.8%), but the enterprise flexibility margin is higher in Case 3 where total absenteeism is partially compressible through socio-economic innovation actions.

Regulation Modes

The study of regulation modes and their economic impact consists of analyzing the distribution of regulation of absences according to the principal modes and types (see Table 2.8). As an example, in an analysis of an electronics factory (Bonnet & Labaume, 1982), 1,348 hours of absences were observed over a two-week period, corresponding to an absenteeism rate of 27.5 percent. This problem was regulated as follows: 13.5 percent of the hours were replaced by calling in additional help from within the enterprise; 13.5 percent of the hours were replaced by a multi skilled employee from the workshop; 27 percent of the hours were replaced by calling in temporary help; and 46 percent resulted in stoppage of the absent employee's machine, which is non-production (missed production).

TABLE 2.8   Classification by Motives for Absence

1. Absenteeism partially compressible through socio-economic innovation actions
    - Illness
    - Work accidents[a]
    - Authorized absence
    - Absence without motive
    - Injuries
    - Internal strikes
    - Lateness
    - Compensatory rest
    - Recovery of additional hours
2. **Absenteeism reflecting the enterprise's internal "social climate"**[a]
    - On-going professional training
    - Delegation (employee-management committee, personnel representative, union representative)
    - Leave for training
    - Sabbatical leave
3. **Absenteeism due to motives external to the enterprise**[b]
    - Leave without pay
    - Family events (maternity, death, marriage, sick children)
    - Strikes for external rationales (nationwide strikes, solidarity strikes)

---

[a] Work accident motives are included when they are not the object of a specific evaluation of work accident indicators

[b] Incompressible through socio-economic innovation actions.

It is then necessary to embark on an in-depth study of the overall impacts caused by each regulation mode, calculating the unitary cost of each regulation mode. Figure 2.5 presents the analysis of absences regulated by double substitution and by workstation stoppage at the end of the production line.

The study of absence regulation in this manner reveals the unitary cost of each regulation mode, and consequently the distribution of costs according to the chosen regulation mode. As another example, in a wire-drawing workshop (Collignon, 1978), we have demonstrated that regulation costs for the same period of absence (8 hours) vary between 74€ when the absence was regulated by overstaffing and 1,200€ when the absence was regulated by double substitution with production stoppage at the end of the production line. The overall cost of absence regulation is thus obtained by multiplying the unitary cost of each regulation mode by its frequency (for an example, see Table 2.9).

Compensation for Absenteeism

Absenteeism has a financial incidence, independently of regulation modes, in terms of compensation salary paid for the absences. This incidence is linked to the motives for absence and the collective agreements

TABLE 2.9   Annual Cost of Absence Regulations in an Electronic Component Assemblage Workshop (58 workers)

Mode of regulation	Frequency (hours)	Unitary cost (1989 Euros)	Total cost (1989 Euros)
Temporary help	6,210	15	93,150
Overstaffing	3,105	12	37,260
Multiskilled employee	3,105	26	80,730
Work stoppage	10,580	26	275,080
Sub-total			**486,220**
Time spent by supervisors reorganizing the workshop[a]			
2 foremen	450	16	7,200
2 supervisors	225	24	5,400
Sub-total			**12,600**
Total			498,820
Cost per person per year[b]			8,600

[a] In this evaluation, time spent by supervisors is relatively independent of the regulation mode chose. Therefore, they were evaluated overall.

[b] This cost is under-estimated because it does not take into account direct productivity variance and quality defects linked to absence regulations. These are entered under other indicators.

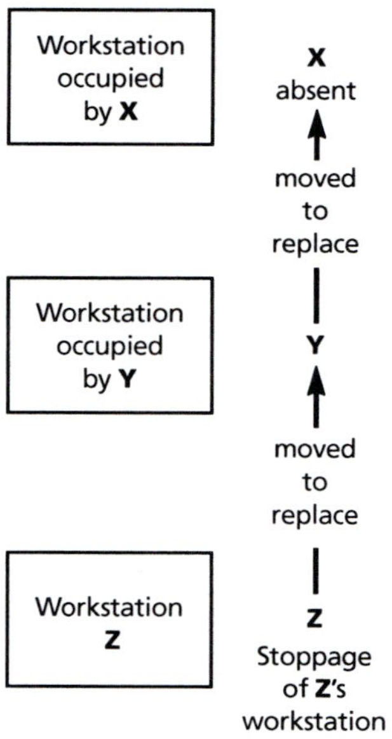

Description of effects	Economic implications	Hidden cost component
• Lateness in starting work	Stoppage of machines or workstations	Non-production (missed production)
• Transmitting instructions to replacement **Y** and additional supervision of his/her work	Indirect time	*Overtime*
• Remuneration of **Y** at a rate of **X**	Payroll costs	Salary variance
• Work done completely by **Z**. Errors of or quality defects	Cost of non-quality	Non-production (missed production) and over-consumption
• Equipment deterioration	Cost of repairs	*Overtime*
• Productivity of **Z** inferior to that of **Y**	Non-production (missed production)	and over-consumption Non-production (missed production)
• Necessary overtime	Payroll cost	*Overtime*
• Delays: client discontent	Commercial damage	Non-production (missed production)

Workstation occupied by **X**

X absent

moved to replace

Workstation occupied by **Y**

Y

moved to replace

Workstation **Z**

Z Stoppage of **Z**'s workstation

Figure 2.5   Analysis of absences regulated through double substitution and by workstation stoppage.

TABLE 2.10   Average Daily Cost of Sick Leave Compensation in a Bank

For an absence lasting less than 3 days and for the first 3 days of every absence:
- Permanent staff member   156€
- Non-permanent staff member   0

For days of absence from the 4th day on:
- Permanent staff member   78€
- Non-permanent staff member   0

currently in effect in the enterprise. Conventionally, these compensation costs are included under the heading of salary variance. Sick leave and, in certain cases, family events, usually entail salaries paid by the enterprise. Let us specify that the portion of compensation costs paid by the Social Security system should be deducted, since we are attempting to calculate the hidden costs paid by the enterprise (as an example, see Table 2.10).

Costs Linked to Absenteeism

The overall cost linked to absenteeism is thus the sum of the: a) compensation paid to absent personnel; and b) cost of regulations implemented to reorganize the unit (e.g., workshop, office, department). It is interesting to highlight the portion of total hidden costs linked to absenteeism, which are partially compressible through socio-economic innovation actions. It is, indeed, this fraction of costs the enterprise can start reducing.

In the example given in Table 2.11, the cost linked to partially compressible absenteeism represents 44 percent of overall costs. This example also highlights a result that is verified in all our evaluations: there is no proportional relationship between rates and costs of absenteeism, and generally speaking, no proportional relationship between rates and costs of all dysfunctions. In this case, 54 percent of the absences generate 44 percent of the costs. This phenomenon can be explained by the economic consequences of the cost of regulations adopted or chosen by company management to fill in the absences.

HIDDEN COSTS LINKED TO WORK ACCIDENTS

The work accident indicator is close to absenteeism in terms of hidden cost evaluation. In the case of overall hidden cost evaluation of a unit, that is using all five dysfunction indicators, there are two possible methods.

TABLE 2.11 Annual Hidden Costs Linked to Absenteeism in the Accounting Department of a Service Enterprise in Telecommunications

	Overall absenteeism	Partially compressible absenteeism
Annual absenteeism rate	10.8%	5.9%
	(100%)	(54%)
Hidden costs		
A. Absence compensation	21,400	13,500
B. Regulation by non-production (missed production)	18,500	15,300
C. Regulation by replacement	41,000[a]	7,000
Total annual hidden costs	80,900	35,900
	(100%)	(44%)
Average cost per person per year[b]	12,600	5,600
Percentage of hidden costs/payroll of the department	31%	14%

[a] This amount is due to the replacement of a maternity leave absence.
[b] Average number of employees: 6.4 employees for the year.

The first method is the specific evaluation of hidden costs linked to work accidents. This method is relevant to companies where work accidents are considered a major dysfunction—essentially in the industrial (manufacturing) sector and, in some cases, certain service activities subject to non-negligible risks, such as hospitals. The second method focuses on the evaluation of costs linked to work accidents included in absenteeism.

This second method, which we often utilize in the service sector, includes work accidents among the motives for absences (see Table 2.8). Since this approach was dealt with under absenteeism, this discussion focuses on the first method, specific to work accidents. In this case, it is important to be sure that double accounting of cost elements does not occur. The assessment of absenteeism should thus exclude absences for work accidents, as well as all regulations made necessary by accidents.

Costs linked to work accidents (see Table 2.12) are broken down as follows:

- Compensation paid to absent employees, after deduction of the amount paid by Social Security;
- Cost of work accident regulations, distinguishing between regulations in the workplace (e.g., industrial accident victims) and administrative operations (e.g., filing accident reports); and
- Social Security insurance installments paid by the enterprise to cover work accidents. Indeed, especially in the industrial sector, the em-

TABLE 2.12   Evaluation of Annual Costs Linked to Work Accidents in a Metalwork Machining Workshop

Cost heading	Total (Euros)
Compensation paid to absent employees	9,400
Regulation through non-production (missed production)	8,500
Cost of administrative operations	Not evaluated[a]
Pro-rata of company installments paid to Social Security for work accidents	33,800
Total hidden costs	**51,700**
Costs per employee per year (30 employees)	1,700

[a] Not evaluated given the time allotted.

Source: Marc Bonnet and Annie Bartoli, under the direction of Henri Savall, *Diagnostic socio-économique dans un atelier de fabrication et dans le service comptabilité d'une usine de métallurgie* [Socio-economic diagnostic in a manufacturing workshop and in the accounting service of a metallurgy factory], ISEOR report, January 1981, p. 90.

ployer's contribution to Social Security, regarding work accidents, is partly calculated in function of the seriousness and frequency of work accidents that took place in the enterprise during the previous year. This evaluation corresponds to four work accidents of varying degrees of seriousness.

Hidden Costs Linked to Personnel Turnover

Personnel turnover can be considered as a dysfunction since employee movement (arrivals and departures in a micro-space: service, workshop, department, agency, including internal company transfers) can readily disturb the unit in question. Technically, costs linked to hiring an employee should be considered an immaterial investment in human resources that are to be amortized within a given period, or "standard lifespan." Thus, we shall not speak about hidden costs for the enterprise except when the employee quits his or her job before the end of that period (see Savall, 1981). In practice, however, enterprises never determine the standard lifespan of the different company employments. Therefore, once again, we evaluate "absolute" hidden costs. Hidden costs linked to personnel turnover depend, of course, on the amount of personnel turnover, whatever the motive, but also on recruitment, hiring, integration and transfer policy.

Personnel Turnover and Instability Rates

Personnel turnover should be analyzed within the perimeter of the studied unit. Thus, when the study concerns a workshop, all arrivals into the workshop and departures from the workshop are taken into consideration, even the personnel coming from or going to other company units. We want to zero in on the hidden costs the studied unit is subjected to, as a means of explaining its level of performance.

Two indicators are calculated to assess the impacts of personnel turnover, after drawing up the unit's table of personnel "arrivals and departures." The personnel turnover rate measures definitive departures from the unit, whatever the motive (e.g., firing, quitting, transfer, retirement). It is calculated as follows:

$$\frac{\text{Number of permanent staff departures}}{\text{Average number of permanent staff members}}$$

The personnel instability rate takes into consideration all personnel turnover: incumbent, definite term, internship and temporary workers. This rate depicts more clearly the extent of disturbances to which the unit is subject, in terms of welcoming new recruits, training, quality defects, and so forth. It is calculated as follows:

$$\frac{\begin{array}{l}\text{Number of employees entering the unit}\\ + \text{Number of employees leaving the unit}\\ + \text{Number of employees entering and leaving the unit}\end{array}}{\text{Average number of employees in the unit}}$$

When the unit has few employees (less than 10 persons), the turnover rate and the instability rate can be high, even if personnel turnover is low. This accurately depicts the disturbance caused in a unit of 3 employees, for example, by the departure of one of its members. Table 2.13 presents several examples of turnover and instability rates, illustrating the complementary nature of these two indicators.

Once turnover and instability rates have been calculated (social module), hidden costs caused by this personnel turnover are identified (organizational and financial modules). These costs derive from three phenomena:

TABLE 2.13   Personnel Turnover and Instability Rates in Different Enterprises

Activity Sector	Bank	Bank	Bank	Socio-educational
Studied Unit	Flying team	Agency 1	Agency 2	Educational team
Number of employees in the unit	6	19	4	16
Annual turnover rate	33%	55%	0%	31%
Annual instability rate	147%	86%	133%	82%

departure of an employee from the unit; arrival of his or her replacement into the unit; and, sometimes, the interval of time between an employee's departure and his or her successor's arrival, which also generates dysfunctions and therefore hidden costs.

Hidden Costs Linked to the Entry of a New Employee

As an example of the ramifications of personnel turnover, the discussion focuses on calculating the costs linked to the arrival of a new employee. Three components can be identified:

- Personnel recruitment costs, which require time on the part of personnel services and unit supervisors. Recruitment often generates consumption of related goods and services (e.g., job advertisements in newspapers, testing). depending on company recruitment procedure.
- Personnel training costs for the new recruits when training is necessary before taking over the job.
- Personnel learning costs in connection with new recruits gaining awareness of what the job entails, becoming acquainted with the production unit and the enterprise as a whole. This learning period usually means under-activity, causing hidden costs due to non-production (missed production), which exists whatever the complexity of the job.

Generally speaking, these three cost components vary in function of the new employee's familiarity with the enterprise (internal transfer) or lack thereof (external recruit).

Table 2.14 presents an example of the entry costs of an accounting department agent in a telecommunication service company, distinguishing between internal transfer and external recruitment. A unit's personnel rotation cost is obtained by multiplying unitary costs (see Table 2.14) by the rotation rate for a period of at least one year (see Table 2.15). It is also possible, when necessary, to carry out an analysis differentiating the principal positions subject to rotation.

Hidden Costs Linked to Quality Defects

There are two separate cases with respect to quality defects, depending on whether or not the enterprise has defined quality norms. The hidden cost evaluation method for non-quality can be broken down into the following three stages:

1. Identifying the principal types of quality defects and carrying out statistical analysis of the frequency of these defects;

2. Studying the regulation of quality defects and the principal regulation utilized by the enterprise (e.g., alteration, repair, rejection, downgrading, scrap return); in the case of quality defects that require complicated regulations, it is possible to draw up graphs of regulations (see Figure 2.6); and
3. Calculating costs linked to quality defects, which include regulation costs and quality control system costs. Indeed, it is thanks to these two frameworks that the enterprise produces a given level of quality (see Hirniak, 1983).

TABLE 2.14 Comparison of Costs Linked to the Arrival of a New Employee in an Accounting Department by External Recruitment and Internal Transfer (Euros)

Hidden costs	External Recruitment	Internal Transfer
Recruitment		
Personnel services	4,200	1,100
Orientation unit	400	100
Training	0	0
Learning period (under-productivity)	9,100	5,300
Total	**13,700**	**6,500**

TABLE 2.15 Examples of Costs Linked to Personnel Turnover (Euros)

Activity Sector	Socio-educational	Telecom services	Metallurgy
Studied Unit	Entire establishment	Accounting department	Machining workshop
Number of employees in the unit (average calculated over one year)	30	6.4	30
Annual turnover rate	40%	36%	26%
Hidden costs:			
recruitment	9,500	9,600	Not evaluated[a]
training	300[b]	Not evaluated[a]	1,300
learning period	200[b]	19,800	3,600[c]
Total	**10,000**	**29,400**	**4,900**
Annual hidden cost/per person	300	4,600	160

[a] Given the time allotted to the study.
[b] These costs are largely under-estimated: they do not include training and learning period costs of recruited educators.
[c] Quality defects were not evaluated.

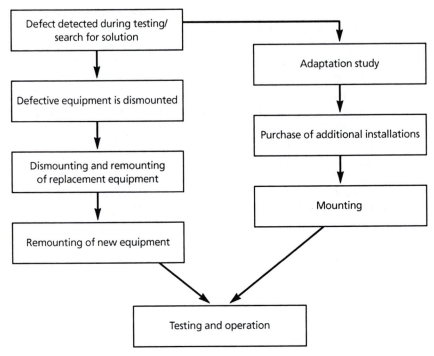

Figure 2.6 Graph of quality defect regulation: "Non-standard equipment" in a textile factory. *Source:* Philippe Petiau, *Socio-economic diagnostic in a weaving workshop: Analysis of the quality indicator,* ISEOR report, March 1983.

The study of the hidden costs related to quality defects in many enterprises reveals certain exorbitant amounts, as illustrated in Table 2.16. The extent of these disturbances can be estimated in terms of time taken away from productive activity. In an analysis of a clothing factory, for example, it was estimated that two full-time employees were devoted entirely to alterations of manufactured clothing, out of a total fifteen employees.

Hidden Costs Linked to Direct Productivity Variance

In a number of instances, various tasks, notably the case in tertiary activities, will not have defined quality norms. The evaluation of non-quality costs is therefore joined to the evaluation of direct productivity variance. The method involves precisely identifying elementary dysfunctions and the time spent regulating them over a period of several weeks. The sum of these times represents the activity that was necessary to produce services at a given level of quality, and which harmed production of additional services. As an example, Table 2.17 presents a detailed inventory of hidden costs due to quality defects and direct productivity variance in a bank agency.

TABLE 2.16   Examples of Costs Linked to Non-Quality (Euros)

Activity Sector	Metal transformation	Metallurgy	Electronics
Studied Unit	Etching (engraving) workshop	Appliance manufacturing workshops	Electronic canon assemblage workshop
Number of employees	43	195	58
Hidden costs:			
quality defect regulation	1,300,000	193,600	632,000
quality control	118,000	Not evaluated[a]	440,000
Total hidden costs	1,418,000	193,000	1,072,000
Annual hidden cost/per person	32,900	900	18,400
Total costs/budget of the unit	31%	(2% of earnings)	32%

[a] Given the time allotted to the study.

Direct productivity can be considered a wrap-up indicator, for it measures the residues of direct under-production that were not included in other indicators. Still, it remains a full-fledged indicator, taking stock of variance measured between a standard, when it exists (e.g., technical standard versus actual productivity, with respect to work hours).

As with all other indicators, hidden costs linked to direct productivity variance can be broken down into key categories: excess salaries, overtime, over-consumption, and non-production (missed production). The discussion now turns to an in-depth calculation of over-consumption and non-production (missed production), which in our evaluations constitute the bulk of hidden costs linked to direct productivity variance.

Over-Consumption

The ISEOR research database shows that the utilization of products, raw material or energy in the manufacturing process can undergo fluctuations independent from product quantities. These fluctuations, or variance, with regard to the theoretical quantities to be consumed, represent part of the hidden costs of direct non-productivity.

As an example, in a highly automated chemical enterprise (Bonnet, 1981), we studied the consumptions of two "utilities" required in the production process: natural gas and steam.

We measured a six-month period for each one of these two utilities: actual consumption of these utilities and actual production of manufactured products, which of course explains part of actual consumptions. Thus, over-consumption of steam and gas was recorded on certain days, while on others one could talk of under-consumption, by reference to a regression line.

TABLE 2.17   Direct Productivity Variance and Quality Defects in a Bank Agency

Type	Time spent on regulation (duration × number of employees)	Time spent annually (hours)
Dysfunctions causing client complaints		
Processing customer requests and complaints (recorded in 1982)		17
Transmitted by Production Management		
in writing: VIP clients		29
by telephone: other clients		81
Rectification following erroneous deposit of checks	15 min/day	56
Rectification following errors (typing errors)	2 min/day	8
Response to client following complaints for rejected means of payment	15 min/day	3
Explanation of bank charges to client, following complaint (misunderstanding of procedures on the part of client)	1 h/quarter	4
Response to client following non-arrival of checkbook	10 min/day	37
Response to client complaints following breakdown of automatic teller machine	15 min/two-week period	6
Various errors		
Search for cash register error	1 h 30/month	18
Record mark, telephone calls for installment errors (administrative service)	4 h/month	48
Search for documents or file components, in the event of loss or following assessment error during constitution of the file)	1 h/week	52
Dysfunctions generated by clients		
Telephone calls to clients when proof of residence not sent by the client	8 h/month	96
Typing salary statements for a client enterprise when payday arrives	2 h 30/month	30
Redirection errors		
Response to phone calls redirected by error (recorded over a period of 10 days)	40 min/day	149
Time spent processing mail sent to the agency by error	15 min/day	56
Total		689
Total hidden costs: Euros		26,700€
Hidden costs per person and per year: (12 p.)		2,200€

Source: Amélioration des prestations commerciales et du fonctionnement interne d'une agence bancaires. Diagnostic et projet socio-économique [Improving commercial service and internal operations of a bank agency. Socio-economic diagnostic and project], ISEOR report, December 1983.

Over a one-year period, over-consumption of vapor represented 85,000 tons, or approximately 2.13 million Euros. This amount corresponds to 83 percent of the utilities' overall payroll. Over-consumption of gas amounted to approximately 3 million cubic meters, or 320,000 Euros, or 23 percent of the overall payroll. The sum of these two costs represented more than 73,000 Euros per worker per year.

Hidden cost analysis shows that incorporation of technical progress provokes a chain reaction of hidden costs. Indeed, the human act becomes rarer yet more costly when it falters: over-consumption costs increase proportionally to the degree of capital-intensive technological progress in the form of equipment costs (sub-form of amortization). Simultaneously, human time (representing human acts) is inversely proportionate to the incorporation rate of technical progress. Thus, we have often observed that new technologies of production or information introduce a factor increasing the level of hidden costs, when the socio-economic operational level of the company is insufficient.

Non-Production (Missed Production)

Non-production (missed production) represents lost earnings linked either to machine stoppage or decreased human efficiency (e.g., dexterity, rapidity). Once again, relevant indicators must be found, taking into consideration company activities and its product quantity measurement indicators. In an industrial sheet-metal shop, for example, we applied the following ratio, which was regularly referred to in the company:

$$\frac{\text{Production express in Euros}}{\text{Number of work hours}}$$

This ratio represents the average hourly production estimated in Euros. The variance should be measured between this and another ratio, which could be either the company's established productivity standard or compared to a previous period of the same measure. In this industrial sheet-metal shop, the comparison was made between two periods: in period 1, the hourly production estimated in Euros was 50 Euros; in period 2, it was 55 Euros. This variance represents a hidden cost reduction of 625,400 Euros.

A Complete Hidden Cost Evaluation in a Work Unit of an Electronics Firm

This section illustrates a complete case of socio-economic evaluation implementing the five dysfunction indicators. This evaluation focused on an assembly and control unit for television tubes (Savall, 1984).

Synthesis of the Hidden Cost Evaluation

The synthesis is presented in Table 2.18 and includes: a) qualitative results, from interviews with the personnel and from observation by intervener-researchers; b) non-financial quantitative results, from statistical analysis of the dysfunctions detected; and c) financial results, from monetary calculation of dysfunction regulation.

Calculation of the Margin on Variable Costs

Overtime and non-production (missed production) are evaluated using the hourly contribution to the margin on variable costs. This method of calculation is presented in Table 2.19.

Costs Linked to Absenteeism

The annual cost of absenteeism amounted to 572,700 Euros (see Table 2.20) in the work unit. This cost is under-estimated to the degree that it does not take into account certain effects, such as under-activity of the sector in downstream position (e.g., packaging, task-sequencing disturbances, in-process material overstocking).

Personnel Turnover

The interviews provided explanations for certain departure causes: 1) the physical working conditions would seem responsible for certain departures, notably for vision and backache problems; 2) rotating 8-hour work shifts sometimes constitute a constraint that is difficult to reconcile with private life; and 3) the work appears belittling, due notably to a lack of information and communication difficulties, which was also a contributing factor to departures.

Statistical analysis of this indicator was carried out in the work unit over the course of a year: out of 54 workers, there were 8 departures, which represents a turnover rate of 15 percent. The departures were replaced either by new recruits or by transferring workers from other sectors of the factory. It is interesting to note that no theoretical training session on the characteristics of work in this particular unit had been organized in the past three years, while half of the personnel had been replaced. The integration procedure for a new employee was reduced to the strict minimum. A few starting tips were given on-the-job by the supervisor or the technician, followed up by supervision by a seasoned worker in the section. This could partly explain the disparities observed among new workers in attaining quantity and quality objectives. Indeed, several members of the supervisory staff mentioned during interviews that there was a connection between investing in a new recruit's initial training, that person's learning difficulties and, consequently, the quality of the individual's products and direct productivity.

TABLE 2.18 Synthesis of a Hidden Cost Evaluation in an Assembly and Control Workshop for Television Components

Indicator	Qualitative results	Quantitative results	Financial results (Euros)	
Absenteeism	• Packaging under-activity • Task-sequencing disturbance • In-process material overstocking	• 13,000 hours of absences in 1983 plus 2,500 additional hours • Partially compressible absenteeism = 11.2% • Total absenteeism = 11.7%	• Additional hours • Sick leave compensation + work accidents • Non-production (missed production) Total:	12,500 100,200 460,000 572,700
Work accidents		• 1,384 stoppage hours in 1983	• Social Security contribution for work accidents	35,700
Personnel turnover		• 8 departures out of 54 workers in 1983 • 1 to 3 months learning period for new recruits	Direct productivity variances taken into account in the evaluation	
Quality defects	Risk of losing clients	• 7.9% recovery of discarded tubes • 3,330 broken necks in 1983		292,200 487,300
	Company's corporate image impaired with respect to competitors	• % 1.5 tubes sold rejected by clients, of which 40% are attributed to assembly + control • 27 employees out of 3 teams occupied with controls	Total:	364,400 1,851,300 2,995,200
Direct productivity variance		69.6 tubes recovered out of 75 tubes (standard)		265,701
		Total hidden costs		3,869,300
		Hidden costs per person per year (67 employees)		57,700

TABLE 2.19   Detailed Explanation of Margin on Variable Costs Calculation

Items of variable cost margin in the workshop (in thousands of Euros)		Amount in Euros
Fixed expenditures directly attributed to the workshop	(1)	2,181,000
		5,513,000
Fixed expenditures indirectly attributed to the workshop		
$1,774 \times 25\%$		443,000
$16,578 \times 25\%$	(2)	4,144,000
Fixed expenditures indirectly attributed to the firm		
$14,338 \times 4.75\%$	(3)	681,000
Total fixed expenditures attributed to the workshop		
$(4) = (1) + (2) + (3)$		12,962,000
Profits		
$(21,680 + 12\ 962) \times 1.91\%$	(5)	661,000
Margin on variable costs for the workshop		
$(6) = (4) + (5)$		13,623,000

Note: This table represents percentages of the studied work unit's cost items, proportionate to the number of employees in the workshop. For example, the company's fixed indirect costs are 14,338 K€. The workshop represents 4.75% of company employees. Thus, 14,338 K€ × 4.75%, or 680,000€, indirect costs are charged to the workshop.

The hourly contribution to variable costs is the following:

$$\frac{13,623,000}{174 \text{ employees} \times 221 \text{ days} \times 8 \text{ hours}} = \frac{13,623,000}{307,632} = 44$$

TABLE 2.20   Calculation of Hidden Costs Linked to Absenteeism

	12,964 hours of absence in 1983	
Sick leave and work accident compensation	Regulations	
	Additional Hours	Non-production (missed production)
10,040 hours representing 100,200€	2,498 hours representing 12,500€	10,466 hours representing 460,000€
	Estimated Total: 572,700€	

Quality Defects

Figure 2.7 illustrates the different routes possible for tubes in function of the decisions made by each actor involved in the quality production process. There were numerous dysfunctions affecting the quality production process in the work unit. First, there was rejection of "at-the-limit" tubes by workers, but which were considered adjustable by the inspector. These tubes required more time to be correctly adjusted and risked being rejected

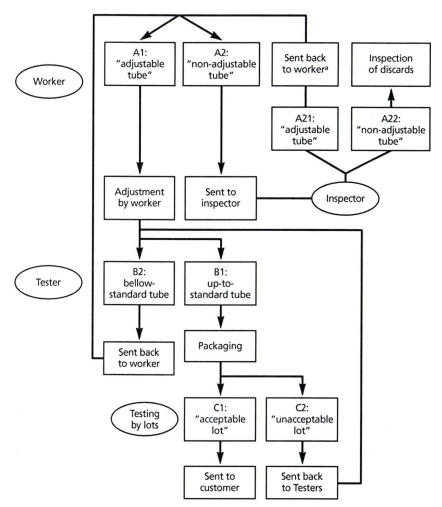

Figure 2.7 Quality production process.

by the quality testers. In some cases, workers adjusted these tubes after having consulted the posted supervisor, who then indicated to the quality testers that they should be more lenient given the slightly-defective character of these tubes. In other cases, these tubes remained on the conveyor belt for several hours, even until the following team arrives. While there were no precise measure of the rejection rate of tubes by workers, interviews pointed out that 50 percent of the tubes rejected by workers were repairable.

A second dysfunction concerned worker-tester conflict over tubes that were considered as scrap heap material by the testers. Given the multiplicity of variables influencing the quality of tubes and the different techniques that intervened between adjustments and quality control stations, quality assessment was difficult for tubes at the limit of quality norms. In many instances, a tester's decision to discard a tube was contested by a worker. These disagreements often resulted in conflicts that required intervention from higher management. It should be noted that interviews conducted with workers revealed strong disagreement concerning testers' capacity to evaluate the quality of tubes, notably due to the wide-spread use of temporary help for testing.

Third, return of more than 1.5 percent of the tubes sent to clients (television manufacturers) and deemed rejects despite the nearly-systematic control of tubes after adjustment. At the time of the diagnostic, approximately 75 percent of the adjusted tubes were tested by testers. The year's objective was to reduce this rate of testing to 40 percent, but management seemed very dubious about attaining that objective, given the client-return rate which was three times higher than that of Japanese competitors.

The estimated cost of product quality defects includes four principal components: the cost of rejected tubes that had been adjusted; the cost of broken necks; the cost of tubes sold and returned by clients because of non-quality; and the cost of time spent controlling quality. The overall cost of quality defects was estimated at 3,835,600E, which was still under-estimated in that the risk of losing clients and the negative consequences for the corporate image were not taken into consideration.

Direct Productivity Variance

Some of the causes of the direct productivity variance were alluded to during interviews:

- *break-down time* was cited as a major factor in production disturbance;
- *supply problems* of tubes to the workshop were considered detrimental to productivity because they implied periods of under-activity for adjustment workshops, testing and packaging;
- *lack of machine maintenance* and *insufficient tools* were also cited as causes of productivity variances; and
- *different rhythms* among workers and production stoppages at the end of the workstation, when most adjusters have finished their work on 75 tubes, were considered to be a source of problems for testers, because this forced them to alternate between over-charged and under-charged periods of activity.

The direct productivity variance was calculated according to two elements: 1) the *reference norm* (i.e., 75 tubes per worker per day) in this application (rather than an official norm); and 2) the *actual number* of adjusted tubes: it is 69.9 tubes per worker per day. This latter number was taken from production reports by the sector's supervisor over a five-week period and extrapolated to one year. Based on these calculations, the direct productivity variance represented 340,200€.

CONCLUSION

The stakes of hidden cost can be very high. A company that can endure high hidden costs is a company that has high potential for improved profitability, which can significantly contribute to its survival and development in the coming years—if the company succeeds in tapping that potential. These estimations, which are based on the framework presented in this chapter, reveal amounts varying between 9,200€ and 65,600€ per person per year. These hidden costs are caused by dysfunctions linked to the five key indicators: absenteeism, work accidents, personnel turnover, quality defects and direct productivity variances. While it is possible to evaluate the costs linked to each one of these indicators on a separate basis, an overall estimation is preferable, because hidden costs "cluster" in places that differ from one enterprise to another.

These sometimes-exorbitant sums are nonetheless usually under-estimated in reality, as ISEOR's long experience has proved. However, they represent costs that are only partially compressible. A part of hidden costs is over-expenditure or excessive spending; the rest corresponds to missed earnings, to lost production. Finally, it is important to remember a key point of the chapter—that hidden costs constitute the financial manifestation of phenomena called dysfunctions. These dysfunctions can be detected and dealt with using the qQFi method, drawing on qualitative, quantitative and financial data in order to avoid missing information that can prove precious for remedial action.

NOTES

1. The complementary nature of qualitative, quantitative and financial datasets is also discussed in connection with the strategic piloting logbook (see Chapter 9).
2. This is the case for many of the diagnostics cited in ISEOR's published work (see Appendix 1). It should also be pointed out that these evaluations can be applied to enterprises considered to be in good health and to those in distress. Regarding the latter, see "Managing endangered enterprises: Lessons learned from socio-economic interventions in two small to medium enterprises following bankruptcy", Masters Memoir, University of Lyon 2, Groupe École Supérieure de Commerce de Lyon, Octobre 1984.
3. It should be remembered, however, that these first evaluations included finetuning and testing the operational method.
4. The gross minimum wage in 1989 (March) was 4,960 Francs (94€), or approximately 59,000F per year (11,200€).

REFERENCES

Bonnet, M. (1981). *Communication, emploie de la ressource humaine et dysfonctionnements dans un atelier automatisé d'une usine de chimie* [Communication, human resource employment and dysfunctions in an automated workshop of a chemical factory]. Ecully, France: ISEOR Report.

Bonnet, M. & Domeur, F. (1984). *Diagnostics socio-économique rapides dans des PMI de la bonneterie* [Rapid socio-economic diagnostics in small to medium garment industries]. Management Research Reports, no. 7, pp 1–25.

Bonnet, M. & Felder, F. (1985). *Diagnostic socio-économique de la qualité globale des produits et des services dans une entreprise de lunetterie* [Socio-economic diagnostic of products and service overall quality in an optical enterprise]. Ecully, France: ISEOR Report.

Bonnet, M. & Labaume, G. (1982). *Parcellisation des tâches, absentéisme et défauts de qualité dans un atelier de montage électronique* [Breakdown into individual tasks, absenteeism and quality defects in an electronics assembly workshop]. Ecully, France: ISEOR Report.

Collignon, E. (1978). *Évaluation financière de l'absentéisme dans une tréfilerie* [Financial evaluation of absenteeism in a wiredrawing plant]. Ecully, France: ISEOR Report.

Hirniak, C. 1983). *L'analyse de la qualité par la méthode de diagnostic: étude comparée de deux approches, l'approche qualiticienne et l'approche socio-économique* [The analysis of quality by the method of diagnostic: A comparative study of two approaches, the quality approach and the socio-economic approach]. Masters thesis in Management Sciences under the supervision of H. Savall, University Lille 2.

Petiau, P. (1983). *Diagnostic socio-économique dans un atelier de tissage. Analyse de l'indicateur qualité* [Socio-economic diagnostic in a weaving workshop: Analysis of the quality indicator]. Ecully, France: ISEOR Report.

Savall, H. (1984). *Rigidité socio-organisationnelle et coûts cachés dans un atelier de finition de tubes de télévision* [Socio-organizational rigidness and hidden costs in a television tube finishing workshop]. Ecully, France: ISEOR Report.

Savall, H. (1979). *Enrichir le travail humain: l'évaluation économique* [An Economic Evaluation of Job-Enrichment]. Paris: Dunod.

Savall, H. (1979). *Reconstruire l'entreprise—L'évaluation socio-économique des conditions de vie au travail* [Reconstructing the enterprise: Socio-economic evaluation of work life conditions]. Paris: Dunod.

Savall, H. (1978). *Analyse économique des conditions de travail* [Economic analysis of working conditions]. Scientific report to the National Delegation for Scientific and Technical Research (DGRST)]. December.

Savall, H. & Bonnet, M. (1985). *Méthode de diagnostic socio-économique de l'efficacité et de la qualité dans les PMI* [Socio-economic diagnostic method of effectiveness and quality in small to medium industries]. Ecully, France: ISEOR Methodology Report.

Savall, H. & Zardet, V. (1992). *Le nouveau contrôle de gestion* [New management control]. Eyrolles: Éditions Comptables Malesherbes.

Zardet, V. (1985). *Diagnostic et projet socio-économiques en vue de la perspective de fermeture d'un service de traitements informatiques dans une banque régionale* [Relational conditions, work organization and dysfunctions: Socio-economic diagnostic of an accounting service in a small to medium international telecommunications service]. Ecully, France: ISEOR Report.

CHAPTER 3

THE SUSTAINABLE REDUCTION OF HIDDEN COSTS

Since 1978, the principal objective of ISEOR's experimental intervention-research has been to demonstrate that hidden costs can be sustainably reduced, by conducting transformation actions. From a pragmatic perspective, one can determine the extent to which company effectiveness can be improved or whether certain hidden costs are inevitable. From a scientific perspective, it is also important to examine the variability of hidden costs. Indeed, the concept of hidden costs becomes solidly justified when their variability is fully demonstrated, the absence of which reverts to so-called "organization slack" theories of Anglo-Saxon origin. These theories have largely been utilized by theorists and practitioners to ideologically justify the necessity of dysfunctions.

In the early 1970s, Savall (1974, 1975) struck out in diametric opposition to these theories, hypothesizing that hidden cost levels measured at a given moment corresponded to *hypertrophied* "slack" due to the enterprise's *historical entropy*.[1] According to Savall (1975), "slack" can be divided into its "physiological" component (a necessary part of the enterprise's life) and its "pathological" component. Incompressible hidden costs are seen as part of the enterprise's physiology, while compressible hidden costs (i.e., costs reduced by the enterprise's socio-economic development actions), are declared pathological, since their elimination improves the enterprise's "state of health."

Mastering Hidden Costs and Socio-Economic Performance, pages 67–88
Copyright © 2008 by Information Age Publishing
All rights of reproduction in any form reserved.

Actions addressing human behavior, however, have proved insufficient to ensure the constancy, or stability, of this new behavior. Actions on employee behavior should be accompanied with actions on company structures. The synchronization of these actions requires the implementation of a company transformation method, an approach that we refer to as the *socio-economic approach to management* (SEAM).

HIDDEN COST REDUCTION

Hidden cost assessments, carried out since 1974, clearly reveal the overlapping nature of work-life conditions of the personnel and the hidden cost levels of the enterprise, affecting economic performance. Thus, Savall's (1975) work2 reflects an integrative, inclusive approach, one that includes the economic and social variables of the enterprise, ceasing to consider them a priori as incompatible or antagonistic objectives. Transformative actions proposed are therefore referred to as socio-economic innovation actions, to underscore the simultaneous search for improvement of both social and economic performance.

The concept of *social performance* (formerly referred to as "work-life conditions" in the ISEOR analytical model) is made up of six components or domains:

- Working conditions: physical conditions and work relationships;
- *Work organization:* distribution of the enterprise's principal functions, work division units, and interdependence between jobs and activities;
- *Communication-coordination-cooperation:* operational and functional articulation among individuals in view of accomplishing their activities, information exchange;[3]
- *Time management:* organization of individual and collective time management, distribution of the individual's time among his or her major activities (e.g., preparation—execution—control, prevention-regulation, daily operation development);
- *Integrated training:* professional training practices, job/training adequacy; and
- Strategic implementation: techniques, methods and practices of transforming, breaking down and translating the firm's strategic objectives into concrete actions toward attaining them.

Social performance is thus defined as the results obtained by the enterprise, or the unit, in each one of these six domains, representative of

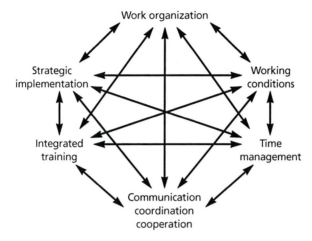

Figure 3.1 The components of social performance.
Source: Henri Savall, "Les coûts sociaux: Importance économique des coûts caches lies à l'absentéisme, la rotation du personnel, la qualité et la productivité directe" [Social costs: The economic impact of hidden costs related to absenteeism, personnel turnover, quality and direct productivity], *Revue de l'École des Mines de Saint-Étienne*, 1983 (April), p. 6.

dysfunctions and actions. Strategic implementation has the particularity of being the guiding outline for innovation actions (or dysfunctions) relative to the other five domains. Furthermore, as illustrated in Figure 3.1 all six domains interact with one another.

Economic performance is determined both by immediate results for the current period (e.g., productivity, profitability) and by the *creation of potential* (i.e., actions whose full effect will be measured in future periods, such as increased human competency). When an enterprise carries out actions for the improvement of working conditions, or for the development of integrated training, it increases its creation of potential. This shows the interrelationships that exist between economic performance and social performance as we define them—hence the reference to performance as *socio-economic* effectiveness, for we are referring to two facets of the same phenomenon.

CHARACTERISTICS OF THE SOCIO-ECONOMIC INTERVENTION METHOD

Construction of the socio-economic intervention method was based on a critical analysis of techno-economic and socio-technical approaches (Savall,

TABLE 3.1 Differential Analysis of Intervention Methods: Techno-economic, Socio-economic, and Socio-technical Approaches

Techno-economic approach (points of difference with respect to the socio-economic approach)	Socio-economic approach (principal positioning points with respect to techno-economic and socio-technical approaches)	Socio-technical approach (points of difference with respect to the socio-economic approach
• *Non participative process:* Decision-making process according to a hierarchical structure	1. *Participative-type process* that includes *training* which we designate with the term "cooperative-training" and not "training" alone.	• *Participative-type process that includes group dynamics and activities*
• *Non-transparent information,* notably concerning result evaluation	2. *More transparent and better-controlled process* following the existing system of relations in the enterprise, without postulating its transformation, seeking amalgamation [hierarchy-trade unions].	• *Discovery of projects by participants themselves through small-group activities* seeking amalgamation [hierarchy-trade unions-workers]
• *Training content,* essentially technical content focused exclusively on *learning orthofunctioning,* affording no consideration to the expectations and ambitions of individuals, nor to dysfunctions.	3. *Time-controlled process* framed by key-dates that limit the different phases. On these dates, *information* and/or *consultation* procedures are implemented with other partners less directly involved in the process. These dates also mark points of *decisions* to pursue the intervention.	• Experimentation process preceded by a *relatively long, undifferentiated diagnostic phase,* small-group activity phase based on group dynamics techniques.
• Absence of preliminary social analysis; absence of social projects • Absence of qualitative assessment	4. *Process assessment:* after the first phase of intervention, a new phase is not undertaken until after *socio-economic performance is assessed:* • from the company viewpoint • from individual viewpoints	• *Confusion between activities of information, expression and participation* both during the "diagnostic" phase as well as during the "project development" phase or the actual training sessions • Absence of quantitative and financial assessment

1975). Table 3.1 presents a differential analysis of the socio-economic intervention method with respect to those two approaches. It highlights the participative characteristics, transparency, and enhanced control, timing and assessment associated with the socio-economic approach.

Spatial Segmentation of the Enterprise

The socio-economic approach promotes an experimental (ethnographic, clinical) procedure for the analysis of dysfunctions, hidden cost calculation and search for causes. Indeed, the variables that explain hidden costs are numerous, whether they concern structures or behaviors. These variables are complex and interrelated, requiring an *in-depth* method of intervention applied in clearly *delimitated spaces* where overall professional work-life conditions can be considered as relatively homogeneous. Application of the socio-economic intervention method in an enterprise therefore requires the preliminary *spatial segmentation* of the enterprise, to locate socio-organizational groups, in function of the enterprise's actual organization chart.

Three categories of groups are identified: micro-spaces, entities and interfaces. *Micro-spaces* (see Figure 3.2) refer to a group of individuals devoted to a group of activities in a given geographic territory (department, work unit) and managed by the same hierarchical authority. There are *simple* micro-spaces: a unit situated at the finest level of the company organization chart comprising shopfloor workers, office workers, a hierarchical manager and eventually, depending on the number of employees in the unit, an intermediary manager (e.g., maintenance service of a factory, branch office of a bank). *Complex* micro-spaces are made up of a group of simple micro-spaces, with a common head manager for the coordinated piloting of the group (e.g., a department made up of several services, a group of bank agencies, a large work unit).

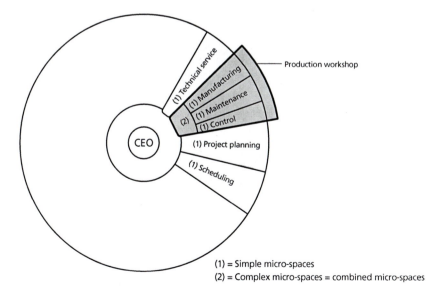

Figure 3.2 Segmentation of the enterprise: Micro-spaces.

Entities are a group of individuals all of whom have hierarchical responsibility and who report to the same superior. What distinguishes entities from micro-spaces is that this group of individuals with equal responsibility is not materially represented in the geography of permanent operating units nor in the daily communication-coordination-cooperation system. Such a group is materialized only in the context of relatively-infrequent periodical meetings. Figure 3.3 illustrates two examples of these entities. First, *the production team*, placed under the responsibility and piloting of the production manager. It includes an engineer in charge of manufacturing and the heads of technical services, project planning, scheduling and maintenance. Second, *the management team*, placed under the responsibility and piloting of the Chief Executive Officer (or Director of the establishment). It includes, in addition to the CEO, the production manager, the sales manager, the financial manager, the manager of social affairs and sometimes other department or division heads.

Interfaces are interstitial spaces between socio-organizational groups, or activity "nebulae" spanning the boundaries between the two groups: a) boundary between two micro-spaces, manufacturing/control; b) boundary between a micro-space and an entity: project planning service/production

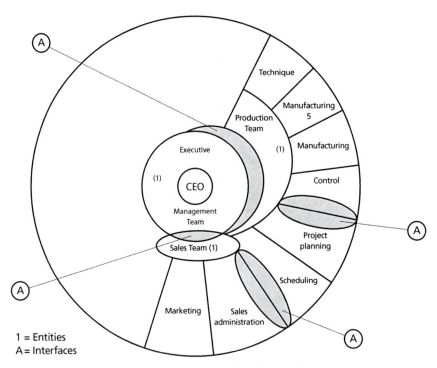

Figure 3.3 Segmentation of the enterprise: Entities and interfaces.

team; and c) boundary between two or more entities: production team/ sales team or production team/executive management team.

In the socio-economic intervention method, micro-spaces and entities are targets for socio-economic innovation actions, implemented in precise order and in a carefully-articulated manner. These procedures are developed in Chapter 4.

Progressive Nature of the Method

In socio-economic intervention, special attention is devoted to interfaces during the focus-group composition phase. Thus, in the example given in Figure 3.3, if socio-economic innovation action is conducted in the Scheduling Department, the focus-group would include, in addition to other department heads, the sales administration head, enabling the project to address dysfunctions situated at the interface between Scheduling and Sales administration.

The socio-economic intervention method is implemented in all micro-spaces and entities following four chronological phases: a) diagnostic, b) project, c) project implementation, and d) assessment of actions. This section briefly introduces the content of these four phases, referring the reader to the second section of this book for detailed explanation of operational methods and their illustrations. These phases are preceded by a long period of negotiation with the top management (for 4 to 6 months or more), which is concluded with the signing of an agreement stipulating precise intervention modes.

Diagnostic

During the initial diagnostic phase (see Chapter 5), intervener-researchers carry out interviews with different personnel members and assess the five hidden cost indicators: absenteeism, work accidents, personnel turnover, product quality defects and direct productivity variance. These personnel interviews (e.g., workers, supervisors, engineers, department heads, executive management, personnel representatives, support service heads) focus on professional work-life conditions and dysfunctions perceived, from the standpoint of the social and economic performance of their micro-space or unit.

The results of this qualitative, quantitative and financial diagnostic are written up in a report presented to the top management during a meeting designed to produce a "mirror-effect," and then to all interviewed personnel (by groups of 30 at the most) as a way of opening a dialogue. Following the review of this report, top management, in agreement with the head of the micro-space, decide to launch the next phase: socio-economic project development.

Project

In the project phase (see Chapter 6), intervener-researchers lead various focus-group meetings inside micro-space management teams. Between focus-group meetings, specialized task-forces made up of managers and supervisors, sometimes including workers, technicians and office employees, hold meetings, to make progress in certain connected areas of work. Project development includes several consecutive sequences:

1. Inventory of the various suggestions emerging from the personnel with respect to dysfunctions identified during the diagnostic.
2. Classification of these suggestions into domains of action.
3. Analysis of these action domains in order to constitute a project with the following three characteristics: internal coherency, social performance improvement, and economic performance improvement.
4. Financial assessment of the material investments and immaterial investments necessary to carry out the project.

The results of the focus-group's work are written up in a report to top management, which makes the decision to implement the different actions proposed. A report is also presented by top management to representatives of the personnel involved in this stage of the process.

Project Implementation

Project implementation (see Chapter 7) is done in two stages: a) scheduling and budgeting for the implementation of the various actions, and b) actually accomplishing those actions, under the constant control and guidance of an *audit* process. During this phase, intervener-researchers assist the enterprise by acting as leaders of piloting meetings, which makes it possible to regularly check progress on implementation.

Evaluation of Actions

The final stage (see Chapter 10) entails drawing up a comparative balance sheet of the social and economic performance generated by the actions. This phase follows the main lines of the diagnostic methodology. It reexamines the interviews of the different partners concerned, as well as quantitative and financial analyses of the evolution of the five hidden cost indicators (absenteeism, work accidents, personnel turnover, product quality defects, direct productivity variance). The piloting of the different phases has the particular characteristic of being rigorously *scheduled* and *assessed.*

Furthermore, it directly involves all categories of the personnel concerned in various ways.

Participative Aspects of the Intervention Method

All concerned categories of personnel participate in various ways in drawing up the diagnostic of the situation, elaborating the transformation project, implementing solutions and assessing their results. In a sense, solutions are constructed *bottom*-up—starting with the analysis of problems as perceived at grassroots level and moving upward toward the different hierarchical levels, with middle management and top management playing a very active role in conducting the project-development process and in implementing the improvement project. Employee representatives are informed about the objectives and methods during the initial diagnostic phase. They carry out their usual functions within the enterprise, in application of regulations (consulted on the project and on integrated training plans) and in keeping with the current state of social relations between the enterprise's top management and its unions (or employees). Thus, "traditional" social partners (e.g., top management and the unions) maintain all of their prerogatives in this process, which requires very close collaboration on the part of the personnel directly concerned by the micro-space transformation project (e.g., workers, staff, supervisors, managers).

The implementation of these decentralized procedures and the monitoring of the organization's evolution according to the socio-economic approach are accompanied with a centralized mechanism at the top management level, which, under the vigilant observation of the unions, ensures a type of quality control of this participative change process. During the 1980s, ISEOR progressively developed its intervention-research work, building a framework for change management. It was no longer a question of simply assisting the enterprise in conducting change actions, but of teaching the enterprise how to manage change itself, in essence creating a *management engineering transfer* process (See Savall & Bonnet, 1994). This evolution was notably characterized by setting up permanent tools in organizations to reactivate the change process, such as the Priority Action Plans and Periodically Negotiable Activity Contracts discussed in this volume.

Just as medical inquiry does not stop at the description of the disease, but pursues its work by searching for remedies, so the proposed method is not limited to the description of change-resistance phenomena that lead enterprises into haphazard evolutions. The explicit goal of the socio-economic method is to manipulate "frozen" energy inside the enterprise and transform it partly into change energy, so as to attain a new state, one that is preferable for all actors involved. Even if all "diseases" in the enterprise are far from being treated, we think current results are encouraging in a wide range of domains, nearly thirty years after ISEOR's first experimental research.

There are four key change management difficulties that the socio-economic approach helps to resolve. The first concerns a heightened awareness of the necessity for change on the part of all actors involved. Such awareness can be obtained through the *mirror-effect* of the socio-economic diagnostic, which demonstrates the link connecting the dysfunctions that organizational members constantly deal with and highlights the waste of economic resources these dysfunctions induce. As ISEOR's experimental research progressed, it became clear that the socio-economic diagnostic was an indispensable stage for creating an "appetite" for change.

Second, the method makes it possible to strike a balance between actor participation, which is necessary for the change to be accepted, and the requisite control and direction for efficient synchronization of actions. Such balance is one of the objectives of the socio-economic project stage.

Third, the methodology of periodically negotiable activity contracts (PNACs) has shown the importance of negotiating change at the collective level as well as at the team level and with individual employees. These PNACs make it possible to reward efforts and make objectives more attainable by tapping the hidden resources that exist in all organizations.

Finally, the socio-economic tools help develop the managerial role of directors and managers, making them "actors of change." During socio-economic interventions, managers become leaders, trainers and negotiators, while increasing their own competency. They evolve toward a more demanding role, for they are increasingly called upon to devote themselves to development actions. Simultaneously, this is an easier role to assume in many ways, for they handle fewer shifts of responsibility and dysfunction regulation on a daily basis.

There are, of course, a number of other difficulties to overcome. In particular, there are often problems in transferring the methodology to internal interveners in large enterprises, especially in terms of multiplying intervention and training capacity while reducing costs. Following training, cooperation with the internal team of interveners is aimed at institutionalizing permanent socio-economic tools within the enterprise. However, the energy of these interveners diminishes over time, while creating dysfunctions linked to competition between internal and external interveners. The "rules of the game" must therefore be clearly defined, as well as the means of productive combination of internal energy (which is typically directly utilizable) and external energy (which has the advantage of not being subject to depletion).

Another problem concerns the case of enterprises that have waited too long to undertake change actions, finding themselves faced with short-term financial difficulties. These enterprises must simultaneously reduce their costs and begin in-depth change actions, if they are to recover economic health and experience new development after restructuring. This difficulty requires convincing evidence demonstrating that certain hidden cost-performances can be mobilized in the short-term.

A third difficulty stems from unequal awareness levels among senior management teams concerning change management. Certain teams are more advanced and achieve remarkable deployment in their enterprise. Others do not put stock in the effort, for lack of training or for lack of opportunity to work with competent consultants (external energy). They adopt classic strategies that encounter implementation obstacles, which result in lost opportunity. In certain cases, managers indulge in fashionable, temporary experiments, but without in-depth change action inscribed in the long-term. They end up discouraged and sometimes harbor ill feelings toward the concept of change management, owing to the low level of success obtained through their amateurish actions.

Assessment

The results of this process, both in terms of the evolution of personnel competencies (e.g., technical, economic and management, group work methods) and the quality of productive behavior (e.g., absenteeism, personnel turnover, work accidents, quality of goods and services, direct productivity) should be *constantly monitored*, so that concerned actors stay informed and can thus modify their activity to attain the desired results. This piloting can be accomplished using the strategic piloting logbooks discussed in this volume.

Stimulated interest for the work and increased responsibility for the different categories of organizational members can be renewed through the use of PNACs. These contracts are created between individual organizational members and their department head, in connection with top management. As discussed in this volume, the PNAC *defines the objectives* to be attained by the personnel (including the department head) with regard to the department's specific area of activity, reduction of dysfunctions and evolution of competency, drawing on the *means* allotted by top management for the improvement of both company operations and work-life conditions. The "contract" also specifies the expected positive repercussions for the personnel if objectives are attained, both in economic terms (salary bonus) and in social terms (improved professional-life quality). The PNAC and strategic piloting logbook thus make it possible to pilot the results of the change process.

This method of socio-economic intervention has been applied since 1979 in industrial and service businesses, and in public and parapublic health, social, sport, cultural and consular organizations. The results of ISEOR's action assessments have shown that hidden costs were reducible, sometimes in considerable proportions.

MAGNITUDE OF HIDDEN COST REDUCTION

As a way of illustrating the socio-economic approach, this section presents an overview of ISEOR's general results, followed by two detailed cases that capture the four stages of the process: diagnostic, project, implementation and assessment.

General Results

Table 3.2 presents six illustrations of hidden cost reduction assessed in different activity sectors. The results displayed are the *variations* of hidden costs between the initial assessment made during the diagnostic and the assessment made six to twelve months after the beginning of project implementation. Furthermore, these results take into account the *cost of actions* carried out: *time spent* in the enterprise in meetings (e.g., diagnostic, focus-group, training) and the *cost of services rendered* by the intervener-researcher team. All costs are expressed in Euros to facilitate comparison.

The magnitude of hidden cost reduction is reflected in Table 3.2—between 3,330€ and 16,300€ per person/per year in the examples cited. Compared to the gross minimum wage in 1989 (the year of these diagnostics), hidden cost reduction represented between 30 percent and 145 percent of the annual minimum wage.

The extent of hidden cost reduction is equally significant when compared to the absolute amount of hidden costs evaluated during the diagnostic. Drawing on the data in Table 3.3, hidden costs were reduced:

- 43 percent in a machining workshop in a metallurgy factory (or 73% if the cost of action was not included);
- 16 percent in a workshop in a glassworks factory (18% not including cost of action);
- 20 percent in a workshop in an electronics assemblage factory (30% not including cost of action); and
- 85 percent in a workshop of an industrial bakery.

Even if these results cannot be generalized without caution, they show *the enormous reserves of potential productivity* that enterprises contain. Furthermore, it appears, in view of the results accumulated over recent years, that

TABLE 3.2 Hidden Cost Reduction Results per Person, per Year in Six Units (Euros)

Sector of activity	Metallurgy	Glassworks	Metallurgy	Electronics	Agri-food	Bank
Unit concerned by the evaluation	Machining workshop team	Molding and firing workshop	Sheet metal workshop	Assemblage workshop	Industrial bakery workshop	Branch office
Number of employees in the unit	4	95	45	22	115	16
Total net reduction of hidden costs per person/per year	9,700	7,700	6,600	5,900	6,300	2,400
Cost of the action per person	6,600	110	1,200	2,900	700	800
Hidden cost reduction per person/per year *before amortization of the cost of action.*	16,300	8,900	7,800	8,700	7,000	3,300[c]
Absenteeism	1,000	800	100	600	—	2,600
Work accidents[a]	not evaluated[b]	100	200	not evaluated[b]	—	
Personnel turnover[a]	not evaluated[b]	—	—	not evaluated[b]	—	700
Quality defects[a]	4,500	11,500	not evaluated[b]	1,100	7,000	not evaluated[b]
Direct productivity variance[a]	10,800	not evaluated[b]	7,500	9,200		not evaluated[b]

[a] Reduction of costs per person-year, not including the cost of actions.
[b] Not evaluated given the time allotted to the financial evaluation of this study.
[c] Amount largely under-estimated in our study which did not include doubled sales performance recognized by the enterprise itself

TABLE 3.3   The Metallurgy Enterprise and Work Unit

Indicators	The Overall Enterprise	The Work Unit
Activity	Metallurgy	Sheet metal works
Number of employees	600 persons	100 persons
Annual sales figure for 1978	51 million Euros	8.5 million Euros
Hierarchical structure	• Site director • Production director • Sales director • Personnel director • Financial director	• One department head and six supervisors
Observations	The enterprise was part of large industrial group when the action took place[a]	The action began in late 1978

[a] The enterprise has since been acquired by a private firm. It is interesting to note that from 1980 through 1985, the sheet metal workshop was the only sector that achieved a substantial profit while the rest of the enterprise was regularly subject to heavy deficits causing three waves of personnel lay-offs.

the *more an enterprise is subject to hidden costs, the more it can maneuver in terms of increasing its efficiency.*

Despite these promising results, any calculation of hidden cost reduction should be based on cautious interpretation. It is important to keep in mind that hidden costs are often *under-estimated.* Thus, hidden cost reduction percentages stem from under-estimation of the original calculation. We have even known the case of an enterprise where hidden cost reduction amounted to 150 percent, compared with original hidden costs evaluated at 73,600€ per worker/ per year. This clearly proved that the original evaluation was under-estimated, even though it was received with much skepticism on the part of executive management when it was first presented. A related point is that the time period between implementation of actions and hidden cost reduction assessment is relatively short, typically from 6 to 12 months. One could advance the hypothesis that individuals are very motivated by the current actions, and that they are consequently very stimulated in their professional behavior:[4] their work is more interesting, they are receiving training related to their jobs, they are better informed, and so forth. Hidden cost levels should therefore be very regularly monitored and a system should be set up enabling on-going piloting and activation of behaviors, far from postulating the irreversibility of improved economic performance. This system takes the form of two management tools: the strategic piloting logbook and the periodically negotiable activity contract, presented in the third section of this book.

Evaluations of hidden cost reduction make it possible to underscore two interrelated explicative factors. Hidden costs decrease either because *dysfunctions decrease* (e.g., declining number of absences, work accidents, personnel departure, quality rejects) or because the regulations set up to compensate for dysfunctions become *less expensive* (or a combination of the two). This essential outcome signifies that even enterprises with few dysfunctions can take action on their hidden cost level. For example, we have encountered cases where hidden costs linked to absenteeism were reduced by 20 percent without variation in the absenteeism rate, as expertise with respect to the regulation of absences had become more effective.

The Case of Hidden Cost Reduction in a Metallurgy Enterprise

The intervention discussed in this section was conducted by Henri Savall and Emmanuel Beck between 1979 and 1981 in a metallurgy enterprise employing 60 persons (see Beck, 1980). It involved a work unit manufacturing industrial equipment (e.g., kitchen and supermarket equipment) with approximately one hundred employees (see Table 3.3). The intervention was extended to include the rest of the enterprise in 1982. At the end of the diagnostic, which had revealed numerous dysfunctions in product quality and direct under-productivity (see Table 3.4), the workshop management team developed a socio-economic innovation project (see Table 3.5) and submitted it to the enterprise's top management.

The solutions that were selected included the creation of operational groups of 4 to 8 workers, taking charge of the nearly complete production

---

TABLE 3.4   Major Problems Identified by the Diagnostic

Identified dysfunctions and hidden costs	• Absenteeism 9%
	• Non-quality
	• Direct productivity variance
	• Excessive manufacturing time
	• Annual hidden costs superior to 960,000€ in 1985
Principal causes evoked	• Workers lack training and multi-skill capacity
	• Lack of motivation due in part to limited opportunities for promotion within the workshop
	• Worn-out equipment and maintenance problems
	• Difficult physical working conditions
	• Lack of coordination among managers

Note: The diagnostic included in-depth interviews with workers, supervisors, top management and personnel representatives. Direct observation was carried out in certain cases (see Beck, 1980).

TABLE 3.5   Development of the Socio-Economic Innovation Project

Workshop

Composition of the authorities participating in project development	• *Project group:* the department head, six supervisors, one representative from the planning and methods department and the ISEOR intervener-researcher.
	• *Executive management group:* CEO of the factory, personnel director, department head and the ISEOR intervener-researcher
Number of meetings	4 meetings spread out over two months
Characteristics of planned actions	• Increased worker autonomy through the creation of four *production operation groups*, later extended to ten groups for the entire workshop
	• Technical and economic integrated training of workers by supervisor following training of supervisors
	• Creation of a work group that met once a week including workshop supervisors, not only to ensure follow-up of the current action, but also to examine improvement ideas regarding security, quality and equipment maintenance

Characteristics of the production operation groups:

- 4 to 8 members
- Relatively autonomous "territory"
- A certain degree of homogeneousness regarding qualifications
- The objective of developing multi-skill capacity
- Rotation among all job positions
- Manufacturing activity of the complete product or family of products
- Own means of operation as much as possible
- Reduced dependency on other employees to finish the job
- Incorporation of the first quality control
- Possibility to store buffer stocks close to the territory
- Capacity to absorb at least one absence without problems, permitting internal regulation
- Weekly production objectives at the least permitting relatively autonomous planning of the week's work

of products or semi-products. After training of the workers by supervisors, the five workshop foremen created a work group that periodically met to better coordinate and cooperate, focusing on the operational monitoring of the different groups and the development of workshop operation-improvement missions. The evaluation of the results of this experiment (1982) revealed a financial surplus of 8,500€ per worker/per year. During interviews to evaluate the action, workers and supervisors stated that they found their work more interesting. Furthermore, they benefited from salary hikes and better opportunities for promotion.

Evaluation of Economic Performance After Implementation of Actions

The intervention's *short-term economic results* are summarized in Table 3.6. The hidden cost reduction of 7,900€ per person/per year represented a reduction rate of approximately 80 percent. *Long-term economic results* (evaluat-

TABLE 3.6 Short-Term Economic Results

Indicators	Qualitative results	Quantitative results	Financial results per worker/per year (hidden cost reduction in Euros)
Absenteeism	• Less absenteeism • Greater facility to replace absent employees	Lowered absenteeism partially compressible 3% (0.2 point)	190
Work accidents	• Fewer accident following the action	Frequency rate lowered by 50% and serious accidents lowered by 29%	245
Personnel turnover	• Personnel turnover almost nil before and after the action	None	None
Product quality	• Fewer rejects • Fewer customer returns • Production time reduced	Not evaluated due to lack of data for the period before the action	Not evaluated due to lack of data for the period before the action
Direct productivity variance	• Less wasted time • Greater agility and faster execution	Average progression of + 9.6%	7,500
Total per person-year			7,900 + elements not evaluated

ed through the creation of potential that will manifest itself, in the coming months or years, as financially-confirmed economic performance) pointed to: increased *flexibility* of the workshop in dealing with unforeseeable events (e.g., absences, machine breakdown, reduced production time); increased *know-how* and *competency* among the employees; improved *receptivity of technological innovations* and noticeable improvement of certain manufacturing procedures; and the work unit's taking charge of medium-term and long-term *development actions*. Each of the core domains of improvement showed improvement as well (see Table 3.7).

Hidden cost evaluations carried out in different sectors of industrial and tertiary activity have shown that hidden cost levels are higher than company managers usually imagine. Our experimentation of innovative socio-economic action has also shown that these costs result from complex phenomena whose causes are multiple and interrelated. It follows that the solution to hidden costs linked to poor working conditions can never be addressed through simple solutions, focused on only one action-variable. The complexity of

TABLE 3.7   Social Performance Evaluation Following Action Implementation

Domains of improvement	Characteristics of the experienced improvements[a]
Working conditions	• Reduction of the physical work at certain workstations • Reduction of the risk of work accidents • Less fatigue linked to the rotation of workers on the most difficult jobs demanding sustained attention
Work organization	• Work content considered more interesting thanks to work enrichment of worker and supervisor tasks and increased multi-tasking capacity
Communication-coordination-cooperation	• Improvement of relations between workers and supervisors thanks to the reduced disciplinary role of supervisor, transformed into a role of aid, information and assistance toward worker groups.
Time management	• Possibility of greater self-organization of time by workers and greater possibility to adapt work-hours • Supervisory staff saved time on distributing tasks to workers and re-allotted the saved time to more interesting functional tasks scheduled in advance
Integrated training	• Improved individual competency and increased multi-tasking capacity among workers and supervisors
Strategic implementation	• Definition of objectives for workers and supervisors over extended long-term periods • Possibility of career advancement thanks to the opening of new career tracks • Increased remuneration by +7% on the average for workers in the workshop compared to the rest of the factory thanks to the workshop's improved economic performance

[a] Opinions expressed during interviews carried out by the ISEOR with workers and supervisors of the workshop, executive management and personnel representatives at the end of the actions.

operating enterprises induces the search for complex solutions that address both structure and behavior, within the company's defined strategy.

It thus appeared necessary to invent "semi-complex" tools, i.e., neither simplistic nor unnecessarily complex, as a means of improving the quality of on-going enterprise piloting. The competency grid, the strategic piloting logbook and PNAC discussed in this volume are good examples of such tools.

The Case of a Branch of a Mechanical Engineering Firm

The results of change in a 3,200 employee branch of a mechanical engineering firm were evaluated by the ISEOR in 1993 at 11.4 million Euros, which corresponded to more than 3,400€ per person/per year. Most of these gains came from micro-improvements identified in every department, such as those shown in Table 3.8. In this case, the evaluation included creation of potential indicators, such as reduction of the delay risks, acquisition of new

---

TABLE 3.8   Example of Hidden Performance Indicators in a Service Branch of a Mechanics Company

Visible performance summary in a large mechanical engineering firm (in Euros)

Results		Explicative hypotheses
Immediate results	*Earnings on lines* • Average earnings of 25 h per equipment on 144 products • T = 3,600 h for 1 year × 36€ = 129,600€ • Average earnings of 730 h on 7 products • L = 5,110 h × 36€ = 183,960€ • less 300 hours of line productivity time not recorded • (at 36€): = 10,800€	• Work groups • Consensus at shopfloor level on time reduction • Just-in-time action
	Earnings on cycles • Earnings of 1,277,000€ in treasury, or a gain in financial fees (10%) = 127,700€	• Standardized supply plan given to suppliers
	• Average earnings of 35 days on the T cycle, or a 680,000€ reduction of in-process materials, or a savings of 68,000€ in financial fees	• Work groups
	• Earnings on supply cycles enabling a reduction of cash requirements by 1,277,000€, or a 127,700€ savings on financial fees	• Supply management actions
	Fewer reworks-rejects • For product T, 30h/month earnings over 8 months = 240 × 36€ = 8,640€ for the workshop	• Quality management actions
	Earnings on external expenses • Disinvestment of approximately 102,000€ per unit × 10% financial fees = 10,200€ • Surface reduction by 6,000 M², or 6,000 × 5€ = 30,000€	• Identification of untapped resources
	Lowered risk of delay penalties • Product T delivery without delays, thus no delivery penalties	• Improved production management
Creation of potential	*New procedures* *New methods* • Implementation of a JIT system. • Automation	

Evoked causes: Work groups—Major just-in-time actions.
Deep causes: Developing the leadership role of the hierarchy—Implementation of the socio-economic diagnostic.

procedures and new models, and transformation of indirect personnel into direct personnel.

As this summary suggests, the interest of an economic evaluation is not merely short-term and financial in nature. It also plays a role in stimulating the pursuit of change for two main reasons. First, showing the initial results encourages continued effort. Operational heads perceive synthetic piloting logbooks as a device that complements budgeting procedures, for it monitors indicators over which they have real control and which constitute good levers for attaining profitability objectives. The second important reason is that economic evaluation results provide the resources necessary for pursuing change. A portion of the recorded improvements enables maintaining the enterprise's competitiveness by reducing market prices and improving self-financing margin. Another portion serves for the financing of intensified change action, for example, financing *creation of potential* or financing the *compensation for efforts* demanded from actors of the change action (e.g., work-life condition improvements, PNAC bonuses).

A qualitative evaluation of results involves three components in ISE-OR methodology: a) an exhaustive inventory of operating improvements perceived by company actors that could be at the origin of the obtained economic results, and b) expert opinion on the external intervention's contribution to the change process; and recommendations in the form of guidelines for pursuing the action. In terms of methodology, it should be pointed out that the assessed economic results are not attributed solely to the socio-economic intervention; rather they should be considered the fruit of overall action on the part of company actors with the aid of external interveners. This methodological point of view permits avoiding undue quarreling between the enterprise and the interveners concerning the origin of performances.

An inventory of observable improvements is carried out through semi-structured interviews with all categories of company personnel and actors affected by the change actions. It employs the same methods used in the socio-economic diagnostic, except the accent is not placed on pinpointing dysfunctions, but on their reduction. Table 3.9 presents the partial synthesis of the qualitative results in this large mechanics enterprise. These results are taken from calculations based on 170 two-hour interviews. They are placed in relation to economic performance, for example, in terms of reducing external expenses and non-quality costs.

NOTES

1. Entropy designates, by analogy to thermodynamics, the ineluctable deterioration of energy within an enterprise. We refer here to *historical entropy*, stressing

TABLE 3.9 An Example of Performance Earnings Interpretation

Immediate results

Indicators	Sum of evaluated performances (in Euros)	Hypotheses on the origin of performances
Earnings on cycles	1.46 M€	Even though insufficient, these earnings show progress with respect to action deadlines and implementation of just-in-time procedures. This is especially noticeable in waiting-period reduction for spare parts.
Earnings on supplies	0.43 M€	Earnings are primarily obtained thanks to actions such as improved management of stocks and operational sequencing efforts in production units.
Earnings on external expenses	1.00 M€	Implementation of budgets and piloting logbooks was accompanied by overall dysfunction reduction actions to eliminate wastes, especially in the domain of consumable supplies. Another major element is that of surface reduction whose impact is evaluated at 0.24€ taking into account only external heating expenses or rent, but with even higher potential earnings if vacated buildings were completely restored for other usages
Fewer reworks and rejects	0.82 M€	In numerous sectors, non-conformity was cut in half compared to 1992. Implementation of qualimetrics began to bear fruit in that anomalies were more and more dealt with through priority actions to pilot the reduction of detected dysfunctions.
Fewer work accidents	0.24 M€	Greater vigilance was exercised by the human resource department in management of company work-accident installments. Many priority actions were performed to improve prevention in the domain of security.

the fact that entropy stems from long-term deterioration, that of the enterprise's history.

2. *Enrichir le travail humain* was subsequently published in English in 1981 by Oxford University Press.

3. *Communication* includes all types of information exchange among actors, both formal and informal, vertical and horizontal, relative to professional activity or not. *Coordination* designates information exchange frameworks and devices among actors, organized in view of accomplishing operational or functional activity objectives. *Cooperation* characterizes the types of information exchanges among actors that make it possible to define common operational or functional objectives to be attained within a defined time span.

4. This observation reflects what has been referred to as the "Hawthorne effect" since the experiments of Elton Mayo, a leader of the American school of human relations in the early 1930's.

REFERENCES

Beck, E. (1980). *Creation of semi-autonomous production groups in a sheet metal workshop.* Ecully, France: ISEOR Report.

Savall, H. (1975). *Enrichir le travail humain* [Job enrichment]. Paris: Dunod.

Savall, H., & Bonnet, M. (1994). *The socio-economic method's contribution to company change education, illustration of the case of two large enterprises.* Paper presented at the International Research Seminar "Change education", IAE Aix-en-Provence, France (May).

• PART II •

SETTING UP SOCIO-ECONOMIC MANAGEMENT

Human evolution is limited both in terms of rhythm and scope. In a mere six-month's time, is it impossible to transform long-standing, extremely-Taylorian work organization into operational production groups where every individual is multi-skilled for a wide range of activities, with teams working on weekly objectives with their supervisors with minimal technical assistance and advice. Such a transformation takes place progressively over a year (if everything goes very fast) or two (usually the case), with some actors never really succeeding in achieving the transformation. Confidence, with regard to management, is therefore indispensable but cautious. It is built through a process of change assistance piloted by executive management and intermediary supervisory staff. Expected change is rarely attained spontaneously and is sustainable only through the vigilant support of the surrounding actors.

In socio-economic analysis, confidence also includes the possibility for evolution and transformation of company *structures*, i.e., the capacity and power of people to modify, through their will, determination, energy and actions, the structure of their company and their environment. Thus, each individual is attributed a status of "*active unit,*" according to François Perroux's usage of that term for designating enterprises in economic sciences. This confidence in the capacity of individuals to modify the struc-

Mastering Hidden Costs and Socio-Economic Performance, pages 89–98
Copyright © 2008 by Information Age Publishing
89

ture of their activities, and *not passively endure their environment,* takes on an especially powerful meaning in large organizations or firms whose operation is bureaucratic in character, according to Weber's use of this term or as used in Crozier's critical analysis. Indeed, pilot-actions carried by the ISEOR in a public service organization have shown that it is possible to enlist decisive action for modifying work organization, work schedules, work content, and management roles, in sum everything considered as immutable by the personnel, the supervisory staff, office managers, and even by certain theorists.

The socio-economic intervention process is *not* based on *blind, naïve confidence* in the evolution of structures and behaviors. Indeed, these partially "escape" from individuals' control; their modification requires, in a certain number of cases, *compelling change energy* injected from the policy-making levels of the organization, progressively shared by more and more actors. At the Post Office,[1] for example, setting up the first periodically negotiable activity contracts (individualized objectives linked to a reward system, discussed in Chapter 8) required more than a year of negotiation among the human resource director, the delegated director of a region with 30,000 employees, a member of the top management who ardently wished to implement the management tool, and finally the financial director, without whose authorization the activity contract rewards could not have been paid, because of the non-miscibility principle (in application at the time) of cost and the fact that it was forbidden to award bonuses to managers. Confidence in the evolution of structures requires steadfast patience and sociologically oriented on-going analysis of individual and collective strategies focused on "change resistance" during the waiting periods and the spread of this evolution. But, this is a *"speedy" patience* that wastes no time.

Corporate strategies (e.g., technical maintenance teams in industries), or local and activity-group strategies (e.g., industrial sites confronting head-office operations directors) are often opposed to the enterprise's overall stakes and strategies. Change resistance is propagated by metastasis, when the demanded change action does not produce visible, positive rewards. Workers, for example, accept training only when they perceive a personal interest in consolidating their experience, or enhanced perspectives for job, career or pay. In the absence of such rewards, the individual effort inherent in all change action remains limited and/or ephemeral.

Finally, one of the primary causes for loss of confidence in enterprises comes from *discrepancies between words and deeds,* in essence, commitments not respected and promises not kept. Time management actions offer a striking illustration, when time management dysfunctions have been identified and their reduction requires changing work habits and acquiring new reflexes. For example, in an industrial firm employing 2,500 persons, the executive management team committed to improving the quality of meeting time by starting and finishing meetings on time, and closing doors during appointments to avoid frequent impromptu interruptions. Such actions, however, demand substantial individual and collective willpower if they are to change professional habits. In this case, very little was actually accomplished, despite the apparent will to change… and the big posters displayed throughout the enterprise on "how to manage our meetings." The *mutual confidence* that could have been fostered by the evolution of these practices had not developed. Beyond the difficulty for individuals to change their daily habits, a deeper root-cause resided, it seemed to us, in the company actors' conception of their personal *margin of liberty* in the organization. This view led to their more or less conscious and deliberate *evasion* of the rules of the team game, to their "*amnesia*" devoid of innocence, and to that *versatility* often observed in enterprises at all levels, in which management teams are so often accused by their collaborators, who do not display exemplary behavior either. These are factors of rapid and lasting deterioration of confidence in an organization.

Socio-economic analysis is based on a supposition, from the start, of confidence in the capacity of all company actors to *make progress in their performance without new external resources*. In a hospital, for example, where dominant claims always concern demanding more means for improved service, this confidence in the existence of sufficient internal resources is very tenuous and not widely spread. One finds an analogous situation in cultural organizations.

The socio-economic diagnostic method we created, based on the identification of dysfunctions and hidden costs, makes it possible to demonstrate the existence of resource pools inside the enterprise, which underscores that this confidence is well-founded. However, the preliminary condition for launching the socio-economic diagnostic and intervention is a minimum of *a priori* confidence, without which a vicious circle or *regressive spiral* develops: *distrust or defiance* with regards to the enterprise's capacity for evolution → voluntary, self-determined *lack of action* → observed *absence of change* accompanied by maintained or *increased hidden costs* → reinforced *defiance*, and so on over time. The alternation of demanding phases with gratifying if not "pleasant" phases is indispensable to continuing the mission (and therefore to the intervener's continued presence in the company) as well as restoring confidence. With the socio-economic innovation process, management tools are progressively set up throughout the organization. Beyond the necessary confidence in the capacity of the *entire* management team to grasp these tools, these tools *contain seeds of confidence*, in their implementation and in their content.

THE NECESSITY OF A SOCIO-ECONOMIC
INNOVATION STRATEGY

How should an organization's management attempt to move from a state of socio-economic under-development (State 1) in the enterprise, characterized by hypertrophied dysfunctions and hidden costs, to a state of socio-economic management (State 2), characterized by greater harmony of operations and increased socio-economic performance? This transformation, which is schematically summarized in Figure II.1, supposes simultaneous and synchronized action of multiple levers of transformation: structures, behaviors and the six domains of dysfunction actions. To put it another way, our hypothesis is that it is necessary to carry out global action, whatever the intervention space: micro-spaces or entities in the enterprise, service, workshop or department.

Enterprises, however, are not accustomed to such wide-sweeping actions, often preferring to concentrate on a particular domain of action (e.g., communication, training) or a certain type of structure (e.g., rethinking the organizational chart, up-grading the technological organization).

Thus, one cannot easily pass from State 1 to State 2 without external contributions, both in terms of *energy* and *time* which are necessary to carry out these actions.

This external contribution is nevertheless necessarily limited in time. It is done in the first phase of change from State 1 to State 2. This first phase is a stage of transition in the course of which change is progressively rooted in the enterprise—referred to as the socio-economic intervention phase—but it is also a phase of internal commitment on the part of the enterprise to accomplish significant transformations over a relatively short period of time. We stress the notion of *transformation* here, as opposed to that of evolution, which is a common phenomenon in enterprises. Innovative transformation includes significant modifications of structures, behaviors and domains of action, carried out within a restricted time span—several months for a micro-space, several years for an enterprise. Our pilot experiments show that implantation of such transformation requires negotiation between the top management and the actors directly concerned, determining, from the start of the intervention, a minimal platform upon which the different categories of actors agree, if they are to really accept the delicate game of transforming the operation of the organization. It is therefore advisable to carry out periodical cooperative evaluations (referred to as "achievement appraisals") in the course of this transition phase, every six months for example.

To prepare the organization for a state of permanent socio-economic management, the transition phase is also the occasion to implant a system and tools of strategic piloting. As illustrated in Figure II.1, the passage from

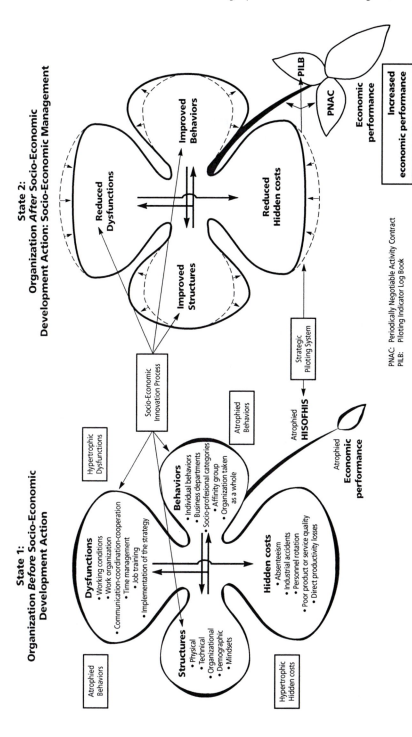

PNAC: Periodically Negotiable Activity Contract
PILB: Piloting Indicator Log Book

Figure II.1 Socio-economic intervention.

State 1 to State 2 can be achieved through an innovative transformation process, referred to as socio-economic intervention, which includes: a) a process of socio-economic innovation, and b) introduction of a strategic piloting system.

THE SOCIO-ECONOMIC INTERVENTION PROCESS

The socio-economic intervention process can be broken down into four phases: diagnostic, project, implementation, and evaluation. Figure II.2 indicates the time necessary to carry out this process, based on an application in a micro-space with several dozen employees (30 to 150). The principal actions of these four phases are presented in Figure II.3. This section of the book provides detailed explanations of the operational methods for these actions, examining successively the phases of diagnostic, project, implementation and evaluation. We shall take, as a schematic example, the case of the innovation process applied to a micro-space (service, workshop or agency). However, the same process can be applied to a broader entity, e.g., to a group of employees sharing the same responsibility, even though their group does not have a recognizable, material existence (see, for example, Savall & Zardet, 1985).

The Three Axes of Socio-Economic Intervention

The effectiveness of a change intervention depends on the articulation of three factors: a) the initiation of change dynamics through a process of social and organizational innovation, b) the implementation of change piloting tools in order to instrumentalize and consolidate the roles of the actors of change, and, finally, c) the contribution of strategy and change energy through the policy axis.

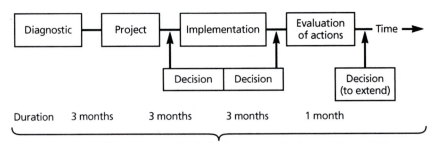

Figure II.2   Phases of the socio-economic intervention process.

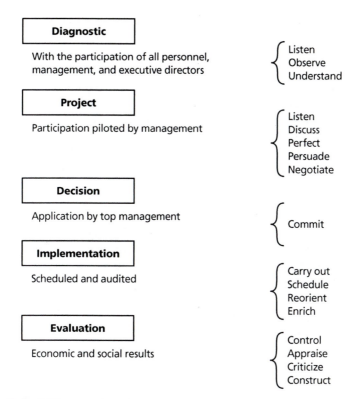

Figure II.3 Different actions in the socio-economic intervention process.

The *process axis* raises awareness of the need for change by evaluating dysfunctions (diagnostic stage), then building a participative improvement project, and finally launching improvements to complete or enhance the project-process. At the horizontal level, this axis notably concerns improving inter-divisional coordination devices and the organizational modifications that this implies. At the vertical level, projects particularly address implementation of more stimulating work organization and responsibilities, as well as implementation of integrated training manuals designed to accompany this evolution of jobs.

The *tools axis* entails developing the managerial dimension of company managers by instrumentalizing their roles as leaders and pilots of change. The six principal socio-economic tools are:

- *Priority Action Plans* (PAP) and Internal-External Strategic Action Plans, the goals of which are to help members of the management team to better articulate their action to company strategy and to make company strategy concrete, comprehensible and foreseeable for the teams they manage.

- *Competency Grids* (CG), which provide a synthetic vision of each team's human potential. They help managers to better anticipate the evolution of skills based on an analysis of a team's vulnerabilities with respect to current and future operations, and by negotiating each employee's evolution in terms of new competency acquisition and multi-skill development.
- *Time Management* (TM), which helps managers and directors better plan their actions and reduce their shift of functions, increasing the portion of their time devoted to change management (e.g., acquisition of new competencies, implementation of new procedures and methods).
- *Piloting Indicator Logbook* (PILB), which helps members of the management team to select relevant indicators for guiding their actions and reporting the outcomes. These indicators are displayed in simple, synoptic and panoramic form so that managers are not overwhelmed by overly-profuse information. The choice of indicators respects the equilibrium between security-management and development-management, in order to avoid concentrating actions either exclusively on immediate results, or conversely, on the pursuit of only creation of potential objectives (future goals).
- *Periodically Negotiable Activity Contracts* (PNAC), which permit members of the management team to manage objectives with their subordinates by ensuring that team objectives and personal objectives are feasible. PNACs offer financial benefits linked to the results, which are evaluated according to piloting logbook indicators.

Finally, the *policy axis* entails defining change orientation, including the underlying strategy, "rules of the game," social policy, choice of participants, and so forth. In contrast with the first two axes, where interveners play an important pedagogical role by contributing their methodology, in this case it is the company's top management that selects options and makes decisions. Within the spirit of this axis, ISEOR has advised and stimulated top managers by sending monthly "conjuncture letters" explaining the points where the change process is going forward (or at a standstill), and the domains where decisions need to be made.

The success of the change process results from a balanced articulation of these three axes, as presented in Figure II.4:

- Change built only around the improvement process-axis can produce long-term economic results, but immediate results are few or inexistent.

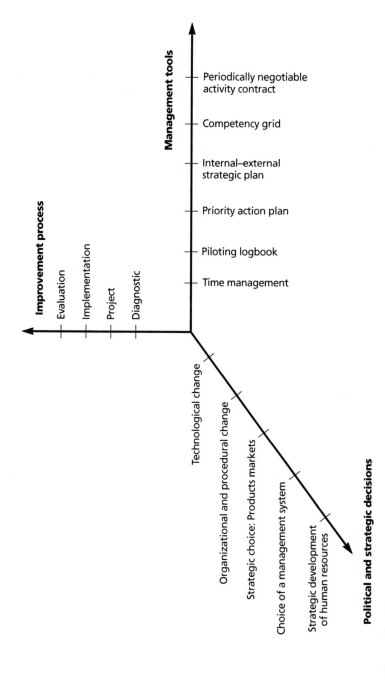

Figure II.4 The three axes of socio-economic intervention.

- Implementing only the *management tools-axis* can lead to weakened innovation and creation of potential in the change process.
- Change that is dominated by policy concerns (political and strategic decisions) eventually exhausts actors and depletes their energy, as early as the end of the first year of intervention.

Implantation of a Strategic Piloting System

The system of strategic piloting includes priority action plans, socio-economic piloting logbooks, and periodically negotiable activity contracts which, as we will see in Section III, enable reactivating behaviors that permit diminishing hidden costs.

In the first section of this book, we analyzed the theoretical foundation and principles of hidden cost analysis, evaluation and reduction. This section is devoted to the process of socio-economic intervention. Chapter 4, devoted to the Horivert method, examines the articulation of the socio-economic innovation process and the implantation of a strategic piloting system. The next three chapters focus on the diagnostic, project and implementation phases of the socio-economic innovation process.

NOTE

1. The Post Office Study was undertaken by Aimé Perret, Director of human resources at the Post Office, "Une entreprise publique: les enjeux et le nouveau management" [A public enterprise: What is at stake with new management], acts of the colloquium Qualité du conseil et mutation du secteur public [Management consulting quality and mutation of the public sector], Economica, 1992, pp. 163–190. See also Jean Pichon, Director of the western delegation of the Post Office, "Stratégie d'extension du management socio-économique dans une région" [Socio-economic management extension strategy in a region], acts of the colloquium Évaluation de l'expert-comptable: conseil en management [Evaluation of public accountants: management consulting], Economica, 1993, pp. 215–237.

REFERENCE

Savall, H., & Zardet, V. (1985). *Processus d'innovation socio-économique de deux équipes d'encadrement d'une banque régionale: Méthodologie et résultants* [Socio-economic innovation process of two management teams in a regional bank: Methodology and results]. Ecully, France: ISEOR Report.

CHAPTER 4

THE HORIVERT PROCEDURE

The socio-economic approach to enterprises aims to generalize socio-organizational innovation within the enterprise. In essence, its goal is to create an overall process of energizing the enterprise. It became apparent that, to achieve this, an intervention method of in-depth, progressive transformation had to be designed.

One can roughly distinguish two characteristics—common and specific—in ISEOR's intervention framework. *Common characteristics* are shared by all interventions (e.g., negotiating the intervention with the top management). These common characteristics constitute the "core" of the intervention method, which will be presented in detail in this chapter. *Specific characteristics* are particular to the intervention in a given enterprise. These specificities are always negotiated between the researchers and the top management, with the two-fold goal of adapting the intervention to the organizational structure and culture, while maintaining coherency between these arrangements and the core of the intervention method. Through examples, the chapter will illustrate the significant degree of flexibility that is an integral part of the core. This process is referred to as *Horivert* because the intervention in the enterprise begins with two simultaneous actions: *hori*zontal action within the executive management team and *ver*tical action in one or two company units.

This socio-economic intervention method has been applied in more than 1,000 enterprises and organizations in 31 countries in Europe, North America, South America, Africa and Asia. It has three fundamental

Mastering Hidden Costs and Socio-Economic Performance, pages 99–126
Copyright © 2008 by Information Age Publishing

characteristics. First, it is a *progressive* method, spanning a period of several years in the attempt to truly energize the enterprise. We shall see, however, that this progressive approach takes on relatively different forms in horizontal and vertical actions. Second, it is a *structured* method, owing to its designer's preference for a strategy of change (see Savall, 1981). This organization is evident in: a) the *sequencing of phases* (diagnostic → project → implementation → evaluation; see Savall, 1982), b) the heuristic search for *effective rhythms* of intervention (e.g., when the time period between the beginning of the diagnostic and the end of the project exceeds a year, entropy effects can hinder the energizing objective),[1] and c) the composition of *participation devices* for company actors taking part in the intervention. The socio-economic intervention method strongly involves all categories of company actors—from shopfloor personnel all the way up to the CEO—yet in carefully studied order and groups. During the diagnostic, for example, the results are first presented to a hierarchical group composed of the head of the unit in which the diagnostic was carried out and his or her hierarchical superiors up to the CEO. Third, it is a method *evaluated with company actors* in that all results provided by researchers are presented for discussion and assessment with the enterprise. Thus, all ISEOR's hidden cost results, which have been calculated over the past 30 years, have been reviewed, verified, discussed, and even modified with the enterprise directly concerned.

The first intervention method—referred to as the *ripple-through process*—was implemented from 1978 to 1983 in nine enterprises.[2] These experiments made it evident that, while having been conceived as a "pincer movement" process, the *ripple-through process* was, in reality, a bottom-up procedure. This set limits with respect to the overall energizing objective. Thus, beginning in 1983, the intervention method was transformed into the *Horivert process*.

Before any socio-economic intervention in an enterprise, ISEOR always conducts a *veritable negotiation* on the methodology to be applied while adapting the tools and concepts to the enterprise, which is considered a unique socio-cultural space. Intervention negotiation between the research center and the director of the partner enterprise defines the research theme and objectives, but above all, the intervention methodology. It could be said, at the risk of slightly over-simplifying, that the "core" of the intervention method is non-negotiable—it is the *sine qua non* condition for carrying out the intervention. However, this core includes devices and modalities that are to be adapted to the enterprise and defined within the negotiation framework between the two parties.

THE "RIPPLE-THROUGH" PROCESS: LESSONS FROM EXPERIENCE

The ripple-through process was conceived through critical analysis (Savall, 1981) of procedures for implanting organizational innovations practiced in French and European enterprises. These intervention method procedures can be classified into two types:

- The descending procedure or "top-down" approach in which "executive management elaborates, under its authority, the discrete study of a project, reserving the initiative to pursue or to interrupt the study at any moment...executive management implements the project following hierarchical channels" (Savall, 1981: pp. 96–107).
- The ascending procedure or "bottom-up" approach, which is "initiated at the summit (top management), directly involving workers who are called upon to expose problems as operators themselves, to express suggestions, and to convey this information in view of studying solutions and the means that need to be available" (Savall, 1981: pp. 96–107).

Combined Ascending-Descending and Iterative Processes

The *ripple-through* process was conceived as a combined ascending and descending procedure, thus creating a "pincer movement" effect and attributing a *specific major role to the hierarchy*. The embedding of two procedure types confers an innovative character to the intervention method, which can be illustrated as follows:

1. The ascending procedure consists of taking stock of problems, dysfunctions and suggestion given by shopfloor personnel (workers, office employees) and the intermediary supervisory staff (foremen, supervisors) to be presented to the executive management team and senior management.
2. In order to accomplish this, socio-economic diagnostic methodology carried out in a unit includes semi-structured interviews with the rank and file personnel, intermediary supervisory staff, the Management and labor representatives to identify dysfunctions relative to the unit.

3. This ascending procedure is then linked to a descending procedure. The Board and top management and senior executives, as first and second rank decision makers in the enterprise, are directly involved in the socio-economic innovation process: they are interviewed in the diagnostic phase; they attend the presentation of diagnostic results; and throughout the development of the project, they play an active role in a focus group whose objective is controlling the coherency between solutions proposed during the plenary group and the enterprise's objectives-constraints.[3] The top management makes the final decision to accept the project, determines the means necessary to implement it, participates in the steering group and are responsible for auditing the implementation of the project.

One can thus affirm that the *ripple-through* process, from the very start of the intervention, involved the top management and senior executives. Together they concentrated on *dysfunctions* and the *search for solutions,* localized within the basic unit. It was only later that the *ripple-through process* addressed the top management problematics.

Two *idées-forces* (pivotal ideas) provide a chronological vision of the *ripple-through* process: progressive extension of the spatial fields of intervention, and progressive extension of actor categories involved in the intervention.

Progressive Extension of Spatial Fields of Intervention

A basic observation was that procedures that studied problems one by one in a large population (e.g., a company concentrating its efforts on communication one year and on training the following year) offered limited efficiency. Moreover, since the socio-economic approach was aimed at the overall level of the enterprise, the principle of spatial segmentation with three successive stages was adopted with the objective to identify all dysfunctions and search for solution to these dysfunctions in that spatial field.

These three successive stages are:

- *Experimentation:* the intervention is applied to a service, office, or agency with approximately 5 to 50 employees;
- *Extension:* a work unit, division, or department employing between 100 and 200 persons; and
- *Generalization:* the entire enterprise or establishment, from 600 to 30,000 employees in the various interventions carried out by ISEOR (in some very large enterprises processes that have lasted up to roughly 5 years).

In each stage, the final objective is the search for more efficient operation in the given field through a succession of the diagnostic, project,

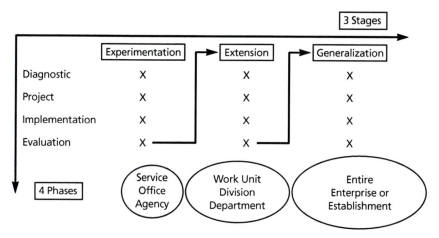

Figure 4.1 Stages in the *ripple-through* process

implementation and evaluation phases. The evaluation phase is critical as it provides the top management with the basic information necessary to decide whether to pursue the intervention into the extension stage and then into generalization. The progressive extension of fields of action in the *ripple-through process* is illustrated in Figure 4.1. The time necessary to accomplish this process in an enterprise employing several hundred people was approximately 5 to 6 years: experimentation, 12 to 15 months; extension, 2 years; and generalization, 2 to 3 years. Today, ISEOR conducts similar interventions in *less than half the time* due to the Horivert procedure.

Progressive Involvement of Actors in the Intervention
If the progressive nature of the procedure can be explained by the complexity of the problems to be handled, it also has to do with finding hierarchical partners who volunteer to accept an intervention, This willingness to participate is a *sine qua non* condition of the experimental stage, where one unit must be the first one to "launch" itself. This premise also holds true for the extension stage. The *ripple-through* process was based on a progressive increase in the number of allies in the enterprise, with respect to interveners and internal opinion-leaders of the pilot action. Although experience has shown that this participative dynamic typically works, in the nine enterprises where the *ripple-through* process was applied, several actors (members of middle or top management) remained staunch adversaries throughout the intervention, which ran from 2 to 5 years depending on the enterprise. This resistance created harmful effects on the intervention's effectiveness, and influenced the development of the Horivert process.

In terms of progressive involvement of actors, it is important to distinguish between actors *associated with* the intervention piloting from actors *directly affected* in their jobs by the intervention. Indeed, if the first group is simply associated with the intervention, they are not necessarily affected by it in their operations. Thus, during the experimentation stage, department heads will certainly be directly and frequently associated with the intervention, but they will continue to carry out their role as department head in much the same manner as before, until the extension stage is applied to their department. For the head of the particular service and his or her personnel, on the contrary, the intervention, by touching them directly, influences their jobs, efficiency, professional behavior, and so forth. Thus, there is often psychological questioning during the diagnostic phase, followed by actual transformations during the implementation of the project, concerning such practices as the distribution of tasks, hierarchical relations, training, leadership, personnel evaluation, and so forth. In other words, the intervention may represent a positive stake, but there is also a certain degree of risk-taking for the head of the unit and, to a lesser extent, his or her staff.

The idea of progressive extension (*Ripple-Through* Process) gradually increases the numbers of actors directly involved in the intervention: they can number from 5 to 50 during the experimentation stage, from 100 to 200 during the extension stage, and from 600 to 30,000 employees during the generalization stage. Whatever the stage, there are three types of actors associated with piloting:

1. The hierarchical superiors of the considered field, i.e., the hierarchical chain of command up to the CEO. Depending on the size of the enterprise, 2 to 5 persons are typically considered.
2. Certain hierarchical superiors from other fields who are associated with the diagnostic phase (interview, data collection), the project phase (participation in the focus group) and the evaluation phase (interview, data collection). These employees, selected for their operational contacts within the field of intervention (e.g., management control of personnel, computer services) are approximately 5 in number during the experimentation phase; their number increases during the extension and generalization phases (up to several dozen).
3. Personnel representation authorities, who are interviewed during the diagnostic phase, and then kept informed in the context of institutional social relations in the enterprise. Personnel representation authorities do not participate as such in the project nor in the implementation phases.[4]

The *ripple-through* process is characterized by its progressive extension into fields and its progressive involvement of actors, structured into the three stages. Generalization constitutes the ultimate stage before the departure of the interveners, during the course of which specific effects were sought.

The Anticipated Results of Generalization

The anticipated results of generalization[5] focus on the maximum globalization of solutions and their effectiveness as well as lessening the costs of the intervention. With regard to globalization of actions and their effectiveness, three types of results are anticipated:

- The strategic aspect of the action becomes increasingly clear, i.e., the will of the CEO and top management to transform company management into socio-economic management;
- The *accomplishment of actions* in all six action domains, notably in "strategic implementation," which is often neglected during the experimentation phase and even during extension; and
- Modification of productive behavior, activated by the implementation of periodically negotiable activity contracts (PNACs; See Chapter 8).

At the same time, despite the objective of an enlarged scope of action, ISEOR and its client organizations have attempted to reduce the unit cost of these transformation actions[6] during the generalization phase due to a "triple effect":

- Economy of scale effect: lowered unit costs through increased product volume for a given phase (scope of actions);
- *Experience* effect: lowered unit costs through increased cumulative volume, due to the progressively increasing number of persons involved over the course of successive phases of the intervention process; and
- Learning curve effect: lowered unit costs through acquisition of know-how on the part of ISEOR interveners and company actors enabling them to attain higher effectiveness more rapidly.

Problems Encountered in the Application of the "Ripple-Through" Process

Although this approach attempts to engage organizational members in the process of bringing about large-scale organizational change, application of the framework pointed to gaps between desired and anticipated results. As an example of these problems, this section draws on two cases—

in the metallurgy industry and in a bank—to illustrate the challenges inherent in the *ripple-through* process: the difficulty in passing from one stage to another; and the complexity of the intervention during the extension and generalization stages.

In all companies studied by ISEOR, the transition from one stage to the next—from experimentation to extension or from extension to generalization—was extremely difficult, despite formal acceptance by the top management. The problem, however, lies with application and implementation rather than with the principles of extension themselves. As an example, an organization can technically be in the generalization phase, but without having attained the necessary conditions for effective action. Depending on the enterprise, the forms and sources of these transition difficulties and complexities can take many forms.

Opposition from New Hierarchical Superiors

In two enterprises that were engaged in the generalization stage (decided by the top management), the actual implementation of generalization activities was hindered by the refusal of hierarchical superiors at the top management team level to commit to actions, both in their divisions and at the top management level.

Incompatible Objectives

In four enterprises, there were contradictions between the intervention's objectives and those of the enterprise. In a bank, for example, the generalization phase was negatively impacted by a contradiction between the profitability objectives inherent in socio-economic intervention (hidden cost reduction) that were accepted by the top management and the "productivity"[7] objectives that were pursued by the top management. This contradiction, which was exposed during the diagnostic of the management team of the commercial network, clearly placed management in a very uncomfortable position. The problem of the incompatibility of objectives arose in other enterprises with the arrival of new, key executives in the management team, when the objectives they pursued were radically different from those of their predecessors.

Insufficient Internal Information

A lack of information about the intervention can contribute to various "blocking" behaviors or opposition to the intervention. This phenomenon was particularly acute in one of the enterprises we studied, where various rumors circulated on the experimentation evaluation results, when the top management, personnel department and unit involved had not even divulged the results of the intervention. In the absence of this information, organizational members began "filling in" the details on their own. The issue of insufficient information occurred in specific departments involved with the intervention (e.g., projects, sales or production departments) and at the management team level.

Broad-Scoped Intervention

A retrospective study found that on a general level the application of the *ripple-through* process resulted in replication of the same methodology at all three stages of experimentation, extension and generalization. The term methodology should be understood here, not as the succession of the diagnostic-project-implementation-evaluation phases, but as the nature of services rendered by the intervener-researchers. Thus, in hindsight, there could have been insufficient questioning on the part of ISEOR researchers about their intervention practices, a lack of resistance toward pressure from the management demanding replication, and intense involvement of interveners, which could have unconsciously led to over-statement and perfectionism.

The challenge of broad-scoped intervention can be illustrated by another case of an enterprise at the generalization stage. During the second year of generalization, 19 actions were carried out by 7 ISEOR researchers in several various units (8 central services and 11 agencies). These actions were carried out according to the same operational method, which had been condensed by the enterprise in an operations manual. Nevertheless, the management team refused on two occasions during the same year to embark on an improvement process of its own operations.

Unresolved Dysfunctions

From as early as the experimentation or extension stages, diagnostics revealed dysfunctions that could only be fully addressed later on, during the generalization stage. These dysfunctions dealt mainly with inter-unit interactions and strategic implementation, which nevertheless affected the micro-spaces. This effect was completely predictable, given the *ripple-through* process concept. The "rules of the game" were clear for the heads of the micro-spaces—they knew in advance that inter-service and strategic implementation dysfunctions could not be dealt with until the generalization stage. Nevertheless, given the goal of enhancing effectiveness, this issue was a clear limitation.

Projects Poorly Linked to Company Strategy

Especially during the experimentation stage, the actual content of specific projects that were under development were, at times, difficult to related to the overall company strategy. In some instances, the project was in blatant contradiction with company objectives (e.g., in several micro-space projects were rejected by the top management because they demanded additional staff, while the strategic objectives included keeping down staffing levels). In other situations, the project lacked sufficient scope with respect to company strategic objectives and were seen as "timid" projects.

It is useful to note that these problems arose even though projects had been developed with the aid of the core-group, including the unit's hierarchical superior responsible for ensuring the compatibility of the project with company objectives and constraints. This difficulty was explained by the existence of up-stream dysfunctions, which included limited knowledge, a lack of commitment to the objectives defined by the top management, a vague company strategy, or the personal strategy of actors promoting their own demands, under the cover of the intervention scheme.

Unit Heads in Uncomfortable Positions

While this issue occurred mostly during the experimentation stage, in many instances it was prolonged through the generalization phase. From the point of view of actors involved in the intervention, it was clearly understood that the head of the unit where experimentation took place was the actor, of all company actors, who was in the most uncomfortable situation. This person was the individual who experienced multiple demands, often being hounded on all sides by demands for additional work or being personally called into question, and faced with multiple objectives that were partially incompatible. Because of this situation, the head of the experimentation unit had to attempt to simultaneously attain a) the objectives assigned by the socio-economic intervention (i.e., improvement of the socio-economic performance of the unit) and b) operational objectives of the short-term action plan dictated by the company's general policy.

We have also observed that, in the course of the intervention process (which can extend over several years), new *general policy* objectives can appear that are partially incompatible with the socio-economic objectives, while at the same time, the top management, adopting schizophrenic behavior (a kind of split general policy), continues to affirm its initial decision to pursue and develop the socio-economic intervention. Even though intervener-researchers can, in this type of situation, "push back" in their interactions with the top management, unit heads unit can nonetheless find themselves "momentarily" torn in two.

Other company actors can also exert significant pressure on their unit heads, which may even take on deceitful forms, suggesting that executive management has devoted little attention to providing information about the intervention throughout the enterprise. Rumors can then run rampant, pointing to the "reasons" that the unit was chosen (e.g., it's the "worst" in the company) or the results of the diagnostic showing the "disastrous" operation of the unit. Although all phases are subject to rumors, which are usually not denied by the top management, such rumors readily affect unit heads, who find themselves as the target of their colleagues' accusations.

Hitches in the Unfolding Process

Stepping back in order to analyze the entire process, from experimentation to generalization, two observations are in order. First, in certain enterprises and organizations the *process* has been interrupted due to the top management's non-renewal decision, even though economic and social results were positive. In a magnet manufacturing company, for example, the top management rejected extension of the intervention, even though experimentation evaluation results revealed gains achieved through hidden cost reductions of 10,100€ per person per year. Other cases of interruption occurred at the end of the diagnostic (in an aluminum enterprise), or the project phases (hospital service, chemical plant), further bringing to light the flaws of the *ripple-through* process. The second observation deals with the length of the time period required for the unfolding process to reach generalization. In too many instances, the passage from one stage to another was chaotic, either in terms of formal decisions by the top management or in terms of *effectively* accomplishing the extension or the generalization phase.

Problems encountered during the application of the *ripple-through* process progressively lead us to adapt certain core aspects of the intervention method. Given the repetition of certain problems, it appeared to us that the *ripple-through* process itself was the origin of those problems. In other words, the problems were due to shortcomings in the conception of the operational intervention method. Thus, starting in 1983, the *ripple-through* process was replaced by the Horivert process for ISEOR's new experimental research interventions.

THE HORIVERT INTERVENTION PROCESS

The Horivert process was conceived by keeping the progressive and structured characteristics of the ripple-through process. However, it was based on three totally new guiding principles.

Guiding Principles

These three guiding principles, which emanated from a critical analysis of the *ripple-through* process, focus on a) launching the intervention in a more coherent and coordinated fashion, b) promoting internal dissemination of the intervention, and c) involving more organizational members during a shorter period of time.

Launching the Intervention

The first principle concerns launching the intervention with two simultaneous and coordinated actions: a) a **horizontal** *action*, involving the executive management team; and b) a **vertical** *action* in at least two basic units (service, agency, office), thus involving operating employees (workers, staff) and the first-line supervisors of those units. The innovation with respect to the *ripple-through* process thus consists of situating the horizontal action much earlier in the process, at the very start of the experimentation phase, while it occurred only during the generalization phase in the original *ripple-through* process.

This double horizontal/vertical action—hence the term "Horivert"—has three objectives. First, to ensure a stronger *link* between the socio-economic intervention and the company's strategy. This objective is facilitated by the horizontal action, which, as we shall see further on, entails defining, activating and energizing the implementation of company strategy. Second, this double action permits identifying and *resolving* so-called "basic" or "operational" dysfunctions and *strategic dysfunctions*. The aim is to re-articulate the problematics that classic literature in management has separated and to demonstrate the interactive effects of strategic and operational problems, which are inseparable. Finally, the double action envelops middle-management with a sort of "pincer" movement representing the two actions. Indeed, certain managers are directly involved in both actions, for example, one or more members of the executive management team who are hierarchically responsible for units involved in the vertical action (see Figure 4.2).

This double-involvement in the presence of one another, combined with the intervener-researchers, fosters coherency between the two actions and limits the practice of double discourse, which was often encountered in the *ripple-through* process.

Promoting the Internal Dissemination of the Intervention

The internal dissemination of the intervention is promoted through training and management analysis tools. The objective here is to avoid subjecting company actors to energy brought from outside the enterprise by the interveners. This is done as early as possible and as swiftly as possible. In order to foster the enterprise's autonomy toward interveners, we have chosen to progressively reduce the tasks externalized to intervener-researchers by helping the management team do the tasks themselves. For example, internal dissemination can involve breaking down certain intervention modules, such as the socio-economic diagnostic and the search for solutions, after training managers in the methodology and periodically assisting them in carrying out the diagnostic and then the project.

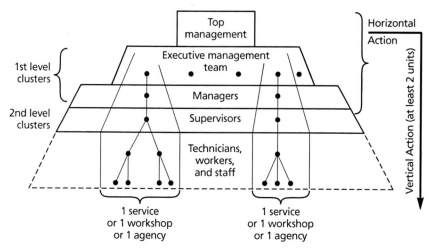

Figure 4.2 The Horivert process (experimentation phase)

This intervention scheme has several advantages: a) it increases management competency in socio-economic management, b) it reduces delay in the intervention's progress, thanks to the multiplication of "internal interveners", and c) most importantly, it significantly reduces the rupture that occurs between the intense moments of the intervention when interveners are present in the enterprise (diagnostic, project day) and daily operations. In other words, the evolution of managers' mindsets is more rapid and profound, and one can rightly speak of an *evolution* of the management culture. Moreover, by involving management in this way they are more likely to create the link between the intervention and company strategy, which is critical as this is one of the axes of strategic implementation.

Involving More Actors Over Shorter Time Periods

In order to fight the entropy and inertia phenomena identified in the *ripple-through* process, the Horivert method strives to involve company actors for shorter time periods. This required modifying the services rendered by intervener-researchers so as to avoid stifling the enterprise with time-consuming schemes. The process can be accelerated by incorporating key piloting tools in the early experimentation stage and helping to break down internal objectives as a means of accelerating the process.

A related way to foster integration and implementation of the intervention process is up-stream training in time management for all collaborative-training clusters. *Time management* tools are introduced in the socio-economic intervention process by the *self-analysis of time grid* (see Figure 4.3). This method consists of entrusting the members of the management and supervision team with the responsibility of observing their workday over a

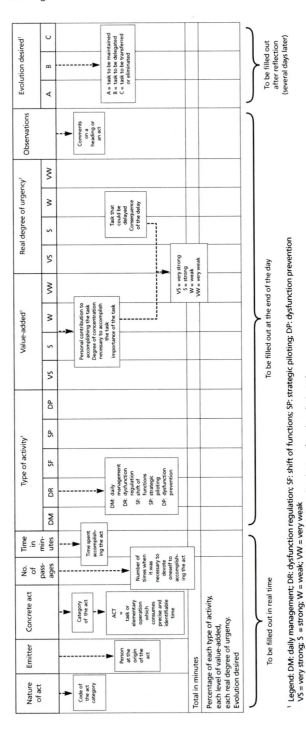

Figure 4.3 Self-analysis of Time Grid.

period of 3 to 5 days and capturing the results on a grid designed for self-analysis of time usage.

This assessment is clearly based on a certain relationship of trust between the top management and the management team, as well as between the intervener-researchers and members of the top management and senior management. It is important that everyone involved endorses this self-collection of data, which helps to generate *authentic* information that can be used and reused by the individual during the intervention. Of course, as an intervener-researcher, one must be aware that data collected in this manner can still be erroneous, imprecise, or even voluntarily manipulated in certain instances. The essential objective is much less perfect "reliability" (one could even question whether data collection protocols exist that permit guaranteeing such a notion) than *rapid access* to a field and its time management, customarily considered by managers as their private domain, since it touches their professional intimacy.

This data collection method simultaneously attains three objectives: a) obtaining a preliminary series of concrete, anonymous data on actual time management practices, creating a foundation for the first stage of time management improvement research; b) acquiring the management team's confidence toward the intervention procedure, materialized by the interveners, with regards to an eminently sensitive and traditionally delicate subject; and c) reassuring company actors (starting with management) against time-schedule "disturbances" that their participation in the different stages of the process could provoke. The time management tool constitutes the first lever in a dynamic change process, for it permits freeing time for the intervention, without over-loading actors' responsibilities and schedules.

Double Progression: Fields of Actions/Issues

The three principal stages of socio-economic intervention have been maintained in the Horivert method, even though their content has been radically transformed. The first substantial modification is the increased numbers and categories of actors involved at each stage, compared with the *ripple-through* process (see Figure 4.4). The second characteristic is that from the very beginning of the intervention, certain actors are involved in horizontal and vertical action (see Figure 4.2). The *experimentation* phase, which extends over the first 12 to 15 months, pursues the objective of implanting socio-economic management tools in two populations: a) the entire top management and senior management team, and b) at least part of the intermediary supervisory staff (if the enterprise employs more than 500 persons).

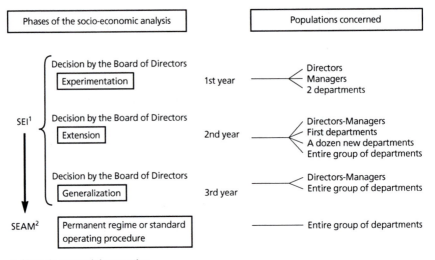

1. SEI: socio-economic intervention
2. SEAM: socio-economic management

Figure 4.4   Socio-economic development strategy in the Horivert process.

Details of the Horizontal Action

Three types of action directly involve the Board and executive management over the course of the first year. The first is *collaborative-training action.* Collective sessions are taught by intervener-researchers to directors, managers and supervisors involved in the vertical action. Groups from 12 to 15 persons are constituted into "clusters" following the actual architecture of management teams, with each group including a director and his or her direct collaborators (see Figure 4.5).

Every group follows exactly the same training program, which is made up of ten half-day sessions every other month, plus six one or two-hour sessions of personal assistance for each participant in the training program. These customized sessions, placed at the intervals between the collective collaborative-training sessions, are intended to assist managers in transposing and adapting tools introduced during the collective session to their own specific cases. The five personal assistance sessions address the use of key socio-economic management tools: the time management tool, the piloting logbook, the competency grid, the priority action plan and the periodically negotiable activity contract.

The second direct action is a *horizontal diagnostic of general dysfunctions* in the enterprise, which feeds into the collaborative-training program as real cases in the enterprise. This diagnostic draws up an inventory of dysfunctions in the form of key-ideas. This is done through in-depth, semi-structured interviews of members of top management. The diagnostic is

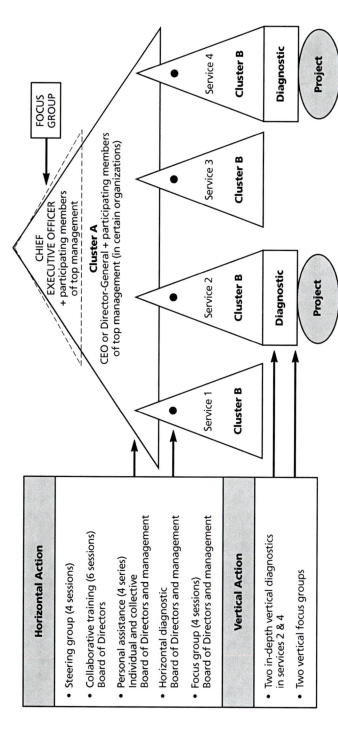

Figure 4.5 Architecture of collaborative training by clusters.

presented to each collaborative-training group and concludes with the intervener-researchers' "expert opinion" presented several weeks later (see Chapter 5).

Finally, the *horizontal project* (see Chapter 6) is developed and implemented over the course of the first year. It represents a group of general, overall solutions focused on helping the enterprise to significantly reduce the dysfunctions revealed by the diagnostic.

Details of the Vertical Action

In the two units chosen for the vertical action, two key actions are carried out. First an *in-depth socio-economic diagnostic* (explored in more detail in Chapter 5) is carried out. This process is based on semi-structure interviews with *all* categories of actors in the units. A qualitative diagnostic of dysfunctions is carried out, which includes creating *competency grid* for the entire personnel of the studied units and estimating the units' hidden costs. These results are orally presented three times: first, to the head of the unit with his or her hierarchical superior, then to the same unit head and his or her personnel, and finally to the entire personnel interviewed. Three or four weeks later, the "expert opinion" is presented to the head of the unit.

The second action is the *socio-economic innovation project*, in essence a group of solutions that aim to reduce the dysfunctions identified during the diagnostic. This innovation project is then broken-down into the unit's PAP, and serves for the preparation of the PNACs of the unit's personnel.

Horizontal and vertical actions are carefully synchronized as Figure 4.6 illustrates. The piloting tools implemented during the vertical action, which aim to pilot the introduced change, are duplicated by piloting tools implemented in all zones of the enterprise during the horizontal action. This second action enables more rapid cultural evolution inside the enterprise due to the cultural-diffusion role played by the members of the top management in the enterprise's everyday operation. Director and manager populations are thus *directly involved* from the beginning of the experimentation stage. They remain involved during the extension and generalization stages, but work issues evolve progressively toward coherency between company strategy and internal operations, notably due to the piloting tools.

This progression is attained by specific actions within each phase. During the experimentation phase, for example, piloting logbooks are constructed and PNACs are adapted to the enterprise. During the extension phase, a diagnostic of strategic implementation is carried out inside the executive management team. It leads to solutions for improving the implementation of company strategy, sometimes even to modifying the strategy itself. At the end of the extension phase, activity contracts are clearly articulated to strategic implementation. Finally, during the generalization phase, the top management develops its program of *internal-external strategic actions* (IESP),

Actions	Month									
	1	2	3	4	5	6	7	8	9	10
Conduct an overall progress procedure avoiding dispersion										
• Piloting group	1			2		3				4
Improvement of company piloting through common and well-adapted management tools										
• Collaborative-training in the 5 directors-managers clusters	1 TM		2 MC	3 DIAG	4 PAP	5 DIAG		6 SPLB PNAC		
• Individual and collective implementation assistance for directors and managers		1		2			3		4	5
Underscoring improvements and performances										
• Horizontal diagnostic of directors/managers		←→								
• Top management's focus group						2		3	4	
• In-depth vertial diagnostics in 2 units: Training and company support				←→						
• Vertical focus groups of the 2 units						1	2	3	4	

Figure 4.6 Synchronization of horizontal and vertical actions during the implantation phase.

i.e., it defines, prioritizes and schedules actions in the environment and inside the enterprise that will enable it to attain the strategic objectives the enterprise defined for itself. Internal actions represent the implementation of company strategy, which are defined by the actions on its external environment.

This program entails progressively equipping the executive management team with the management tools it will need to accomplish its function. Thus, the permanent socio-economic management regime, once the interveners have left the enterprise, is prepared and equipped with three coordinated tools: the IESP, the piloting logbook and the periodically negotiable activity contract. The principal actions and outcomes of the different stages of the Horivert process are summed up in Figure 4.7.

Vertical Action in the Horivert Process

A hasty analysis of the evolution of ISEOR's intervention processes could suggest that top-down procedures are increasingly preferred to bottom-up procedures. Indeed, horizontal action, as conceived in the Horivert process, emphasizes treating the top management's dysfunctions. However, if this upper-level analysis is to be successful, it must include dysfunctions that affect the base of the company, because more than thirty years of socio-economic diagnostics in all kinds of enterprises have shown us that top managements *always* have a *distorted vision* of the base. With that in mind, it seemed to us a fragile stance, in methodological terms, to be subjugated to the company's discourse on its own operations. Maintaining the vertical action thus appears indispensable.

Furthermore, the two actions interact and "feed" one another. Horizontal action is fed by the results of vertical action. Members of the executive management team are thus successively presented with the results of the diagnostics carried out in the units: the opinions expressed by the personnel, the hidden costs, the content of the project, and, periodically, the evaluation results following implementation. The vertical action is fed by horizontal action. Vertical input is clearly evident at the project stage where hierarchical superiors, members of the small-group, are ready to fix precise strategic objectives at the plenary focus-group meeting. These objectives will have been previously discussed within the executive management team (horizontal action). Finally, in a more subtle, on-going way, the units involved in the vertical action appear to be more actively supported by the top management and executive management, both toward their colleagues as well as toward their own subordinates.

Ultimately, the question of how to choose the units that will be involved in the vertical action must be posed. We have already evoked the problems

Populations	Experimentation	Extension	Generalization
Top and middle managers	• Training in socio-economic analysis • Construction of piloting logbooks for each and everyone • Discussion on the policy of activity contracts in the firm • Diagnostic and project on: [communication-coordination-cooperation], time management and strategic implementation	• Diagnostic and project, strategic implementation • Setting up activity contracts	• Development of the PASINTEX: program of internal-external strategic actions • Activity contracts (continuation)
2 units	• Diagnostic • Project • Construction of piloting logbooks • Implementation • Evaluation of results	• Setting up logbooks and activity contracts for all personnel	• Same action as the extension (continuation)
10 other units	Training of management personnel in socio-economic analysis	• Light diagnostic • Rapid project • Setting up logbooks and activity contracts • Implementation	• Logbooks and activity contracts for all personnel (continuation)
All units combined		• Setting up piloting logbooks	• Light diagnostic • Concise project • Setting up activity contracts • Implementation • Evaluation of results

Figure 4.7 Principal actions in the different stages of the Horivert process.

experienced by the heads of the first units involved in an innovation process. It seems indispensable to us to launch the vertical action in *two* units. This offers two advantages. First, two members of the top management are thus engaged in the vertical action, which can increase their influence during the horizontal action. Second, the results of the vertical action are not limited to the suggestion that they are an "isolated case." *Conversely*, we have observed that when only one unit was selected, dysfunctions exposed by the diagnostic provoked a cultural shock among the unit's personnel, which was misinterpreted by other units that were not involved. This dynamic often led to remarks such as, "That department is the worst." When two units are involved, especially if they are very different from one another, this perverse effect is radically reduced.

APPLICATIONS OF THE HORIVERT PROCESS

Since 1983 the Horivert process has been applied by ISEOR in over 1,000 enterprises and organizations, including industrial groups and tertiary companies, SMEs, liberal professions and public administrations, in 31 different countries in Europe, North America, Latin-American, Africa and Asia. The resulting data base provides a useful foundation to examine the effectiveness of the process's application, notably evaluating recently-observed effects in comparison with the *ripple-through* process. Our assessment points to four principal effects.

Strategic Implementation

It is important to address the domain of strategic implementation early in the process, from the perspective of dysfunctions as well solutions and related piloting tools. This positioning of the socio-economic intervention, which is now presented and negotiated with the top management, becomes a method and process of strategic implementation in the entire enterprise or organization in the case of a large group.

To illustrate the critical role that strategic implementation plays in the process, this section presents four examples in very different types of organizations. In each case, the intervention produced significant results within a relatively short period of time. In an agro-food group with 2,600 employees, actions completed over a 14 month period engaged a significant part of the enterprise. The top management and senior management team, made up of 220 persons, plus 150 supervisors were trained in the socio-economic approach, equipped with time management tools, strategic piloting logbooks,

PAPs, PNACs and competency grids for their collaborator. In addition, 600 technicians, workers and staff members had PNACs, and vertical diagnostics had been carried out in 9 units representing 700 employees (550 had taken part in individual or collective interviews). A horizontal diagnostic, based on 150 interviews with the top management and senior management, was followed by a horizontal project and individual and collective actions in time management improvement. Finally, a "network" of 10 trainer-interns and assistants had been created and trained.

In a city hall employing 2,500 persons, after 6 months, priority action plans had been implemented for the first time in all departments and services, approximately 60 in all. They had been prepared by the head of every unit, and then negotiated with the top management.

In a telecommunications service, the executive management team undertook a revision of the company's "project" (strategy) only one year after the beginning of the intervention, with ISEOR's methodological assistance and the application of the diagnostic method, followed by the search for solutions in focus groups. Reflecting back on the *ripple-through* process, this type of horizontal action did not occur until the generalization phase, 3 to 5 years after the beginning of the intervention.

Finally, in a public housing management firm, 20 managers were equipped with decentralized piloting logbooks adapted to their responsibilities after 9 months of intervention. Six months later, the firm's entire personnel, representing 360 employees, had PNACs, each one of which had been prepared and discussed between the employees and their immediate hierarchical superior, in a pyramidal contract structure. By then the firm instituted both collective and individual piloting tools designed to be closely linked to the firm's medium-term strategic plan, which the top management had developed over the course of the first year of intervention.

Another outcome of strategic implementation is *greater commitment* on the part of executive management regarding decisions related to the unfolding process. This underscores the important role early strategic involvement plays. It greatly reduces hesitation on the part of executive management, which we had been confronted with in the *ripple-through* process. Thus all preliminary negotiations, before any intervention begins, should address the practical organization of the intervention process and the advisability of setting up periodically negotiable activity contracts. This means that launching an intervention is contingent upon executive management's agreement on a collaborative training program for managers, designed to test the feasibility of the intervention and prepare the implementation of the activity contracts, based on a system of remuneration incentives for the personnel that are financed by hidden cost reduction.

Dissemination of Socio-Economic Culture

Instilling a true socio-economic culture in an organization seems to emerge from horizontal actions that focus on the collaborative training of the top and senior management in the socio-economic approach following the schema of clusters (see Figure 4.5). The role of management as part of this process has continually evolved over time. In 1979, for example, during ISEOR's first transformative research, there were no training devices. Numerous problems, especially a type of cultural shock experienced by management during the diagnostic and project, led to the creation of a management training phase in the socio-economic approach. From 1981 to 1983, managers received several days of training between the diagnostic and project phases. The main positive impact that we observed reflected the emergence of an overall vision of the socio-economic approach, which they had initially been compelled to piece together painstakingly like a puzzle. However, overt and covert blocking by certain actors, in addition to the slackening of the process, led to watering down the intervention method once again. Thus, since 1983 collaborative training of the top management and management has become the *first* stage of horizontal action. In any case, training usually takes place *before* presentation of the diagnostic results in view of vertical action, in order to reduce the cultural shock created by revealing dysfunctions through knowledge of the phases that follow the diagnostic.

This cultural effect is further facilitated when top management ensures open and extensive communication about the intervention. Indeed, experiencing the damaging effects provoked by insufficient information about an intervention has led us to emphasize the critical role that top management plays in organizing the content, forms and scheduling of messages communicated to the different social groups of the enterprise, including senior management, middle management, shopfloor personnel, personnel representative bodies (labor-management committees, personnel representatives, trade union representatives), and, in some enterprises, even to shareholders and board of directors (board of trustees in certain public establishments).

Management Taking Charge of Innovation Actions

Management's impact is not limited to the transformation of mental structures through cultural change. It becomes concrete reality when managers take charge of operations and acts that were formerly delegated to the intervener-researchers. In this sense, *taking charge* essentially means that the managers become the *internal interveners*. This is made possible by earlier, more rapid and more economical introduction of piloting tools (e.g., log-book, PAP, PNACs) as well as through a less time-consuming intervention process. Based on our field work, it appears that this version of the intervention was what companies actually wanted. In some instances, executive management considered this appropriation as a way to activate managers through integrated training.

As an example, in the public housing management firm referred to above, during the design of socio-economic logbooks for managers, methodological assistance to each manager was delivered partly by ISEOR intervener-researchers and partly by the head of personnel and the assistant managing director. This configuration served a threefold objective: a) enabling these two company-members to play the role of *internal reference*, thus fostering progressive autonomy of the firm vis-à-vis the research center; b) providing in-depth methodological training for the two company members in piloting logbook design and utilization; and, finally, c) ensuring solid coherency between the company's strategic objectives, of which both were keenly aware, and the logbook indicators that were under construction;

Similarly, in a telecommunication service firm, following two vertical actions of socio-economic innovation (diagnostic-project-implementation), executive management wanted the other department heads to conduct their own diagnostic and project. Once again, a twofold objective was served. First, this process ensured the integrated training of managers in socio-economic methods of analysis and management, since they alternated in-depth training sessions with "practical application." Second, it encouraged the managers to directly take charge of the dysfunctions in their departments, in order to find solutions.

It is important to underscore that despite the success cited in these two experiences, there can still be difficulty, deviation and delays during this process. Thus the evolution of this process is important to pursue and develop, especially due to its potential and positive impact.

Rapid Intervention Rhythms

Our last observation concerns one of the priority objectives assigned to the Horivert method, focusing on the importance of rhythm and its effects on the energy of internal actors. It is important that key actors understand executive management's determination and that they are stimulated to play an active role. One way in which this can be accomplished is through reducing the time involved in the intervention. In a socio-educational establishment with 50 employees, for example, the diagnostic and project process concerning the *entire* establishment was successfully carried out in just one year, despite a fair amount of resistance and reticence on the part of the personnel and executive management at the beginning of the process. In a telecommunications service firm, experimentation involving horizontal action and two vertical actions was completed in six months. At the end of that period, executive management decided to carry out the generalization phase over the course of the following year. The entire intervention lasted approximately 15 months. In an agro-food group employing 2,600 persons, all tools, including the periodically negotiable activity contract, were generalized in two years.

It is important to note that such rapid implementation and the rhythm it creates are, to a large degree, outcomes of the three principal effects discussed above. By closely linking the intervention with the strategic objectives of the enterprise, instilling a socio-economic culture and encouraging managers to take charge of the process, making it their own, the intervention will create its own rhythm of success.

CONCLUSION

Originally conceived as an overall management procedure, the socio-economic approach was initially tested in several firms using the ripple-through process, based on preliminary pilot-actions in workshops, agencies and services. Extension to an entire sector of the enterprise, followed by generalization to the whole company, proved feasible and fruitful, but the process was too slow and too complicated, despite executive management's active involvement from the very start. Drawing on the lessons learned from these first experiments, we perfected the Horivert method which combines: a) global action directed toward the entire top management team, beginning with collaborative training action, initially launched within the top management and based on the diagnostic of their own dysfunctions; and b) in-depth action in at least two sectors of the enterprise (depending on its size and complexity), involving the entire personnel (managers, supervisors, technicians, shopfloor and office workers).

This method embodies the principles we set out for ourselves from the very inception of the socio-economic approach. The numerous pilot-actions we have carried out in all types of enterprises and organizations indicate that the Horivert method is an efficient and effective operating method, one that eliminates many, if not most, of the inconveniences usually encountered in the course of organizational change, notably resistance and withdrawal.

NOTES

1. The term *entropy* designates, through analogy to thermodynamics, an irreversible deterioration of energy. In the domain of business management, energy

is the capacity to accomplish effective decisive acts with regards to company objectives. Deterioration of energy constitutes a loss of information (information that does not lead to effective decisive acts) as well as wasted human, technical and financial resources, which constitute the compressible portion of hidden costs and of dysfunction regulation activities.

2. Six of the enterprises were in the industrial sector (glassworks, mechanics, foundry, metallurgy, chemicals, electronics) and three were service enterprises (consumer credit, banking and a hospital).

3. In socio-economic management, the concept of objective-constraint designates all concrete objectives and actual constraints that constitute the field of action where the strategic implementation will take place. The systematic association of the words "objective" and "constraint" intends to signify the fact that formulating an objective implies *ipso facto* formulating at the same time the constraints connected to that objective. A typical problem in strategic implementation is precisely determining and carrying out decisive acts whose two-fold goal are the objective itself (e.g., increase sales) and the constraints or obstacles to be overcome (e.g., design a new product ahead of competitors, despite production technique difficulties and within the framework of a limited publicity budget).

4. This does not exclude the fact that certain employees associated with cooperative training clusters and in the focus groups, as hierarchical superiors, can also be selected as personnel representatives. This also applies to workers, office employees and technicians who participate in task groups or satellite focus groups.

5. For a detailed analysis of generalization, see Bartoli (1983).

6. The unit cost of transformation actions is understood to signify the ratio of expenses undertaken to accomplish actions during a certain period divided by the number of persons involved during that period. These expenses are evaluated according to total-cost principles and include the cost of the intervention, the cost of time spent by company members, and, in some cases, the cost of material accommodations. These expenses can be considered as human resource investments (e.g., redeemable over a three-year period).

7. In the bank case, productivity was defined as deposits for savings (savings accounts and savings plans for housing) over the average number of clients; in essence, effectiveness was measured by the collection of monetary resources by the bank and its network of agencies.

REFERENCES

Bartoli, A. (1983). *Socio-Economic Innovation Actions in Industrial Enterprises: Analysis of the Generalization Phase and Piloting Methodology.* Doctoral thesis in Management Sciences, under the direction of H. Savall, University of Lyon, Lyon, France.

Savall, H. (1981). *Work and People: an economic evaluation of job enrichment..* Cambridge: Oxford University Press. P275.

Savall, H. (1982). *Les quatre phases de l'expérimentation de solutions socio-économique au sein des entreprises et des organisations* [The four phases of experimentation of socio-economic solutions inside enterprises and organizations], *Les Cahiers de Recherche en Gestion* [Research Notebooks on Management], 3(Summer), 53–55.

CHAPTER 5

THE SOCIO-ECONOMIC DIAGNOSTIC

The socio-economic diagnostic is first and foremost a process of listening to all actors involved. Indeed, every individual, regardless of his or her job and hierarchical position, witnesses dysfunctions. All individuals in an organization cause dysfunctions and put up with them in their day to day activities, but they are also capable of emitting suggestions, sometime very concrete ones, for reducing those very dysfunctions. This dynamic is what we refer to as the "living idea-box" principle, which we have applied at ISEOR since 1974 as we built a methodical inventory of all dysfunctions encountered by shopfloor personnel. Furthermore, since every member of an enterprise harbors a different vision than his her colleagues or hierarchical supervisors, it is instructive to confront these differing visions, studying their convergences and their specificities, for they can, in themselves, be a sign of dysfunction of communication-coordination-cooperation or of strategic implementation.

THE FUNCTION AND CONTENT OF THE DIAGNOSTIC

The socio-economic diagnostic, by listening to a wide diversity of actors from all categories, initiates the renewal of a certain kind of confidence among actors. First, there is the confidence that employees have toward

Mastering Hidden Costs and Socio-Economic Performance, pages 127–156

the hierarchy, because they are involved in the interview process and encouraged to express their opinions on company operations. Second, there is confidence of the people being interviewed toward the intervener-researchers, because the interveners practice very open-minded listening and do not select a priori the ideas they want to hear. In addition the employees are also promised anonymity and the questions are centered on organizational problems and dysfunctions, and not on the employees themselves. The interveners assure the actors that "We're searching for dysfunctions, not for culprits. There are only problems to be solved, problems that are created and maintained through interaction among actors." Finally, there is confidence of intervener-researchers toward each one of the interviewees, convinced that what they have to express merits attention. An underlying premise of the socio-economic diagnostic is that every actor, whatever the level of his or her qualifications and hierarchical position, has relevant observations to make about operations and dysfunctions, observations that will contribute to a platform of improvements for the organization.

The Critical Role of Critical Listening

The intervener-researcher's attitude of confidence is nevertheless coupled with an attitude of critical and lucid listening, which facilitates accurate interpretation of the information. In essence, listening intensely does not mean believing *everything*. The *expert opinion*, which is developed by the intervener-researchers, enables them to express their own opinions on the major dysfunctions they perceive, beyond what is expressed directly by the actors themselves. In this process, the intervener-researchers help to identify the root-causes of dysfunctions, eventually pointing out dysfunctions characterized by a lack of confidence among company actors, which is typically difficult for the actors to admit. In this instance, the interveners are in a stronger position to detect and report the dysfunctions (the spokesman function of the intervener's intermediation).

Actor discourse provides an important foundation for intervention (e.g., basis for the mirror-effect), but its effectiveness for changing practices is limited—words lead to more words, while only *acts provoke acts*. The attitudes of actors during change action are, of course, expressed through their words, but they can only be "seen" through their professional acts. Thus, the stimulus role played by the intervener-researcher, mirroring exemplary practices, is a determining factor for *renewed confidence* throughout the organization.

Dysfunctions and Their Consequences

The objective of the socio-economic diagnostic is to highlight dysfunctions and their effects, as outlined in Figure 5.1. It reflects a process of estimating the reserves of potential effectiveness that are present within a given micro-space, by measuring the amount of the (so-called absolute) hidden costs it experiences. In terms of intervention strategy, this basic methodological option, which consists of selecting only the company dysfunctions, rests on a willingness to *create a cultural shock* or new level of company awareness, with the goal of motivating employees to search for solutions (project phase). Dysfunctional analysis possesses strong incentive power for stimulating human behavior, which a classic diagnostic of "Strong Points vs. Weak Points" does not possess, as satisfaction with the "strong" points often annuls the impact of the "weak" points.

Seeking the Causes of Dysfunctions

The socio-economic diagnostic endeavors to bring to light the causes of dysfunctions, without making this outcome the top priority. Indeed, the search for causes is conducted in a more in-depth and systematic manner during the project phase (see Chapter 6), once consensus has been established on the inventory of dysfunctions and their effects. However, the diagnostic enables a preliminary quest for causes, based on information gathered by the intervener-researchers.

The diagnostic is useful to isolate three types of dysfunctions:

- *Dysfunctions provoked* and *regulated* by the micro-space itself.
- *Dysfunctions externalized* by the micro-space. They begin inside the micro-space, but part of their regulation involves their environment. For example, a computer system in a bank that prints erroneous documents and sends them to branch offices for customer use will create problems (e.g., inappropriate decision-making in branch offices, customer complaints).
- *Dysfunctions internalized* by the micro-space. Their causes are to be found in the environment, for example, from another micro-space, but the consequences fall upon the former micro-space.

Because internalized dysfunctions are responsible for the micro-space's hidden costs, people often think they cannot take action on them. How-

Figure 5.1   The socio-economic diagnostic.

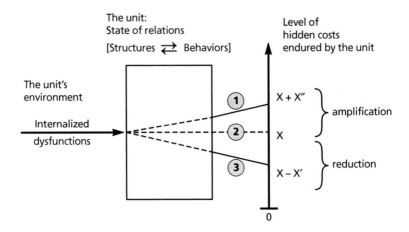

① The quality of unit's relations [Structure ⇄ Behaviors] leads to deterioration of internalized dysfunction levels.

② The quality relations [S ⇄ B] is neutral in terms of final hidden cost levels. This case is only theoretical, yet it represents a frequent mental schema among the unit's internal actors.

③ The unit's good operating quality succeeds in reducing the initial impact of internalized dysfunctions.

Figure 5.2   Internalized dysfunctions.

ever, our in-depth studies on multiple micro-space operations show that the operational quality of the micro-space that internalizes exogenous dysfunctions (those of external origin) has a "prism" effect. This effect either provokes an amplification of the dysfunctions or contributes to their reduction (see Figure 5.2). Thus, the micro-space, by improving its own operations, can *take action* on the levels of hidden costs caused by *externalized dysfunctions*.

Typical Content of a Socio-Economic Diagnostic

The final result of a diagnostic phase can be divided into two parts (see Figure 5.3). Part I includes all results that are orally presented to the enterprise in order to solicit its opinions and observations. This collective oral presentation permits completing the diagnostic. This part is named the "mirror effect." Part II, named the "expert opinion," is an analysis carried out by the intervener-researchers based on Part I and the oral presentation of results. Part I and Part II are combined in a written document that is presented and discussed in the enterprise. It is important to note that the

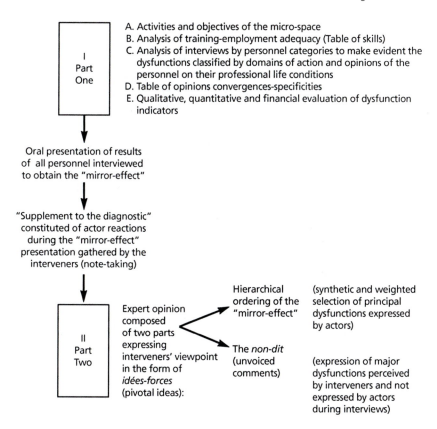

Figure 5.3 Typical content of a socio-economic diagnostic.

final report submitted to the enterprise is anonymous. It can thus be distributed to those who request it, based on a principle of sharing research center results. Enterprises are, of course, informed on the rules of research dissemination.

DATA COLLECTION TECHNIQUES

The socio-economic diagnostic is based on an extensive collection of data, carried out on the appropriate "terrain" (enterprise, workshop, service, agency) using three techniques implemented by intervener-researchers: interviews, direct observation of work situations (micro-spaces), and analysis of documents. The main problem posed here, which is generally speaking a fundamental methodological problem in social science research, concerns the quality of the information gathered, particularly its reliability. Thus, these data collection techniques are utilized out of a constant concern for improving the quality of information collected.

As a way of improving information quality, examples of the tactics employed at ISEOR include: a) obtaining a minimum of two informants for a given theme, b) simultaneously using interviews and document collection, c) diversifying the levels of informants by grouping shopfloor and office workers with supervisors, middle managers, executive managers and personnel representatives when composing *informant pools*, d) avoiding short-circuiting the hierarchy (by interviewing them right from the start so as to avoid possible blocking from their part, e) obtaining systematic validation of information necessary for hidden cost calculation (see Chapter 2 on the SOF Method), and f) distinguishing between reliable information and discourse by resorting to quantitified indicators. Chronological succession of these different data collection techniques should be designed with the goal of information quality constantly in mind. Figure 5.4 illustrates ways in which these techniques can be combined.

If these various techniques are complementary to one another, each one can also be associated with specific types of information. Thus, interviews constitute the preferred technique for gathering descriptions of dysfunctions; direct observation is indispensable for studying the regulation of dysfunctions; and finally, document analysis is fundamental for unitary cost calculations (e.g., hourly contribution to margin on variable costs).

Interviews

In the context of a socio-economic diagnostic applied to a micro-space, there are three groups of employees that should be interviewed: a) employees within the micro-space, b) key personnel external to the micro-space, and c) key individuals outside the enterprise.

Personnel within the Micro-Space

It is essential to interview all categories of the personnel working in the micro-space, including shopfloor and officer workers, second-line management and the head of the micro-space. If the time-budget allotted to the diagnostic is limited, it is possible to sample the shopfloor and office workers (the most numerous category), being careful to ensure that the employees selected reflect the diversity of jobs, opinions and behaviors in the micro-space.

Company Personnel External to the Micro-Space

Selecting people external to the micro-space should be based on an analysis of the organizational chart and the operational relationships practiced in the company. However, *in all cases* it would seem advisable to interview

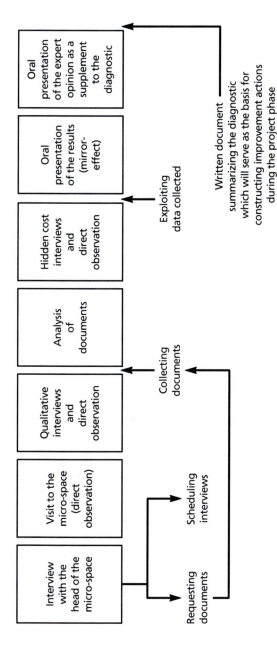

Figure 5.4 Timing of different data collection techniques during the socio-economic diagnostic.

the hierarchical superior of the micro-space, the personnel/HR director, the company CEO (especially if this is the first diagnostic in the enterprise), and key personnel representatives (e.g., labor-management committee members, trade union delegates, personnel delegates). The other respondents, who can be chosen either at the beginning or over the course of the diagnostic, are usually responsible for operational and functional services at the interface of the micro-space being studied. For example, in diagnostics of production workshops, interviews are frequently conducted with the heads of the basic service areas (e.g., maintenance, sequencing, quality control, dispatching, methods, management control, sales).

People External to the Enterprise

It can prove useful, depending on the theme and research hypotheses, to collect information from people who are part of the enterprise's relevant environment, even though they may be external to the enterprise. This group could include, for example, the organization's clients in a broad sense (e.g., patients in a hospital) or people who, based on their function, exert a certain impact on the enterprise's operations (e.g., in a hospital: suppliers or medical consultants). The data collected outside the enterprise should be limited to the context of the diagnostic that is being performed. The priority objective should remain focused on operations analysis and improvement through *internal human potential*, rife with information on the external environment, as well.

Carrying Out Qualitative Interviews

Interviews are usually conducted with the individual, although they are also done in small groups with shopfloor and office workers (3 to 6 people), making sure that these groups are diversified in terms of the participants' jobs. Some groups should be homogeneous, while others can be heterogeneous to provide a more complete picture of the organization. Interviews last from 1 to 1:30 hours, depending on whether they are individual or collective, and according to the complexity of the problems discussed. This duration is due to the semi-structured nature of the interviews. The intervener conducting the interview is typically confronted with a disorderly flow of information from the respondent and attempts to maximize insights from that discussion, through probing and reflective interviewing techniques, into useful information for the diagnostic.

This useful information, collected during actor interviews across the board, can be hierarchically ordered into three domains (see Figure 5.5):

- Information on dysfunction descriptions: These are facts which are rarely disputed, in comparison with the other two domains. Interviews attempt to collect dysfunction descriptions in priority,

	Description of dysfunctions	Analysis of effects	Analysis of causes
Prioritizing the intervener's time and energy allotted to interviews	① absolute priority	② second-ranking priority	③ third-ranking priority
Nature of the information	Facts	Opinions	Opinions
Degree of acceptance of the information (during oral presentation for example)	Rarely disputed	Relatively rarely disputed	Very controversial
Objective pursued through the diagnostic	*Indispensable* maximal solid platform	*Necessary* mini-platform (to quantify)	*Micro*-platform sought (threshold to attain on psychological impact)
Priority technique during interviews	High priority	Priority for • regulation graphs • hidden cost evaluation	Non-priority (in-depth inquiry during the project phase)
Source of analysis	ONLY source: the actors	ADDITIONAL source: the intervener's socio-economic analysis model	BASIC source: the intervener's socio-economic analysis model
Degree of directivity on the part of the intervener during interviews	Strong	Very strong	Weak

Figure 5.5 Domains of useful information during diagnostic interviews.

for company actors are usually the only source for collecting this information. The degree of directiveness can be high, if the interview fails to spontaneously produce dysfunction descriptions. This type of direct questioning is implemented following the interview guide (discussed below).

- Information on *dysfunction effect analysis*. These data are essentially actor opinions and require precise expression to enable reconstituting dysfunction regulation graphs, which contribute to the financial evaluation of hidden costs. Direct questioning is typically needed to collect this type of information, for actors do not spontaneously take stock of dysfunction effects. This is one of the reasons why actors often underestimate hidden costs. Conducting interviews for this type of information is done with reference to the socio-economic model: the intervener strives to obtain, for example, precise expressions on dysfunction effects in terms of over-consumption, overtime, excess salary, and non-production (missed production).

- Information on dysfunction cause analysis: This third type of information belongs to the domain of opinions to be validated; it is not a priority during diagnostic interviews. In-depth analysis of causes is carried out during the project phase (see Chapter 6), the essential goal of the diagnostic being to draw up an inventory of dysfunctions and their effects. The degree of directivity is thus weak in the domain of causes, the basic source for interveners being the socio-economic analysis model: dysfunctions result from the interaction between structures and behaviors.

In sum, the intervener's degree of directivity in interviews is linked to the domains discussed with the respondent. If the latter spontaneously expresses him or herself on dysfunctions and their effects, the intervener only probes to obtain more precise, quantified information (e.g., phenomena such as the frequency of a given dysfunction, the time spent regulating it). However, if these domains are not mentioned, the intervener probes with direct questions.

The Interview Guide

Interviews are conducted using an *interview guide* pre-established by the intervener in the context of the theme being studied and the socio-economic analysis model. The guide consists of a list of themes and sub-themes to be discussed during interviews, in any order, as long as all themes are discussed. The intervener-researcher uses it as a control list; what is essential is that no point is omitted. Figure 5.6 presents an interview guide that was used with managers for the diagnostic of an "executive management" unit,

Checklist, Observations	Themes discussed	Examples of points to be developed, questions to be asked, only in the event that spontaneous expression is sufficient	Objectives of the themes (for intervener use only: What are they trying to find out?)

Approximate time during the first interview 10 min.	1. Training/employment
	1.1 Training
	  1.1.1 Initial training
	  1.1.2 Personal training, integrated training
	1.2 Employment
	  1.2.1 Professional itinerary
	  1.2.2 Physical conditions of work
	  1.2.3 Description of current job and evolution
		- Local
		- Material
		- What are your activities?
		- What should your activities be?
		- Tasks not assumed, poorly assumed
		- Regulations set up by the person concerned, by others
			- Incidence of eventual problems: the functioning
			  a) effective functioning
			  b) definition of institutional function
			  c) desired functioning
			  - a/b differential
			  - a/c differential
			- Causes of these differentials
			- Degree of multi-tasking

10 min	1.2.4 Work organization	-Distribution of tasks within the group
		  - the interviewee
		  - other actors
			- Autonomy
			- Critical analysis
			- Improvement suggestions

	1.2.5 Remuneration	- Current procedures that pose problems (delegation systems, others …) - Level - Evaluation system	- (Critical analysis rather than descriptive analysis)
	1.3 Training/job adequacy	- What are the tasks for which you experience lack of training? - What are your competencies that are not used? - What are the concrete problems that result from these differentials?	- Poorly assumed tasks - Delays, backup - Economic under-performance - Quality of functioning

10 min.	2. Time management	- What is your typical work schedule at the moment?
		  - internal activity
		  - external activity (clientele)
		- What perceived constraints trouble your time organization?
		- Routine utilization (or not) of a personal datebook?
		- Do you regularly schedule ahead of time, or do you use your personal time from one event to the next?
		- In the latter case, what concrete problems are encountered?
		- Try to give numerical elements that describe your work load
		- Does time management of personnel exist in your branch office (for heads of branch offices)
		- What would your ideal time schedule be?
			- Work scheduling practices
			- Flexibility in organization of one's personal work time
			- Waiting lines
			- Canceled or postponed work
			- Overtime
			- Distribution by major types of activities (credit, branch office promotion)
			- Differential with regard to the current time schedule

Figure 5.6 Example of an interview guide: Diagnostic of a group of bank branch offices.

Checklist, Observations	Themes discussed	Examples of points to be developed, questions to be asked, only in the event that spontaneous expression is sufficient	Objectives of the themes (for intervener use only: What are they trying to find out?)

10 min.	3. Communication-coordination-cooperation system
	3.1 in the branch office
	3.2 in Sector X
	3.3 in the group
	3.4 in the enterprise
	   - with other services
	   - with executive management
		- What kinds of formal contact exist (meetings, appointments, written communication, telephone calls)?
		
		- What are the existing contacts and circuits of informal information (= unplanned)?
		- What is your opinion on the effectiveness and articulation of these systems?
		- What improvement suggestions would you make?
			- With whom?
			- Who initiates contact?
			- Frequency
			- Themes discussed
			- "Taboo" themes

	4. Strategy 4.1 Strategic orientations	- Do you think that general policy is not perceived in the same manner by everyone? - For you, what are the priority axes of general policy? - Who decides what they will be? - Do you feel you are an actor in the strategy? - Would it be necessary to clarify certain objectives? Which ones?	- Objectives (communication? coordination? Cooperation? - Operating mode (bottom-up? discussion? top-down?) - Perceived usefulness and declared objectives of these systems
	4.2 Strategic implementation 4.2.1 in the branch office 4.2.2 in the group 4.2.3 in the enterprise	- Are there any objectives you find questionable? Or lack compatibility with actual branch office operation? - Specificities of the market: needs? Competitor practices? - What axes did you especially monitor last year? This year? - If you notice a discrepancy between objective/accomplishment on one of those axes, what do you do? - For you, what are the main obstacles to implementation of the strategy? - Are the means allotted to you for strategic implementation sufficient (delegations, group support, various assistance...)? Are they adequate with regards to the objectives, etc.? - For you, are there problems of coherent strategic implementation at the different levels (branch offices, group, enterprise)?	- Degree of knowledge of objectives - Assimilation, acceptation - Usefulness of information campaigns
	5. Expectations - jobs - training - remuneration	- Evolution of job content - Promotion (horizontal, vertical)	- Autonomy/search for support

Figure 5.6 Example of an interview guide: Diagnostic of a group of bank branch offices (continued).

focused on the effectiveness of piloting in dealing with communication-coordination-cooperation problems and strategic implementation.

The semi-directive interview form and the utilization of an interview guide make it necessary for interveners to take exhaustive notes. Each interview, which lasts between an hour and an hour and a half, is captured in approximately 10 handwritten pages. This *exhaustive note-taking* is indispensable if the data are to be fully utilized, drawing on the fieldnotes for quotes from the actors in their own words for their illustrative and representative character.

Conducting Hidden Cost Interviews

Following qualitative interviews, additional interviews with managers (middle management, supervisors) are organized to calculate hidden costs. These more directed interviews enable the collection of additional information on the frequency and modes of dysfunction regulation, in essence "validating" the existence of those dysfunctions pointed out in the course of qualitative interviews.

Direct Observation

Direct observation seeks to identify information on the effects of dysfunctions, in terms of regulations and induced cascading dysfunctions. Depending on the time budget allotted to the diagnostic, direct observation can be focused, diffuse or delegated:

- *Focused*: The intervener devotes several hours, sometimes several days to observing dysfunctions and their effects. This technique has the inconvenience of being costly.
- *Diffuse:* The physical presence of the intervener on the work site offers ample opportunities to directly observe dysfunctions (e.g., passing through a workshop an intervener might observe a pile of rejects, an interview might be interrupted by an employee reporting a dysfunction).
- *Delegated*: The intervener asks the management team of a micro-space to observe and write down dysfunctions and their effects over a period of several days.

Whatever form it takes, direct observation should, first and foremost, be *organized* to produce relevant and reliable information. This is particularly true when it is delegated. Figure 5.7 presents an example of a direct observation grid and an illustration of a delegated observation by the head of the accounting service in a bank.

Dysfunctions	Regulations		Incidences (+ observations)
	Nature	Time	
1. *Delays in follow-ups* (tallying accounts)	The employee responsible for the work has a longer period of reference for checking off accounts Phenomena of accumulation		Suspended or abnormal operations belated detected (time for regulations much longer—interlocutor reactions are slower when asked questions)
	When major delay occurs, redistribution of priority tasks		More written entries submitted to check off Adjustment more difficult
2. *Absence of or defective filing of documents and files* ☐ absence of "bibles" (official instruction manuals for procedures and operations) ☐ absence of a central filing system ☐ deterioration of the filing system rationale ☐ files not returned to their places	Several employees search for documents and are disturbed *Or* Employees momentarily renounce to dealing with the file (which will be dealt with later on) *Or* Employees search for the missing information outside the office in order to deal with the problem		Direct and indirect losses of time Disturbs operations in the service Inconvenience and discomfort until the file or information or problem has been found.

Figure 5.7   Example of a direct observation grid.

Information obtained through direct observation should be validated during interviews, which is why it is useful to alternate direct observation and interviews (see Figure 5.4). This validation permits verifying the unique or repetitive character of dysfunctions and their effects.

Document Analysis

The objective of document analysis is less that of collecting "official" documents than of finding information attesting to and describing dysfunctions and their effects in precise terms. This type of document is rarely official, other than reports concerning absenteeism, occupational injuries and, more rarely, direct productivity, which, of course, poses difficulties not only in obtaining the data but ensuring the quality of the information as well. Managers, however, often have "work" documents that can be very useful to the intervener who knows how to find them and how to gain access to them. These "subterranean" documents, which are impossible to fully list due to their nature, include private note-taking on various dysfunctions (level of rejects) or problems raised during meetings.

There are also a number of documents that are *indispensable* for carrying out the socio-economic diagnostic. These include: the organization chart of the enterprise and the micro-space; the list of the personnel of the micro-space, mentioning their age, sex, seniority, qualification and salary; absenteeism distributed by employee, mentioning the motive and duration of the absence, covering a period of at least six months; personnel turnover covering a period of at least six months; and the profit-and-loss accounts or the budget of the micro-space and of the enterprise. Other documents, which are worth collecting if the enterprise possesses them include: the collective bargaining agreement; the social progress report; the enterprise's strategic plan; the piloting logbook of the micro-space; and more generally, all documents relative to the activities, operations and dysfunctions of the micro-space.

Documentary analysis is essential for evaluating hidden costs. This type of information is also useful in describing the micro-space's activity and can contribute to identifying certain dysfunction causes (e.g., in terms of demographic structure, age, gender, academic background and so forth).

Interview Analysis

As noted above, interviews serve the technical objective of describing dysfunctions and their effects, for the purpose of orienting the hidden cost evaluation. They also serve another objective, no less important in terms of intervention strategy. Interveners strive to create a "mirror-effect" among their respondents and the interviews can be presented in a form that permits the respondents to recognize themselves despite the anonymous presentation. This mirror-effect is an important lever for progress in the innovation process. If it is not obtained (i.e., if actors do not recognize themselves during interview analysis), the status and competency of the interveners will be seriously questioned, which drastically hinders the effectiveness of the process. *A contrario*, successful mirror-effect constitutes "credibility" for the intervener-researchers who find themselves endowed with a certain degree of confidence on the part of company actors.

In order to obtain this mirror-effect, and to detect a maximum number of dysfunctions and regulations in actors' discourse, analysis of the interviews is carried out according to a precise, original method.

The Method of Interview Analysis

This method, which is characterized by its in-depth, rigorous procedure, was created and developed by Henri Savall, with the participation of the ISEOR team. With fieldnotes taken during interviews as the starting point, fieldnote quotes illustrating dysfunctions are selected and classified. The subsequent analysis can be outlined in the form of a tree structure (see Figure 5.8) that includes:

- *Themes*: Six domains of dysfunctions constitute the families of themes in the socio-economic analysis model: working conditions, work organization, time management, Communication-Coordination-Cooperation, integrated training and strategic implementation (see Table 5.1).
- *Sub-themes* (and "sub-sub-themes"): Breaking down the themes into specific areas (see Table 5.2).
- *Key-ideas:* These are generic ideas, formulated by the intervener to amalgamate fieldnote quotes.
- *Fieldnote quotes:* Unmodified excerpts from the interviews, within the limits of understandable expression, with the possible exception of obscure slang words or injurious statements that are translated to reduce cultural shock. The number of fieldnote quotes selected from one interview can vary between ten and fifteen. For a diagnostic including thirty interviews, which is a common case, basic research material is thus composed of 300 to 450 fieldnote quotes. These are classified, grouped together and categorized into key-ideas. This process provides an illustration of the method's rigor, which certain company members do not hesitate to describe as "painstaking" and "meticulous."

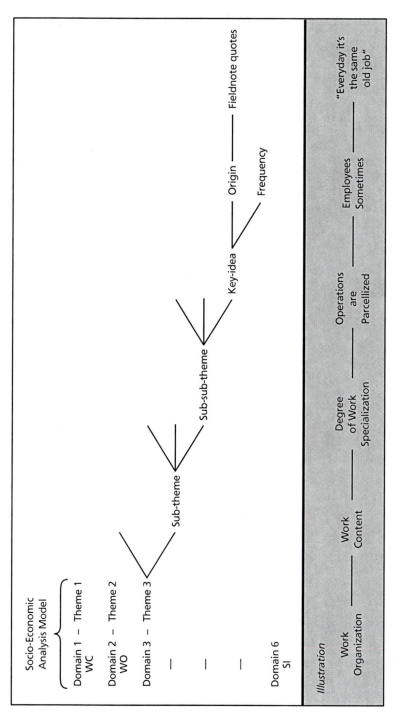

Figure 5.8 Tree form structure for breaking down information gathered during interviews.

TABLE 5.1 Definitions of the Six Domains of Dysfunctions

Working conditions	"Working conditions" covers both the physical conditions of work (work space, environmental annoyance, physical demands of the job, security) and the technological conditions of work (equipment and supplies, available tools, etc.)
Work organization	Work organization includes organizational structure (organizational diagram), task distribution and job design (specialization…)
Communication-coordination-cooperation	• *Communication* designates all types of information exchange among actors (both formal and informal) whatever the subject and the goal (professional or extra-professional) • *Coordination* applies to information exchange frameworks among actors, organized in view of carrying out an operational or functional objective of the activity • *Cooperation* characterizes all types of information exchange among actors to define an operational or functional objective to be carried out in a determined period of time
Time management	Individual or collective time management includes methods of work-time organization (scheduling methods, programming methods…), scheduling of the individual's time around major tasks: prevention time, dysfunction regulation, daily management, shift in functions, strategic piloting

Integrated training	• Two types of integrated training (job-training adequacy) generally utilized in companies can be distinguished:
	   – "On the job" training organized on the workplace under conditions that often limit its contribution to rudimentary learning
	   – External training organized by specialists often poorly informed about real job content and whose contribution is not applicable on the job
	 • *Integrated* training, regarding workers, is done by their immediate hierarchical superior and is usually preceded by pedagogical training and the preparation of a training manual. The content of integrated training action is based, in priority, on the dysfunction identified during the diagnostic

Strategy implementation	This domain includes the clear formulation of company strategy and its breakdown into concrete, operational actions to be carried out in order to attain the strategic objectives. Strategic implementation also includes the financial and technological means and the human resource policies necessary to carry out the actions.

TABLE 5.2   General Nomenclature of Dysfunction Themes and Sub-Themes

Themes	Sub-Themes
1. Working conditions	Equipment and supplies
	Layout of office and work space
	Disturbances
	Physical conditions of work
	Security
	Work hours
	Work atmosphere
2. Work organization	Distribution of tasks, missions, functions
	Interest of the work
	Workload
	Autonomy in the work
	Regulations and procedures
	Organizational chart
	Absenteeism regulation
3. Time management	Respect for delivery times
	Poorly assumed tasked
	Planning, scheduling of activities
	Disturbance factors in time management
4. Communication-Coordination-Cooperation [3C]	3C Horizontal
	3C Vertical
	Information transmission
	Relations with the surrounding services
	3C at the executive director level
	3C between main office and branch office
	3C internal to the service
	3C framework
	3C between elected officials and civil servants
	3C between network and home office
5. Integrated training	Training-job appropriateness
	Training frameworks
	Available competencies
	Training needs
	Training and technical change
6. Strategic implementation	Strategic orientation
	Authors of the strategy
	Breakdown and organization strategic implementation
	Information system
	Personnel management
	Strategic implementation tools
	Modes of management
	Means of strategic implementation

- *Origin of fieldnote quotes:* Interviews are processed by separating the personnel interviewed into the principal professional categories (e.g., workers, supervisors, managers, executives). This segmentation enables the analysis of similarities across the organization or the specificities of key-ideas that come from specific personnel categories. A table of similarities (referred to as "convergences") and specificities of key-ideas between management and executives, executives and supervisors, supervisors and workers or employees, multi-skilled and unskilled workers can thus be drawn up (see Table 5.3).

- *Frequency of key-ideas:* A quantitative indicator of the frequency of the appearance of an idea in a given personnel category. Frequency is noted in qualitative terms: rarely, sometimes, often, always; each of these categories corresponds to a precise range of percentages of the occurrence of the key-idea in a given category. "Sometimes" as a frequency indication means from 15% to 29% of the personnel interviewed. Frequency is useful for measuring the dissemination of dysfunctions. But its significance must be kept relative: high frequency can be explained by a strong inclination for "unofficial instructions" emanating from trade union representatives, managers or executives. Conversely, low frequency can indicate the existence of "taboos" in the enterprise. This second degree of analysis is separated in our methodology and it is carried out in the expert opinion stage (discussed later in the chapter).

A Computerized Method with an Expert-System Software Program

Having carried out more than 1,000 diagnostics over a 30 year period, ISEOR has developed a high level of expertise in organizational intervention research. This knowledge has been captured in an expert-system software, a socio-economic diagnostic aid program that offers multiple functions:[2]

- *Qualitative analysis:* The software facilitates designating themes, sub-themes and key-ideas based on a database of nearly 2,500 types of dysfunctions that are entered in the form of pre-identified key-ideas. It automatically calculates the frequency of these key-ideas and edits convergence-specificity spread sheets.

- *Quantitative and financial diagnostic* (hidden costs): The model facilitates the identification of elementary dysfunctions and regulation modes based on pre-identified nomenclature. It leads the user through the procedure of calculating unitary regulation costs, and enables a regular updating of hidden cost results.

- *Socio-economic project:* The software proposes socio-economic innovation projects, complete with concrete actions, in the context of the enterprise's specific parameters and dysfunctions.

TABLE 5.3 Table of Convergences and Specificities of Opinions among Supervisors and Workers in a Metal-work Works

	Themes	Convergences	Specificities	
			Workers	Supervisors/Technicians
Domains of dysfunctions	Working conditions and work organization	• Lack of space/maneuvering • Noise and dust • Interruption of series • Insufficient personnel • Overloaded swing tray • Faulty packing machines	• Lack of hygiene • Working rhythms • Equipment maintenance poorly done • Lack of renewable supplies	• Uninteresting worker jobs • Existence of tasks poorly assumed by supervisors • Hierarchy among workers • Worn-out equipment
	Integrated training	• Extensive needs for worker training • External training unsuitable	• Desire to understand the manufacturing process	• Training problems on the Kitchenware Assembly Line
Hidden cost indicators	Product quality	• Numerous quality defects • Insufficient quality control • Defective metal	• Permissive attitude among supervisors	• Supervisor awareness
	Absenteeism	• Difficult regulation of absenteeism	• Inconvenience for the "fill-ins"	• Lack of multi-task skill to deal more easily with absenteeism
	Security	• Few security problems • Risks in connection to stacking	• Lack of qualified first-aid workers	• Work hazards during press assemblage
Implications for the project	Expectations	• More fairness • Reward for effort	• More information and communication	• Evolution of the supervisor function • Salary raise
	Suggestions	• Numerous technical suggestions	• Suggestions to better manage team composition in accord with affinities	• Motivate workers

This software package, which is referred to as SEGESE®, provides two major advantages: a) it simultaneously increases the quality and the speed with which diagnostics are carried out, and b) significantly enhances the enterprise's acquisition of the socio-economic method and encourages the practice of periodical diagnostics. Three versions of this module are currently available: the *expert* version, which possesses all functions and is intended for consultants who have been trained in the method; the *didactic* version, for learning purposes, destined to beginners and students in training for utilization of the expert version; and the *basic functions* version, for limited use.[3]

Case Illustrations

Drawing on several *excerpts* from interview analyses, this section illustrates how this approach has been used in different sectors of activity and personnel categories and the various themes that have been analyzed. Key-ideas are indicated with a dot (•) and fieldnote quotes are between quotation marks.

Case of a Technical Support Service in a Telecommunications Firm
Theme: Working conditions
Sub-theme: Physical conditions: workshop, equipment
Category: Technicians
Key-ideas (•) *and fieldnote quotes:*
- Technicians suffer from the heat and from lack of space:
  "It's as hot as a furnace in here, especially in the summer; there's no ventilation."
  "There isn't enough room in the shop; you can never find anything."
- Equipment and supplies seem insufficient:
  "We need more workbenches to test equipment."
  "We often have to wait before doing repairs because we don't have the spare parts."

Case of an Automated Production Workshop (38 Employees) in a Chemical Factory
Theme: Communication-Coordination-Cooperation [3C]
Sub-theme: [3C] between daytime supervisors and production-line foremen
Category: Production-line foremen
Key-ideas (•) *and fieldnote quotes:*
- Communication between daytime supervisors and workers often short-circuits the production-line foremen:

Often:

"When it's the workers who tell us about certain manipulations the daytime supervisors have requested, it's unpleasant for us."
"Daytime supervisors should let us know when they plan to intervene with the workers."
"We should be better coordinated with the daytime supervisors."

- Production-line supervisors lament the lack of quality in Communication-Coordination-Cooperation [3C] between daytime supervisors and workers:

Sometimes:

"Daytime supervisors should spend more time in the control room."
"Workers have the feeling they are separated from the daytime staff. There is a lot of misunderstanding between the personnel and daytime supervisors. Workers feel like too much is demanded from them."
"There is a wall. Workers never approach daytime supervisors."
"Daytime supervisors should spend more time talking with workers."
"The daytime supervisors completely disgusted the workers by mistreating them at the start. They wanted to keep them in line, but they antagonized them.
"Workers have lost interest in production-line equipment because no one pays any attention to them."
"When daytime supervisors work alongside employees, confidence is renewed."
"When a daytime supervisor works with the line-personnel, the sector operates better."

Case of Computer Department in a Bank

Theme: Work organization
Sub-theme: Interest of the work
Category: Technicians
Key-ideas (•) and fieldnote quotes:

- The console operator's work is less interesting since processing-controller jobs were created:

Sometimes

"Now, the job of console operator seems like unskilled labor to me"
"The console is assembly-line work and being a console operator is not interesting."
"Before, there was a lot of work to do, problems to solve, I liked that."
"I do less and less."

Case of Bank Branch Office
Theme: Integrated training
Category: Office workers
Key-ideas (•) *and fieldnote quotes:*

- The dominant opinion is that the best training is done on the job and based on actual needs, which is not the case:

  Often:

  "The first training session was a waste of time, because I had only been working in the bank for six months. Training is essentially done on the job, and that's the best training."

  "When I started, I didn't realize what banks are about. I had no idea there were so many operations. I learned on the job. It took me a year or two to master teller operations."

  "Most of my training wasn't provided by my current bank, but by the previous one."

  "Since my arrival, I attended a daylong training session on "stocks and bonds" and another on "credit". Actually, not much training goes on, it's mostly information distribution."

  "The "quick sales" training session wasn't bad. The sales pitches were really interesting.

  "I haven't attended a training session in several years. Every time one takes place, the director says to me, "You don't mind if I don't send you to the training session, do you; I'm going to send someone else." I don't have a choice!"

  "I attended the 'Level 2' training session without having attended the 'Level 1' session. It wasn't for me."

  "No one has ever asked me if I wanted to attend a training session, just like no one asked me if I wanted to work this position. No one chooses anything around here."{\BSL}

Case of a Bank Agency
Theme: Strategic implementation
Sub-theme: Customer service quality
Category: Office workers
Key-ideas (•) *and fieldnote quotes:*

- The arrival of a customer is seen as a privileged occasion for establishing contact, but an occasion not sufficiently capitalized upon:

  Sometimes:

  "We often miss occasions to sell, simply because we don't know the rates by heart and don't have time to look them up."

- Customer reception and accompaniment do not appear to be entirely satisfactory:

Often:
"When the agency is full of customers, employees should not be talking to one another elsewhere."

"Customers are pleased with the reception, even if they have to wait 5 minutes while having a cup of coffee. But this waiting period should not be exaggerated.

"Overall, customers are satisfied, some would no longer consider leaving the agency."

"Sometimes, a single customer is seen by 3 different bank employees and is evaluated differently and given contradictory information."

"Even if I know how to give customers the explanations, I am still compelled to refer them to another employee to fill out the paperwork. This doesn't seem right."

- This can sometimes be explained by lack of training:

Rarely:
"Yesterday, a customer asked for information about bonds. I couldn't understand a thing. The customer had to wait 20 minutes, while the explanation took only a few minutes."

"Often, customers call for information we are not prepared to provide and we have to ask them to call back."

Case of an Electronics Component Finishing Workshop

Theme: Strategic implementation
Category: Executive management[4]
Key-ideas (•):

- The short-term strategic objective of the unit to which the workshop belongs is improving its quality-results with customers, so as to come closer to the much higher performance levels of competitors, especially the Japanese.
- Maintaining a 100 percent quality control system for components following a 1982 product innovation may have contributed to lack of responsibility among producers regarding quality.
- A system of incentives was progressively set up to motivate workers to improve productivity and quality. This incentive system does not motivate new progress: a "threshold-ceiling" of 75 good components per day has progressively become established as current practice.
- This incentive system does not take into account absenteeism, which can have significant impact on weekly sales quantities, given the sector's key position inside the workshop, plus the fact that currently it is almost impossible to replace absent workers.

Case of a Technical Maintenance Service In A Telecommunication Service Enterprise

   Theme: Integrated training

   Category: Personnel representative authorities[5]

   Key-ideas (●):

- Personnel competencies not implemented
- Training-job inadequacy for certain personnel: the same work could be done by lesser-qualified personnel, thus at lower cost.
- Lack of competency among middle and executive management for piloting the enterprise.

THE ROLE OF HIDDEN COST ANALYSIS IN THE SOCIO-ECONOMIC DIAGNOSTIC

The interview synthesis constitutes only a portion of the diagnostic, which also includes hidden cost evaluation (see Chapter 2). The hidden cost evaluation has particular impact on company actors, which can be clearly noted during the oral presentation of the diagnostic. By feeding back the information to the participants, this part of the diagnostic gives perspective to the information created in the interview syntheses. Although this impression can be partly explained by the methodological option of selecting only dysfunctions at this stage of the diagnostic, it is also shaped by the qualitative character of the information gathered during interviews. The hidden cost evaluation, in contrast, is often seen by company actors as a more "objective" analysis. This perspective signifies that the financial language, chosen for the evaluation of hidden costs, permits key decision makers—executive and middle management—to better position themselves with respect to indicators and information they deal with on a daily basis. Indeed, hidden cost calculation can be placed in relationship to the cost of company products and eventual competitiveness problems linked to excessively-high selling prices or insufficient quality in comparison with competitors.

The evaluation of hidden costs also has direct operational utility: application of the SOF method (see Chapter 2) reveals "solidarity" among all personnel in creating and propagating hidden costs, and thus the necessity of actions touching *all company actors.* Hidden cost evaluation therefore incites the search for more efficient regulations. As ISEOR projects have underscored, the presentation of hidden costs sometimes incites management to modify, literally the very next day, its behavior and decisions concerning regulations. From a scientific point of view, this rapid transformation of certain behaviors is explained by the fact that hidden cost evaluation and dysfunction inventory considerably enrich actors' *basic knowledge.* The interview synthesis and hidden cost evaluation are thus highly complementary, in terms of both the types of information they provide as well as their impacts on actors.

EXPERT OPINION

The expert opinion is given to the enterprise following the oral presentation of results and constitutes what could be called a "second-degree" analysis. It is based both on the information collected in the organization and ISEOR's past experiences and knowledge base. The expert opinion has high value-added in the eyes of company actors compared to the first part of the diagnostic, probably because it is very synthetic and, at the same time, demands more involvement on the part of the intervener regarding his or her positions.6 It is important to note that there has been an evolution in the diagnostic with respect to the use of expert opinion. Prior to the early 1980s, we were reticent to the idea of presenting our expert opinion to the enterprise, largely based on the fact that we wanted to give sovereignty to the mirror-effect. The first expert opinion intervention dates from 1981 (Zardet, 1981) and it was further developed into a tool over the next several years in connection with a diagnostic of a bank agency group. During this period, we considered that the mirror-effect had been sufficiently formalized and structured that it was useful to develop the expert opinion as the last point to wrap up the diagnostic.

The expert opinion on the diagnostic includes a highly-condensed synthesis of the diagnostic, based on material from the first phase (interview synthesis, hidden cost evaluation, job-training adequacy), and recommendations for conducting the follow-on project and implementation phases.

Selection of Major Key-Ideas Expressed

This first phase in developing the expert opinion consists of selecting, and then arranging in hierarchical order, the key-ideas formulated during the exploitation of interviews. Emphasis is placed on the key-ideas that appear to be the most important, and which, in the opinion of the intervener-researcher, call for precise, substantial responses in the project. This selection can take into account notably the frequency of these key-ideas, knowing that this can correspond to a company "*hobbyhorse*" (i.e., expert opinion consists of analyzing and "screening" discourse in terms of organizational "hobbyhorses-taboos-disputes").

Highlighting Unformulated Key-Ideas
In addition to interviews, interveners can draw on other sources of information—direct observation, informal interviews, knowledge about the

enterprise—which can permit them to detect key-ideas that may not have been directly expressed by actors or expressed in obscure or cloaked fashion, because they touch on a company *taboo* or a company *dispute* (i.e., a latent conflict more or less verbally expressed).

Expression of Synthetic Idées-Forces (Pivotal Ideas)

The formulation of *idées-forces* (pivotal ideas) is based on the key-ideas selected at the end of the two preceding phases. At this point, the intervener adopts more critical distance in formulating hypotheses based on information coming from different sources, for example the "double language" practiced by certain members of the management team. These *idées-forces* (pivotal ideas) can, in certain cases, contradict beliefs held by the top management and senior-level management.

As an example, in a "group of agencies" in a bank, the group's Director felt strongly that the "discipline" of his management team would facilitate the follow-on project phase. The expert opinion, however, accented the "risk of anesthesia that represents the perception of an *apparent* 'no problem' acceptance." This risk was revealed during interviews, but in a *highly concealed* fashion.

Monitoring During the Action Phases

The diagnostic often accentuates potential dysfunctions (risks) that could hinder the dynamics of the engagement process. Thus, points that should be monitored include: a) *current dysfunctions* that executive management does not seem to perceive; b) *predicted dysfunctions* with high blocking-risk, due to usual company dysfunctions that can be exacerbated during the intervention; and c) *high-risk points* of deviation or inertia (i.e., apparently discrete dysfunctions, such as the attitude toward discipline referred to above).

The expert opinion also serves as the basis for developing improvement actions for members of the project-group, which will be further discussed in Chapter 6.

FINAL WORD: PRECAUTIONS IN THE DIAGNOSTIC

The principal difficulty to be mastered during the diagnostic phase is the cultural shock that is linked to the dysfunctional analysis. It is therefore essential that the intervener-researcher keep this risk constantly in mind, in order to adopt preventive procedures. Such preventive procedures begin with the negotiation of the intervention with the top management (see Chapter 4), which notably stipulates the nature of the diagnostic method and the focus on dysfunctions and hidden costs.

This type of informed prevention is also present in the framework of the oral presentation of diagnostic results, which was progressively perfected to avoid placing the head of the concerned micro-space in a precarious position between his or her hierarchical managers and personnel. The framework calls for an initial discussion with the head of the micro-space, a second presentation with that person's manager(s), and finally a third with the personnel, usually in the presence of the micro-space's hierarchical superiors. Cultural shock, however, can equally come from non-hierarchical personnel, whose anonymity the intervener is committed to respecting.

As a way of dealing with these concerns, ISEOR has adopted a deontological position of refusing all requests to delete an idea, once we have verified that the idea was actually expressed and correctly transcribed in its context. This position is applied regardless of the hierarchical position of the person making the request. However, *additions* and *precisions* can be made if the concerned individual(s) feels that he or she failed to express him or herself well or inadvertently exaggerated their remarks.

Another difficulty is when diagnostics do not include hidden cost evaluation, as was the case during the first years of our research at the ISEOR. Enterprises often underestimated the financial impact of dysfunctions, due to the fact that impact was indicated only qualitatively. Clearly, this void hindered the acquisition of heightened awareness of the economic and financial stakes in the innovation action. The cultural shock created by the dysfunctional analysis and the "anesthesia" created by the absence of a realization of hidden costs point to the critical role of the Horivert Process (see Chapter 4, in which Executive Management is, from the start, much more involved in the innovation process of the enterprise's operation.

NOTES

1. The first structured presentation of this interview approach is in Véronique Zardet's ISEOR Report, *Socio-economic analysis of a national television group: Working conditions, organization and quality*, ISEOR Report, August 1981, 164 pages.
2. The expert system was constructed by ISEOR in collaboration with a team of computer science researchers under the direction of Professor Jacques Kouloumdjian, with the active participation of Mrs. Nouria Harbi, head of the ISEOR computer department and professor at the University of Lyon.
3. The SEGESE® software, which was tested on nearly one thousand diagnostics, has been made available for commercial licensing to enterprises and man-

agement consulting firms with ISEOR certification (approximately 50 user-licenses have currently held in France and other parts of the world).

4. There are a number of specific versions of this software: SEGESE® Strategic Vigilance, SEGESE® Marketing, SEGESE® Audit and SEGESE® Training. SEGESE® is available in several languages: French, German, Spanish and Portuguese.

5. For use in this book, the executive management interviews in this case have been summarized in the form of key-ideas alone.

6. Interviews have been summarized only as key-ideas in this case.

7. Such views, however, are relative, for the first part of the diagnostic is also supported by methodological positions and options.

REFERENCE

Zardet, V. (1981). *Diagnostic du système de gestion socio-économique d'une société nationale de télévision: structures, procédures et ressources* [Diagnostic of the socio-economic management system of a public television corporation: structures, procedures and resources]. Under the direction of Henri Savall. Ecully, France: ISEOR report.

CHAPTER 6

THE SOCIO-ECONOMIC INNOVATION PROJECT

The socio-economic innovation project phase is fundamental to start restoring confidence within the enterprise. During this part of the intervention, executives, managers and intervener-researchers co-produce socio-economic innovation solutions as a way of reducing the dysfunctions faced by the organization. This is a crucial moment where the organization's management places the first marks of its confidence in the change action, by their capacity to imagine and to believe in new, concrete forms of more effective work organization: confidence in themselves to find alternatives, confidence in the shopfloor personnel to envisage its evolution, and confidence in the top management to accept the project that will be proposed, step by step during sessions in which it is involved.

The objective of the project is to *reduce dysfunctions* identified during the diagnostic, and the resulting *hidden costs* faced by the enterprise by reinforcing and building on the micro-space's *strong points*. The first project phase consists of proposing and initiating a development, by *each* individual, of his or her capacity for socially useful production (economic performance) and for self-production of one's professional well-being and that of those around them (social performance; quality of professional life conditions). The second phase is a reflection stage that leads to a proposal, focusing on an overall transformation project for the micro-space's operation and addressing the six variables of action, structures and behaviors. All actors in

Mastering Hidden Costs and Socio-Economic Performance, pages 157–182
Copyright © 2008 by Information Age Publishing
All rights of reproduction in any form reserved.

TABLE 6.1   Illustrative Project Objectives in an Industrial Work Unit

Project objectives:

- Improving overall *productivity*
- Improving *work life conditions*
- Improving personnel *satisfaction* by increasing *qualifications* and *work interest*
- Improving effectiveness by providing more *scheduling flexibility* and by *reducing* production *time* to *market*

---

the micro-space (workshop, agency, service) are thus personally involved with these actions.

Overall, the project entails planning *synchronization* of the different actions envisaged, with an emphasis on their *synergy* (e.g., training provided by supervisors for workers with a goal of increased competence, enhanced communication-coordination-cooperation [3C] between workers and supervisors). Project construction emphasizes the integration of existing structures, whether these are the enterprise's economic and social situation, the current state of its structures, or existing projects for the evolution of structures. Table 6.1 provides an example of a project's transformation objectives in an industrial workshop, as they were defined at the beginning of the project phase.

As this chapter will discuss, one of the sub-objectives always found is *to consolidate the role of management* in the very short-term by the active role it plays in the project phase and in the medium-term by transforming its function inside the overall transformation project. Management thus participates in all "construction sites," evolving toward a mission of profession development, leadership, training and information sharing.

PROJECT CONSTRUCTION

The piloting group validates the political orientations of the intervention, oversees the intervention calendar, and monitors the successive results of project implementation. The project itself is developed by a hierarchical work group, referred to as the focus group, which is led by the head of the micro-space, who is called the project manager.

Workgroup Framework: The Focus Group

The focus group (see Figure 6.1) is composed of two or three sub-groups, depending on the size of the enterprise: a core group, plenary group and senior management group. The *core group* keeps abreast of the state of ad-

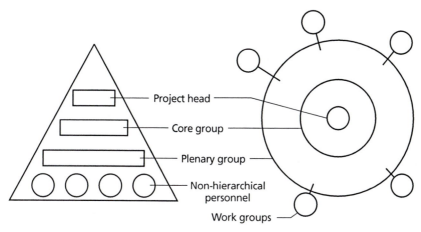

Figure 6.1 Structure of the focus group.

vancement of the plenary group's work, guarantees the coherency of the plenary group's preliminary efforts to draft solutions with respect to the company's strategic objectives-constraints, and prepares the plenary group's agenda. The *plenary group* is responsible for seeking solutions to transform the micro-space and studying their implications on other company micro-spaces. Although this group is thus responsible for implementing a creative approach, in comparison to the creativity advocated by the psycho-sociological study of organizations, we refer to this work as *channeled creativity*, both with regard to company objectives-constraints and to the socio-economic analysis model. Finally, the *senior management group*, which exists only in large enterprises with complex structures where several hierarchical levels exist between heads of micro-spaces and executive management, has a role essentially the same as the core group. Its primary purpose is to physically involve the top management *in the process* of developing the project, and not simply to listen to the final phase of overall project presentation. In enterprises with less than 3,000 employees, executive management directly participates in the core group.

Middle management plays an important role in this working framework. They are, of course, part of the focus group (which includes middle management or supervisory staff) and propose solutions and studies during the project phase. They also regularly provide information to the personnel on the state of progress of the solutions that have been undertaken. As we shall see, this role readily increases during the solution implementation phase.

An important point to underscore is that the "project group" includes *only* members of *management* with appropriate hierarchical power. Indeed, it is essential that the socio-economic project, which necessarily includes actions involving company management, be openly supported by the organization's management, since it legitimately constitutes part of their job. However, this focus does not exclude the *participation* of shopfloor (non-hierarchical) personnel in the process, especially since they have already voiced their comments and concerns during the diagnostic. Indeed, these organizational members should be kept informed, consulted, and even grouped together to form work groups on certain aspects of the project where their suggestions can be precious contributions toward accomplishing the project group's task. However, they are not members of the "project group," which is responsible for making proposals to top management. This is an essential point of difference between the socio-economic approach to management conceived in 1974 and designed in 1978, and "French-style quality circles" which appeared in the early 1980s, often considered to be "living suggestion boxes" working on very narrow problems.

Composition of the Project Group

Two (or three) sub-groups are led by the project head. The *core group* includes the one or two hierarchical superiors of the project head and executive management (CEO) or representative of the top management, as well as the human resource director in most cases. It should be kept in mind that this group is invested notably with the mission of ensuring compatibility between the solutions and the company's strategic objectives-constraints. The *senior management group*, when it exists, includes the same members of the core group plus the general director or the person performing a comparable function. Finally, the *plenary group* is composed of the project head (responsible for the micro-space), his or her internal management personnel and the heads of other departments, both functional and operational, who are at the interface of the studied micro-space. The choice of these heads is done in cooperative manner, after consulting the project head, his or her hierarchical superiors and the intervener. Table 6.2 provides an example of a project group composition for a socio-economic innovation process in a bank.

The composition of the project group should be handled with special care, because evidence has shown that it constitutes one of the decisive factors that explain the quality of solutions and contribute to the success of the socio-economic efficiency improvement action. However, heads of micro-spaces sometimes prefer to choose members of the plenary group based on personal ties rather than on the substantial contribution expected. Affinity criteria are, unfortunately, not the most productive in terms of creativity, in fact, they can even curb the potential conflict that is provoked by the association of actors who are *a priori* reticent or opposed to one another. Such conflict can be important, often leading to the most imaginative and durably effective solutions.

TABLE 6.2   Composition of a Project Group in a Bank

Core group	Plenary group
• Project head: the director of the agency • Director of a group of agencies (the direct hierarchical superior of the agency's director) • Representative of the personnel management service • Intervener-researcher	• Project head: the director of the agency • The agency's internal management: the head of Administrative Management and the head of Commercial Management • The head of Business Engagement division • Head of computer services • Head of private accounts division • Head of personnel management services[1] • Intervener-researcher
Total: 4 employees	Total: 8 employees

---

[a] The presence of the head of personnel services in the plenary group is explained by the particularly important role that was assigned to personnel services by the bank's Director, in terms of piloting the socio-economic innovation process in the micro-spaces and entities.

Duration of Plenary Group Activities

At the end of the diagnostic, the number of project group meetings and their precise dates are set. This prevents the process from becoming overly drawn-out, which would be detrimental to the desired dynamics of the action. On every one of our "job sites," the number of meetings varies from 4 to 6, with sessions held at three to four-week intervals. This schedule helps to support the intermediary work that needs to be carried out, and limits the "risks of forgetfulness."

In general, these sessions last a day each and include four sequential phases: a) small-core group meeting [2 hours]; b) project head and intervener-researcher [1 hour]; c) plenary group meeting [2 to 3 hours]; and project head and intervener-researcher [1 hour]).

The intermediary meetings between the project head and the intervener-researcher were established to improve the efficiency of the project group meetings, with the goal of ensuring that all preparatory work is completed beforehand.

The follow-on core group meeting is devoted to quickly analyzing the agenda of the core group, selecting information to be reflected in the plenary group, and setting the agenda and time allotted to each point of the plenary group meeting. The objective is to establish a precise distribution of roles between the project head and the intervener. The next plenary group meeting consists of taking an inventory of points investigated and resolved, those still pending, those requiring clarification at the next core group meeting, and the intermediary tasks to be accomplished before the next project group.

These two meetings, which should be held on every project, have been shown to develop a certain alliance between the intervener and the head of the micro-space, not without certain moments of tension between them. This bond can provide important support for the project head, especially during the delicate process stage.

Themes of the Plenary Group Meetings

During the project phase, a key part of the framework is the project group. However, it should not be forgotten that technical groups can meet during this phase to seek in-depth solutions. Furthermore, the project phase requires that the project head devote personal time between meetings, as well as at the end of project group's work, to reformulating solutions that are proposed, negotiating their implementation, and evaluating their financial impact.

Plenary group meetings are divided into three stages. The first stage (the first meeting) entails *completing and updating the diagnostic,* with the essential goal of establishing an *information platform* and a *common language* among the different members of the group. During the follow-on sessions, the plenary group should constantly refer to the dysfunctions revealed by the diagnostic as they search for ways to reduce them.

The second stage is devoted to *researching solutions.* The plenary group can organize this research by successively examining each of the six domains of action, related dysfunctions, and the different baskets constituted following the mirror-effect and the expert opinion (see Figure 6.2). For example, the second meeting can be devoted to the domains of "working conditions" and "work organization," the third to "communication-coordination-cooperation" and "time management," the next to "integrated training," and so forth.

The third stage (the last meeting) is devoted to studying the *coherency and coordination of the various aspects of solutions* proposed during the second phase, as well as *calculating the means* necessary for implementation (e.g., technical, financial, informational). Finally, during this last session, *a scheduling outline* is drawn up. This final stage is crucial, since it can expose the incompatibilities between the various solutions proposed or point to dysfunctions that are not resolved by the proposed solutions.

Financial Study: Economic Balance of the Project

The operational method of the project includes carrying out a financial study. This assessment is a provisional calculation that evaluates whether the proposed project will render sufficient earnings in comparison with the means necessary to implement it over a given period of time. This financial study, which is carried out by the project head with the methodological assistance of the intervener, is called the *economic balance* because it includes: a) the evaluation of investments related to the proposed solutions (e.g., equipment, material, training, salaries in the cases of projects formulating

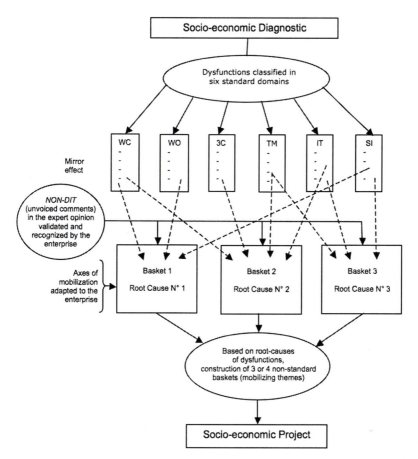

Figure 6.2 Sequential process from diagnostic to project.

the request for supplementary employees); and b) the evaluation of hidden cost reduction related to the implementation of the actions proposed.

This economic balance constitutes an essential element of the project file that is submitted by the project head to his or her manager. It is the counterpart of the hidden cost evaluation in the diagnostic. It also, more importantly, constitutes a type of commitment, an activity contract between the heads of the micro-spaces and their hierarchical managers. Such a commitment signifies that once the project is accepted by the top management it will enable, once it is implemented, a reduction of the hidden costs by a defined amount.

Table 6.3 presents an example of an economic balance for a factory. The economic balance method, including the evaluation of hidden performances, can be applied more generally to all change projects (as an example, see Tables 6.4 and 6.5). The financial evaluation demonstrated

TABLE 6.3 Project Economic Balance in a Fabric Dying Entreprise

Economic balance (at the stage of change impact evaluation)

Basket N° 1: Cleaning up working conditions and work organization (excerpt)

Concrete actions	Dates	Dysfunction example	Dysft. costs	Reduction rate prognostic	Earnings Qualitative	Quantitative	Financial
Establishing an improvement process for the reliability of repairs and implementing a CAMP (computer-assisted manufacturing and production) to enable tracking breakdowns and improving preventive machine maintenance	End 2002	Repairing low-quality machines (excess time) 2 employees spend 5 minutes doing urgent repairs on machines that rapidly break down: 2 employees × (5/60) hrs. × 227days × 21.5€	813€		Utilizing an itemized operations chart to capitalize certain maintenance service interventions		270€
Resolving the temperature problem of the packing machine overheating by: • establishing a protocol for utilizing the temperature potentiometer; • studying the possibility of installing a temperature regulator on the packing machine (cf. economic balance): (1 employees × 20 hrs.) + (1 employees × 15 hrs.)	Oct. 30, 2001 End Feb. 2002	Plastic packing of fabric quickly come undone (excess time) 1 employee wastes approximately 20 minutes per day redoing packing with defective dielectric closure: 1 employee × (20/60) hrs. × 227 days × 21.5€	1,627€		Avoiding eventual client purchase returns due to soiled fabric	Reducing time spent redoing defective packing Reducing consumption of plastic wrap	1,627€
TOTAL for all combined actions in Basket N° 1			120,100€		Reduction	54%	64,850€

TABLE 6.4 Economic Balance by Root-Solution

Actions	Elementary dysfunction	Dysfunction costs	Reduction rate	Earnings		
				Qualitative	Quantitative	Financial
Concrete actions to be implemented to reduce the dysfunctions identified in the expert project	Dysfunctions (evaluated or non-evaluated) identified in the diagnostic	Total amount of hidden costs due to dysfunctions	Predicted total amount of hidden costs reductions due to dysfunctions	Qualitative improvements that the action will provide (e.g., improved customer reception)	Quantitative improvements induced by the action (e.g., reduced number of customer complaints)	Estimated total amount of predicted hidden cost reductions

Types of project investment costs:
• Time: time spent by the focus group, evaluated by hourly contribution to margin on variable costs.
• Supplies: necessary supplies or investments,
• Other expenses

Types of investment costs induced by the project:
• Time:
• Supplies: } Cost of permanent framework to be implemented
• Other expenses

TABLE 6.5   Overall Economic Balance for a Socio-Economic Innovation Project

Axes of the project	Solutions	Investments	Results of 1st year after amortization
Working conditions	Small supplies	117,000€	410,000€
	Pauses in conditioning	—	105,000€
	Physical working conditions	257,000€	8,000€
Upgraded role of supervisors	Cooperation within the hierarchy	4,000€	50,000€
	Time management and workload of supervisory staff	2,000€	61,000€
	Offices	46,000€	52,000€
[3C] between production and connected services	Supplies	105,000€	171,000€
	Small parts	—	—
	Relationship with maintenance	—	—
Decompartmentalization of production	Information circulation down the line	10,000€	61,000€
	Self-control of quality	530,000€	186,000€
	Line organization	792,000€	88,000€
Cost of the focus group		326,000€	
Total		2,189,000€	1,192,000€

Other performances evaluated qualitatively:
• Improved quality and reduction of complaints
• Improved social climate and sense of belonging to the enterprise
• Increased capacity of the factory to adjust to its environment (new products, new technologies, etc.).

that the investment in new machinery would be amortized in one year and four months by reducing the work unit's hidden costs.

PROJECT CONTENT

This section contains illustrations of the content of the project phase, drawing on three projects that were focused on transforming the operations of micro-spaces. The discussion focuses on the principal actions of these projects, which is why the six domains (working conditions, work organization, time management, communication-coordination-cooperation [3C], integrated training and strategic implementation) are not systematically represented in each of the three projects. Drawing on this discussion, the analysis turns to an underlying characteristic that is common to most projects—the changed role of the supervisory staff and middle management.

A Project in a Consumer Credit Corporation Agency

In this 15-employee agency, *work organization* was very fragmented: the complete processing of a credit request file demanded up to 21 manipulations, calling for the intervention of 12 different employees. Dysfunctions were numerous; they mainly concerned the quality of the work and service provided and included long client response time, poor customer reception, and an extremely high numbers of errors.

Project Objectives-Constraints

The principal objective-constraint established by executive management was *improving the quality of services.* The two key outcomes selected were reducing waiting periods in answering customers and personalizing the agency-customer relationship. The enterprise also wanted to develop multi-tasking and personnel responsibility as a way of introducing and efficiently commercializing new products.

Project Content

Three action items were proposed, focusing on work organization, integrated training and the delegation of power. In terms of *work organization,* emphasis was placed on:

- "A to Z" processing by the same employee (monomial processing) for direct credit files;[1]
- Setting up binomial processing for indirect credit (i.e., credit requests transmitted to a vendor);
- Self-organization of work inside the various teams;
- Increased personnel responsibility;
- Quality improvement in reception for a more personalized agency-customer relationship; and
- Multi-tasking of the personnel throughout the entire process.

In this intervention, personnel responsibility meant that all employees, regardless of whether they were involved in monomial or binomial procedures, were responsible for the files they processed, in terms of the quality of the services provided and the waiting periods for responses and processing. This responsibility is part of empowering employee decision, which in turn is linked to financial delegation.

The activities of the (monomial and binomial) processing units concerned tasks that were directly or indirectly linked to processing files. Nevertheless, priority was given to those activities whose non-execution or differed execution would harm the quality of services provided to customers.

The internal operation of binomial processing units was based on the principle of self-organization, which is based on two conditions: a) the satisfactory acquisition of multi-tasking skills, acquired through mutual training between members of the binomial unit; and b) non-creation of new dysfunctions that would impair service quality, notably in terms of delayed responses to the vendor. Previsions were also made in the project for co-operation between binomial units, notably in cases of work overload or absence of one of the employees in the binomial unit.

Integrated training activities were related to restructuring jobs and were proposed in three areas: a) an information program (e.g., visits to company headquarters, introductions to home-office contacts, information meetings); b) three training units before launching the new work organization (technical and administrative procedures for processing files; work organization; and technical and administrative procedures for customer follow-up); and 3) two training units following the launch (credit training; new-client welcoming and first-contact training).

Finally, the power to accept or refuse requests for credit was *delegated* to the agency's personnel, based on the employee's competency. In both binomial and monomial units, empowerment was given according to the employee's delegation level. If the employee did not have decision-making delegation, the file was first submitted to the other employee in the unit with higher empowerment or to the head of the agency.

A Project in an Electronic Component Finishing and Control Workshop

Table 6.6[2] presents a synthesis of the actions proposed in the project of a work unit with 67 employees. This synthesis is based on the negative points identified in the intervention, focusing on the dysfunctions recognized during the diagnostic and the solutions that were created during the project and classified according to the six domains of action. The discussion focuses on two of the domains of action during the project—work organization and communication-coordination-cooperation.

In terms of *work organization*, the focus group studied three alternative solutions: diversifying tasks, enriching work and setting up operational groups. As Table 6.4 indicates, certain dysfunctions can only be resolved through one of these three solutions. Diversifying tasks consisted of rotating personnel between adjuster and controller workstations. Job enrich-

TABLE 6.6 Project Synthesis Grid

Negative points[a]	Time management (TM)	Work organization (WO)	Communication Coordination Cooperation (3C)	Integrated training (IT)	Working conditions (WC)	Implementation of strategy
Soiled tubes					• Protection conveyor graphite • Plastic film packaging	
Irregular delivery of supplies	Task →;[b] Display of supervisor coordination	• Worker/controller rotation[4] • Employees distributed according to production				
Incomplete deviator recycling				IT on components + workshop organization		
Evacuation conveyor saturation		Operational groups		IT on workshop organization	• Conveyor installation project • Customize evacuation swing trays	
Insufficient toolkits		Job enrichment 1st interview			New tools	Credit for tools
Visual fatigue		Worker/controller rotation			Study by a specialist	
Backache					Adjustable flooring	

(continued)

TABLE 6.6 Project Synthesis Grid (continued)

Negative points[a]	Time management (TM)	Work organization (WO)	Communication Coordination Cooperation (3C)	Integrated training (IT)	Working conditions (WC)	Implementation of strategy
Contact problems workers performing adjustment controls	Task ↑: Information to the personnel	• Worker/controller rotation • Targeted adjustment control • Operational groups • Job enrichment, info about quality	Quality analysis meetings	IT on defect causes, their costs and reminder of regulation and control procedures	Conveyor installation	
Problems changing machines	Task ↓: Workstation change in event of breakdown	• Operational groups • Job enrichment 1st interview		IT on production cost and cost of non-production		• Group objectives • Financial counterpart?
Lack of autonomous workers	Task ↓: Operator replacements	• Operational groups • Job enrichment 1st interview	Quarterly meetings of worker supervisory staff on results	IT on new tasks		Possibility of activity contract
Dichotomy adjustment workers-controllers	Task ↑: Display supervisor coordination	• Operational groups • Targeted adjustment control • Rotation adjustment control		IT of adjustment and control workers and workshop organization	Dismantling office and partitions	
Control distribution 100% control sample	Task →: Final product quality follow-up	• Targeted adjustment control • Operational groups • Worker/controller rotation		IT on the cost of quality defects		

Non-respect of adjustment procedures	Task ↑: Personnel training			• Update procedures • Reminder adjustment & control procedures • Cost of quality defects		Group objectives
Insufficient links among teams	Task ↑: Team reporting			Cooperative preparation of training		Group objectives
Lack of mutual assistance among workers		Operational groups		IT on workshop organization		Group piloting logbook
Information delay control/workers	Task ↑: Liaison between QC personnel and workers^c	• Targeted adjustment control • Operational groups		IT on cost of quality defects	Installation conveyors	
Insufficient cooperation supervisor/management	Task ↑: Relationship with the department head		Proposal of a meeting + regularity of existing meetings			
Technical services research	Task ↓: Maintenance replacements (Fob) Task ↓: Maintenance replacements (Tech)	Job enrichment 1st interview				
Differences in worker rhythms		Operational groups		IT on workshop organization	Installation conveyors	Group objectives

(continued)

TABLE 6.6 Project Synthesis Grid (continued)

Negative points[a]	Time management (TM)	Work organization (WO)	Communication Coordination Cooperation (3C)	Integrated training (IT)	Working conditions (WC)	Implementation of strategy
Tubes at quality limit not adjusted		Operational groups				Group objectives and piloting logbook
Insufficient information on tube rejects	Task ↑: Final product quality follow-up	• Targeted adjustment control • Operational groups				
Absence scheduling of supervisory work	Utilize TM synthesis tables	Job enrichment				
Insufficient quality improvement studies			QC meeting + manufacturing[c]			
Problem solving follow-up	Final product quality follow-up	Operational groups	Monthly meeting supervisory staff of workers			
Insufficient initial training	Task ↑: Personnel training			Reminder procedure—factory visit, enterprise economy and environment		
Insufficient on-going worker training	Task ↑: Personnel training	Operational groups	Monthly meeting supervisory staff of workers			Possibility of activity contract

[a] The notion of negative points has evolved in socio-economic theory: henceforth it refers to the concept of "principal elementary dysfunctions."

[b] Task →: maintain task. Task ↓: reduce task. Task ↑: develop task.

[c] QC = quality control.

TABLE 6.7   Communication-Coordination-Cooperation [3C] in an Industrial Work Unit

Framework	Period	Employees involved	Theme
Meeting	Every three months	Managers—day supervisors—workers	• General information • Quarterly results
Meeting	Monthly	Executive management—managers	General information
Memorandum	According to needs	Manufacturing personnel service, quality control service and technical service	Modifications concerning remuneration
Appointment	Every three months	Personnel service and line supervisors	Progress report on personnel management (absenteeism)
Meeting	According to needs	Quality service and manufacturing supervisors	Quality analysis

ment entailed having the workers take charge of first level maintenance. Operational groups were also composed of two binomial groups of controllers and four groups of adjusters.

Five specific frameworks were proposed in *communication-coordination-cooperation* and they are summarized in Table 6.7.

A Project in a Bank Agency[3]

Seven negative points were revealed by the diagnostic of this agency with personnel of 17 employees, including: excessively long waiting periods for processing and answering client requests; a high rate of personnel turnover (90% instability rate); inappropriate job training; under-motivated personnel; customer complaints; insufficient commercial prospective; and problems related to promotion, qualification and remuneration.

The Guiding Principles and Main Actions of the Project

The project was constructed around three principles, considered to be the causes of dysfunctions: a) reduction of the dichotomy between administrative activity and commercial activity; b) improvement of the organization's flexibility to enable a better absorption of work overloads; and c) substitution of an organizational focus on tasks to a focus on the clientele.

The main actions of the project focused on work organization, communication-coordination-cooperation, and integrated training. In terms of *work organization*, the personnel were divided into three work groups, each one in charge of initiating, following-up and making decision on all problems and operations related to the business assets they were responsible for. The agency's business assets were therefore divided into three groups: private clients, small businesses and enterprises (see Figure 6.3). The only exception was for bank window-tellers who, in order to simplify customer reception, welcomed all clients without distinction. A system of job rotation inside each work group made it possible to progressively increase personnel multi-tasking skills.

1. During the diagnostic phase:

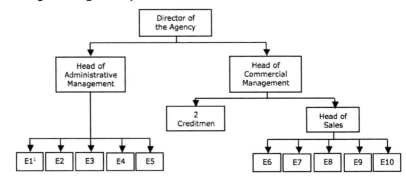

2. After the project:

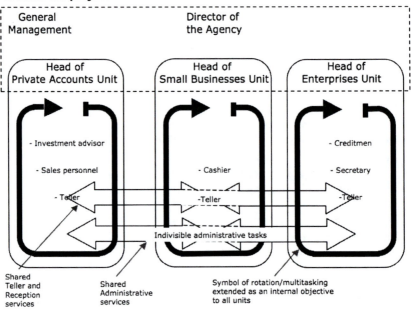

[1] E = Employee

Figure 6.3 Comparison of a bank agency's organizational diagram before and after the project.

Communication-Coordination-Cooperation centered on the creation of a framework to periodically bring the head of the agency and the heads of the three work groups together. Two objectives were assigned to this management unit: a) ensure good internal communication and coordinate activities among the three work groups; and b) enable the head of the agency to accomplish an external representation mission, set at 50 percent of that person's time. The management unit met at varying intervals: every day, for a brief moment (approximately 15 minutes), to deal with pending operations; every week, for one to two hours, to pilot the agency in function of activity results and observed dysfunctions; and every month or quarter, to envisage commercial and internal actions of a wider scope and to inform agency personnel on the results obtained.

Integrated training involved the creation of an ambitious training program that was designed to implement the new work organization in the work groups. Even though part of the training program was provided by the bank's own training department, most of the training was done by the heads of the work groups.

THE EVOLUTION OF THE MANAGER'S ROLE

The content of a project, three illustrations of which are provided in this section, always includes an axis of enlarged multitasking as well as increased worker and office personnel autonomy. Such change raises questions about a portion of the tasks carried out, up until then, by intermediate or top management. For example, self-organization within binomial teams eliminates the task of distributing daily work, previously attributed to the hierarchy. Furthermore, the reduction of dysfunctions has an impact on the role of managers, an important part of whose job is often devoted to regulating dysfunctions. In some case, we evaluated as much as 75 percent of management working time as devoted to regulation.

Thus, projects developed include specific actions concerning the role of managers within the overall project.[4] Let us cite two cases where dysfunctions specific to management were studied in depth.[5]

Action Addressing a CEO's Time Management

In a bank in the process of generalizing socio-economic management (Savall & Zardet, 1985), in-depth research was conducted on the CEO's time management dysfunctions. The time management dysfunctions that were identified included: work overload; fragmented work-time (i.e., a multitude of subjects dealt with at short time intervals, from 2 to 15 minutes; processing a large number of operations having little or moderate importance, in light of the CEO's job; and a large number of vitally important operations on hold or late or processed over the weekend.

An extremely precise analysis of the CEO's time management, conducted over a two-week period, enabled developing solutions to remedy the dysfunctions identified. These solutions simultaneously addressed the three key areas of work organization, integrated training and communication-co-ordination-cooperation. In terms of *work organization*, attention was placed on setting up procedures for *actual delegation* to the CEO's collaborators. This collaborative delegation required a precise manual of specifications between the two parties, as well as integrated training actions for the delegated party (carried out by the delegating party), in order to implement the specifications manual. The objective of the *integrated training* was to make delegation possible. Integrated training actions for senior management raise specific difficulties, since senior managers rarely recognize their weaknesses in terms of competency. Thus, the training should be done in the form of shared work sessions, alternating between dealing with *generic* questions (e.g., how to deal with a suspicious client) and specific, concrete cases (e.g., how to solve the problem of Mr. X., a suspicious client).

Finally, a number of actions were undertaken that increased the time dedicated to *communication-coordination-cooperation*, which resulted in a modification as to how the CEO functioned. Changes to his schedule included: alternating between plenary meetings and two-person team meetings; reducing contacts, namely unplanned meetings (involving two or more people) that created havoc with work-time organization and consumed more time than necessary. An emphasis on improved communication-coordination-cooperation frameworks made it possible to prevent this type of dysfunction.

Actions Addressing the Role of Supervisors in an Industrial Work Unit

In an industrial enterprise in the process of generalizing socio-economic management, a work program was carried out with the supervisory staff in view of a three-fold improvement objective: improved supervisor work methods; improved time management and scheduling of supervisor tasks; and improved internal and external communication-coordination-cooperation among supervisors. The discussion will focus on detailed aspects of time management.

Characteristics of Supervisor Time Management

Supervisors determined the time involved for every task they carried out, whether these tasks merited being developed, maintained or reduced, in order to attain dysfunction-reduction objectives for the workshop and enhance multitasking among workers. Table 6.8 presents the synthesis of these

TABLE 6.8 Distribution of Tasks

Evolution sought by the supervisor	Task to be reduced	Task to be maintained	Task to be developed
Administrative work	• Distribution of hours • Preparation of follow-up charts	• Controlling daily charts • Filling out various coupons • Declaring work accidents	• Checking-up on new employees • Controlling various measurements • Follow-up of production curves • Verifying salary and new employees ratio • Analyzing personnel tasks • Preparing manuals for new machines
Manufacturing follow-up	• Searching for metal and raw materials for supplies • Handling • Minor break-downs of equipment • Replacing adjusters • Replacing workers • Searching for means of correcting defects	• Walking the workshop rounds (approx.) • Following-up on machine operation • Certifying break-downs • Searching for improved adjustments	• Follow-up of manufacturing in the workshop • Verification and follow-up of quality
Communication—contacts	• Searching for additional information on suspicious product lines • Discussing final adjustment of tools at startup • Method contacts to search for new or modified lines of products	• Contacting technical and administrative services • Discussions with personnel • Telephone calls to other services or workshops • Meetings • Various interviews	• Contacting the personnel • Cooperation among supervisors • Contacts with the hierarchy • Consultation of supervisors by the head of the workshop regarding salaries and classifications
Organization and scheduling	• Searching for available labor inside the workshop (depending on needs) • Modifying the daily schedule	• Work provision for the next day • Work provision for teams • Distribution of the day's work • Follow-up on missing workers	• Medium-term work provision
Improvement and development		• Services rendered inside the factory	• Reflect on various improvements • Participate with installation of new machines • Orientation of new personnel • Training of personnel • Inform. supervisors on new techniques

evaluations, which revealed: a) the large number of tasks that could be reduced, representing from 1 hour 25 minutes to 4 hours 45 minutes per day, depending on the supervisor; b) the dysfunctional character of these tasks, most of which were dysfunction regulation tasks; and c) the concentration of improvement and development actions on poorly-assumed tasks (or on tasks to be developed). Moreover, the collection of quantified data revealed the fragmentation of their work-time, including numerous short tasks (6 to 26 per day) and or interrupted tasks carried out in discontinuous manner (average number of sequences for one single task was 2.2).

Improvement Actions Envisaged

There were five key improvement actions that were highlighted. First, it was agreed it was important to reduce simple regulation actions and liaisons in favor of action and liaisons focused on prevention. Second, emphasis was placed on reducing the number of short tasks and the number of sequences for the same task. Third, attempts were made to improve and develop the work unit's operations, focused on personnel training, updating knowledge on new technologies, improving on-the-job security, and so forth. Fourth, the number of planned and prepared appointments and meetings (follow-up on results) were increased, especially among supervisors. Finally, the supervisors determined the priority of the tasks to be scheduled.

These actions were carried out at the same time as the workshop's operation transformation project. Thus, developing worker autonomy, after setting up operational worker groups, facilitated the progressive delegation of simple tasks classified by supervisors as "tasks to be reduced."

DIFFICULTIES IN THE PROJECT PHASE

The main difficulty in the course of the project phase can come from a lack of creativity on the part of the plenary group, which can fail to imagine solutions that depart too drastically from current operating modes. In other words, the solutions proposed in many cases are more often rearrangements of the current situation than innovative solutions. Paradoxically, however, our experimentation has demonstrated the need for significant transformation of work situations in order to truly mobilize human energy.[6] This blockage, which can come from the plenary group as a whole or from the project leader alone, demands that the intervener deploy pedagogical know-how, notably supported by the successful experimentation already completed by the ISEOR. In certain cases, a visit can even be organized to the sites of these experiments, which augments the veracity of the predicted outcomes.

During the project phase, the intervener should systematically alternate between "shock" and "cultural conformity" behavior. In this context, *shock* consists of suggesting solutions judged *a priori* unacceptable by the focus group, such as bringing up operational worker teams when the micro-space is currently organized in a highly fragmented and specialized manner. *Cultural conformity*, which can be indispensable to avoid rejection, is exercised by taking into account technical specificities or the cultural values of the focus group members.

A second type of difficulty can appear at the *end* of the project phase, entailing the *refusal of the proposed solutions.* Refusal can come from the top management. This has occurred in the few rare cases, when core groups played their role poorly due to ignorance or a misevaluation of the strategic objectives-constraints. Such was the case, for example, when a project called for recruiting (increasing the work force), while the enterprise was under the constraint of not hiring anyone that year.

Refusal, however, can also come from workers or employees impacted by the project. This has also occurred in a few rare cases, when the project leader failed to supply information to the personnel between the end of the diagnostic and the end of the project. This information void created anxiety as well as unreasonable expectations that were ultimately disappointed. Thus, it is essential to inform and interact with the personnel between focus group sessions. It is recommended to regularly provide information with concrete examples in the company newsletter (when it exists), or to create such a communication device for the socio-economic intervention.

Finally, refusal can be more isolated. It can come from one person or from a category of personnel. The main reason seems to be that people feel disadvantaged by the proposed project, either because a task, a function, or a "flattering attribution" is taken away from them. They can also feel that the project does not offer them enough in comparison to others. To avoid such problems, it is important to undertake a coherency analysis of the project, carried out during the last session, which addresses the proposed evolution of every micro-space regarding actions on working conditions, work content, training, increasing competency, and so forth.

It also seems important to point out that the presentation of the project by the project leader to his or her hierarchical managers, and then the personnel, can be conceived as a veritable commercial action, a relation of negotiation carefully prepared in advance that attempts to respond to latent needs or explicit requests. It is worth mentioning, from this point of view, that certain CEOs report having seen project leaders present their project with a "loser's attitude," without any real effort to be convincing.

Given these concerns, the *problem solving cycle* proposed in the socio-economic analysis should coincide with the process of *restoring confidence* as discussed in Chapter 5. Nevertheless, the quality and the effectiveness of the problem solving cycle depend on the degree of legitimacy attributed to the external intervention team, which requires a basic level of *confidence* between the *CEO* and the external interveners. Such confidence can be problematic, however, largely due to the reality that the stakes of the intervention are not strictly identical for both parties. There are also the inevitable fluctuations of confidence levels over the course of the intervention process.

Clearly, there must be confidence on the part of the company CEO in the competency of the interveners to help the company improve itself, as well as and confidence in the necessity to call in experts to help to solve certain dysfunctions. This confidence manifests itself as and absence of company resistance to problems and objectives-constraints during change actions, and an absence of resistance on the part of the different categories of actors during diagnostic interviews in their comments and willingness to provide company documents. This type of confidence needs to be earned and validated though such deontological practices as *discretion* and *respect of anonymity* on the part of interveners. This confidence is also manifested in facilitating access for the intervener-researcher to confidential sections of company strategy.

All of this not without deontological problems and moments of faltering confidence or suspicion. Indeed, absolute discretion concerning such information is to be observed, even when the intervener is sometimes led to work with managers on certain projects despite knowing how fragile they are, and sometimes knowing the outcome or decision made at higher levels. It is a case of being torn between the absolute necessity for secrecy and the confidence accorded to the intervener by managers, who sometimes feel "betrayed." Notwithstanding, it is also true that the intervener does not remain totally inactive in such situations. It is critical to head off deception, sensitizing the top management to the presumed incongruity and ineffectiveness of certain decision intentions and situations in which organizational members will be negatively impacted by the project. Thus, the intervener should strive to adopt a dual focus on the intrinsic *quality* of his or her mission and the *effectiveness* of the intervention (or quality of service) as perceived by the client enterprise, following a path illustrated in Figure 6.4.

CONCLUSION

The ISEOR method for developing socio-economic effectiveness improvement projects in businesses and organizations includes a number of particularities. First is the focus on overall actions, because the sustainable reduction of dysfunctions requires concrete actions touching all employees

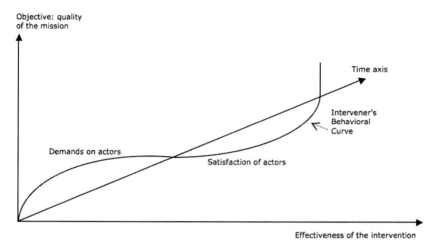

Figure 6.4 Intervention objectives and effectiveness.

in a given unit, sometimes involving even several neighboring units. It is vain to attempt improvement by limiting the intervention territory and by relying, for example, on a small group of volunteers to find solutions. Second, the nature of solutions is multidimensional. All solutions to dysfunctions and all reductions of hidden costs imply concrete actions touching several, sometime all, domains of action as we have defined them: working conditions, work organization, individual and collective time management, communication-coordination-cooperation frameworks, integrated training (adequacy between training/job), strategy implementation. Third, the development of the project is entrusted to the project leader, the hierarchical head of the unit involved. This person, of course, may be assisted by his or her internal managers and representatives of managers from other company departments, plus supported by periodical meetings with his or her manager and the top management.

Following these tenets, projects are developed as the result of a triple negotiation: with the top management, with the other departments and with the collaborators of the unit. The unit's project is thus a veritable company project—in line with company reality (bottom-up procedures), but also in line with company strategy (top-down procedures). This explains why ISEOR's socio-economic projects developed to date have led to considerable achievements and results. The project method constitutes an *original problem solving method*, involving a participative search process for a composite basket of concrete solution that correspond to a rigorous inventory of major dysfunctions. It also provides for the development of a carefully prepared action plan for implementing precise company strategic objectives.

NOTES

1. This discussion is based on ISEOR Reports: Rennard and Uzan (1980) and Breney (1981).
2. Table 6.6 "Project synthesis grid" is excerpted from *Intervention socio-économique et préparation du changement technologique dans les grandes entreprise industrielles. Cas d'un atelier d'électronique* [Socio-economic intervention and technological change preparation in large industrial enterprises. The case of an electronics workshop], masters thesis in Organizational Management under the direction of Henri Savall, University of Lyon 2 and the Graduate School of Commerce of Lyon, October 1984, 167 p.
3. This case is drawn from "Projet de restructuration dans une agence d'un établissement bancaire" [Restructuring project in an agency of a banking establishment], ISEOR report, June 1981, 54 pages.
4. On this topic, see Marc Bonnet, et al, under the direction of Henri Savall, "Transforming the role of management: Case study of ten enterprises in a French industrial group." Research carried out with the participation of the National Foundation for Management Education (FNEGE), June 1985, 21 p.
5. It can be noted that these three domains of management dysfunction emerge from more than 1,000 diagnostics of enterprises and organizations carried out by the ISEOR in more than 36 countries and in nearly 60 sectors of activity: time management, communication-coordination-cooperation and strategy implementation.
6. American professors and experts who have discovered the ISEOR methodology, notably in 1998 at the Academy of Management Conference in San Diego (USA), have characterized the socio-economic method as being a forerunner and a more humane, "nonviolent" version of "reengineering."

REFERENCES

Breney, C. (1981). *Restructuration des emplois en milieu tertiaire dans une optique stratégique* [Restructuring jobs in the service sector from a strategic perspective]. Lyon, France: Graduate Studies in Management Sciences.

Rennard, M. & Uzan, O. (1980). *Projet d'amélioration de la qualité des services par la restructuration des emplois dans une agence de crédit* [Service quality improvement project for restructuring jobs in a credit agency]. Ecully, France: ISEOR Report.

Savall, H., & Zardet, V. (1985). *Improving time management: Tools, concepts and operational methods. Case of the senior management team of a regional bank.* Ecully, France: ISEOR Report.

CHAPTER 7

IMPLEMENTATION

The project phase ends with the proposal of a coherent group of actions that, in their current state of development, still lack sufficient detail to enable their concrete application. Thus, the follow-on implementation phase is broken down into two steps: preparing for action, and then carrying out the actions themselves. The separation of these two steps, however, mainly concerns the "major" actions of a strategic nature, which are often complex actions requiring extensive cooperation across the various company divisions. Numerous micro-actions, set off in the process of the project development phase, facilitate the reduction of dysfunctions and hidden costs without awaiting the end of the project phase. This initial implementation focus makes it possible to gain momentum for a stronger change dynamic and helps to manifest the first positive concrete effects, which stimulate and encourage further actor commitment to the innovation process. The result is considerable progress in cooperation frameworks among actors, both vertically and transversally.

PREPARING FOR ACTION

This initial step involves constructing a detailed project for specific actions based on those proposed in the project. This job requires the analysis of the value of operations, to avoid unnecessarily adding new tasks and missions to those that already exist. This value analysis should be carried out in a

Mastering Hidden Costs and Socio-Economic Performance, pages 183–197
Copyright © 2008 by Information Age Publishing
183

rigorous, structured manner, successively studying the different domains of action. Preparing for action also includes the essential scheduling and programming of the different actions, which constitute a substantial factor of implementation success. Figure 7.1 presents an illustration of a coordinated implementation plan for the project of a workshop in a glassworks factory.

THE ACTION

This second step of implementation consists of actually carrying out the different actions proposed. In general, this sequence is a relatively long one, since it extends over several months (see, for example, Figure 7.1). Also, this concrete action phase supposes regular dissemination of information to the concerned actors, as well as regular follow-up and audit of the process.

This section focuses on: a) the construction of the detailed project of concrete actions; b) integrated training actions, with an assessment of both preparation and delivery; c) information distribution to actors; and d) follow-up and audit of the implementation process.

Detailed Project Actions

Project content must include an additional, highly-detailed analysis of the work (work organization), integrated training (which will be discussed in the next section), physical layout of facilities, and the specific means and resources necessary for implementation, based on the economic balance drawn up at the project stage.

Analysis of the Work

This process consists of defining, in highly precise fashion, the distribution of the tasks that result from the overall solutions proposed in terms of work organization, then remodeling the definition of job profiles. This study, carried out by management under the conduct of the project leader, can be done in conjunction with the human resources department, when the project is likely to lead, immediately or ultimately, to increasing job-related qualifications.

The study of the new distribution of tasks should include the analysis of the value of tasks accomplished, in order to avoid simply adding new tasks, which would consequentially provoke work overload. Analysis should notably consider eliminating useless tasks, in either the old or the new operating procedures, or modifying the procedure for accomplishing certain tasks by improving individual and collective work methods.

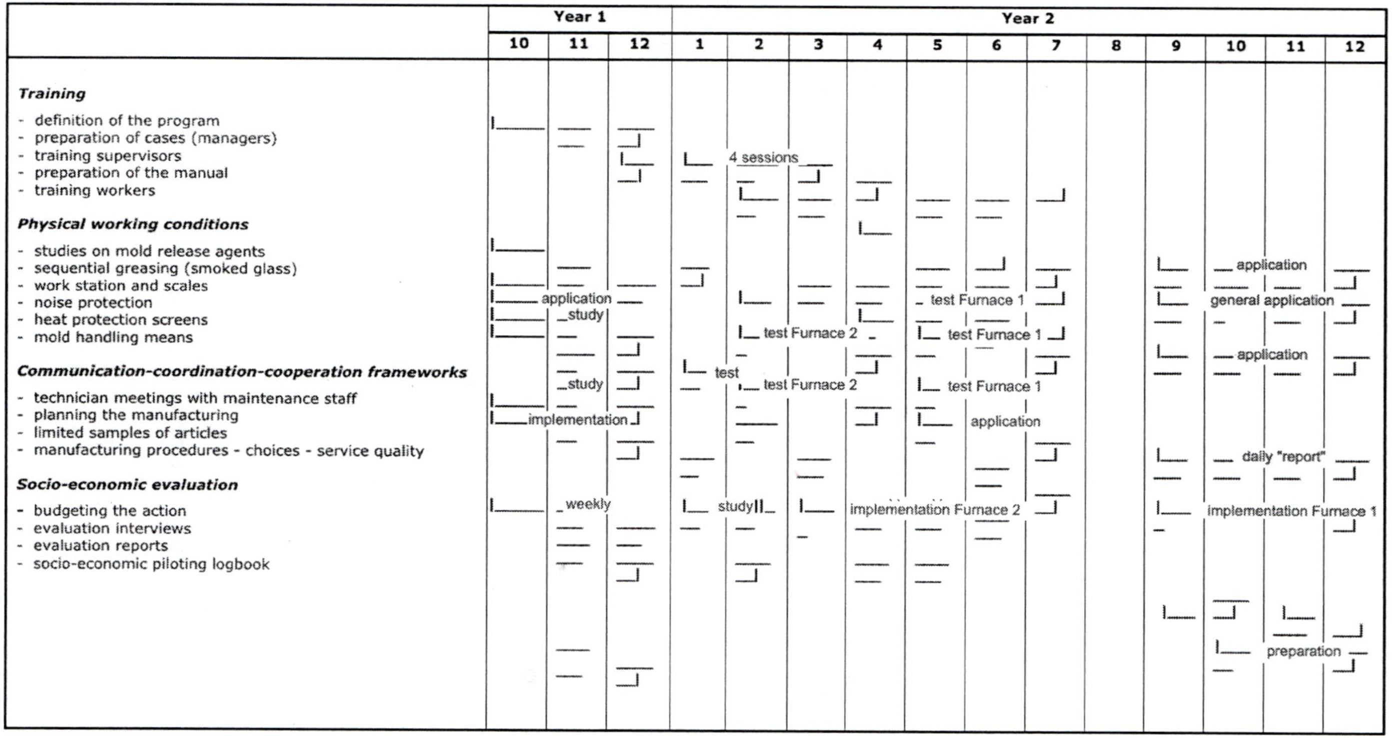

Figure 7.1 Coordinated plan for project implementation in a glassworks factory.

Finally, analysis of the work includes coordinating procedures with operational departments, when these are concerned with modifying actions. In industrial organizations, this particularly concerns processes and scheduling, which could include an in-depth modification of the work if the manufacturing unit is to be reorganized into operational worker groups with weekly production objectives, instead of the typical daily objectives. This can also concern the quality control service when the work project entails job enrichment by incorporating quality assessment. In the service sector, the main areas concerned would be different, for example, in a bank this might involve the computer department, central credit service and so forth.

Plant Layout

Modifications in the physical layout of facilities can stem either from actions proposed in terms of working conditions improvement, or come indirectly from work organization actions. A precise study of plant layout is important because it has been proven that modifying physical structures always has a strong, symbolic impact on organizational members. Indeed, these modifications are immediately and directly observable, in contrast with actions in other domains, which can be drawn out over several months and can seem more abstract. As illustrated in Figure 7.2, plant layout refers to machines, workstations and circulation in the industrial sector. It can also focus on people, for example, circulation of customers in the service sector.

Implementation

This assessment requires in-depth work on the preliminary sketch provided by the project group, which serves as the basis for developing the economic balance. Emphasis is placed on material means (e.g., purchase, adaptation, installment, equipment distribution) and human means (e.g., evaluating the time necessary to accomplish the actions proposed, determining whether that time can be provided by the time made available through improved productivity, whether it is necessary to consider temporary personnel support). Table 7.1 presents an illustration of this *inventory of means*. The inventory can include the search for exterior financing to carry out the actions.

Integrated Training Actions

Integrated training actions are critical since they exert a significant influence on the success of job restructuring. Going from limited, precise individual tasks (Taylorism) to work groups is typically based on the assumption of increased employee competency, which requires both training and

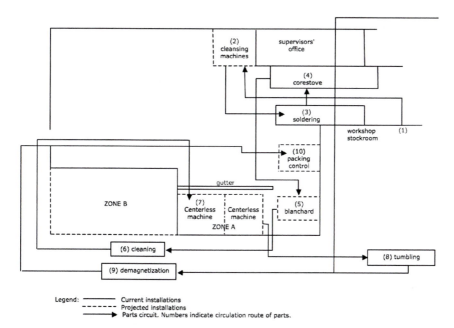

Figure 7.2 Project for installation of machines necessary for the first operational work group. *Source:* Marc Bonnet, *Elaboration d'un projet de restructuration des emplois avec formation intégrée dans une usine de métallurgie* [Development of a job restructuring project with integrated training in a metallurgy factory]. ISEOR Report, February 1981.

regular practice of new tasks. Successful training programs require several successive preparation phases, including: a) *programming action* (e.g., forming training groups, developing training schedules, providing for stand-ins, arranging visits to departments and fieldtrips to other enterprises); b) *developing the training program* (e.g., drawing up an inventory of training needs, setting up cooperation between supervisors, managers and the company training service, determining pedagogical materials, when needed training supervisors in pedagogical methods); and c) *creating pedagogical materials* (e.g., writing the training manual(s), creating or gathering pedagogical material for training sessions).

Integrated Training and Pedagogical Tools

It is essential to coordinate the training program with the job restructuring actions. The training itself should be based on three core areas. First, emphasis should be placed on the *list of dysfunctions* drawn up during the diagnostic. Training actions action should raise awareness of the existence of dysfunctions, training organizational members in how to avoid them or regulate them in the most efficient manner possible. The second focus

TABLE 7.1 Inventory of Means for Project Implementation in an Electronics Factory

Action Domain	Material Means	Human Resources
Work organization	• Displacing machines to enable implementation of the groups • Setting up a meeting room for the groups with table, chairs and blackboard • Repairing 2 microscopes • Marking production by groups • Interchangeable electrode blocks	• Learning time for new tasks
Integrated training	• Setting up a classroom for training	• 100 salaried hours • 200 hours of supervisor leadership + preparation

Communication-coordination-cooperation framework	• Intercom at the "cannon" service	• Professional evaluation appointments supervisors/workers:
		  – Supervisors' time: 100 hours/year,
		  – Workers' time: 100 hours/year
		• Supervisor/group meetings: 2 hours per week

Physical working conditions	• Eliminating mechanical relays to K1 machines: 40,000€ for 11 machines (estimation) • Installing suspended ceilings • Neons with light intensity regulation • Individual potentiometer/lighting • Armrests on tables	• Time spent on studies and achievement follow-up

is on the *job restructuring action*. The training should permit personnel to progressively acquire the competencies for the new operations that will be entrusted to them. Finally, a key tool is the *competency grid*, which enables taking stock of each individual's weak points regarding current and future operations, in connection with the job restructuring (Chapter 1 examines the competency grid is detail).

The competency grid fits together with the other two tools for developing training programs. While other tools exist, their functions are to support the competency grid, enabling an in-depth understanding of that concept in view of preparing an "integrated training plan" (ITP) and "integrated training manual" (ITMA). As an example, a useful tool is the operational units grid (OPU). These satellite tools also facilitate the capitalization of company knowledge and know-how, in the double perspective of knowledge management and quality certification (e.g., ISO 9000 - 2000 version). Finally, the training program should include company *strategic objectives*, thus making training action a precise and direct tool of strategy implementation. Table 7.2 lists some training themes defined in reference to the dysfunctions analysis, the job restructuring project and the company's strategic objectives.

It is interesting to point out that among other program themes, management often plans for an "initiation to economics" training session for workers and office employees, introducing them to the economic mechanisms of operating an enterprise: how production costs are determined, what incidence production cost and quality levels have on the enterprise's competitiveness, and so forth.

The Training Manual

Once the program has been defined, creating the training manual is an essential step. Resorting to pre-existing manuals is, of course, a possibility, but they should never be the sole source, since the manual should not only supply theoretical elements of knowledge (e.g., "What is our savings plan?"; "How does such and such machine function?"), but manuals should also adapt this knowledge to the needs of the work unit in terms of dysfunction reduction or procedures to be implemented to prevent or regulate the dysfunctions.

TABLE 7.2   Integrated Training Themes in an Industrial Setting

Dysfunction analysis
- Review of adjustment and control procedures
- Workshop organization
- Visits of the factory and of new installations
- Pay slip

Job remodeling
- Porpis measure (technical term)
- Screwdriver adjustment
- Impedance modification
- Adjustment of the viewer
- Operating rules for operational groups
- Controlling

Strategic objectives
- Analysis of quality defect causes
- Operating mechanism of a new factory (investment project)
- Production cost of products and quality defect costs
- The enterprise in its environment

Thus, the training manual is constructed in cooperation with the managers of the micro-space, the technical services involved and the company training service, and, as needed, an external training center. The manual takes the form of information cards, each one highlighting a key idea or a key problem. In some cases, part of the manual is based on an inventory of incidents or break-downs that the personnel are confronted with. The information card format makes it possible to *transform training manuals into operating manuals* once the training has been accomplished. In this way, organizational members can refer to manuals in the course of their job activity, in order to consolidate their knowledge, review forgotten points, and to complete the manual. In this sense, the manual thus becomes a "living" tool.

Creating a training-operating manual is therefore an investment that has short-term and long-term returns: it not only provides a document for the integrated training of the personnel, it also provides the opportunity for them to increase their technical competency. Thus, it represents a chance to gather together in written, transmittable form both management and personnel "know-how," which in many enterprises is only inscribed "in the minds" of actors.

Implementation

Numerous socio-economic diagnostics have revealed complaints about professional training institutes, whose programs are often disconnected from the reality of the job. If the training program is to succeed in providing solutions to the dysfunctions uncovered during the diagnostic, the timing and duration of the sessions are critically important. The *duration* of the training sessions must be carefully chosen: most enterprises opt for short sessions, from 1 to 3 hours long, but in some cases, training occupies the entire day, even entire weeks. *Synchronization* of training sessions with other project actions is also important, so that acquired training can be consolidated and reinforced through regular practice of operations. This is the principle of alternating between training-working, which has become very popular today, which ISEOR has been implementing for almost twenty-five years.

Finally, the composition and size of groups seem to be another criterion for effectiveness: the number of trainees, ultimately a choice made by the company, hovers between 4 and 7 participants. An attempt is made to constitute inter-categorical employee groups, the leaders of which are supervisors. Indeed, one of the objectives is to create a common language that addresses both practical operations and individual knowledge of employees having different jobs and functions yet belonging to the same operational activity group (principle of functional cooperation). Integrated training action thus contributes to developing the micro-space's internal communication-coordination-cooperation.

Roles of the Different Actors in Integrated Training

The role of supervisory staff or middle management is essential to successful implementation of the project, especially with regard to integrated training actions. Three categories of actors need to work together in these actions: a) *workers and staff* for whom the training offers a framework for developing their professional relationship with supervisors; b) *managers* who assist supervisors in developing programs and training manuals; and c) *supervisors* who, knowing the micro-space better than anyone else (e.g., its structures, behaviors and dysfunctions) are best equipped for creating manuals and leading sessions. Also, in certain cases, supervisors have received training in pedagogical techniques, which increases the effectiveness of their leadership. Thus, integrated training can also enhance the status of middle management—it enhances their mission with leadership and training responsibilities as well as their relations with other managers, senior management, and technical and operational services.

Case Illustration of an Integrated Training Action

The case (Bonnet, 1980) is based on an integrated training action carried out in a glass fusion work unit in a glassworks factory (25 employees). On the average, workers possessed a training level equivalent to primary school education. Preparation for the training action took place over a six month period, beginning with the *pedagogical* training of supervisor-instructors (10 half-days of training over a three month period) and development of the *training manuals* (prepared by the supervisors containing the theoretical and practical knowledge necessary to operating the workshop installations [e.g., furnaces]).

The *training program* itself was the object of four themed manuals addressing: glass-making technology, glass composition (e.g., feeding in component raw materials, operating the composition equipment, equipment maintenance tasks), glass fusion in Furnace 1, and glass fusion in Furnace 2. As part of the preparation phase, related *pedagogical materials* (e.g., diagrams, samples of raw material components, demonstration equipment, visits to glassworks factories using different glass-making equipment) were also created. A *budget* for the training was also developed, 40 percent of which went to preliminary studies and preparation and 60 percent for the training action itself.

The program was implemented over a two month period. Faced with the potential risk of refusal on the part of workers who might consider the training useless to them, in light of their age or seniority, senior management brought workers together to introduce them to the objectives of the action, the content of the programs and the importance of the training. Despite some initial reticence, all workers agreed to participate. The training action took the form of three sessions (lasting 1 week, 2 days and 3 days) and repeated four times. Thus, 24 workers were trained in groups of 5, for the equivalent of approximately 1,000 trainee-hours.

In the course of training, several workers requested the development of procedural manuals derived from the training manuals. Thus, three procedural manuals (Furnace 1, Furnace 2 and glass-composition machine) were created and installed in workstations. They were mostly made up of schemas, but also, at the demand of workers, included economic information such as the cost of various raw material components.

In *evaluating* the training program, drawing on qualitative and quantitative measures,[1] workers felt that the training action had *increased their competency* at their jobs and *improved working conditions* regarding certain points. These outcomes were confirmed through a comparative study of competency grids before and after the action. The training also affected job content. It brought about *higher levels of responsibility* because workers were now equipped to intervene in case of problems, and *take charge of ongoing maintenance tasks* and *reporting,* tasks formerly attributed to the supervisor alone.

INFORMATION DISSEMINATION

As the decisive phase for application, during the implementation stage it is important that regular information about actions from senior management and micro-space management is disseminated throughout the organization.

Micro-Space Personnel

Even when organizational members have been regularly informed over the course of the focus group's work, it remains indispensable to organize, following project approval by the top management, a meeting bringing together all personnel where the project leader presents the content. It is interesting to note that the presence of the CEO has a positive impact on the personnel, to the degree that personnel thus directly perceive the company's determination, in terms of strategy and policy-making by the top management.

The staff is then involved in preparing the implementation, being kept regularly informed about its state of advancement, in which they participate directly. This information feedback is essential, for it enables the personnel to keep measure of their progress, which could be under-estimated in their minds, given the difficulties and the effort required for implementation. This represents an implementation piloting action, which rounds off the piloting group's job.

Human Resource Representation Bodies

These bodies should be informed of project content through the framework of institutional relations that exits in the enterprise. For example, the labor-management committee should be provided with the opportunity to give its opinion on the training actions that are part of the project, as is provided for in their attributions.

Other Actors

Depending on the enterprise, we have observed different behaviors on the part of senior management regarding information distribution to the entire enterprise about the project and its implementation in a micro-space. As a guideline, we have found that the less information is circulated, the more the micro-space is isolated, especially the head of the micro-space, literally becoming an organizational "ghetto." It therefore appears preferable, to avoid this isolation and the rumors triggered by uninformed imaginations, to organize information feedback to top management and, eventually, to the top management. The *Horivert* architecture includes a minimum of two divisions having undergone in-depth diagnostic, with 30 to 60 percent of line personnel participation. This makes it possible to avoid the inconveniences provoked by the fact that only one company division exposes its dysfunctions and hidden costs in front of the whole company ("voyeurism" effect) or, conversely, is the only division to demonstrate progress (effect of organizational "jealousy").

It can also be beneficial to inform the company's clients, either to solicit their indulgence at the beginning of implementation (primarily in service sector cases) or as part of a publicity strategy, showcasing the socio-economic innovation actions conducted by the enterprise.

FOLLOWING-UP

The implementation phase appears to be the "most nerve-racking" of the entire process. This is understandable as it entails preparing and applying innovative actions, all the while maintaining daily operations. In addition, this phase requires major energy expenditure on the part of all members of the micro-space, from undergoing training and performing new tasks, to using new tools and learning how to coordinate efforts and work together. It is therefore indispensable, at the risk of running astray, as soon as the project phase is completed, to set up a follow-up and audit framework of the implementation process. This tactic can help to protect the project leader and his or her project management team from isolation in front of the rest of the company during this crucial phase of action. This framework takes on two forms, one with the piloting group and the second based on personal assistance to the project leader.

The Piloting Group

The composition of the piloting group is the same as the focus group, set up during the previous phase (see Chapter 6). Its role, however, is different as it has two principal missions. First, the piloting group follows the actual state of progress of actions compared to the programmed schedule. This summons the directive aspect of piloting, destined to limit calendar deviation, which constitutes a major dysfunction in itself. Second, the group also audits the process. This step involves the participative aspect of piloting. It consists of drawing up an inventory of concrete problems encountered during implementation and finding solutions—at the level of top management, responsible for conducting company strategic actions and the promoter piloting socio-economic innovative intervention. These problems can be diverse in nature (e.g., the unexpected departure of a company employee, delay in the delivery of the equipment that was ordered, vacations). The piloting group, which can engage in in-depth work or only modification of certain points of the innovation process, typically meets roughly once every three months.

Personal Assistance to the Project Leader

In addition to the piloting group, ISEOR has developed forms of individual assistance for project leaders who, experience has shown, often find themselves in need of support during the implementation phase—in addition to the support provided by the piloting group. Besides a psychological dimension, this personal support also has a methodological content. These assistance meetings facilitate preparation for focus group meetings, by prioritizing the points to be studied and maximizing their benefit (e.g., drawing up an inventory of in-depth work to be accomplished, selecting an operating method to accomplish it).

This type of individual assistance also provides the occasion to help project leaders to develop personally, within the context of the collective project and their own methods of work (e.g., time management, communication-coordination-cooperation. Thus, in a certain sense, project development is continued and fine-tuned during the implementation phase.

IMPLEMENTATION CHALLENGES

The main implementation difficulties deal with discrepancies in scheduling and the content of the project itself. A major problem at this stage is the risk of "going astray" time-wise in preparing actions and carrying them out. In some rare, yet pathetically spectacular cases, up to eight months were wasted between the end of the project phase and the beginning of implementation preparation, which can obviously have a disastrous impact on implementation effectiveness and efficiency. As a way of attempting to control this problem, the intervention agreement should include a provisional schedule, rigorously negotiated and annexed to the contract, which can significantly reduce such implementation delays.

A related problem is that certain enterprises consider the presence of the external interveners as no longer important during the implementation phase. Drawing on our experience, however, in these cases when we returned to the enterprise following implementation, we observed that the implementation had been carried out without synchronization of the different actions, which is a major factor of failure or reduction of the action's impact. When ISEOR has taken part in implementation, its intervention is much lighter, but extends over a longer period, approximately two days per month.

In terms of scheduling, it is important to *actually do* the scheduling (which is far from being standard business practice) and ensure its *follow-up*, thus enabling regular adjustments to the calendar. It is also important to *inform* the personnel about the schedule and its periodical adjustments. While these three guidelines might appear to be common sense, our experience has shown that they are not necessarily common practice.

As for *discrepancies in project content*, there appear to be two basic types. In some cases, we observed that project leaders, feeling too "pushed" by focus groups, did not actually adhere to the project. In essence, they were not convinced *a priori* of its efficacy or feasibility. As a result, the project leader was inevitably little inclined to implement it. When this occurs, the project leader must be "guided," with the support of his or her hierarchical superiors and personnel, to change his or her position, potentially adapting certain aspects of the project if necessary. A second type case comes from the difficulties encountered during implementation, which were underestimated during the project stage. This second case, more frequent and simpler than the first case, requires modifying the project, with support from the steering committee, for example, by staggering actions over longer periods of time. Professional experience has shown that firms often find it difficult to actually implement the carefully planned projects they have designed.

Our research and experimentation have convinced us that the breadth and swiftness with which the results appear through innovative action are increased when *actions are conducted methodically*, following a rigorous schedule, carefully prepared with the various actors directly concerned by the action and periodically reactivated through *stimulation techniques* based on a strategy of information, communication, attentive piloting and intermediary evaluation (e.g., inventory of concrete actions actually accomplished; evaluation, or even partial evaluation of results). Pilot actions have shown that *time* and *resources* invested in the quality of implementation are quickly self-financed thanks to the more rapid reduction of hidden costs.

The audited implementation method perfected at ISEOR not only includes operational techniques; it is also based on the *scientific principles* that we have acquired from evaluations of our numerous experiments. These assessments revealed the existence of *flexible yet relatively stable rules*, notably regarding the effectiveness of *rhythms* for conducting change actions.

The Role of Internal Interveners

In order to perpetuate implementation actions, the tools and methods implanted in the organization, as well as alleviate intervention costs (in terms of time and money), ISEOR systemically trains internal interveners and has done so since 1987 (for an overview of the extensiveness of these programs, see Buono & Savall, 2007). These individuals are employees who, owing to their organizational function (e.g., Human Resources) or out of personal motivation, invest themselves in the transformation project of their organization. These employees are thus involved at two levels of the intervention process: a) as company actors, taking part in diagnostics, projects and collaborative training clusters; and b) as internal interveners, receiving additional intensive training on the intervention method (process and content).[2] They thus become capable of taking charge, following a progressive integration plan, of part of the intervention alongside ISEOR interveners (during the first phase), and ultimately with complete autonomy in specified micro-spaces (services, departments, subsidiaries).

In application of the synchronization principle of socio-economic intervention, internal interveners participate in all communication-coordination-cooperation meetings of the intervention team. In addition to their function of perpetuating the intervention and alleviating its cost, as mentioned above, internal interveners largely contribute to acclimatize the intervention in the enterprise. Thus, they may be in charge of adapting training documents or internal communication, in order to reduce the "cultural shock" that can be induced by external intervention in a firm. As years go by, these internal interveners remain the link and privileged relay for all "clean-up" actions undertaken by the ISEOR or additional training in socio-economic management.

NOTES

1. The economic evaluation of hidden cost reduction was presented in Chapters 2 and 3.
2. Several training seminars on the consultant role are organized every year by the ISEOR. These seminars include four 2½ day sessions, long spread out over 6 months and are open to senior managers, middle managers, internal consultants, professional consultants, experts and instructors who wish to learn the methods and tools for piloting change. More than one thousand participants have attended these training seminars since their creation in 1987.

REFERENCES

Bonnet, M. (1980). *Evaluation socio-économique d'une restructuration des emplois avec formation intégrée dans une usine de verrerie* [Socio-economic evaluation of job restructuring in a glassworks factory]. ISEOR Report, under the direction of H. Savall. Ecully, France: ISEOR.

Buono, A.F., & Savall, H. (Eds.) (2007). *Socio-economic intervention in organizations: The intervener-researcher and the SEAM approach to organizational analysis.* Charlotte, NC: Information Age Publishing.

PART III

TWO TOOLS
FOR THE CUSTOMIZED
MANAGEMENT OF THE ENTERPRISE

CHAPTER 8

SOCIO-ECONOMIC MANAGEMENT, HIDDEN COSTS, AND THE PERIODICALLY NEGOTIABLE ACTIVITY CONTRACT

Socio-economic management, which can be viewed as an overall approach to business management, is founded on the development of human potential as the fundamental lever of economic performance. It follows ipso facto that a certain a priori confidence in the capacity of actors to develop their potential is the indispensable condition for introducing socio-economic management into an enterprise.

The fundamental hypothesis of socio-economic analysis considers that improvement of a firm's economic performance is made possible, without new external financial resources, by enhanced interaction between the company's structures and its human behaviors. As suggested in Chapter 5, the rationale underlying this position lies in:

- Confidence in people, in their capacity for personal growth;
- Confidence in the capacity of human beings to develop their inter-individual relations with a view toward improving collective effectiveness;

Mastering Hidden Costs and Socio-Economic Performance, pages 201–254
Copyright © 2008 by Information Age Publishing
201

- Confidence in the capability of people to influence work structures, modifying them necessarily despite the magnitude and difficulty of this task; and
- Confidence in the organization's capacity to follow through on these changes, with the intent of improved economic performance for the enterprise.

It is realized, of course, that there are barriers that can prevent certain actors from influencing such progress at any point in time. This is why socio-economic theory considers that conflict management, under its various forms (e.g., tension, covert conflict, overt conflict), is at the heart of business management.

The human actor is at the core of socio-economic analysis and management. The fundamental hypothesis is that every individual is capable *under certain conditions* to grow and develop—in terms of both his or her own progress and the progress of the organization. We have endeavored to discover these conditions for more than 30 years through experimentation-research programs at the Socio-Economic Institute of Firms and Organizations (ISE-OR) (for an extensive overview of this approach and its application see Buono & Savall, 2007).

The individual, in his or her professional situation, can be analyzed through the lens of several complementary grids of analysis that capture: personal statements, discourses and professional practices; competence, know-how (whether it be technical or managerial) and related behaviors; and individual behavior with regard to relations with others (e.g., hierarchical relations or transversal relations with colleagues in the same department or between departments).

The principle of integration led ISEOR researchers to a new principle formulated as follows: the ability to synchronize actions in a firm is a fundamental factor of effectiveness. Priority was thus placed on developing tools that could help to integrate the multiple dimensions that traverse the phenomenological field of management. Such research findings, upheld as principles of action, would enable enhanced synchronization of company practices and thus improve company performance.

The socio-economic theory of organizations focused on two innovative concepts of management: the fundamental theoretical concept of SIOF-HIS, and the operational tool PNAC, the *periodically negotiable activity contract*. The "SIOFHIS degree" (*humanly integrated and stimulating system of operational and functional information*) of an enterprise designates the capacity of that organization to stimulate effective behavior among its members, in order to attain the enterprise's collective objectives. This is an innovative concept in that it places psychological and sociological considerations at the very core of the information system, whose quality and effectiveness are consequently measured in terms of its real impact on the actual behavior of the organization's actors or agents. The SIOFHIS concept is a good illustration of the integration principle and the synchronization principle, because it represents a scale model of the entire socio-economic theory, which explains the mechanisms and sources of economic and social performance in organizations. In socio-economic theory, theoretical elements do not follow traditional management segmentation criteria founded, grosso modo, on the clear differentiation among company functions (e.g., sales, production, finance, administration) and among their respective employees (both individuals and groups of individuals). As illustrated in Figure 8.1, this theory cuts across the traditional domains of management and is holistic and multidimensional.

The effectiveness of a firm depends on three fundamental factors: its *SIOFHIS*, its *synchronization* and its *cleaning-up* practices. The SIOFHIS concept, which is a condensed version of the theory of socio-economic management, focuses on synchronizing actions, the primordial source of ef-

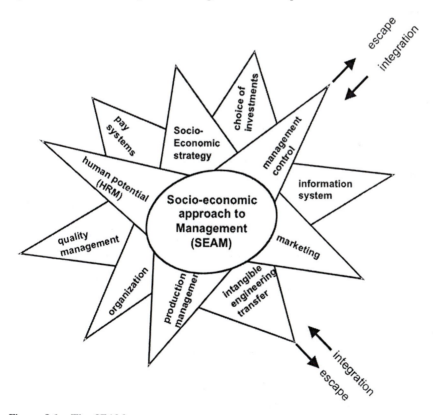

Figure 8.1   The SEAM star.

fectiveness and performance. *Cleaning-up* constitutes a secondary source of effectiveness and performance. It designates the periodical examination and revision of objectives, priority actions, procedures and company organization. Depending on the needs and the nature of problems, cleaning-up should be performed at regular intervals ranging from a week to a semi-annual basis. This assessment is indispensable because every enterprise is affected by "pollution" phenomena—from a loss of human responsiveness and volatile shifts in the environment, to changes in company strategy and so forth.

After having identified the essential factor(s) for performance (SIOF-HIS), the next step, as with therapeutic remedies, is to construct a technology capable of "curing" the diagnosed malady: in other words, making it possible for organizational members to *sustain* the ability of their organization to increase its performance by decreasing its *reducible dysfunctions*. One such tool is the periodically negotiable activity contract (PNAC), created in 1977 and perfected through extensive experimentation carried out by ISEOR researchers. It is a simple, operational method that enables a firm to simultaneously (synchronization principle) manage different problems and attain economic and social objectives in a coordinated way.

Socio-economic theory is based on the concept of dysfunction, perceived as a result of the informal powers of resistance that actors interacting with work structures possess. Such dysfunction has economic consequences, referred to as "hidden costs" which damage the company's overall economic performance. These costs are said to be "hidden" because they generally do not appear in the firm's information systems (e.g., accounting, budgets, logbooks). They are partially reducible through innovative socio-economic actions, as the many experiments conducted in businesses by the ISEOR have shown (see Chapter 5).

Let us suppose that a firm has determined its major hidden costs and has set the overall objective of reducing these hidden costs as part of its strategic framework. As we will explore in the next section, through the use of Periodically Negotiable Activity Contracts (PNACs), the firm can then set personnel objectives so that *overall economic savings* from reduced hidden costs *finance the salary rewards* offered in the PNACs and *generate adequate surplus to self-finance investments and to improve the competitive advantage of the firm's product's* (goods, services).

THE PERIODICALLY NEGOTIABLE ACTIVITY CONTRACT

Within a company, the PNAC is a "game" with explicit rules designed to regulate the professional relationships over a given period (e.g., semi-annual) between each individual in the enterprise and his or her hierarchical superior. The underlying focus is to stimulate both short-term and long-term productivity improvements through direct dialogue (called negotiation) between two consecutive hierarchical levels. In essence, the PNAC is composed of a selection of several individual and collective priority activity objectives (less than 10) for a limited period (6 months) in application of the company's dysfunction diagnostic (sources of hidden costs) and of the company's pluriannual strategic plan. The PNACs of a particular unit (service, department, workshop) are coordinated in a decentralized piloting logbook, enabling management to co-pilot all activities within that unit. This logbook is, in turn, coordinated into executive management's piloting logbook.

The PNAC has proven to be an excellent incentive for organizational members, because it clearly stipulates in advance (at the beginning of the period) the improvement objectives for performance and operating quality, the carefully studied means allotted, and the rules for evaluating the results at the end of the period, as well as the levels of additional salary granted based on each individual's attained results. This *synchronization a priori* of the elements that are usually disconnected in the firm's observed operations produces stimuli on productive behavior and triggers enhanced performance in the forms of lower overhead and higher production.

At the end of the period, the evaluation of past results coincides with the preparation of the next period's PNAC. With each new period (milestone), the rules of the PNAC game (e.g., objectives, means, evaluation, fringe benefits) may be slightly different since they are adapted to fit the environment (strategic analysis), overall company results, and each unit's results (service, agency, workshop), as well as in the learning curve of actors who progressively learn to "play" better and consequently are better positioned to influence PNAC content.

The PNAC is, thus, a tool of strategic implementation, operations control and human resource management. It facilitates the ability to undertake multiple synchronizations of company activities, which contributes to enhanced performance, as ISEOR experimentation in firms has demonstrated. *Multiple synchronizations* allow the organization to focus on objectives and means, the different levels of hierarchical responsibility and different units in the enterprise. Synchronization is performed both during the initial PNAC implementation (intervention phase) and during its institutionalization (the permanent operating procedure phase).

The process starts with an emphasis on improving the coordination of various company actors (synchronization of space or human groups). This implementation is done through *collaborative-training* action at the various hierarchical levels representing all company units (services, agencies, workshops). These sessions bring together two or three consecutive levels (e.g., department heads and employees, senior-level management and department heads), facilitating creation of a common language around two major themes: the PNAC "charter" that specifies the company rules of the game and the general framework of *individual wage incentives.*

Synchronization (the source of effectiveness) also results from the co-operation between individual actors and their hierarchical superior. This assessment is performed at the beginning of each period (semi-annually as a general rule) and is conducted according to the following sequence: proposal of PNAC content by the hierarchical superior, discussion with the concerned collaborator, then determination of final content for the period (see Figure 8.2). At the end of the period, the evaluation of attained objectives is completed and related compensation adjustments (bonuses, additional salary) are distributed. The information produced and exchanged during the *evaluation* serves as the basis for preparing the next period's PNAC (see Figure 8.3). The evaluation in t_i (t_{i-1}, t_i) is a *diagnostic* that serves as a basis for the *project* (improvement objectives for activity results) for the following period (t_i, t_{i+1}). In this way, synchronization of different activity periods (temporal synchronization) is achieved.

Experimentation through ISEOR projects has shown that this type of synchronization is effective from a socio-economic point of view because a) organizational members buy into well-coordinated, productive approaches and b) the fine-tuned operational method makes it possible to achieve this synchronization with considerable economy of time and means (principle of economy of information costs). The PNAC was designed as a tool aimed at stimulating productive behavior in all members of the firm, whatever

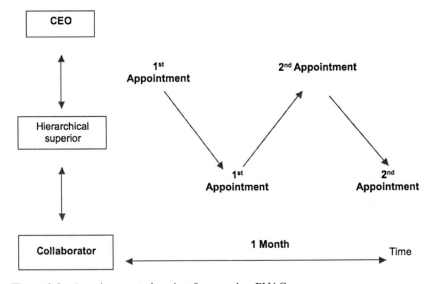

Figure 8.2   Appointment planning for creating PNACs.

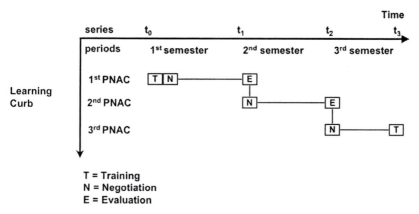

Figure 8.3 PNAC synchronization over time.

their hierarchical level or function. Questions, of course, can be raised about the extent to which this approach is different from other objective assessment systems (e.g., Management by Objectives). The next section focuses on the foundations of the PNAC and what differentiates this approach from other methods.

Foundations of the Periodically Negotiable Activity Contract

The socio-economic theory of organizations[1] considers the enterprise (or units that comprise the enterprise: divisions, departments, services, workshops) as an overall work structure (S) interacting with the behaviors of its members (B). This relationship [S ←→ B] engenders the enterprise's operations, which socio-economic theory breaks down into two groups: a) "properly conducted" operations, or *orthofunctions,* that correspond to the operations expected by the enterprise, and b) *dysfunctions,* which represent phenomena whose effects are contrary to the objectives pursued by the enterprise. Orthofunctions, like dysfunctions, result from the relation between work structures available to individuals or groups and the behaviors of the personnel in work situations. This relationship [S ←→ B] therefore defines, in every enterprise, the activity contract established between the enterprise and its members. This contract, however, is usually informal, insomuch as the terms of the contract have not been clearly stipulated.

The periodically negotiable activity contract is based on the fundamental idea of a *prior agreement* by both parties (personnel and enterprise) on the socio-economic performance to be attained. In this sense, the PNAC constitutes the keystone of *socio-economic management,* the mode of management advocated by the socio-economic theory (see Savall, 1975, 1979). It is designed, through its formal characters, to modify the *conflict-cooperation dialectics* in the organization, enlarging the zone of convergence among actors (e.g., executive directors, management, shopfloor personnel, labor representatives). In principle, the PNAC seallocates part of the informal power of resistance of organizational members, which can cause dysfunctions, by making it formal power. This emphasis creates a foundation for both increasing economic effectiveness and activating people's energy. By aligning personnel behavior with the firm's economic effectiveness, the PNAC has a dual function, serving as a tool for: a) "piloting" the firms, facilitating the implementation of company strategy; and b) managing people, both in terms of a wage incentive system and an operational tool for measuring and increasing personnel participation in company development.

The concept of the PNAC tool is based on the fundamental hypothesis that activating employee energy (increasing work motivation) requires three conditions: a) additional financial reward in exchange for additional performance; b) explicit rules for running the "game," expounded in great detail by both the personnel and the hierarchy, in order to foster effective behavior; and c) some degree of participation on the part of personnel in the implementation of strategic decisions, perhaps even in preparing these decisions or having the confidence to ask one's superior to explain a decision). Within this context, confidence refers to the ability to really talk to one another during the PNAC negotiation and evaluation discussions, making them true dialogues. The PNAC is not restricted to legal or contractual obligations captured during annual interviews; its rationale is embedded in implementation, participation and involvement.

PNACs also permit negotiating contracts with the spirit of *confidence* referred to earlier (e.g., entrusting an organizational member with a task that he or she been awaiting for a long time and agreeing to evaluate progress in six months, focusing on the observable effects of the confidence accorded). Performance improvement contratualization is thus embedded as a source of confidence, for this periodic evaluation permits gradually adjusts both parties' objectives to the other's and to major events that affect them. Mutual obligation, the fundamental value and basic principle of socio-economic management, has proved itself, through our pilot actions, to be a source of fruitful development and a way to regenerate confidence.

The purpose of this chapter is to introduce the fundamental principles of the PNAC, at the drawing-board and evaluation stages (first and second sections), drawing out the impacts that PNAC implementation has on company human resource policy. Based on these principles and the work at ISEOR since 1980, a number of firms have set-up PNACs for themselves. Even if strategic decision making is (or is thought to necessarily remain) the prerogative of senior-level managers, attaining strategic objectives requires information, understanding, and cooperation from organizational members throughout the hierarchy.

The periodically negotiable activity contract (PNAC) is a customized *objectives-means* system (group, team and individual) with wage incentives coupled with a device for biannual dialogue, discussion and resolution. A PNAC requires *confidence* from the start, first in *self-evaluation,* and then in bilateral, hierarchical and transversal *relations:* the face-to-face interview affords the occasion to really listen to one another, making it possible to address delicate, often taboo subjects. As we have found, with ISEOR methodological assistance, organizational members are enabled to raise issues about behaviors that have created dysfunctions. These cases have been addressed in other publications (e.g., Savall & Zardet, 1985) that endeavored to point out the specificities of each PNAC application, in the context of each firm's general policy and human resource policy.

Principles for Creating a PNAC

A PNAC is an agreement between an employee and his or her immediate hierarchical superior. Every employee, whatever his or her job or hierarchical position, can have a PNAC, all the way up to the executive level. This PNAC agreement concerns two items: a) objectives for growth of the individual's effectiveness; and b) counterparts furnished by the enterprise to the individual, both in terms of the *means* necessary to attain the aforementioned objectives (training, organization, information networks, budgets, material resources) and in terms of *additional salary.* The terms of the PNAC, objectives and counterparts, are determined in *precise detail and prior to* the beginning of the PNAC. At the end of the PNAC period, success in attaining objectives is evaluated. This evaluation activates the total, partial or non-payment of the additional salary, depending on the degree of success in attaining objectives.

The notion of *means* necessary for attaining objectives is understood here in the broad sense—it could indicate means *already present* in the enterprise, which might have been forgotten or "ignored" by the concerned person, or that may not be readily available or accessible. Allocating resources in this case would mean mobilizing *existing* resources, a factor of performance improvement. It could also concern, though rarely, additional means of diverse nature—human means (human hours and competencies), technical means (tools, procedures, methods), material, financial, and pedagogical means (training, information). As will be discussed, these supplemental means are "self-financing" in nature, covered by the reduction of *hidden costs* they entail.

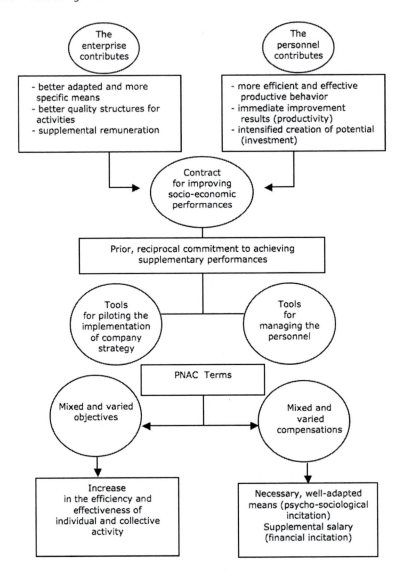

Figure 8.4 The periodically negotiable activity contract.

The PNAC is not a substitute for work contracts, collective agreements or labor laws; rather the PNAC is a complement to them. Indeed, the objectives fixed by the PNAC constitute an *additional effectiveness* requested of an individual in the context of his or her job responsibilities; effectiveness that requires, in principle, an effort or supplemental commitment. In other words, the objectives that are fixed for an individual prior to the implementation of the PNAC (in his or her work contract for example) are not mentioned in the PNAC. The only objectives mentioned are those about which require additional effort and *increased results* beyond the individual employee's usual activities.

The PNAC is said to be *periodical* because it is established for a limited duration *a priori*, determined by the senior management during the implementation of PNACs in the firm. This period, specific for every firm (or at least for every given category of employees), would seem to be best defined by the firm in function of two organizational objectives:

- The duration of PNACs should correspond to segments of the firm's strategic plan, since the objectives fixed in PNACs are inferred from the firm's strategic objectives; and
- the duration should furthermore represent a relevant horizon for the employee who concludes a PNAC, regarding work periods relative to his or her job.

The duration of a PNAC, which should minimally be several months in order to correspond to strategic implementation horizons, should not exceed one year. Indeed, if we refer to the notion of *relevant horizon* for employees, PNACs of six months could be envisaged for blue-collar and white-collar workers whose typical work horizons rarely exceed a week. For managers working in reference to more distant horizons, implementing PNACs can choose yearly assessments.

A PNAC is said to be *negotiable* in the sense that it foresees and organizes adjustment procedures between the individual and his or her immediate manager, before the terms of the PNAC have been agreed upon. However, the adjustment does not concern all terms of the PNAC (see Figure 8.5). Indeed, in all cases, the amount of additional salary is unilaterally fixed across the entire firm by senior-level managers. In the same way, other conditions could be relevant to policy decisions made by key executives, such as the weighting principle for objectives. The document drawn up by the executive directors that summarizes all of these terms and conditions is referred to as the *PNAC chart*.

"Negotiation" between the individual and his or her hierarchical manager should be understood in a different sense than joint consultation: a) the manager presents and comments on the objectives and the corresponding means that he or she proposes; and b) then a discussion is engaged between the two actors, concerning the coherency and feasibility of the objectives and means. At the end of this discussion, either an agreement is reached about the objectives and means or a disagreement subsists, in which case the PNAC becomes a *unilateral proposal* made by the manager to the subordinate. The fixed objectives then become the conditions to be fulfilled by the end of the period by the subordinate to obtain the bonus.

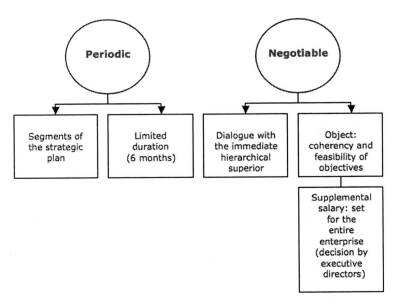

Figure 8.5 Defining the PNAC.

In this case, the PNAC is no longer a reciprocal contract; rather it is a conditional fringe benefit unilaterally proposed by management in an overall framework defined by the organization's senior managers.

This applies also to personnel who reject the PNAC principle. In these cases, objectives are determined by the hierarchical superior. If the concerned person fails to attain them, that individual does not receive the wage reward; if he or she attains them, logically, the wage reward would be given.

As illustrated in Figure 8.6, the PNAC thus constitutes a tool for assessing the appropriateness of assigned objectives and allocated means, as well as the scope and feasibility of the general effort demanded for the period. Within this context, it is important to emphasize the choice of the supervisor for establishing PNACs. Indeed, the socio-economic development solutions proposed by the ISEOR for improving organizational effectiveness are based on the development and strengthening of the piloting role of all management levels in the company, in order to reduce the discrepancies between the company's strategic objectives and their actual implementation. In this spirit, the PNAC was conceived as a concrete means for helping the organization to more effectively guide its strategic planning. Another reason that argues in favor of PNACs being established by supervisors is that this person is best-informed about the real operating practices of the unit and its members. Thus, the objectives that he or she proposes, in terms of effort and means, come from knowledge and insight about the individuals involved and the priority objectives of their unit.

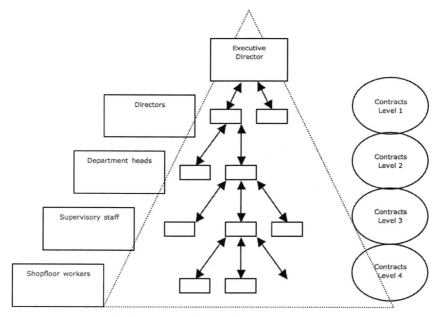

Figure 8.6   The architecture of PNACs.

Priority Action Plans and Internal-External Strategic Plans

The priority objectives of a work unit should come from its priority action plan (PAP). The PNAC is an inventory of actions to be accomplished within a given period, generally on a semi-annual basis, in order to attain the priority objectives. An *action* is distinguished from an objective by three characteristics: it is *understood* by all actors of the unit, it is *concrete*, and it is *planned* (i.e., estimation of time necessary to accomplish it). Two sources make it possible to construct a PAP: a) the firm's strategy and b) the dysfunction diagnostic of the unit.

The firm's strategy, in socio-economic management, is made up of two types of objectives:

- Actions focused on the firm's external environment, which are the expression of the firm's will to act upon its market. These objectives constitute what are referred to as superstructure actions. They are visible, relatively organized and planned by the firm; and
- Actions focused on the firm's internal environment, notably, actions to reduce major dysfunctions. These are infrastructure actions, which can be broken down into six domains: working conditions,

work organization, communication-coordination-cooperation, time management, integrated training and strategic implementation (see Chapter 6 for detailed discussion). The infrastructure usually represents the hidden, non-planned, and poorly organized part of the strategy.

Socio-economic strategy is expressed in an Internal/External Strategic Plan (IESP) for the medium term (pluriannual). The IESP is a socio-economic tool that translates strategic objectives into clusters of actions, which produce an "image" of the firm's desired strategic situation over a 3- to 5-year time-span. The IESP is the instrument that points out which actions must be undertaken to attain the Strategic Plan's objectives. The IESP is two-fold since it: a) reduces dysfunctions in the organization (which constitute a strategic brake); and b) formulates improvement actions (a strategic motor for the firm). The IESP thus describes actions on the firm's internal and external environments. It takes into account the quality of information (*qQFi*) of the selected objectives (see Table 8.1).

The IESP includes three supports: a) a tri-annual table for planning strategic objectives that makes it possible to visualize the time-span for the completion of every objective; b) synoptic tables of strategic objective breakdown; and the breakdown cards of priority actions (see Figure 8.7). Indeed,

TABLE 8.1 Improving the Quality of Information (qQFi) System

	Information		
Characteristics	**Qualitative**	**Quantitative**	**Financial**
Units	Key words	Numbers	Monetary units
Stage of development	1st	2nd	3rd
Quantities available	Very abundant	Abundant	Rare
Properties	• Semantic richness • Adaptability to the object	• Wide variety of possible measures • Semantical stability	• Homogeneous form • Direct measurement of the stakes
Difficulties	• Ambiguity or semantic plurivalence • Versatile or temporal instability	• Heterogeneous • Uncertain aggregation • Uncertain formal synthesis	• Knowledge concerning functions of costs and of performances

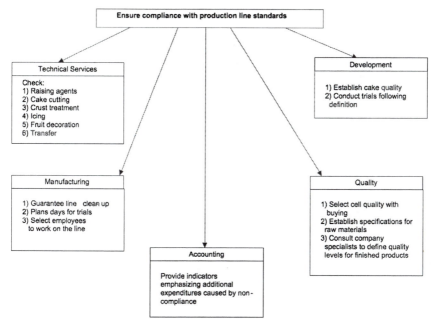

Figure 8.7 Example of one line of a priority action plan breakdown in a bakery.

as an implementation of the decentralization principle of socio-economic management, the IESP is broken down into different PAPs—by company, then by unit. These PAPs are then linked to each individual's PNAC.

As noted above, the IESP time-span is commonly 3- to 5-years, but with yearly updating to respond to new constraints and opportunities generated by the firm's internal and external environment. Figure 8.8 provides an example of an IESP in terms of both formulating (e.g., double productivity in manufacturing and packaging, increase domestic market share, implement an efficient social policy), and planning the firm's strategic objectives.

Constructing Priority Action Plans

As illustrated in Figure 8.9, shifting from an internal/external strategic plan to priority action plans requires several stages: a) objectives are first broken down into actions; b) actions are then cut into bi-annual segments; and c) the time necessary to accomplish actions for the first semester is then planned (time volume estimated) and then programmed (dates scheduled).

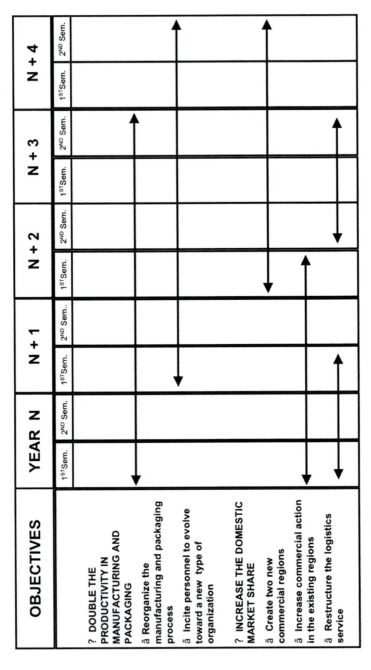

Figure 8.8 Example of an IESP.

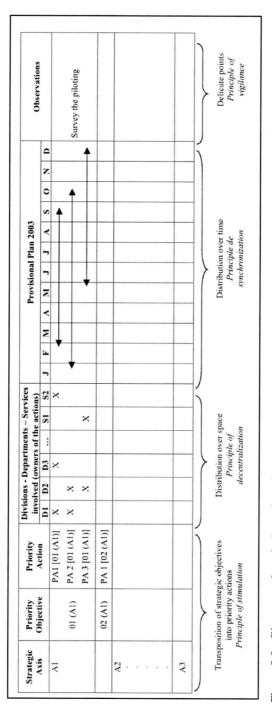

Figure 8.9 Elements of a priority action plan.

This planning is carried out through a synoptic table (see Figure 8.10) that illustrates the four fundamental principles of socio-economic management:

1. *Simulating principle*, translating strategic objectives into actions (see Figure 8.11);
2. *Decentralizing principle*, breaking down these actions into PAPs and then into PNACs;
3. *Synchronizing principle*, ensuring that the actions are distributed over time; and
4. *Vigilance principle*, identifying the points to be kept under surveillance.

The vigilance principle constitutes a test of the PAP's feasibility in terms of time management. This is an essential phase, for a PAP is only valid when it is feasible in terms of the allotted time for the activity, which constitutes the principal resource necessary. The other eventual resources pertain to budgetary procedures, which are usually better structured.

An illustration of a PAP is presented in Figure 8.12. When a unit's PAP is elaborated, it becomes particularly useful to the unit's manager, enabling that person to work out his or her personal plan. Indeed, a manager's time is allocated to both the period's priority actions and everyday management operations.

There are several advantages of this procedure, which has been put into regular practice by several thousand managers in different businesses. First, constructing a PAP enables managers to deal with priorities instead of focusing on emergencies, one after another. It also places the

Strategic axis	Priority objectives	Priority actions
Desired result for the long-term (3 to 5 years or more)	Desired result for the medium-term (approximately <3 years)	Concrete actions to be accomplished during the semester to attain all or part of the objective
Example: Guarantee the perenity of the enterprise	• Develop the human and technical competencies of the executive management team	• Develop grids of competencies • Define and launch a three-year training program, etc.
	• Increase productivity	• Define a development plan for the site, etc.
	• Ensure the preservation and transmission of know-how	• Draw up an inventory • Develop an implementation plan, etc.

Figure 8.10 Synoptic table of strategic objectives breakdown

Priority objectives	Priority actions
1. Obtain greater commitment from personnel in the attainment of production objectives	• Starting in January, set up monthly themes: set monthly objectives and monitor accomplishments in every source of production (e.g., agencies, customer counters, mail).
2. Increase the traffic at Agency Y: go from 12 to 20% average (agency open half a day per week).	• Visit all units with more than 50 employees not yet visited since their opening; gather information about the agency and display information.
3. Attain complete staff versatility at customer counters and a 70% capacity to manage property damage.	• Continue until the end of January 1988 the internal-partner training plan started in September 1987. • Draw up and display a monthly calendar of occasional tasks (3 days per month minimum: cf. grid of skills).
4. Reduce the number of outstanding accounts for production: go from 250 to 100 (intermediate objective for the of the 1st trimester = 150).	• Distribute the outstanding accounts among the following persons. • 10 per day for Ms. X • 15 per week to the other counter staff.
5. Reduce payment delays and increase the rate of closures on claim files.	• Assign 10 claim files per day and per staff member for revision. • Debrief each staff members every week.

Figure 8.11   Working from priority objectives toward priority actions: the case of an insurance agency.

emphasis on *choosing* priority actions when strategic ambitions cannot be satisfied within the available time resources. Second, once completed, a PAP gives executives and managers the courage to refuse certain actions that are not provided for, in order to honor PAP commitments. Finally, a PAP enables making mutual commitments, with internal (e.g., other services or departments, top management) or external (e.g., clients, suppliers) partners about realistic delays and deadlines for accomplishing actions (see Figure 8.13).

Breaking Down a Company's PAP

Constructing a PAP is done following a downward movement, according to the way in which the firm is divided into various department and units (see Figure 8.14). Company "pilots" (i.e., manager or supervisor responsible for a unit) prepare their PAPs, and then consult with their hierarchical manager on the priorities and choices to be made. However, this top-down procedure makes room for local actions. Every PAP should contain local

Strategic axes	Priority objectives	Priority actions	D	G	M	G	S	D	B	X	A	M	A	M	J	J	A	S
Improve service to users	Reorganize the interface between IT service/users	Define and implement a welcome service:																	
		• special telephone n°			X	X	X	X	X										
		• formalize requests			X	X	X	X	X										
		• follow-up on requests		X															
		• establish a diagnostic	X	X															
	Inform users	Present the new service structure	X	X															
		Inform users with regular work-in progress reports																	
		Monitor IT usage indicators by profit centers		X	X														
	Train users	Instruct in printer and keyboard usage			X	X	X												
		Test development and maintenance before launching the service				X	X												
		Train database users					X												
	Improve internal teamwork	Define a piloting indicator logbook	X	X															
		Up-date the budget in function of the new PAP	X	X															

Figure 8.12 Excerpt of a priority action plan (PAP) for the director of IT services in a firm with 1000 employees.

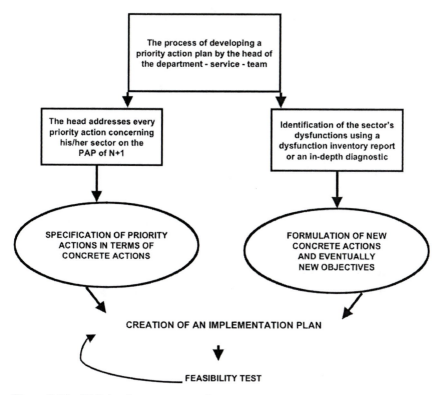

Figure 8.13 PAP development procedures.

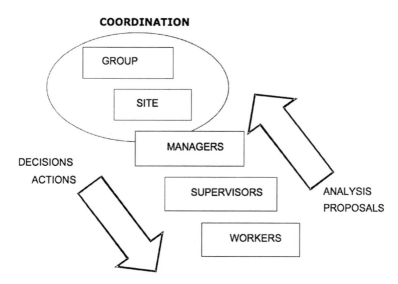

Figure 8.14 Preparation of a PAP.

diagnostics and local projects (for either development or dysfunction reduction). As the following illustration indicates, these insertions fall within the specific province of each local pilot.

Drawing on our case studies, in a company with 450 employees, the PAP breakdown began with 4 strategic objectives for the coming 3-year period. The breakdown discerned 800 priority actions to be performed by the firm's internal service sectors (see Figure 8.15). Progressing from the priority actions at the company level (56 actions in this example) to the priority actions at the service level (252 actions), then to the priority actions for each local sector (800 actions), is necessary for actions to become a reality at each consecutive level. This process also enables the organization's managers to draw up precise plans. As illustrated in Figure 8.16, one line of company priority actions could thus be broken down into 15 lines distributed among the PAPs of the 5 services responsible for performing company priority actions. Another illustration of this type of progressive breakdown is presented in Figure 8.17.

Breaking down PAPs in this manner leads to more rigorous coordination. In this sense, the PAP is a real tool for cooperating and contracting between services or units (like PNACs between individuals). Every communication-coordination-cooperation device becomes an occasion for this cooperation, as Figure 8.18 illustrates.

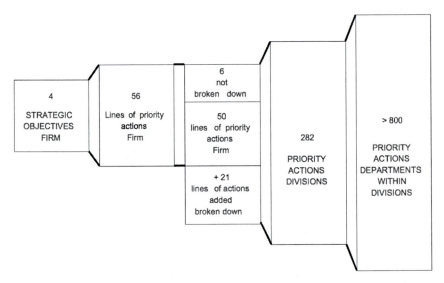

Figure 8.15 Breaking-down priority actions: the case of a metallurgy enterprise.

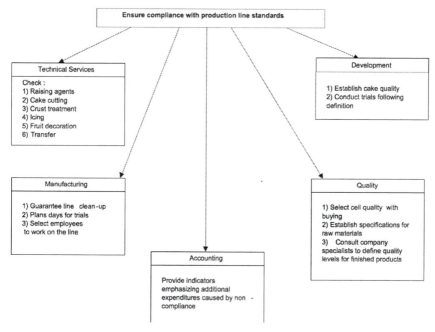

Figure 8.16   Example of one line of a PAP breakdown.

OBJECTIVE: *"lower the production costs of the product line"*

1. Ensure compliance with line standards

2. Control materials and processes

3. Analyze operating time

4. Train the personnel

5. Manage the discrepancies

Figure 8.17   Example of a factory objective breakdown.

Points of Special Attention in Developing a PAP

It is necessary to identify comprehensible, concrete actions that are coherent with the objective to which they are linked. Expressing them should be a stimulating exercise, in essence, finding verbs to illustrate the action. Furthermore, it is important that each action on the PAP for N addressing N-1 be discussed and broken-down in the PAP for N-1. The insertion of local dysfunction reduction and development actions should

People (decision-makers and co-pilots)		Occasions for communication-coordination-concertation (=3c) (collective interfaces)		Cooperation face-to-face bilateral (individual interfaces)
Chief executive officer	CEO	Top Management meetings	TMM	
Top management (ex.: director of a division, department, or branch)	DBD	Industry management meetings or Branch management meetings	INMM BAMM	
Directors of a factory	DF	Factory management meetings	FAMM	Piloting interviews between every superior and each one of his/her collaborators
Managers of a sector	MS	Sector management meetings or Service management meetings (or sector meetings)	SMM SRM	
Managers of a service	MSR			
Supervisors of a service	SS	Supervisor meetings (or service meetings)	SUPM	
Blue-collar workers, white-collar workers and technicians	BWT	Personnel meetings per semester	PEMS	

Figure 8.18   PAP as a tool of cooperation.

be respected at every level, as well as the combination of immediate-result actions and creation-of-potential actions. It is imperative to designate a leader for every action. And finally, the actions selected should be planned and programmed.

Articulating the PAP With Other Socio-Economic Management Tools

For the given period, a half-year for example, three tools—the PAP, PNAC and the piloting indicator logbook (which will be further discussed in Chapter 9)—should be strongly interconnected, because each one works with the others. First, a firm's PAP is subdivided into PAPs for its services. In each department, the PAP makes it possible to prepare the PNAC for the head of the department, by selecting particularly strategic or particularly vulnerable actions that demand special vigilance or highly skilled piloting. The evaluation criteria for these actions are precisely stipulated in the PNAC, for example, in terms of respecting delays or budgets. In completing the PNAC, objectives that are more personal can be added (e.g., personal training, behavior improvement), which may be independent of the PAP.

Second, the PNAC and the PAP are studied to identify the piloting indicators necessary to set up the piloting logbook, in addition to the regular management indicators:

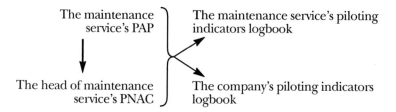

As an example, throughout this period, the unit's piloting indicator logbook is useful for tracking and verifying (i.e., "piloting") the progressive accomplishment of the PAP and of the PNACs of the unit's personnel (see Figure 8.19). The PAP provides structure and facilitates the implementation of the overall strategy, while the PNAC provides stimulation at the individual level (see Figures 8.20 and 8.21). They are complementary to one

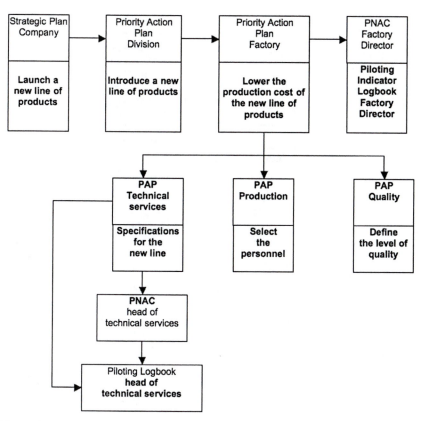

Figure 8.19 Overall linkage of priority actions.

2 Tools of Strategic Implementation

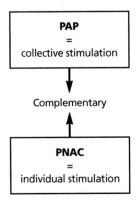

Figure 8.20 Articulation between PAP and PNAC.

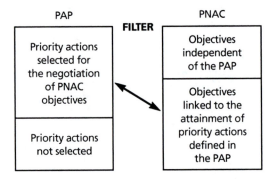

Figure 8.21 The articulation principle.

another. A concrete illustration of the complementary links between these tools is provided in Figure 8.22.

To guarantee a coherent transition from one period to the next, an inventory of accomplished PAP actions is taken at the end of every period. First, this inventory keeps factory personnel informed on actions accomplished over the previous semester. Second, it creates a list of actions that remain to be accomplished. Logically, these actions will be inserted into the next period's PAP, which may be inflected by the emergence of new dysfunctions or by new strategic orientations.

Thus, the manager is well equipped for selecting the objectives where each team member should invest priority effort, in order to attain sufficient economic improvement to self-finance salary rewards. Nevertheless,

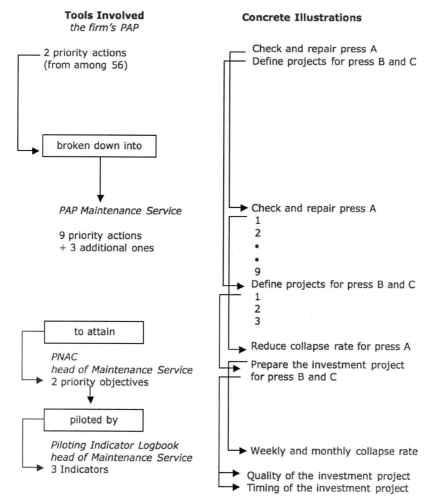

Figure 8.22   Articulation between PAP and PNAC Tools: The piloting indicator logbook—example of a factory.

negotiating with the immediate hierarchical superior (director, service manager, supervisor) supposes a prior overall framework, provided by the PNACs drawn up by the executive management. This overall framework is one of the components of the company's social strategy and, as we shall see, PNACs constitute, by their very principle, a *growth system for the company's net economic improvement.*

The Financial Principle and Economic Effectiveness of the PNAC

The PNAC can be conceptualized as a lever for creating economic surplus, as well as a device for distributing this surplus to the firm and its employees. It is a *self-financing system* in that it does not require additional financial or human means (see Figure 8.23). Using a simple example, we shall attempt to illustrate this self-financing system. It should be remembered that hidden costs, as we have defined and calculated them in numerous firms, are composed both of supplemental *overheads,* which burden the debit side of the firm's profit and loss account (e.g., personnel expenses related to compensation payments for absent personnel), and *non-production* (missed production), which results in a loss of earnings, thus coming under the credit side of the profit and loss account. Non-production results from time diverted

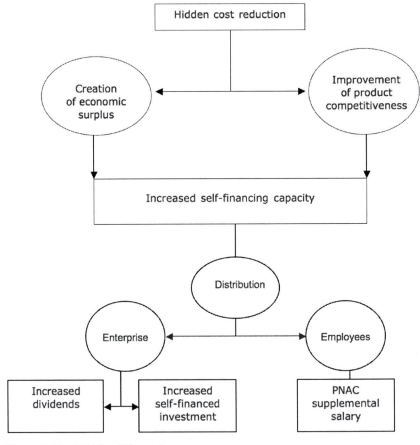

Figure 8.23 PNAC self-financing.

from "proper" production activity, time spent touching up quality defects or non-productive time wasted, for example, during machine breakdowns.

To illustrate the self-financing system of PNACs, let us examine two successive periods: *Year 0* (i.e., year without PNACs) and *Year 1* (year of PNAC implementation).

Year 0
Profit & Loss Account

	Overhead	Products
	100	102
Self-financing Capacity	2	

In *Year 1* (beginning of the year) the firm decides to set up PNACs.

Year 1
Provisional Profit & Loss Account

	Overhead	Products
	96	105
Supplemental Salaries lined to PNACs	1	

This provisional profit and loss account shows that the firm has set the objective of reducing hidden costs by 7, distributed as follows:

- Reduced overheads: 4 (100 – 96)
- Increased products: 3 (105 – 102)

This general objective of the firm is spread out in the different personnel PNACs in successive waves: initially distributed at the level of the firm's various directors, then different services and units, then different sections, and finally shared among individuals (see the discussion on Principles for Determining PNAC Objectives). These PNACs provide for the distribution of salary rewards of 1 if all objectives are attained. The predicted increase in net economic performance thus comes to 6:7 earnings from hidden costs minus 1 for salary rewards.

	Overhead	Products
	97.5	104
Supplemental salaries linked to PNACs	.5	102
Self-financing	6	

The objective of reduced hidden costs was only partially attained:

- Lowered overheads : 2.5 instead of 4,
- increased products : 2 instead of 3

Accordingly, salary rewards were only partially distributed (0.5 instead of 1) since individuals only partially attained their objectives.[2] Hidden cost reduction is thus 4.5; with 0.5 being distributed, net economic performance comes to +4 in comparison with year 0.

This example illustrates one of the important characteristics of PNAC implementation: it appears that the first implementation of PNACs would require the firm to budget the maximum amount of supplemental salaries offered. Indeed, in order to avoid perverting and distorting this device, the objectives set down in the PNAC should be attainable by the personnel if they are to have a truly stimulating effect. Furthermore, since PNACs are "negotiated" directly between the two parties involved, they have a better chance of succeeding. If objectives are attained, the firm thus has every interest, for its own financial security, in having reserved the sums corresponding to the maximal amount of supplemental salaries.

Starting with the second wave of PNACs, this reserve no longer draws on the firm's own equity capital, but is funded by the previous and current net economic performance, by the fraction of non-attributed salary rewards from the first series of contracts (PNAC operating capital). If we refer to the above example, supplemental salaries to be budgeted for the year 2 are self-financed by acquired funds (6) and by the amount not distributed the first year (0.5). It can happen that the firm makes a poor showing for reasons related to its external environment (e.g., commercial circumstances, insolvent clients, money market) while the personnel attains their PNAC objectives.

This phenomenon could be explained by the mode of determining objectives, which we shall study further on. In any event, it appears that supplemental salaries should be paid, firstly, to avoid massive demotivation of personnel faced with playing rules that have not produced the rewards anticipated and justified by the effort exerted; and secondly, because it is logical to consider that the firm's substandard performance would have been worse had the personnel not attained their objectives (see Figure 8.24). Indeed, attaining objectives by the personnel permitted, in this case, to *alleviate the consequences* that unfavorable exterior circumstances had on the firm.

Supplemental Salaries: Amounts and Forms

The amounts and forms of supplemental salaries linked to PNACs are determined by the firm's senior-level managers prior to the implementation of the PNACs (see Figure 8.25). Indeed, one of the fundamental principles of PNACs is *announcing in advance both the objectives* proposed to employees *and the amounts and forms of supplemental salaries* that will be attrib-

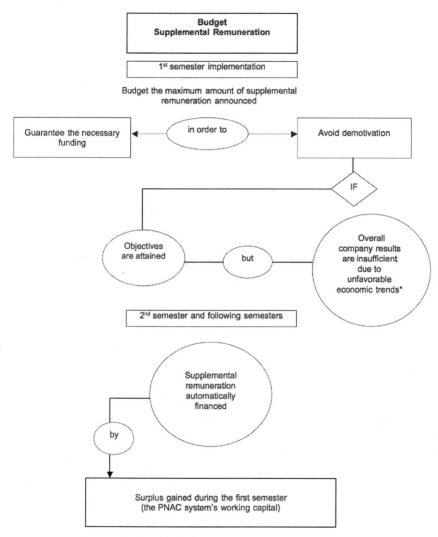

Figure 8.24 Budget of supplemental remuneration.

uted if objectives are attained. To determine a general idea of the sum of supplemental salaries to be linked to PNACs, it appears to us indispensable to determine the *amount* that would be *significant* in relation to current salaries, in order to make them a real incentive. Most of our experiments have shown this amount to be approximately 5 percent of the salary, otherwise stated, one half of a monthly salary per year.

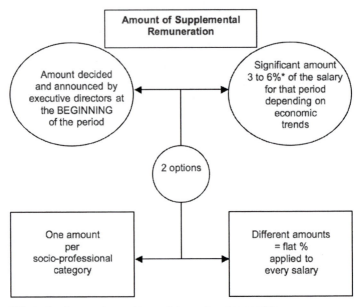

* Illustrative figures: observed in a certain number of companies.

Figure 8.25 Determining the amount of supplemental remuneration.

Furthermore, experimentation showed that it is necessary to avoid supplemental salaries being totally devoid of reference to company hierarchies, because in every case, this provoked blocking on the part of managers. As far as concrete modes of calculation are concerned, several options are possible.

- *Option 1*: A small number is determined (2 to 5 for example) of levels of supplemental salaries corresponding to the principal professional categories (e.g., workers, supervisors, managers).
- *Option 2*: A fixed percentage is applied either to each person's salary or to the coefficient of that person's position, according to whether or not an acute differential between salaries and salary scales exists in the firm.

It also became clear that the forms of these supplemental salaries should be diversified. Indeed, as we shall see further on, a PNAC becomes logically articulated over time to the firm's system of classification and promotion. The different forms could thus be:

- A *bonus*, that is, a sum awarded without a character of automatic repetition. This mode is chosen by firms for the first PNACs;

- A *classification raise* when a person has completed several successive contracts, thus attaining an increased level of competency. This mode consists of augmenting the wage base. It constitutes a ratchet effect, triggered only by the regularity of improved performance results; or
- A *promotion* when the successful completion of several contracts by the same person results in an actual, permanent increase in responsibilities.

Various other modes are also possible, if they correspond to the needs of personnel (e.g., extra vacation, pension units). However, experience has shown that this type of reward *cannot be the only incentive* and that it is better to propose them as options.

These different forms, of course, are not mutually exclusive; they can be complementary to one another. What seems important when a firm is setting up PNACs is that it carefully defines its policy and system of complementary remuneration (see Figure 8.26). For example, according to what criteria can a bonus be replaced by a raise, a promotion or by extra vacation

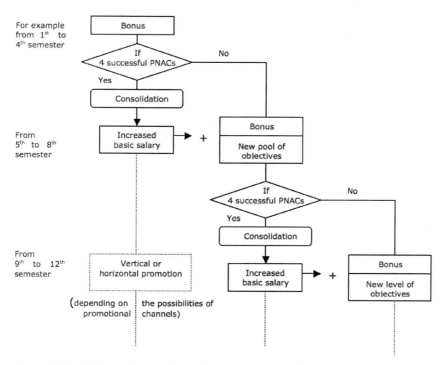

Figure 8.26 Different forms of supplemental remuneration: The case of a service company.

time? As much as the amount, the *form* of supplemental salary should be announced to personnel, to avoid misunderstandings, problems and serious disappointments during PNAC evaluations.

Determining Objectives

What types of objectives should be set for PNACs? How should they be selected? Where should we set our sights? Should objectives be differentiated by weighting principles?

The Nature of Objectives

The first stage in developing a PNAC is selecting the objectives towards which efforts and results will be demanded over the period: should product quality be the priority, or should it be productivity, or the acquisition of new competencies? The choice of objectives represents an especially important stage in setting up the first series of PNACs in the firm. It is then revised, at least partially, with each new contract.

Thus, the PNAC is an eminently flexible and decentralized system that permits choosing the nature and level of objectives *in function of each employee's specificities*. Having said this, it is important to highlight some principles for guiding the selection of objectives, with the goal of avoiding undesirable effects. For example, in order to ensure that the selected objectives permit substantially reducing hidden costs, it is useful to assess, for each individual, *pockets of under-effectiveness* (e.g., high level of absenteeism, major quality defects, insufficient productivity) and their causes (e.g., inadequate job training for the job, lack of interest in the work).

Once these pockets of under-effectiveness have been identified, the selection of several objectives can follow. These objectives should include both immediate and longer-term goals (see Figure 8.27): *immediate result* objectives, that is, in conjunction with cost headings (hidden costs and visible costs) and with the products in the current profit and loss account; and *creation-of-potential* objectives, relative to actions that will have positive effects in subsequent periods (e.g., increased competencies, technological upgrading, preparing new products). If the selected indicators cover both types of objectives, they will better guarantee attaining simultaneously short-term and long-term effectiveness and efficiency. The *number of objectives* selected for the same PNAC also deserves careful attention. Indeed, it has been shown to be indispensable for the number to exceed one sole objective; however, too many objectives runs the risk of having a dissuasive effect on the personnel (caused by too much complexity), concerning the feasibility of attaining objectives, even if the level for each objective is very

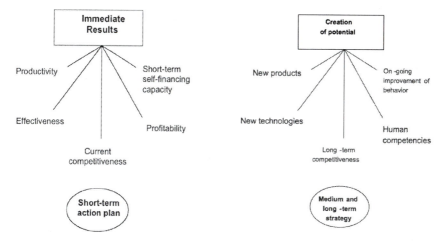

Figure 8.27   The nature of PNAC objectives.

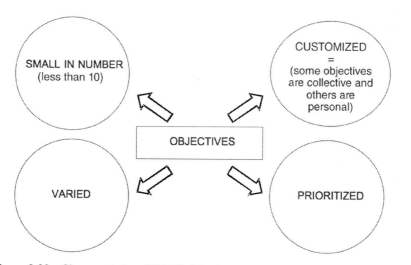

Figure 8.28   Characteristics of PNAC objectives.

modest. We would recommend a number well under 10, especially for rank and file employees.

Let us briefly return to the risk inherent to fixing only one objective. The danger resides in the deterioration of other objectives not stipulated in the PNAC, which might provoke new dysfunctions whose economic effects cancel out the performance attained by the PNAC objective. As an example, it is common knowledge that fixing only objectives related to direct productivity (work performance) incites personnel to neglect product quality. In other words, excessive increase in direct productivity can lead to increased costs linked to quality defects. Similarly, a single immediate performance objective (whether it be quality, productivity, absenteeism) would tend to ignore creation-of-potential targets, which are characterized by being both the most poorly handled and the most critically vital objectives for the firm's long-term economic performance (e.g., strategic investment) (see Figures 8.29 and 8.30).

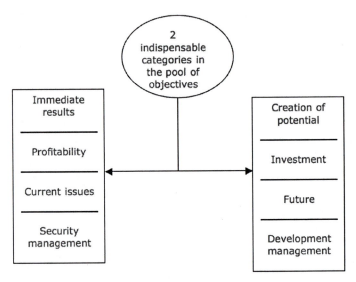

Figure 8.29   The pool of PNAC objectives.

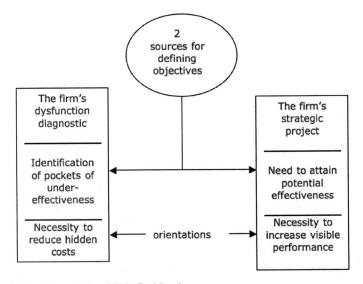

Figure 8.30   The origin of PNAC objectives.

One last factor could also guide the choice of objectives: the *feasibility of measurement*, quantified whenever possible, of the selected objectives. Indeed, the numerous socio-economic diagnostics we have conducted with rank-and-file personnel have shown that doubts are created by too subjective or too qualitative criteria for personnel evaluation. Thus, the reliability of a PNAC is dependent on its *method for measuring the objectives*: a quantified objective whenever possible guarantees greater rigor in the evaluation of attained objectives at the end of the period. Moreover, this supposes that the firm has or is in the process of creating an information system for the selected objectives, thus enabling the selection of PNAC objectives from the strategic piloting logbook. Thus, at the end of the PNAC, the attainment of objectives can be *verified* by examining the strategic piloting logbook.

Levels of objectives

Once the nature of objectives has been determined, the next step is to establish the levels to be attained by the end of the PNAC period. A mechanical approach of equal attribution for a general objective (or fixing an identical level for all persons occupying similar positions) has shown itself to be too discordant with the reality of operations in firms. Indeed, for the same situation, significant disparities can exist among employees in terms of effectiveness, energy, commitment, competencies and so forth.

It therefore seems more relevant to base the level of objectives for a given person, in dialectical fashion, on both the level currently attained by that person and the level expected by the firm (strategic objective). This method makes it possible to take into account the employee's previous efforts as well as specific difficulties linked to the person, his or her job, working conditions, and the individual's history with the firm. For example, in a low-income housing management agency that set up PNACs, the following reasoning was adopted by the top management: one of the agency's strategic objectives was to reduce by 5 percent the number of vacant apartments. This objective was included in the PNAC of the three top managers of delegations (the authority governing the apartment buildings), but each one at a different level:

- Delegation A: 3% reduction, because the level they had attained at the time PNACs were being developed was better than the company average; therefore, the reduction of vacancies appeared more difficult.
- Delegation B: 8% reduction, as the level attained prior to PNACs had been mediocre, making major readjustment an urgent necessity;
- Delegation C: 4% reduction, because the previously attained level was close to the company average and because the delegation had encountered particular problems, which fully justified its difficulty

in reducing the number of vacant apartments (e.g., dilapidated buildings situated in poor neighborhoods with high percentages of immigrant population).

In all three cases, it would be necessary to evaluate whether the objectives could be attained without further specific means. For example, a special building-rehabilitation budget could be allocated for Delegation C, which would be mentioned in the PNAC as part of the means supplied by the firm to the head of that delegation.

Weighting of Objectives

Determining objectives should lead, as we have seen, to the creation of a *pool of objectives* (individual and group). The next question concerns whether these objectives should be weighted or not, that is, be recognized as having different levels of importance in the overall evaluation of the attainment of these objectives that determines the quantity of supplemental salary to be attributed. Two basic options are possible: a) the manager considers that the *sum of all PNAC scores* for each objective attained is equal to the overall score, which makes it possible to determine the overall evaluation level; and b) PNAC objectives are considered as having *different values*. For the latter option, two weighting methods are possible. The first option is to classify objectives according to primary and secondary categories. *Primary objectives or priorities*, which should only be a few in number (between 1 and 4), are those considered to be vital to the firm's strategic implementation (as would be the case for the rate of vacant apartments in the example cited above). The other objectives are called *secondary objectives* because their total or partial non-attainment has less impact on the firm's overall performance.

Every category of objectives is attributed a corresponding weighting coefficient. For example, 8 objectives could be broken down as follows:

2 high priority, primary objectives:

P_1	coefficient	3	
P_1		3	Sub-total 6

6 secondary objectives:

S_1	coefficient	1	
S_2		1	
S_3		1	
S_4		1	
S_5		1	
S_6		1	Sub-total 6

In this example, two choices have been made: a) every priority (P) objective is three times more important than the secondary (S) objectives; and b) the sum of the two priority objectives has the same importance as the sum

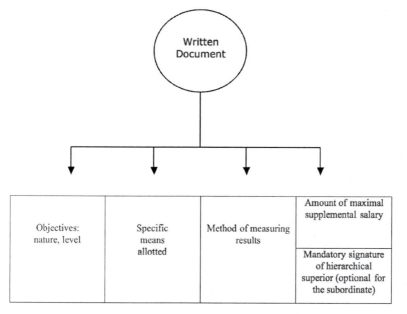

Figure 8.31   Tangible support for the PNAC.

of the six secondary objectives. Stated otherwise, attaining only secondary objectives, to the exclusion of the two primary objectives, activates payment of only half of the supplemental salary.

The *total sum* method has the advantage of being simple and avoiding bargaining on each objective's coefficient during PNAC preparation. Imbalance in the relative weighting of certain objectives is potentially problematic with this method. The use of different *weighting coefficients* attributed to each objective provides a flexible application, but it can have the disadvantage of provoking protracted and complicated discussions on the classification of objectives and their weighting.

Materializing PNACs

Since the goal of the PNAC device is greater transparency and commitment, we strongly recommend that PNACs are laid out in a written document, typically only a few pages in length (2 to 4 pages) (see Figures 8.33). This written document includes all aspects agreed upon in advance by the two parties and constitutes the terms of the PNAC:

- List of the objectives, including their nature and level to be attained at the end of the PNAC;
- Specific means allotted;

PERIODICALLY NEGOTIABLE ACTIVITY CONTRACT

LAST NAME
FIRST NAME
POSITION

TEAM

PERIOD

FROM

TO

CONTRACTING AGREEMENT ON POINTS 1 AND 3

DATE

EMPLOYEE   HIERARCHICAL SUPERIOR

CONCLUSIONS ON CONTRACT EVALUATION

AGREEMENT ON POINT 2

DATE

BONUS AMOUNT ATTRIBUTED

OBSERVATIONS:

3) SUPPLEMENTAL SALARY

3.1 PROVISIONAL MAXIMAL AMOUNT OF BONUS

MONTH OF ACTIVITY	BASIC SALARY	
Month 1		
Month 2		
Month 3		
Month 4		
Month 5		
Month 6		
TOTAL		x at % = €uros

3.2 CALCULATION OF THE ATTRIBUTED BONUS

ATTRIBUTED FRACTION = /3 X = €

TO BE PAID ON DATE:

1) OBJECTIVES SET AND SPECIFIC MEANS ALLOTTED BY THE ENTERPRISE

N°	OBJECTIVE	INDICATOR	CALIBRATION OF FINAL LEVEL			SPECIFIC MEANS ALLOTTED	WEIGHTING %
		INITIAL LEVEL ON DATE	EXPECTED ON DATE				
			3/3	2/3	1/3		
1							%
2							%
3							%
4							%
5							%
6							%
7							%
						TOTAL	100 %

2) OBJECTIVES ATTAINED

LEVEL ATTAINED ON DATE	CONCLUSIONS ON OBJECTIVES ATTAINED	OBSERVATIONS (eventually, causes of discrepancies in the means actually allotted)
Objective N° 1		
Objective N° 2		
Objective N° 3		
Objective N° 4		
Objective N° 5		
Objective N° 6		
Objective N° 7		
	TOTAL OF WEIGHTED COEFFICIENTS	OVERALL EVALUATION RATE (ROUNDED-OFF)

Figure 8.32   Example of a PNAC form.

- The amount and form of the supplemental salary that will be awarded to each individual if all objectives are attained (maximal sum); and
- The scoring method for each objective, mode of overall evaluation (weighting) and method for calculating supplemental salaries distributed in function of overall evaluation.

In the experiments carried out, *it did not appear indispensable to require the subordinate's signature on his/her PNAC*, to avoid suspicion about the impact of PNACs on legal work contracts and to avoid the reticence of rank-and-

Col 1	Objectives set at beginning of the period						Objectives attained at end of the period	
	Col 2	Col 3	Col 4	Col 5: Scoring system[a]			Col 6	Col 7[b]	Col 8
	Nature of objective	Level attained	Weighting	2 positions	3 positions	Mixed	Level attained		
Priority objectives (or primary)	P_1	L_1	k_p	0 or 1	0-1/3-2/3-1	0 or 1	N'_1	2/3	$2/3\ k_p$
	P_2	L_2	k_p	0 or 1		0 or 1	N'_2	1	$1k_p$
	P_i	L_i	k_p	0 or 1		0 or 1	N'_i	13	$1/3\ k_p$
Secondary objectives	S_j	L_j	k_s	0 or 1		0-1/3-2/3-1	N'_j	1	$1\ k_s$
	S_z	L_z	k_s	0 or 1		0-1/3-2/3-1	N'_z	2/3	$2/3\ k_s$
								Total	$xk_p + yk_s$

[a] The 3 sub-columns in Colum 5 represent the 3 scoring system options discussed above.

[b] Actual scoring should be consistent with the selected scoring system (see Column 4). The example here applies to the 4-position system.

Figure 8.33 An example of an overall evaluation of PNAC objectives

file personnel and their official representatives. However, the *indispensable signature of the hierarchical superior* has the advantage of materializing and making credible the firm's prior commitment towards the employee, concerning both the supplemental salary rewarded for personal performance and the means necessary for the realization of objectives.

Evaluating PNACs

Evaluating the PNAC is a crucial activity, for it triggers the payment of supplemental salaries and constitutes a one-on-one debriefing between managers and their subordinates. This dialogue provides the opportunity to assess the results for the period, beyond the sole consideration of salary rewards. The PNAC evaluation principles should be determined and announced *in advance* to personnel, that is, before the beginning of the PNAC.

PNAC evaluation is done at the end of the period. It has become clear to us that a certain amount of cooperation should take place at this time between the immediate hierarchical supervisor and the employee, in the same way as during the PNAC preparation stage. As an example, the procedure could be conducted as follows:

1. The evaluation is prepared by the hierarchical manager;
2. The results are presented to the concerned employee, with an opportunity for feedback and discussion to assess initial observations and reactions;
3. Time is allowed for consideration by both parties, and the hierarchical manager *simultaneously* prepares the new objectives and means (for the next PNAC period) and the evaluation of the terminated PNAC period;
4. Final evaluation by the hierarchical superior and calculation of the supplemental salary to be paid, after listening to the employee's final observations; and finally
5. Presentation of the next PNAC period.

This five-step sequence synchronizes the two individuals and the two periods, which is an essential factor of effectiveness.

Evaluating the Attainment of Objectives
Two stages of the evaluation process should be distinguished: a) the scoring of each objective, one by one; and b) the overall evaluation of the entire pool of objectives, enabling the calculation of the supplemental salary.

Scoring each objective: Several options are possible, with a small number of score levels for each objective:

1. 2-position system: Has the objective been attained (yes or no);
2. 4-position system: Has the objective been attained fully, partially, insufficiently, not at all; and a
3. Mixed system composed of 2-positions for some objective and 4-positions for others. For example, the 2-position system could be applied to high priority objectives, or to qualitative objectives that are more difficult to assess, such as "cooperation with colleagues in the event of justified work overload."

Overall evaluation of objective attainment: After each objective is scored, the next step is weighting the scores in function of the weighting system determined at the beginning of the PNAC period. The sum of the weighted scores produces the overall score (see the calculation below). The score obtained through the addition of the weighted scores (see column 8 Figure 8.33) permits calculating the overall evaluation (O.E.):

$$O.E. = \frac{xk_p + yk_a}{ik_p - (z-i)k_a} \times 100$$

O.E. is thus between 0 and 100%.

The overall evaluation therefore represents a nil (0), partial or total (100) attainment of PNAC objectives. However, O.E. does not determine *ipso facto* the amount of supplemental salary to be paid: instead it is often preferable to avoid over-diversifying supplemental payments by establishing a few O.E. classes that correspond to percentages of supplementary salaries. As an example, this small number of payment levels could be between 3 and 6:

- Level 3 signifies: 0%, 50% or 100% of the supplemental salary;
- Level 4: 0%, 33%, 66%, 100%;
- Level 5: 0%, 25%, 50%, 75%, 100%;
- Level 6: 0%, 20%, 40%, 60%, 80%, 100%.

Figure 8.34 summarizes the respective advantages and disadvantages for each option. Thus, if one were to apply the level 4 (0–33%–66%–100%), a O.E. score of 20 would correspond to a supplemental salary of 1/3 of the amount stipulated in the PNAC, a score of 53 to 2/3, a score of 90 to 100%, and so forth.

Number of levels	3	4	5	6
Echelons (in %)	0 – 50 100	0 – 1/3 2/3 – 100	0 – 25 – 50 75 – 100	0 – 20 – 40 60 – 80 – 100
Advantages	• incites decisive judgment about the objective level actually attained	• avoids the ambiguous center position (50%) • more flexible than the 3-position system	• gives *more* flexibility than the 4-position system	• maximizes flexibility and avoids the central position (50%)
Disadvantages	• risk of inciting the evaluator to frequently assigning the ambiguous central position (50%)	• negligible	• *risk* of provoking *bargaining* on the level to be assigned • risk of inciting the evaluator to frequently assign the *ambiguous* central position (50%)	• *high* risk of provoking *bargaining* on the assigned level: does not incite the evaluator to adopt a clear *position* about the objective level actually attained
Order of preference*	3	1	2	4

Figure 8.34 Comparative table of level options for global PNAC evaluation.

Flexibility in the Scoring System

The scoring system for objectives proposed in Figure 8.33 could be used according to two different perspectives: one of them a "*mechanical*" tendency, and the other allowing for a more *flexible system* with more independence from the hierarchy.

If the firm opts for the "mechanical" calculation, it is enough to arithmetically score the objective (Figure 8.33, column 7) as close as possible to the quotient (the closest value in column 5):

$$\left(\frac{N'}{N} \frac{\text{column } 6}{\text{column } 3} \text{ of the table} \right)$$

If the firm opts for more realism and flexibility, and allows management to use qualitative criteria for evaluating the level of objectives attained, a more *intuitive* framework of evaluation could be set up. One could then

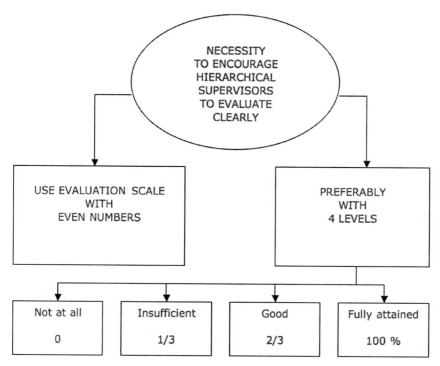

Figure 8.35 Evaluation positioning.

determine that the quotient N'/N, when different from 0 or from 1, does not determine ipso facto the score (column 5) by simple numerical approximation. For certain objectives that are particularly difficult to attain (for example taking into account the means supplied by the firm), a quotient N'/N of 0.75 would be scored 100 and not 2/3 (in the hypothesis of a 4-position scoring system).

The three primary criteria for managing the events that could justify this flexibility are: a) an environmental occurence that diminishes the probability of full attainment of the objective; b) partial or delayed supply by the firm of the particular means stipulated in the PNAC; and c) substantial modifications during the period of strategic implementation: modification of objectives, temporary shift in function.

Objectives not Provided for in the PNAC

When a firm wants to take into consideration objectives that were not identified in the PNAC, but are recognized as consistent with the firm's strategic implementation or introduced by management in the course of the PNAC period to improve strategic implementation (principle of "good initiatives recognized"), two solutions are possible. The first case is when the overall PNAC evaluation does not attain the maximum (100%), but the person attains three other objectives that are *recognized as important* by the organization. If the firm admits the principle of *compensation*, it could score *a posteriori* the three additional objectives, and the overall evaluation could then reach or approximate the complete (100%) objective. This assessment comes down to the consideration that the lack of completion of specified PNAC objectives have been compensated by the supplementary achievements on other objectives—which are judged beneficial for implementing the firm's strategy. The second case is when the overall PNAC evaluation has already attained the maximum (100%). In this situation, the results attained on other objectives could be carried over to the following PNAC, with recourse for a compensation effect. It is important, however, for managers not to *exceed the maximum* provided for in the overall evaluation of the previous period, since the firm does not yet know what hidden costs could be entailed in such over-spending—for other individuals, for other sectors of the firm, or for perhaps even more important company objectives.

Bringing Possible Perverse Effects Into Line

If it is observed that attaining the PNAC objectives over a given period creates dysfunctions in meeting other objectives *not listed* in the PNAC, but that make up part of the employee's job description, managers have two means of action at their disposal:

- *Preventive piloting*: The supervisor's piloting indicator logbook, which is more complete than the PNAC, should alert him or her to the need for rectifying potential conflicts, which should be discussed with the employee; or
- *A posteriori actions*: The next period's PNAC could include, among its primary objectives, the previously unfulfilled objective(s). This action is a way to trigger recovery or provoke a compensation effect, with regard to the current period where the overall evaluation might have been over-evaluated.

Payment of Supplemental Salary

Once the PNAC evaluation has ended, following discussion with the employee, the next step is payment of the supplemental salary. To guarantee the incentive character of PNACs, especially the supplemental salaries, it is important to avoid fragmented payments and any delay between the evaluation and the payment (e.g., during the following month), so that material remuneration for the efforts exerted by organizational members becomes a *concrete reality*. It is also wise to avoid payment of PNAC-based supplemental salaries that coincide with payments of other salary rewards based on different reasoning (e.g., "thirteenth month" payments, participation in the company's profit sharing scheme). This precaution makes it possible to better emphasize the individual performance criteria that preside over the attribution of the PNAC supplemental salary.

The principles of PNAC development and evaluation, which we have just presented in the previous two sections, have allowed us to illustrate the PNAC as a tool for strategic implementation, of course, but also a tool of human resource management. The final section of this chapter turns to the fit between PNAC implementation and the firm's human resource policy.

PNACs AND HUMAN RESOURCE MANAGEMENT SYSTEMS

Different PNACs can be grouped together in a "charter," in essence the PNAC policy framework—a component of the firm's human resource strategy, which should be coherent with the firm's other strategic components. In order for this to happen, there are a number of key elements that should be clarified prior to formulating and implementing the PNAC process:

- *Line of Command,* an organizational diagram of PNAC contracting and scheduling, focusing on the co-contracting pairs in the firm (e.g., the director of a service, the head supervisor, the foreman);
- *Time Frame,* the PNAC periods, focusing on the dates of their beginning and endings;
- *Weighting,* the nature and principles of any weighting for the objectives;
- the amount of *supplemental salaries;* and
- *PNAC evaluation rules,* including the method for calculating the attainment of objectives, the scale of supplemental salary payment, articulation between the PNAC evaluation and the negotiation of the next one.

Several other aspects should also be progressively clarified by the end of the second or third series of PNACs. It is important to secure the successful resolution of issues, such as classification, basic remuneration and promotion acquired through the first few PNACs, as well as choosing whether to maintain, adapt or even discard other personnel assessment tools.

The PNAC, like every tool of business management, is constructed on the hypotheses that constitute the firm's policy base. For example, we have shown how the PNAC is based on the hypothesis that energizing employees is based on three conditions: supplemental salary, explicit "rules of the game," and active participation. In other words, a company that decides to implement PNACs should also be a company that adheres to these hypotheses. The question that immediately arises, therefore, concerns the compatibility between these assumptions and those underlying the firm's human resource (HR) policy and management system. In the event of major incompatibility, experience has shown that it is necessary for the firm to reexamine, reconsider or redefine its current HR policy, without which the PNAC would be seen by organizational members as being incoherent with other tools, which would immediately affect its credibility. In this case, its incentive function would be seriously diminished.

Harmonizing personnel policy can, of course, be done progressively: it is *not a prerequisite* to PNAC implementation. In this case, however, executive directors should announce the precise schedule (approximately one year after the first PNACs) of general HR policy revision. This overall revision of the HR management system, like PNAC implementation itself, should be carried out in the course of regular dealings between upper-level management and company HR representatives (e.g., labor-management committee, HR delegates, union representatives). If the PNAC process is to reach its potential, it has significant implications for the firm's HR policies, especially dealing with salary, classification and promotion, and performance appraisal.

Salary Policy

The implementation of PNACs introduces certain modifications that affect the principles underlying various elements of a company's salary policy (see Figure 8.36). Indeed, if certain elements remain unchanged—for example, basic salary or salary linked to seniority—they can be redefined, modified or even canceled out by the PNAC. This could be the case, for example, with productivity or attendance bonuses and rewards or advances linked to the performance appraisal system.

PNACs constitute an *individual* motivation system, in contrast to other contractual profit-sharing schemes, which are *collective* in nature. Any supplemental salary payments linked to the PNAC are attributed to the individual's performance, while profit-sharing plans are typically attributed to the firm's overall performance. The two types of motivation systems thus correspond to two different types of reasoning, which should co-exist. Additionally, simply replacing a collective motivation system with PNACs could lead to eliminating an important source of negotiation and contribute to unanticipated problems and dysfunctions—in essence the very type of hidden costs the PNAC process is attempting to avoid.

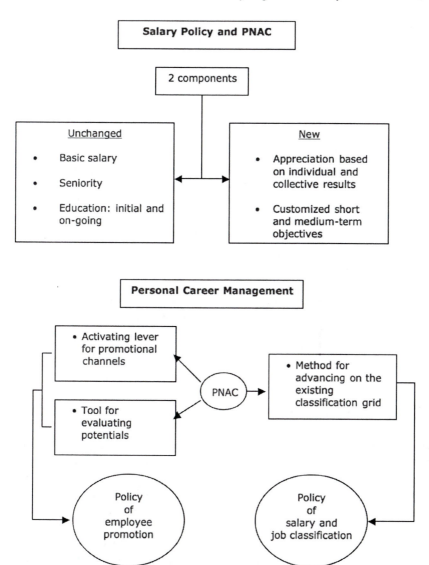

Figure 8.36 PNACs and salary policy.

Job Classification and Promotion Policy

In so far as the objectives set by the PNACs constitute individual effort, the attainment of those objectives, reiterated over the course of several successive PNACs, typically results in an actual evolution of the job held and shaped by the employee (in terms of increases competency, initiative, autonomy, responsibility). These factors represent the criteria that are often taken into account, whenever possible, in job classification systems and efforts to rate company positions.

For the PNAC process to work, it is important to articulate that process within the context of the current classification system, creating a precise scheme (defined by the firm) that links PNACs with the firm's usual practices and its development strategy. Such harmonization becomes indispensable, based on ISEOR's PNAC implementation experience, especially *after the third* PNAC.

In the same spirit, individuals who have successful showings on several PNACs often prefer more rapid career evolution compared to those without such involvement. In this case, PNACs constitute levers for activating promotion, which the firm should be prepared to handle, especially determining the relationship between the PNAC process and promotion: For example, does the firm prefer that PNACs become the sole means of promotion? In this case, the organization could compose a *portfolio* of PNACs for each person, which would constitute a tool for assessing the firm's overall potential and for piloting its evolution. In other instances, firms might prefer, more modestly, that past PNACs become a database on personnel performance, providing management with a flexible decision-aid tool for promotions. Both options are plausible as part of a strategy for improving the firm's socio-economic effectiveness.

Impact on Performance Appraisal Systems

The nature of the criteria used in the performance appraisal process should also be compared with PNAC objectives, in order to avoid incompatibilities and even flagrant inconsistencies. In many of the socio-economic diagnostics carried out by the ISEOR, however, we have found—in all types of organization (industries, profit-making service companies, public service agencies)—that such appraisals often have an exclusively qualitative character, to the point where meaningful assessments are rarely carried out.

Within this context, there are two basic paths for linking PNACs to the performance appraisal process (see Figure 8.37). The first approach is when the company views PNACs as a complement to other assessment criteria. In this case, it is important to guarantee that this complementarity regarding criteria is prolonged by complementarity regarding the impact on salary raises and promotions. A second approach is when the company relies on PNACS as the only tool for assessing personnel, thus avoiding compatibility problems. This second option has the advantage of containing the amount of time spent on personnel assessment, avoiding possible tensions from the co-existence of differing performance appraisal systems.

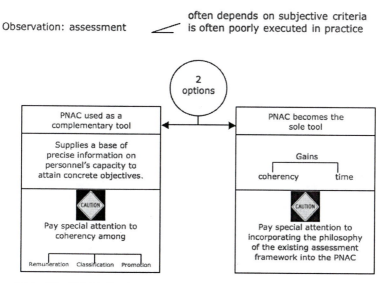

Figure 8.37   The PNAC: Tool for personnel assessment.

CONCLUSION

The PNAC is a management tool that is characterized by its two-fold property of being dynamic and decentralized (see Figure 8.38). For the employee, this property is materialized by its customized pool of objectives, which makes it possible to take into account the employee's personal objectives, his or her career track, and the linkage between the individual's private and professional lifestyle.

For the firm, the PNAC constitutes a tool for nurturing strategic company decisions and imperatives, while revitalizing its human potential. The PNAC is thus a tool of decentralized strategic implementation and follow-up. It fosters responsibility among all levels of personnel categories, particularly those groups of employees that are typically ignored by traditional MBO (management by objectives) initiatives (e.g., blue-collar workers, white-collar workers, supervisors, technicians). PNACs embody annual evaluation interviews while ensuring their orchestration in management and decentralized strategic implementation frameworks. The PNAC tool also contributes to ongoing dialogue, due to its robust managerial characteristics: regular and half-year reviews, diversity of compensation (qualitative and financial), and strong adaptability to the strategic context of the firm or organization. Drawing on ISEOR's long-term experience with this approach, the first companies to have implemented PNACs dating back to 1979 and 1984 are still using this management tool...almost thirty years after the initial interventions.

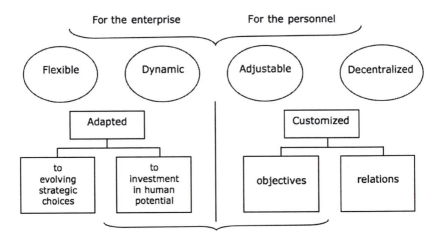

Fostering responsibility of *all* categories of personnel

Figure 8.38 Advantages of the PNAC as an integrated tool.

NOTES

1. This section is based on work by Henri Savall and Véronique Zardet, which has been copyrighted by the INPI (Institut Nationale de Propriété Intellectuelle) since 1985.
2. The ratio chosen for this example between the attained results and the level of supplemental salary awarded is of no particular significance. The amount 1 is merely an indication; generally speaking, the prevailing principle in PNACs for sharing surplus is not a mechanical rule, but rather the notion of threshold of incentive. The relationship between attained results and salary reward levels will be explored more fully later in the chapter.

REFERENCES

Buono, A. F., & Savall, H. (Eds.) (2007). *Socio-Economic intervention in organizations: The intervener-researcher and the SEAM approach to organizational analysis.* Charlotte, NC: Information Age Publishing.

Savall, H. (1975). *Enrichir le travail humain* [Job enrichment]. Paris: Dunod.

Savall, H. (1979). *Reconstructing the Enterprise.* Paris: Dunod.

Savall H., & Zardet V. (1985). *Préparation de la mise en place des contrats d'activité périodiquement négociables: Cas d'une société anonyme de HLM.* [Preparing the implementation of periodically negotiable activity contracts: Case of a low-rent apartment building constructor]. Ecully, France: ISEOR.

APPENDIX

The Appendix contains two examples of PNACs—for an office and industrial worker.

Example of an office employee's Periodically Negotiable Activity Contract

Last Name:
First Name:
Position: Office employee

Period:
From: December 1, 2002
To: May 31, 2003

Contracting agreement on points I and III

November 28, 2002

Employee: Hierarchical Superior :

Conclusion on contract evaluation:
Agreement on point II

Date

Bonus amount attributed* :

* Maximal amount: 300€.

II. Attained Objectives

Level attained			Conclusion on attained objectives	Observations (eventually, causes of discrepancies in the means actually allotted)
0	X			
1/3-2/3	weighting			
3/3	coefficient			

I. Set Objectives

Objective (from 4 to 6)	Indicator at its initial level on December 1, 1990	Indicators at their final levels attained on May 31, 1991			Specific means allotted	Weighting coefficient (10-20-30)
		1/3	2/3	3/3		
Immediate results Resolve litigations on a weekly basis	1 month late	+ 6 litigations in one week	+3 to +5 litigations in one week	0 to +2 litigations in one week	Meeting with the head of the department every Tuesday afternoon	20
Re-distribution of cashier's work	20% of cashier's free time occupied	30% of cashier's free time occupied	65% of cashier's free time occupied	100% of cashier's free time occupied	Allotted cashier's free time. Coordinating file-office entries in cashier's office	20
Creation of potential Train 1 person in data entry and cooperation	2 persons competency grid	1/3 program achieved competency grid updated	2/3 program achieved competency grid updated	3 persons data entry and cooperation	Competency grid _ day per week	30
Behavior Comply with and enforce procedures	non-compliance	from 11 to 15 cases of non-compliance	from 6 to 10 cases of non-compliance	from 0 to 5 cases of non-compliance	Procedures: -storage, -accounting, -safe, -reception, -teller's booth	30

Figure A8.1   An office employee's activity contract.

Types of objectives	Objective-Indicator in Logbook	Allotted Means	Coefficient	Level		Performance Level		Weighting (4 X 8)	Observation (eventually, cause for discrepancies of means actually allotted)
				Beginning level	To be attained	Attained	Score		
	Use of individual protective clothing suited to the workplace – protective glasses, reinforced shoes, etc. 6 checks, 3 of which by the head of the workshop.	All protective clothing necessary + machine security instruction cards	5	3 faults	0 faults = 3 2 faults = 2 >2 faults = 0				
Immediate Results	Compliance with work hours -work at the machine until __:30 o'clock, -from __:30 to __:20 put away and clean up of workstation, -departure from workstation at __:20, -arrival workstation at __:00 + 5 maxi.		5	5 faults	0 faults = 3 2 faults = 2 >2 faults = 0				
	Reading and applying instructions concerning the line. ⋯⋯⋯⋯ Ex: compliance with indicated temperatures, bracings, controls. Modify if necessary, contribute improvements. Workshop technician, supervisor.	Pink Line Job ticket Pyrometer Workshop technician Workshop Supervisor	5	30%	80% = 3 50% = 2 30% = 1 <30% = 0				
Creation of Potential	Multiskilled team, head of the press replaced when he/she is absent. Well-crafted line. Supervisor, workshop technician.	Replacement of person X when absent from the team	5	between 0 and 1	good = 3 fair = 2 passing = 1 refused = 0				

To be filled out at the end of the period

Figure A8.2 Example of an industrial worker's activity contract.

CHAPTER 9

THE STRATEGIC PILOTING
INDICATOR LOGBOOK

Socio-economic diagnostics performed by the ISEOR with management personnel—from top management and middle management to supervisory staff—reveal a specific type of dysfunction for these populations: the strategic implementation dysfunction, that is, the gap between the strategic objectives or the intentions the enterprise sets for itself and the firm's actual achievements. These gaps, often considered as severe by both managers and directors, can concern sales objectives, client and trademark objectives, financial objectives such as cost containment and revenue increases, or social objectives such as increased competency, improved working conditions, and so forth.

Attempts to analyze the source of these strategic implementation gaps lead to highlighting the conditions under which the piloting of the enterprise is exercised. Indeed, strategic piloting, which consists of seeking *compatibility between the enterprise's daily activity and its strategic objectives*, is often judged by managers as being a poorly-performed task. In a typical situation, daily operating tasks and functions and the challenge of dealing with dysfunction problems, consume all of the manager's time, forcing him or her to carry out any development work under, at best, challenging conditions (e.g., hurriedness, long work hours beyond one's regular hours).

Mastering Hidden Costs and Socio-Economic Performance, pages 255–282
Copyright © 2008 by Information Age Publishing
255

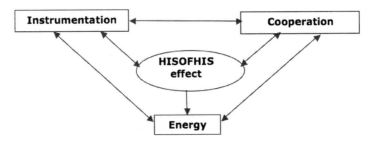

Figure 9.1 The HISOFHIS effect.

Based on our intervention research at ISEOR (Savall, 1983), there are three basic types of actions that are necessary for improving the piloting (strategic management) of enterprises:

- The principle of company energy to "act out" strategy, i.e., implementing strategic decisions;
- The principle of *cooperation*, which communicates the content of strategic decisions to organizational members and is indispensable for the application of strategic decisions; and
- The principle of instrumentation, i.e., utilizing a well-conceived, easy-to-use logbook of strategic piloting indicators.[1]

This chapter, even though it is centered on the principle of instrumentation, will demonstrate the interactions among these three principles of energy, cooperation and instrumentation. These three principles (Zardet, 1985, 1986) work together to trigger what we refer to as the "HISOFHIS effect" (humanly integrated and stimulating systems of operational and functional information systems). The HISOFHIS effect refers to the *accomplishment of efficient management actions driven by information understood and analyzed by the receptors* ("humanly integrated") in reference to the enterprise's strategic objectives. Thus the HISOFHIS effect implies both a piloting logbook and cooperation with other members of the enterprise in putting decisions into action. In order to accomplish this, the piloting logbook applies the principles of composition and utilization that have been mapped out and experimented by the ISEOR in a number of interventions across a wide range of industries and organizations.

DEFINITION OF THE STRATEGIC PILOTING LOGBOOK

The principle of a piloting logbook is to furnish an image of the company's strategic and budgetary decisions, sufficiently detailed, yet simple and pedagogical enough to enable real-time piloting in all circumstances. It is made

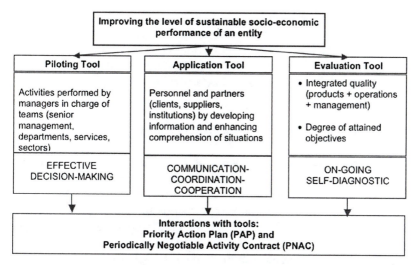

Figure 9.2 Objectives of the strategic piloting logbook.

up of qualitative, quantitative and financial indicators, clearly displayed so as to increase their visibility among all company "co-pilots", (i.e., directors, managers and supervisory staff) and to the entire body of company actors whose activities include numerous micro-piloting decisions

The strategic piloting logbook is based on the notion of *indicators* more than on information per se. An indicator is calculated from a *small amount* of information that is particularly *significant* regarding the enterprise's strategic objectives, and they are regularly updated and analyzed. An indicator is thus an item of information that is particularly charged with meaning for its user.

A *logbook* is a system of indicators, constructed and organized in view of a precise goal: accomplishing the missions and attaining the objectives of its owner. These missions and objectives constitute the filters utilized by the actor for selecting certain information items from the enormous amount of data embedded in an enterprise. An indicator is thus a *warning signal*, calling for decisive action when the alarm system goes off, that is, when a gap is recorded between measured reality and the objective. It can also indicate quality when the indicator notes that the measured reality is in accord with orthofunctioning. The *form* of indicators should therefore be carefully designed and positioned in relation to the objective: piloting is done by comparing the present against the past and the future.

It can be difficult, however, to choose the appropriate form. As an illustration, consider the challenge in selecting an appropriate form for the financial piloting of customer accounts. In order to survey the number of defaults in payments, for example, is it better to choose a) the number of defaulting accounts that attain *X* thousand Euros or b) the ten largest defaulting accounts? In piloting the sales figure, should directors choose volume or financial indicators, or again percentages of progress toward a given objective? It is always necessary to ask oneself what precise objective is being sought and to choose the indicator that will best trigger the alert and the subsequent *decisive piloting action* (HISOFHIS degree).

Who Should Have a Strategic Piloting Logbook?

All company actors face *decisive actions*. All company actors therefore need to rely on indicators, even if they are informal and poorly oriented toward making decisions and taking action. For production-line workers, for example, indicators would be abnormal machine functioning or visible product quality defects. Some indicators have already been humanly integrated through experience and do not require visible formalization. Nonetheless, for certain other indicators, a strategic piloting logbook is very useful, whatever the rank or responsibility of the employee. However, the content and size of piloting logbooks will depend on the employee's job, especially on its complexity. Temporarily formalizing certain indicators that have not yet been integrated can enhance explicit awareness of their effects on company efficiency. During this learning period, the formal indicator functions as a support, which can facilitate: memorization, piloting and transmission of information. In this way, the piloting logbook constitutes a type of *permanent training manual*. After the learning period, the physical support can disappear, be reduced or used at longer intervals, as long as the decisive act that was sustained by the formalized indicator has become an *automatic reflex*.

We have already stated that everyone in the enterprise would benefit from having a piloting logbook. However, given the division of labor practiced in French enterprises, the *managers* should be considered a *priority category*, especially when the enterprise disposes of limited information systems. Indeed, managers are often asked to make decisions based on previous "in-depth" analyses, owing to the complexity of the problems and interactions involved in management concerns. Furthermore, the absence of "living," effective logbooks at the management level often engenders the same phenomenon at the shopfloor or office worker's level. This void also disturbs coordination between workers and directors, due to the absence of substantial information.

Composition and Utilization of the Strategic Piloting Logbook

Strategic piloting is undertaken by the management team, ideally involving everyone who has some degree of responsibility within the enterprise.

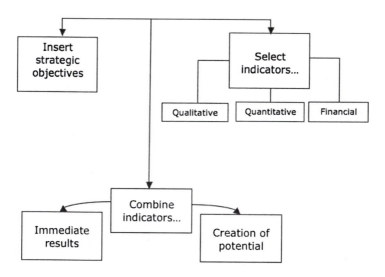

Figure 9.3 Strategic piloting logbook composition principles.

Each one of these managers is made responsible for strategic piloting in his or her zone (division, department, unit, branch). They are therefore considered as *co-pilots* in reference to the enterprise's directors. Thus, all company co-pilots should have a piloting logbook that is adapted to their responsibility in their zone.

The purpose of this section is to emphasize the *common principles* that determine both content and utilization of piloting logbooks (see Figure 9.3), rather than to examine logbooks per responsibility level. These broader principles have served as the basis for implementing logbooks in the different enterprises in which ISEOR contributed its methodological assistance. These cases of application were the objects of experimentation reports (e.g., ISEOR, 1984, 1985), which pointed out logbook specificities in function of the activities and overall policy in the different enterprises.

Inserting Strategic Objectives into the Strategic Piloting Logbook

The piloting logbook is an instrument to help managers pilot their unit (e.g., services, division, enterprise). This means attaining the objectives that were assigned to them by the top management, while at the same time ensuring the daily operations of their units. Piloting logbooks should therefore help co-pilots to understand their zone of responsibility and to constantly analyze their operations, in order to decide on actions that can improve the link between daily operations and strategic objectives.

The selected indicators that compose the piloting logbook should thus be relevant with respect to the strategy chosen by the enterprise. For every co-pilot, the piloting logbook should *explicitly specify the strategic objectives* that have been assigned, whether these are objectives in connection with the enterprise's external strategy (customers, for example) or its internal strategy (toward the personnel). This explicit statement of strategic objectives requires careful choice of indicators as well as their titles. In some cases, this may even entail requiring the top management to clarify its strategy, especially in terms of its strategic implementation.

As an example, let us suppose an enterprise producing goods and services has fixed "improving the image of the company's trademark" as a strategic objective to be progressively attained over several years. Formulated in this manner, this strategic objective stands little chance of actually being attained because it fails to a) identify the actors—individuals or groups— that are expected to contribute to this attainment and b) stipulate what actions the directors intend to take in order to achieve the objective. Thus, as formulated, this objective is of limited use. It is necessary to express in precise terms the concrete actions— even if the list remains open—which the top management wants to embark on to attain this objective. These actions, globally envisaged, constitute the *strategic implementation.* Thus, in this case, in order to improve the image of its trademark, the company might want to reduce its delivery delays, increase the reliability of its products, or customize the relationships between clients and the company. These three options—which can be mutually exclusive or combined—constitute three different sorts of strategic implementation, each one necessitating very different concrete actions and mobilizing different co-pilots. Reducing delivery delays would directly involve production services, packaging and transport, while improving product quality would engage Research and Development, production and quality control services. Thus, in order to improve strategic piloting, it is necessary to precisely identify the *strategic implementation*, which enables the co-pilots who will be directly concerned to include the *operational strategic indicators* into their logbook.

Clarification of the strategic implementation and its coordination are the responsibility of the chief executive officer together with the appropriate hierarchical levels of the enterprise. This is done through coordinated teamwork across the different levels: CEO/top management, top management/department heads, department head/supervisors, supervisors/ technicians, workers and other employees. Thus, continuing the example above, in the case of reducing delivery delays, the operational indicators would be: production time (for production department heads), average time required to move a product through the service (for packaging department heads); and delay between the time the product enters the service and its delivery to the client (for transport department heads).

This example illustrates that there are two types of strategic indicators that enable monitoring the results of strategic implementation actions: a) *local indicators*, or indicators for piloting the specific actions of a unit; and b) *global indicators*, or indicators destined to feed into other logbooks in order to consolidate results at the summit of the hierarchy and create synergy in the company (see Figure 9.4).

Inserting strategic-objective indicators aims to facilitate co-pilot decisions on *daily operational adjustments to the strategy*. In other words, the piloting logbook should permit the co-pilot to analyze all aspects of his/her unit's operations. However, a unit's operations are rarely that simple, and, in most instances, cannot be described or explained by one or two indicators. For example, measuring the production level attained by a unit often requires several productivity indicators (e.g., quantity of products by type of goods or services). Furthermore, in order to explain production levels (in the event of major increase or decrease variations), the co-pilot would probably need to know such factors as absenteeism rates, machine stoppage times, time spent dealing with quality defects, and so forth.

To enable concrete piloting at all times, the piloting logbook should include a *combination of daily operational management and piloting indicators* (short-term), as well as *strategic management and piloting indicators* (medium and long term). This second type of indicator is aimed at piloting the im-

Figure 9.4 Types of strategic indicators.

plementation of the enterprise's strategy, as well as coping with eventual strategic shifts related to evolutions in the environment. Thus, in order for the piloting logbook to be an operational tool for the co-pilot, its content should:

- Include both *immediate-result* indicators and *creation-of-potential* indicators. Immediate-result indicators permit ensuring that the unit *is not regressing*, or that it is maintaining its strategic position; creation-of-potential indicators testify to the enterprise's improved strategic position: they report on the fact that the enterprise *is going forward*, that it is actually preparing its future.
- Reports not only on quantified phenomena (e.g., financial outcomes), but also on more qualitative phenomena, which are often critical in assisting managers in their piloting role.

Combining Immediate-Result and Creation-of-Potential Indicators

Economic performance in an enterprise is defined as the socio-economic analysis of two components: a) immediate results for the period; and b) creation of potential. *Immediate results* are those that directly affect the profit-and-loss statement for the current period. These immediate results are constituted both by the costs supported by the enterprise and by the products it records. Logbooks already in use in enterprises usually display immediate result indicators in the form of visible costs and performance. We propose adding *hidden cost* and *performance indicators* to immediate result indicators. Hidden costs are caused by the dysfunctions an enterprise experiences (Savall, 1975), that is, phenomena whose effects are contrary to the objectives pursued by the enterprise (e.g., absenteeism, quality defects). These indicators detect other results not generally monitored by the enterprise's information system, but which actually affect its profit-and-loss statement. For example, costs incurred by quality defects constitute hidden costs, and, as such, should be monitored through a piloting logbook if the enterprise suspects it has major quality management problems.[2]

Creation of potential refers to the intermediary actions and results whose positive impacts on the profit-and-loss account will not fully and clearly be felt until the coming financial years (see, Figure 9.5). For example, training actions constitute a creation of potential in that the enterprise anticipates that its effects will extend beyond the current financial year regarding quality and productivity improvements. Nevertheless, this same training action will directly affect the operational costs in current financial year (e.g., increased personnel costs) and perhaps even entail a decrease in company revenue through a drop in production.

Immediate Result Indicators	Creation of Potential Indicators
(Final Results)	(Intermediate Results)
1. Number of checks deposited 2. Number of cash operations 3. Number of loans approved 4. Number of stocks and securities deposited 5. Number of accounts opened 6. Number of credit cards 7. Number of salaries domiciled with the bank	8. Number of interviews with business customers 9. Number of interviews with private customers

Figure 9.5 Direct productivity in a bank.

There are four principal reasons for explicitly including creation-of-potential indicators in a strategic indicator logbook:

1. *Creation-of-potential indicators permit explaining part of the immediate results for a given period.* In the case of training action, if creation-of-potential indicators are not included in the logbook, the co-pilot will lack the information necessary to explain, for example, the source of a temporary fall in productivity, or a temporary rise in personnel costs.
2. *Creation-of-potential indicators permit distinguishing between two units whose immediate results seem similar.* From this point of view, a piloting logbook constitutes concrete support for assessing managers regarding the management activities in their units.
3. *Creation-of-potential indicators permit anticipating immediate results for the following period.* They provide information that enables foreseeing future vulnerability or good anticipation reflexes in a unit or an enterprise faced with evolving environments and technologies. This also applies to the enterprise's future strategies. Thus, a training action carried out in Period 1 should logically be detected in Period 2, either through increased direct production or increased quality (e.g., a drop in rejects, waste, customer service returns, delivery delays) or through the production of a new product or service, both internal and external. The nature of the anticipated effects will, of course, depend on the objective or nature of the training action.
4. *Actually displaying creation-of-potential indicators in the logbook works as a strong incentive for management and executive personnel behavior.* We have observed that company actors appreciate the idea of creation-of-potential, which they often equate with their own *personal development.*

Creation-of-potential indicators make it explicit that the enterprise is investing in its human potential, through training and encouraging new activities (e.g., products, methods, technologies). The personnel are thus energized because they are incited to participate both in creation-of-potential actions and in immediate-result improvement actions. This makes it possible to immediately discern what resources are necessary to realize creation-of-potential actions for the future.

Findings from our pilot actions also show a better comprehension of fundamental economic mechanisms among company actors. Strategic piloting logbooks thus have a *double function,* which is both prospective and retrospective, in analyzing the effectiveness of creation-of-potential actions.

To make this second function possible, one should choose sufficiently detailed immediate results indicators that enable co-pilots to establish *cause-and-effect links* between *creation-of-potential actions* and *immediate results.* Indicators should be carefully selected; piloting logbooks developed in several different enterprises show that one cannot be content with measuring immediate results through total costs and products for a given period. These two overall indicators, even though necessary, should be supplemented with indicators relative to specific cost items—visible and hidden—and to specific products. Consequently, a piloting logbook will include a relatively large number of indicators, regardless of the co-pilot's hierarchical position. Experience with piloting logbooks shows that managers typically wind up with between 20 and 40 logbook indicators, and sometimes with as many as 60.[3]

It should be made clear, however, that following up on these indicators should be distributed among appropriate individuals. Thus, the overall logbook is divided into individual logbooks, designed to make entering information very simple. Consequently, the number of indicators monitored by any one person is also relatively small, from one to ten. This makes it possible for the department head to less frequently monitor the entire group of indicators. The frequency can vary from once a week, for all current management indicators, to every three to six months, for strategic management indicators representing long-term objectives.

The number of indicators should not transform the piloting logbook into a bureaucratic tool whose end would deviate from that of providing concrete and effective piloting aid. To avoid this deviation, the management team should assist in *re-formatting indicators that are already in use* but that in practice are used in an irregular or instable fashion, which generates dysfunctions. Inscribing these indicators in the piloting logbook therefore consists of adopting a more methodical practice, which increases effectiveness between the department head and the co-pilot. This greater effectiveness is the result of improved communication-coordination-cooperation, increased work quality, and reduction of poorly-assumed tasks.

Another way to avoid the perverse effects of work overload is to choose an adequate measure for the indicator, that is, a measure that will provide sufficiently enlightening information to assist the co-pilot in analyzing the operations of his or her unit and in making effective decisions. To achieve this, certain logbook indicators could be qualitatively measured, others quantitatively measured and still others financially measured.

Choosing Qualitative, Quantitative and Financial Indicators: The "Qqfi" Principle

One often observes a correlation between the types and units of measurement used in logbooks and the hierarchical and functional levels of the enterprise. For example, the Chief Executive and Financial Director's logbooks might only include financial indicators, whereas production managers' logbooks (especially supervisors' logbooks) are essentially made up of non-monetary quantified indicators. Unfortunately, such disparate indicators can contribute to major difficulties in piloting the enterprise. Co-pilots with only quantified information are typically unaware of the financial consequences of their unit's operations, since they are unfamiliar with relationships between quantities of factors and costs of factors. When logbooks for different functions in the enterprise are heterogeneous and disarticulated, there can be *communication-coordination-cooperation* difficulties within the management team responsible for piloting the enterprise. As a result, there is often a *lack of synchronization* and *insufficient synergy* among the various co-pilots of the enterprise.

The objective pursued through the combination of qualitative, quantitative and financial indicators (as an example, see Figure 9.6) in *every* piloting logbook is three-fold. First, there is better *coordination* of different logbooks, which increases the effectiveness of the enterprise's strategic piloting logbook system. Second, this integrated view develops the *piloting function* at all enterprise levels, through the special impact that financial information has on the behavior of company actors (referred to as the *HISOFHIS effect* discussed earlier). Finally, it counterbalances the *complexity* of numerous indicators by *simplicity* in the measurement methods of those indicators. Indeed, the HISOFHIS effect appears to increase with the simplicity of tools, and it is therefore strongly advisable to periodically simplify tools and measurements, which can be done once indicators trigger "healthy piloting reflexes." These periodic simplifications can, for example, be linked to evaluations of periodically negotiable activity contracts (see Chapter 8), which are carried out every six months (or every year depending on the enterprise).

1- Operating Products
  11-Earnings France
    Compared monthly earnings
    Compared weekly earnings
    Order books
  12-Earnings Export
  13-Gross operating margin
  14-Treasury
    Treasury table
    Bank position
  15-Pricing
    Price per product
2- Operating Costs
  21-Raw materials
    Liquid air expenses
    Manufacturing cost per product
  22-Transportation
    Denrées limousine tariffs
  23-Temporary help
  24-Overtime
    Total overtime hours for year 2000 overall
    Total overtime hours for year 2000 by type of
    hours
  25-Personnel
    Follow-up salary cost per person, contract
3- Quality-Productivity-Delays
  31-HCMVC (Hourly contribution to
    value-added on variable costs)
  32-Hidden cost reduction
  33-Bacteriology-Hygiene
    Hygiene follow-up per type of bacteriology and
    per day
    Surface control
    Statistics of bacteriological results
  34-Product Appearance-Texture-Taste-
    Consistency
  35-Delivery delays-partial delivery-orders
    refused-litigations
    Number of complaints per month and per
    client
    Order book (dysfunctions, delivery delays)
  36-Productivity
    Follow-up production per line and per day
    Certificate of destruction (form)
  37-Breakdown rates-repair delays
    Interview follow-up
4- Material and Immaterial Investments
  41-Markets-Professional Fairs-Order Books
    411- Professional fairs-strategic alert
      Estimation of samples per fair
    412- Catalogues-Commercial documents
    413- Negotiations- Price defense
    414- Security-Dependency on clients
    415- International development
      Export point

42-Human potential
  421- 3C and frameworks
    Activity nomenclature
    Competency grid
  422- Training/multitasking
    Personal training follow-up card
    Training plan
  423- Number of employees-New competency-
    Roles and functions-Job insecurity
    Computer competency grid
    Supervisor job definition card
    Paying suppliers
    Hierarchical group
  424- Working hours – Work scheduling -35 h
    Example of a manufacturing workday
    Personnel scheduling by month and by
    person
    Administrative personnel scheduling
    Example of individual working time pay
  425- Absenteeism/Regulation –
    Accidents/ Job Safety –
    Personnel Turnover/Stability
    Follow-up hours per person and per type
    of hours
    Scheduling of employees per day
    (monthly) and per person
43-Technology-Maintenance-Equipment
  431- Acquisitions – installations
    Follow-up on investments
  432- Computerizing - automating processes
  433- Formalizing know-how –Procedures-
    Operating modes
    Measuring results of cryogen tests
  434- Number of employees – Hours –
    Maintenance competency
44-Products
  441- Research and development
    Catalogue of research and development
    projects
  442- New products
    Activity report
  443- Stocks
  444- Product control – food safety
    Sample testing cost measurement card per
    sample
45-Strategic implementation
  451- Incentive system
  452- Formalizing and breaking down the strategy
    IESP (Internal - external strategic plan)
  453- Information systems
  454- Total quality approach – Quality approach -
    Professionalism
  455- Socio-economic procedure
    Example yellow memo
    Example AIFG (Action item follow-up grid)
    Example meeting resolution sheet
    List internal numbers
    Example of IOS (Itemized operation sheet)

Figure 9.6 Examples of indicator nomenclature: The case of a SME industrial pastry.

Furthermore, the first piloting logbooks should be looked upon as learning tools for *improving decision-making* in view of improving company results. This entails taking stock of all company activity and dysfunction indicators, learning the principles of socio-economic piloting, and creating a training manual for the management team. These first piloting logbooks, which initially tend to be exhaustive, are periodically revised by applying a *value analysis procedure* to them. The only logbook indicators that are maintained are those the management team is still in the phase of learning to monitor and pilot. Conversely, those indicators whose mastery has forged concrete and well-assimilated piloting know-how—in essence, turning them into automatic reflexes—can be eliminated from the formal logbook. These reflex indicators no longer need to be explicitly displayed to trigger efficient piloting actions.

What *criteria* should be taken into consideration when choosing qualitative, quantitative or financial information? This question is not simply an issue of proposing a typology of criteria according to the objectives pursued. One should determine, for each individual enterprise, what type and unit of measurement are most relevant to concrete piloting assistance, based on the company's current information system (see the example in Figure 9.7). This information system should be submitted to a detailed critical analysis,

Internal management	Nature (1)			Support	Issuer	Data entry (2)					Piloting (3)				
	q	Q	F			1	2	3	4	5	1	2	3	4	5
ABSENTEEISM															
-Absenteeism without replacement		X		Schedule		X						X			
-Absenteeism with replacement		X		Schedule	Service leaders	X						X			
for maternity leave		X		schedule		X									
for sick leave		X		Schedule		X									X
PERSONNEL TURNOVER -Rate		X		Personnel status	Service (manual entry)										X
WORK ACCIDENTS -Rate		X		Personnel status	Service										X
QUALITY-PRODUCTIVITY -Number of interventions (operating room)		X		Operating schedule	Service	X						X			X
-Scale of emergency -Number of beds/RN (1), without counting RNs in the operating room		X		(operating room head nurse)	Service	X						X			
+general nurse		X		Schedule	Service							X			
-Analysis of patient discharge chart (care quality)	X			Discharge chart	Director	X		X				X			
-Number of interventions average personnel in the operating room		X		To be created	Service			X				X			
(1) Registered nurse															

Creation of potential	Nature (1)			Support	Issuer	Data entry (2)					Piloting (3)				
	q	Q	F			1	2	3	4	5	1	2	3	4	5
WORKING CONDITIONS															
WORK ORGANIZATION															
COMMUNICATION-COORDINATION-COOPERATION -Number of meetings held with head nurse per month -Attendance of head nurses to meetings (number, quality)		X		Schedule	Service				X				X		
TIME MANAGEMENT -Number of requests to the person in charge for regulation of replacement by the head nurse	X	X		To be created (ex: minutes of the meetings)	Service	X						X			
INTEGRATED TRAINING															
STRATEGIC IMPLEMENTATION		X		To be created	Service	X						X			

(1) q = Qualitative; Q = quantitative; F = financial
(2) 1 = daily; 2 = weekly; 3 = bi-monthly; 4 = monthly; 5 = trimester
(3) 1 = weekly; 2 = monthly; 3 = trimester; 4 = semester; 5 = annually

Figure 9.7 Piloting logbook of a health service establishment.

in order to identify what indicators are lacking and to judge which existing indicators do not work properly.

Qualitative information should be chosen when the cost of producing numeric information (in quantity or monetary units) is judged too high, given the usefulness of that information for piloting purposes. As an example, the personalization of contacts between clients and the enterprise can become the object of qualitative assessment. It may be necessary, however, to limit the qualitative information in a logbook, due to its subjective judgment and because it is relatively difficult to make operational decisions based solely on this type of information.

Quantitative information is useful for monitoring certain phenomena whose cost functions are well known in the enterprise. It can also be useful when the enterprise is just beginning to regularly monitor those phenomena. In this case, the cost of information production is already relatively high and the enterprise can choose to progressively improve its piloting logbooks. For example, in production activities *quantities produced* and *rejection rates* can be sufficient for assessing the level (quantity and quality) of production. But, it could be necessary to fine-tune the indicator by listing the different types of products, or the principal types of rejects.

Finally, *financial* information is necessary for at least three reasons. First, in every enterprise, at least some of the strategic objectives are evaluated in monetary terms. Since the piloting logbook aims to improve consistency between daily activity and strategic objectives, it is logical that logbooks supply financial information. Second, cost functions for certain activities can vary widely from one period to another. In this case, quantitative information lacks sufficient reliability, for example, in the case of changing transportation cost for a team of sales representatives. Finally, as we have already pointed out, financial information provokes special impacts on the behavior of company actors responsible for co-piloting the enterprise. These impacts are materialized through acts aimed at improving economic efficiency in their responsibility areas. Conversely, non-financial information runs the risk of provoking the *erosion of the HISOFHIS effect*, because co-pilots progressively lose sight of the financial impacts of non-financial signals, even if the financial impact constituted shared and stimulating knowledge in the beginning. For example, we have observed that the choices made by the supervisory staff of a factory workshop to regulate absenteeism had very different financial repercussions according to whether the supervisory staff was informed (or not) about the cost of the different modes of regulation it employed.

In the absence of financial information, choices are usually based on habit or convenience. The same person is often asked to replace absent employees, because that person has the reputation of being helpful, or a machine is stopped because of the assumption that this "solution" is the least expensive. However, when hidden cost evaluation is linked to absenteeism, we have been able to demonstrate that the cost of regulation of one day of absence can vary on a ratio of 1 to 5. Conversely, when supervisors are aware of the costs of the main regulations, they are able to take these economic criteria into consideration in their decision-making process, thus making their piloting more profitable.

Qualitative, quantitative and financial information are not mutually exclusive. The same phenomenon can, if the enterprise finds it useful, be identified under the three different forms. As an illustration, the socio-economic evaluation of work accidents can involve all three types of information: qualitative (e.g., good awareness of safety issues among the personnel), quantitative (e.g., 20 work accidents: 10 with sick leave, 10 without sick leave), and financial (e.g., the cost partly generated by work accidents is $19,000: $5,700 employee compensation, $13,300 missed production).

Finally, the form of information can evolve over time, with the on-going effort to simplify the strategic piloting logbook: a) qualitative information can become quantitative to make it more operational, more precise and more incisive; b) quantitative information can become financial for the same reason; and c) financial information can become quantitative when the cost function is well known, or when the usefulness of the information for piloting purposes declines. As an example, a dysfunction can be financially monitored when it corresponds to a major issue for the management team, while the form of assessment could become simply quantitative once the dysfunction is considered resolved. Consequently, piloting would then require less intensity and less financial precision. Figures 9.8 and 9.9 illustrate excerpts of a piloting logbook relative to the indicator "absenteeism," under its financial (Figure 9.8) and qualitative (Figure 9.9) forms.

Constructing a Piloting Logbook

As we have seen, the choice of indicators for a piloting logbook is oriented according to three principles: a) indicators of the *unit's* implementation of strategic objectives, b) immediate result indicators and creation-of-potential indicators with links between them, and c) indicators based on qualitative, quantitative and financial information. The piloting logbook should be developed by the manager of a given responsibility area in conjunction with the *overall architecture* of the enterprise's logbook set up by the CEO and top management. The process should involve that person's manager because such cooperation a) makes it possible to stipulate the strategic and budgetary objectives that are assigned to the co-pilot and b) enables a determination of the global indicators that should appear, under similar headings and forms, in all the enterprise's logbooks in order to consolidate

Elements of cost	Partially reducible absenteeism		Total absenteeism	
	Annual time	Annual cost (€)	Annual time	Annual cost (€)
Cost of absence compensation	6 days	1 000	162 days	26 500
Cost of regulations				
10. reorganization time	$\frac{1}{2}$ hour	7	3 hours	95
11. non-production time			64 hours	1 900
Cost of training by courses				
12. Type 1				
13. Type 2			12 days	640
14. Type 3			15 days	1 440
15. Type 4			45 days	4 850
16. Type 5			60 days	8 550
Total (number of employees: 5)		1 000		44 000
Ratio $\dfrac{\text{Hidden Costs}}{\text{Total Payroll}}$		0.9%		40%
Average cost per person per year		200		8 800

Figure 9.8   Example of a hidden cost grid linked to absenteeism in a department of a telecommunication service company (in 2001 Euros).

indicators at higher levels. This cooperation is thus both "political" (i.e., the will of the CEO and top management) and instrumental (or "technical," a necessity for a well coordinated and synchronized system).

As an illustration, three principal stages of the logbook construction could include the following. Stage 1 would focus emphasis on the co-pilot's strategic objectives both in terms of immediate results and the creation-of-potential. For example, immediate-result objectives could be lowered costs or higher numbers of products or higher profits. Creation-of-potential objectives (or deferred results) could be investments to lower costs (e.g., energy economies, reduction of personnel costs related to absences) or investments in growth and development (e.g., new products, new markets).

Stage 2 would translate these objectives into indicators, that is, creating categories that correspond to concrete, tangible phenomena and determining the mode of measurement (qualitative, quantitative and financial). This stage usually requires that certain objectives be clarified by the CEO and top management in charge of strategic implementation.

Finally, Stage 3 would seek out internal operation and management indicators that have the power to explain the unit's operation. These indica-

Cause of absence / 1982	Illness	Strike	Absence without justification	Sub-total t1	Training	Meetings	Compensation for courses	Employee meetings	Sub-total t2	Family events	Pre-retirement	Missions	Sub-total t3	Total t1+t2+t3	Anticipated days	Legal paid vacation
December 1981	24.5			24.5	2				2				-	26.5	243	26
January 1982	15.5			15.5	4	1			5	-			-	20.5	220	14
February 1982	3			3	4	1			5	2			2	10	200	20.5
March 1982	12			12	4	1			5	3			3	20	230	8
April 1982	12			12	4	1			5	1			1	18	205	37
May 1982	4			4	4	1			5	5			5	14	195	12
June 1982	10			10	8	1			9	1			1	20	220	4.5
July 1982	-			-		1			1	12			12	13	205	40.5
August 1982	-			-		0.5			0.5				-	0.5	210	77
September 1982	-			-		1			1	2			2	3	220	25
October 1982	1			1	9	1			10				-	11	210	0.5
November 1982																
Total	82			82	39	9.5			48.5	26			26	156.5	2358	265
Absenteeism rate	3.47			3.47	1.65	0.4			2.05	1.10			1.10	6.62		

Figure 9.9   Piloting logbook: Example of an absenteeism cause grid for an administrative department of a bank (Unit of measure: one day).

tors should be enhanced with additional indicators relative to phenomena exterior to the responsibility area, coming from other company units and from the external environment that can have an influence on the unit. For example, the quality of the HR department's work depends in part on the transmission of information by other company units concerning absences, vacation and training needs, and so forth. The HR department head could therefore regularly monitor through the logbook information transmission from other departments with the goal of a) explaining eventual deterioration in work quality (delays, errors, etc.) as a *permanent self-diagnostic function* or b) piloting the creation of corrective actions in cooperation with colleagues from other departments as a *co-piloting function*. One of the possible grids of analysis for researching both internal and external management indicators that are capable of explaining the operations of a zone of responsibility could be obtained by drawing up an inventory of the principal dysfunctions that affect it, which should be better mastered or reduced, as well as the determining factors in attaining strategic objectives.

Key questions to ask in constructing a Piloting Logbook include: a) what indicators do I need to make decisions in my zone of responsibility; b) what indicators are useful in reporting to my hierarchical manager; c) what information should I regularly transmit to my subordinates; d) what data is required to respond to the questions of my external partners (other company departments or in the external environment); e) what information should I format to make it more accessible and easier to understand; f) do I need to monitor certain indicators on part of the environment (constraints or opportunities); and g) based on what indicators can I evaluate my actions, and what are evaluations of my actions based on?

Let us suppose, for example, that one of the strategic objectives is the reduction of manufacturing deadlines by X days. If attaining that objective entails implementing actions to reduce absenteeism, increase quality (which calls for training to develop the personnel's competency) and reduce delivery delays and response delays to markets, the piloting logbook could include the indicators summarized in Table 9.1.

Choosing the Monitoring Intervals

Not all indicators need to be monitored at the same interval. A good criterion for choosing the piloting frequency is the possibility to make readjustments before the end of the strategic implementation period. Logbooks we have experimented with include indicators whose piloting intervals vary between one week and three months. The usual period for immediate result indicators (costs and products) is once a month and once every three months for creation-of-potential indicators.

TABLE 9.1   Illustrative Indicators

Indicators	Types of indicators	Measurement[a]		
		Qualitative	Quantitative	Financial
Manufacturing deadline	Immediate results		Number of days	
Absenteeism	Immediate results		Number of days of absence/number of days anticipated	
Quality	Immediate results	Rejection rate		
Competency	Creation of potential	Competency[b] grid		
Training	Creation of potential		Time spent in training	

[a] The measurements given here are merely examples.
[b] See Chapter 5.

The three stages proposed above do not necessarily lead to a fixed pi-loting logbook. Logbooks must remain susceptible to being *adjusted, recti-fied, completed and simplified* whenever it becomes necessary. This is especially the case when *new strategic objectives* are fixed, *new dysfunctions* appear, and indicators require *too much time* to produce information, in light of the in-formation's usefulness. A value analysis procedure should also be applied, retaining the essential information from a functional standpoint while sim-plifying the form and content of these indicators as much as possible.

STRATEGIC PILOTING LOGBOOKS AS A MANAGEMENT-AID SYSTEM

In this first section of this chapter, we have seen that the logbook is a pilot-ing-aid instrument for managers. Taken as a whole, the combination of an enterprise's logbooks constitutes a management-aid system in two respects: a) they constitute a tool for facilitating the actual assumption of responsi-bility by the management team; and b) they represent an instrument for implementing company strategy at all organizational levels including shop-floor and office workers. These two aspects of the piloting logbook lend it a function of coordination between external strategy (e.g., clients, suppliers, external partners, government) and the company's internal strategy, espe-cially in terms of driving and reinforcing management competency.

Facilitating the Assumption of Responsibility

The piloting logbook was not conceived to be the same throughout the enterprise. On the contrary, it was designed to be *adapted* to the activity and objectives of *every unit* in an enterprise. Every unit manager will thus have a specific tool, which can be coordinated with his or her colleagues and hierarchical managers. The tool's purpose is to inform managers about past and current operations of their responsibility area, providing information that will enable them to anticipate future operations, in order to facilitate decision making. The use of piloting logbook thus enables managers to better *define* and *understand* their *area of responsibility* through the use of concrete indicators. For example, strategic indicators in the piloting logbook should correspond to objectives fixed by the board, that is, those indicators which will be used by the board of directors to evaluate the manager. Local indicators constitute primarily a local piloting tool for the manager, situated in his or her field of autonomy and permitting him/her to attain the objectives upon which he/she will be evaluated.

Within this context, the piloting logbook is simultaneously a tool of *individual* and *collective* use. On an individual level, it constitutes a tool for the unit's manager, facilitating the decision-making process within that person's realm of responsibility. Since the logbook also reflects a particular unit's operations, it can be used for piloting *groups of actors*. It enables the top management to hold meetings with managers in various responsibility areas, allowing them to more fully understand the activities involved in that area, based on the information in the logbooks. Logbooks thus also provide support for concerted piloting, referred to as *co-piloting*. Logbooks enable a management team to inform the personnel in their area about operating outcomes and to explain, and perhaps even reflect together on, solutions for modifying operations in the event of a fall in certain indicators. In this sense, it becomes a tool for motivating and energizing, as the information and feedback serve as an effective means of stimulation. From a managerial perspective, the logbook is thus a tool for motivating personnel, a tool that is completed by and can be linked with periodically negotiable activity contracts (as discussed in Chapter 8).

Links with Periodically Negotiable Activity Contracts

As a reminder, activity contracts are agreements concluded between an employee and his or her direct hierarchical manager, based on the fundamental idea of a commitment, on the part of both parties, to attain improved socio-economic performance over a determined period of time defined within a framework prepared by the board for the entire enterprise. Every periodically negotiable activity contract (PNAC) is concluded on two *previously-defined* terms: a) the specific objectives for the improvement of the individual's effectiveness; and b) trade-offs by the enterprise to the individual, both in terms of allotting the means necessary to attain the objectives (e.g., training, structuring, information systems, budget, material means) and providing supplementary salary (i.e., employee profit-sharing scheme based on improved performance resulting from hidden costs reduction).

Managers thus have two tools that are linked together—PNACs and the strategic piloting logbook—to assist in the active management of their personnel. The objectives that are fixed by managers in the PNACs of their personnel can be selected from the indicators of the strategic piloting logbook. The piloting logbook makes it possible to follow the collective evolution (the entire unit), whereas the PNAC is more gauged to reporting on individual performance. For example, if the objective of lowering an individual's absenteeism rate is assigned, the manager would dispose of two supplementary information items: the individual's absenteeism rate and the absenteeism rate of the responsibility area. Since the number of indicators selected in the activity contract should be limited (10 at the most), the piloting logbook permits the manager to detect eventual slippage in indicators that are not in the activity contract, and to engage in preventive actions with the employee. This action could mean, for example, alerting the employee that the attainment of the objectives of his or her activity contract is being achieved to the detriment of other objectives, that while not explicitly mentioned are still part of the employee's job definition.[4]

If the piloting logbook facilitate managers assuming responsibility, piloting decisions are nevertheless still limited by the enterprise's decision-making procedures. Different modes of piloting always co-exist within an enterprise:

- *Autonomous piloting by the manager.* The manager makes and implements a decision alone after analyzing the results of the piloting logbook; the terms "alone" and "autonomous" signify the existence of autonomy of the responsibility area with regard to the rest of the company. However, this so-called autonomous piloting (with reference to hierarchical levels) is often concerted piloting between the manager and his or her collaborators;
- *Concerted piloting.* The manager makes a decision after consulting with colleagues (co-pilots of the same hierarchical level piloting other units, or with his or her hierarchical managers); and
- *Piloting by the next hierarchical level.* After analyzing the results of his or her logbook, the manager informs the hierarchical managers and eventually proposes a piloting action, but the final decision is made by the hierarchical manager. In this case, the manager's role is essentially to alert his or her superiors and request their piloting.

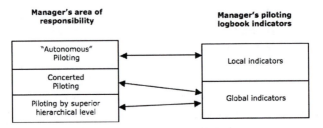

Figure 9.10 Piloting modes and indicators.

A manager's area of responsibility always contains these three modes of piloting, which correspond to dividing logbook indicators into *local indicators* and *global indicators* (see Figure 9.10). Autonomous piloting areas are linked to local indicators, which are specific to the manager. Concerted piloting areas and piloting by upper-management are linked to global indicators, which are common to several piloting logbooks requiring the coordination of the company's various logbooks.

Coordinating the Strategic Piloting Logbook

Coordination of the logbook is carried out in two stages. First, each co-pilot identifies and selects the local indicators that will help in piloting his or her responsibility area within the field of autonomous decisions. Second, all company co-pilots then coordinate and cooperate in selecting the indicators that correspond to the enterprise's strategic objectives. If the enterprise has a clear vision of its strategic objectives at the time the logbook is constructed, the first phase would be a coordinated, cooperative search for strategic indicators. If this is not the case, the procedure is reversed and the coordination of logbooks follows the search for local indicators.

The articulation of piloting logbooks can be separated into two different categories, depending on whether the strategic objectives are assigned to all company units or to one single responsibility area. Strategic objectives that are assigned to all responsibility areas are featured in each co-pilot's logbook (common core principle). These indicators channel feedback up from the lowest hierarchical level and synthesize information into each logbook at the managerial level, all the way up to the CEO's logbook, which displays information *relative to the entire* enterprise. For example, if lowering absenteeism is one of the enterprise's strategic objectives, the rate of absenteeism will be displayed in all logbooks. Information will be collected at the department level (the smallest unit of the enterprise). All department heads transmit their unit's absenteeism rate to their hierarchical managers, who then aggregate the various data and add the absenteeism rate of the group they manage to their own logbooks, and so on. The strategic objectives assigned to all responsibility areas thus require *strict harmonization*, in the operating modes of information collection, processing and transmission.

Strategic objectives that are assigned to only a division (or a *single responsibility area*) are displayed in the piloting logbooks of the other areas concerned. Information relative to these indicators is collected by these different areas and then transmitted to the next hierarchical level, all the way up to the CEO, without that information necessarily undergoing aggregation. This information can be simply reported. For example, if the CEO has fixed the strategic objective of lowering the rate of returned products to the customer complaints department, the indicator "return rate" is displayed in the logbook of the complaints department head, who reports the data to the sales department head, who in turn reports to the CEO. In this case, the return rate would be indicated in all three logbooks. The strategic objectives assigned to certain responsibility areas thus require *harmonization in the choice* of indicators, and in data processing and transmission.

In sum, company piloting logbooks can be coordinated through general strategic indicators and specific indicators. This coordination is consistent both in logbook tools and in co-piloting frameworks (e.g., communication-coordination-cooperation) for transmission and analysis of information and subsequent decision making. Figure 9.11 illustrates the articulation of a company's piloting logbooks

Strategic piloting logbooks thus function as periodic evaluation of collective performance in the company and its units (e.g., divisions, subdivisions, departments). This evaluation is useful for piloting purposes, but also for

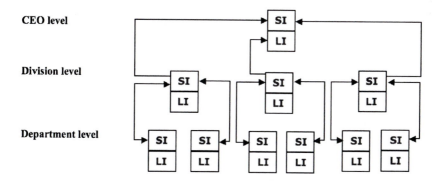

Arrows symbolize information transmission as feedback into logbooks.
SI: strategic indicators (general and specific: utilized at the superior level);
LI: local indicators (utilized in the actual activity area).

Figure 9.11 Articulation of a company's piloting logbooks.

motivating the unit in an informal, simple manner that can result from more or less conscious reflexes prior to decision making. In any case, it should be done before any individual evaluations of the personnel. Indeed, it permits sketching the contours of the general evaluation framework for individual performances. It enables weighting, adjusting and considering collective accomplishments in the assessment of individual accomplishments, which

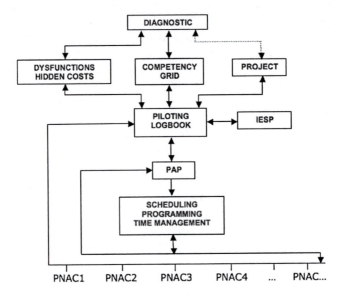

Process for engaging socio-economic intervention

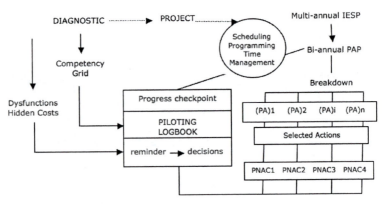

IESP: Internal-External Strategic Plan
PAP: Priority Action Plan
(PA)1: Priority Actions of employee 1
PNAC1: Periodically Negotiable Activity Contract employee

Figure 9.12 Linking socio-economic management tools.

are based on well-documented results. The principal tools of socio-economic management are thus articulated among one another to ensure synchronized management of the enterprise (see Figure 9.12).

The piloting logbook is a management-aid tool, enabling managers to better assume their management and piloting functions, in both the short, medium and long term. In order to effectively fulfill this objective, several directives should preside over the composition of logbooks: a) insertion into all piloting logbooks of the strategic objectives assigned to the responsibility area under consideration; b) articulation of immediate result objectives and creation of potential; and c) joint utilization of qualitative, quantitative and financial measures. These directives leave room for very different and adjustable logbooks, according to the enterprise, but also according to the functions and objectives of the different units that compose it, each one being equipped with its own strategic piloting logbook.

This differentiation implies, consequently, the harmonization and coordination of the enterprise's different logbooks, to ensure good communication-coordination-cooperation among the management team in its mission of strategic piloting of the enterprise.

PILOTING LOGBOOKS AND INTEGRAL QUALITY

The piloting logbook is furthermore a support-tool enabling greater self-controlled management for every member of the enterprise. We have shown (Savall & Zardet, 1992) that mastering hidden costs-performance necessarily requires a high level of commitment on the part of the operational hierarchy. Such commitment can only be attained by radically transforming the role of management controllers, perceived until now as "visible cost compressors," endowing them with a mission of support and assistance toward the operational hierarchy, facilitating better interpretation of economic performance, and most importantly, developing the contributive margin or value-added, either by reducing costs or by augmenting marketable production (see Figure 9.13).

Once again, confidence is the very foundation of these new management control practices: a) confidence, first and foremost, in one's managers (e.g., "Will they succeed in learning these principles? Will they be tempted, consciously or not, to 'falsify' data feedback in logbooks?); and b) confidence in management controllers as part of the hierarchy, beginning with the top management (e.g., "Will they accept transferring part of their duties to the hierarchy and transforming their role becoming more 'advisors' and less 'censors,' a pedagogical role for which they are not typically prepared?).

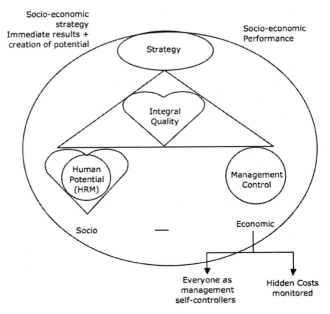

Figure 9.13   Integral quality.

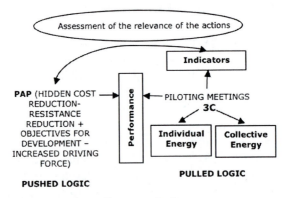

Figure 9.14   Socio-economic performance logic

Our pilot–actions in socio-economic management have demonstrated that this is possible (see Figure 9.14), that this relationship based on the confidence produces results, that it is *efficient* from an economic point of view (assuming it is built progressively and based on a contractual agreement) and *effective* from a social perspective in motivating and energizing organizational members.

NOTES

1. This instrument will be discussed using three slightly different names, each of which corresponds, depending on the context, to the three essential characteristics of the instrument: piloting logbook, strategic piloting logbook and socio-economic logbook.
2. Intervention-research work carried out by ISEOR for more than 30 years in numerous enterprises has shown that if hidden costs are at a high level, they can be contained through socio-economic intervention (see Buono & Savall, 2007). This explains why certain enterprises attempt to fix the strategic objective of reducing hidden cost, as a means of improving their short-term profitability.
3. However, this does not mean that the CEO's piloting logbook includes all indicators in all company's logbooks. As the chapter will further explore, every piloting logbook includes local indicators which are not relevant to higher hierarchical or co-lateral levels. Only global indicators feed into higher level logbooks.
4. Periodically negotiable activity contracts (PNACs) do not replace work contracts, collective conventions, or labor legislation. Rather, they function as supplements to them. Objectives fixed in PNACs deal with additional effectiveness requested of the individual within the framework of his or her job and with reference to the manner in which it is usually carried out. In other words, the objectives assigned to the individual before setting up activity contracts (work contract, for example) are not repeated in the activity contract.

REFERENCES

Buono, A. F., & Savall, H. (2007). *Socio-economic intervention in organizations: The intervener-researcher and the SEAM approach to organizational analysis.* Charlotte, NC: Information Age Publishing.

ISEOR. (1984). *L'élaboration de tableaux de bord de pilotage pour l'encadrement: Cas d'une société anonyme de HLM* [Drawing up piloting logbooks for managers: Case of a private social housing agency]. Ecully, France: ISEOR.

ISEOR. (1985). *Conception et mise en place d'un système de gestion décentralisé en secteur hospitalier, sanitaire et social* [Conception and implementation of a decentralized management system in the public health and hospital sector]. Ecully, France: ISEOR.

Savall, H. (1975). *Enrichir le travail humain* [Work and people]. Paris: Dunod, 1975.

Savall, H. (1983). Le rôle des cadres dans la mise en œuvre de la stratégie de l'entreprise [The role of managers in the implementation of the enterprise's strategy]. *ISEOR Management Research Reports, 5,* 3–25.

Savall, H., & Zardet, V. (1992). *New management control: The hidden costs-performances method.* Eyrolles: Éditions Comptables Malesherbes.

Zardet, V. (1985). Des systèmes d'information vivants: Etude des conditions d'efficacité à partir d'expérimentation [Living information systems: A study of the conditions for efficiency through experimentation], *Revue Sciences de Gestion,* 6, 1–229.

Zardet, V. (1986). *Contribution des systèmes d'information stimulants à l'efficacité de l'entreprise. Cas d'expérimentation* [The contribution of stimulating information systems to the efficiency of enterprises, cases of experimentation], Doctoral dissertation, University Lyon 2, January.

• PART IV •

CONCLUSION

CHAPTER 10

EVALUATION OF RESULTS

Evaluating the effects of intervention and implementation is of interest for two basic reasons: a) for scientific purposes, verification is obtained on whether or not hidden costs were reduced; and b) for operational purposes, the primary interest is providing new information, which is the counterpart of the diagnostic, on organizational improvement efforts. Such insight can also stimulate new behaviors on the part of the micro-space and, more generally, the entire firm. An evaluation can also reactivate the process, notably in the event that problems occurred during implementation. It also provides general direction for continued actions, in that it enables pointing out unsolved dysfunctions, the expectations of new or veteran employees, and sometimes detecting new dysfunctions that were created in the process. In other words, the evaluation triggers an on-going process of perfecting the micro-space. Finally, evaluation provides concrete support for dialogue among supervisors, workers, staff and top management.

The evaluation process also represents the first step toward attributing supplementary compensation to the personnel, notably in the framework of the periodically negotiable activity contract, in the event, and only in the event that positive economic results are verified.

Mastering Hidden Costs and Socio-Economic Performance, pages 285–296
Copyright © 2008 by Information Age Publishing
All rights of reproduction in any form reserved.

EVALUATION CONTENT

The evaluation is carried out with the same operating method as the one used for the diagnostic, since the goal is to compare former and current operations, in order to measure whether improvement of socio-economic performances actually took place. As such, an evaluation is composed of three elements. The first component is an analysis of job/training adequacy. This consists of measuring, by means of competency grids, the competency evolution concerning both the operations already in place and the new operations (see Figure 10.1 for an example of competency evolution). The second element is a synthesis of interviews with staff, workers, intermediary and senior managers that highlights the contributions and limits of the action, as well as suggestions for next steps. Table 10.1 presents a synthesis of interviews with workers in an electronics workshop.

The third component is an evaluation of *hidden cost reduction*. This focus makes it possible to measure the *timespan for reimbursement of investment* on costs for services and time spent on the project and its implementation. Several illustrations of calculated hidden cost reduction were captured in Chapter 3, showing that the timespan for reimbursement of the action is always short and usually less than one year.

As examples of this type of project evaluation, this section presents two cases, one from the services sector and one from the industrial sector.

Evaluation of a Socio-Economic Innovation Action in a Bank

During the diagnostic, internal training in a bank[1] was mainly done in the form of classes, more or less related to actual jobs. Integrated training was carried out from the beginning of project implementation. The head of every micro-space conducted training sessions answering to the needs of the members of his or her micro-space, which could also be attended by members of other micro-spaces. In all, approximately 120 training hours were dispensed to bank personnel.

The most impressive competency improvement took place in the unit that was the first to organize itself; it was also the one that supplied the greatest training effort. In general, competencies were broadened and perfected through integrated training and job enrichment, creating a learning curve effect.

Synthesis of Staff Interviews

The project was perceived as being a source of motivation. However, some employees complained about the gap between the type of organization they

1. Competency grid established before change

Workers	Preparation of profiles	Welding outside template	Implementation template n°1	Argon welding	Implementation template n°2	Control	Straightening and leveling	Sanding Piercing	Door assemblage	Handling	Scheduling and follow-up of work pending	Raw materials	Stockroom management and supply ordering	Preventive maintenance of equipment	Reading schemes and layout	Warehousing and controlling finished products	Follow on worktime hours and objectives
A	■	◪	■		■	■	■	■	■	◪	◪				■		
B	■		■		■	■	■	■	◪	◪							
C	■	◪	■	◪	■	■	■	■	◪	◪			◪		■		
D	■	■	■	■	■					◪					◪		
E	◪	■															
F	■		■	■			■	■									

2. Competency grid established after change (for the same group)

Workers	Preparation of profiles	Welding outside template	Implementation template n°1	Argon welding	Implementation template n°2	Control	Straightening and leveling	Sanding Piercing	Door assemblage	Handling	Scheduling and follow-up of work pending	Raw materials	Stockroom management and supply ordering	Preventive maintenance of equipment	Reading schemes and layout	Warehousing and controlling finished products	Follow on worktime hours and objectives
A	■	■	■	■	■	■	■	■	■	■	■	□	□	□	■	■	■
B	■	◪	■	◪	■	■	■	■	◪	◪	■	■	■	□	◪	■	■
C	■	■	■	■	■	■	■	■	■	■	■	■	■	■	■	■	■
D	■	■	■	■	◪	■	■	■	■	◪	■	■	■	□	◪	■	■
E	■	■	◪	■	◪	■	■	■	■	◪	■	□	□	□	◪	■	■
F	■	■	■	■	■	■	■	■	■	◪	■	■	■		◪	■	■

Traditional operations carried out by workers — New operations carried out by workers

Legend: ■ Frequent practice with mastery; ◪ Occasional practice or not entirely mastered; □ Knowledge of principles without practice; [empty] No knowledge or practice.

Figure 10.1   Competency evaluation in a work unit.

TABLE 10.1 Synthesis of Interviews Carried Out with Workers in an Electronics Work Unit

Domain of actions	Contributions	Limits
Working conditions	• Some modifications considered to be improvements: – Electronic scales – Rearranged bases	• Little physical improvement of working conditions • Certain improvement expected did not occur (machine improvement, breakdown reduction)
Work organization	• Work organization by groups is done without problems • Difficult tasks become easier with experience • Working in groups is more interesting and more motivating	• Some tasks were judged more difficult to assume than others: – Accounting for supplies/ stockroom accounting.
Communication-Coordination-Cooperation	• Better coordination among worker regarding job (production, quality control) • Team leader is more aware of workers' problems • Weekly meetings between workers-supervisors judged useful	• Relations between team leader-workers was little modified • Worker-supervisor weekly meetings are shorter and shorter
Time management	• Task distribution among the team without problems • New tasks executed more and more rapidly	
Integrated training	• Certain themes considered very interesting and useful • Training was well understood	• Certain themes were considered useless or poorly explained • Certain themes were not addressed
Dysfunction indicators	*Absenteeism:* • Workers are more aware of absenteeism • Some workers reduced their absences *Quality:* • Quality awareness • Some wastes were reduced • The regulator problem was partly solved *Direct productivity:* • More work than before	*Absenteeism:* • Organization by groups did not influence absenteeism behavior *Quality:* • Problems in taking charge of temporary worker training

were introduced to during the integrated training and the way in which the organization actually functioned. Working in teams was very much appreciated, as it facilitated exchange between employees and heads of units, enabling better distribution of tasks and increasing competencies. Group solidarity and working dynamics were thus created within each unit.

Certain positions required better definition. Window tellers and first-line sales personnel, for example, suffered from a lack of work coordination, which created a malaise in client services. Despite some adaptation difficulties, it seemed that the staff generally appreciated the new organization and considered that client service quality had improved.

All agreed that the integrated training was a positive element of the restructuring, but it was still considered to be insufficient. They also pointed to several elements that needed improvement, such as inter-unit relations, relations with central services, and contacts with senior management. Finally, certain expectations on the part of the personnel were also unfulfilled, particularly setting up a remuneration scheme based on the efforts to date and a career path for each individual.

Synthesis of Senior Management Interviews

One of the themes that emerged from the interviews with senior managers was that project implementation was resulting in increased competencies. The resulting multi-tasking capacity facilitated the bank's ability to deal with absenteeism. The assessment also pointed to certain individuals with a "flare for selling." However, personnel commitment to the new organization was seen as being hindered by the departure of two employees who had been "advocates" of the project from the start.

Within centralized administrative management (see Chapter 6, Figure 6.3), tasks were viewed as being well distributed between business units and staff/line units, which significantly contributed to helping to keep important deadlines. A problem, however, emerged that was related to the competency of heads of units with respect to their personnel management capacity. Finally, although the staff was seen as participating in the evolution of the units by proposing improvements, delays in implementing periodically negotiable activity contracts was having a demotivating effect.

As a result of these observations, the training was adapted and the senior managers felt that the resultant acquisition of needed competencies was facilitated. Responsibility also improved, with the attribution of numerous delegations. Good team spirit reigned within the units, but three-pronged structure was becoming visible among the different units. Overall, productivity was improved, with a higher quality of client services.

Hidden Cost Evaluation

Comparative hidden cost evaluation was undertaken, comparing the traditional organization as it existed before the intervention and unit-based organization that was currently being implemented. It involved a comparison of two dysfunction indicators that permit an estimate of the overall efficiency variance, provided that performance is maintained over a longer period: absenteeism and turnover.

In terms of absenteeism, there were two sources of performance improvement that were detected in the new organization: the level of absenteeism was lowered and regulation of absences was made easier. Table 10.2 shows a favorable differential of 2,600€ per person/per year for the agency under the new unit-based organization. This financial discrepancy might have been even greater had we been able to evaluate the time spent by senior management regulating absences under the former organization, in addition to extra wage expenditure caused by replacing absent employees with more qualified personnel.

TABLE 10.2   Evaluation of Socio-Economic Efficiency Compared per Person/per Year Under the New Organization

Indicators	Qualitative results	Quantitative results	Financial results (Euros)
Absenteeism	• Greater motivation for attendance	The rate of "reducible"[a] absenteeism went from 4.5% to 1.5%	2,600
Personnel turnover	• More adequate match between Training-Job • Training made easier	Turnover rate went from 90% to 11%	700
Quality	• Fewer errors • Improved reception • Better client follow-up • More attention to innovation	Not evaluated[b]	Not evaluated[b]
Direct productivity	• Improved sales • Reduction of time spent carrying out certain operations	Not evaluated[b]	Not evaluated[b]
Total	• Improved socio-economic efficiency	Under-evaluation of certain indicators	3,300
	Absenteeism and turnover/wage mass = 7.9% improved performance		

[a] This refers to absences considered to be partially reducible through actions addressing working conditions and work organization (illness, strikes, absence without motive), see Chapter 2.

[b] Because improvement was considered obvious by the enterprise (sales of certain priority products were doubled).

Interviews also pointed to two sources of performance improvement linked to turnover as practiced under the new organization: stabilization of personnel turnover in the agency and taking charge of new employees inside each unit, notably for integrated training. The comparative evaluation of costs linked to turnover presented in Table 10.2 shows a surplus of 700€ per person/per year in favor of the new organization. We should highlight the fact that these costs did not take into account vacation replacements and backup bank personnel. Finally, it should be noted that this differential could have been even greater if it had taken into account time spent by senior management regulating turnover under the traditional organization.

In addition to the financial surplus obtained via absenteeism and personnel turnover indicators, a non-quantified *qualitative progress* could also be added, in terms of a) the quality of services made available by increased competencies and b) enhancements in direct productivity, explained mainly by better sales behavior of the personnel following job restructuring.

Evaluation of a Socio-Economic Innovation Action in an Industrial Work Unit

The *diagnostic* (see Bonnet, 1982) carried out in a work unit with 50 employees led to three principal conclusions. First, the absolute hidden cost of dysfunctions amounted to more than half of the work unit's pay package. Second, the lack of qualified personnel made it difficult to regulate absenteeism. Finally, the working conditions were judged as poor on part of the personnel.

The resulting three main axes of the *project* were:

- Physical work condition improvement (noise-reduction and draft-control systems);
- Integrated training actions destined to equip the personnel with the theoretical and practical knowledge necessary to carry out all machine operations of the workshop; and
- Job restructuring action with job enrichment and the creation of semi-autonomous production groups by types of parts and types of machines.

In the work unit, the first semi-autonomous group was set up with the task of manufacturing three simple product types. A simulation of annual production of these types of magnets had led the focus group to proposing *four employees* per group. The tasks given to the group covered almost the entire manufacturing process of the magnets, from cleansing to foundry to quality control to packing. This operating procedure brought together tasks that had previously been carried out, in part or in whole, by nine different work positions. Despite several problems that occurred over the first few weeks due to technical breaches, the group operated within weekly objectives by the second week of its existence.

After two months of group operation, the first *socio-economic evaluation* was carried out.

Evaluation of Competency Evolution

The evaluation was carried out according to two methods. The first approach focused on the factory indicators themselves, based on the criteria of training, work quality, work attendance and behavior. This evaluation measured progress from one to two positions per person on a five-position scale of classification 170 of metallurgy during that period. The second approach focuses on competency grid updating, based on the tasks carried out by members of the group. It revealed moderate progression for all operations by more than one position on a competency grid with four positions (see the previous discussion in Chapter 1).

Synthesis of Staff and Management Interviews

In terms of worker attitudes toward the integrated training, almost all employees reported satisfaction with the training they received, having learned or reviewed extensive subject matter. However, it appears that training had different effects on workers depending on whether their jobs had been restructured or not. Workers in semi-autonomous groups, plus a few workers on the replacement team, were able to put the new learning into practice on the job and thus expressed marked satisfaction. The interest in the training and its impact, however, were less evident for those who found themselves in the same position as before.

Furthermore, it appears that workers preferred more in-depth training during the first weeks following training sessions, in the form of personal assistance (as discussed in Chapter 7). Finally, the workers expressed their desire for an evaluation and its counterpart in terms of salary or classification, which suggested the existence of informal self-appreciation among personnel with regard to their own progress and their need for the hierarchy to recognize their effort.

The *training instructors* (supervisors and technicians) felt that, despite the general feeling of having suffered from a lack of time necessary for quality training, the effects were positive both for workers and for themselves. In addition, most instructors considered that elements of the training action, taken from their context and transposed elsewhere under other conditions, would run the risk of being less effective.

Some top and middle managers considered the training to be effective in terms of acquiring knowledge. The training also appeared to have triggered positive behavior modifications among training instructors. Overall, the managers were pleasantly surprised at the workers' capacity to learn and evolve during the training.

Opinions on the new Organization

All interviewed workers express outright satisfaction regarding the new semi-autonomous group organization. All admitted to having experienced difficulties and doubts in the beginning, but these diminished little by little with experience. Overall, they considered that results were positive in terms of enhanced quality, keeping on schedule and direct productivity. They were all clearly opposed to the idea of backtracking.

The supervisory staff and technicians felt that the job redesign actions together with integrated training for workers would also have positive effects on the role, responsibilities and work conditions of the supervisors, which is one of the reasons why certain supervisory staff members thought that the experimentation should lead to an extension of the action. Middle and top management reported that the main advantage was an increase in employee interest in the job and the demonstration that problems can be solved. Nevertheless, most managers interviewed preferred taking a pause before engaging in an eventual extension of the project.

Evaluation of Hidden cost Reduction

Table 10.3 presents a synthesis of the results of the hidden cost assessment. Hidden cost reduction permitted writing off some of the action costs in less than six months, which amounted to 6,600€ per person/per year.

Two sources of improved performance were revealed in terms of a reduction of absenteeism and an enhanced ability of the operational worker groups to regulating absences. Integrating quality control tasks into the manufacturing process and giving greater responsibility to the personnel also increased motivation to produce high quality items.

The operational worker group made it possible to save time based on a more flexible internal coordination of tasks and movements. In addition, production time was shortened. Thus, statistics on delayed completion of items indicated a gain of an average 2.5 weeks in manufacturing time. This could be attributed to the fact that in-process items no longer had to wait one or two working day between each workstation.

Finally, it was also possible to evaluate the gap between the unitary costs of the two periods and quantities delivered in the second period. The surplus represents a 16.2 percent increase in productivity. Furthermore, the reduction of manufacturing time constituted a reduction of stock immobilization costs.

TABLE 10.3 Comparative Evaluation of Socio-Economic Efficiency of the Operational Worker Group (Euros per person/per year)

Indicators	Qualitative results	Quantitative results	Financial results (Euros)
Absenteeism	• Greater motivation for attendance • Customized work schedule	• Simulation of reduced absenteeism due to illness was 3%	1,000
Work accidents	• Better training and awareness of accident risks • Less recklessness		Not evaluated
Personnel turnover	• Lower risk of turnover of new recruits • Training made easier		Not evaluated
Quality	• Fewer defects • Better regulation of defects • Fewer articles lost	• Rejects were to reduced by 50%	4,500
Direct productivity	• Increased speed • Shorter production time	• +16.2% for the period • reduction of production time by 2.5 weeks	10,800
Total			**16,300**

INDICATORS

As a way of extending these project actions, ISEOR has developed three strategic vigilance indicators:

- *Hidden costs/visible costs ratio:* An increase in hidden costs in relation to costs identified in an organization's accounting scheme suggests dysfunctions and a loss of company energy. This indicator is a warning signal.
- *Externalized costs/internalized costs ratio:* Externalized costs are those costs that are diverted outside the enterprise in order to free itself of certain charges. An inordinate increase in this ratio should not be left unattended. Traditionally, a good policy consists of such reasoning as "all expenditures paid by others constitute an advantage for us." This reflects "good" management, except if one admits that a boomerang effect can occur. When costs are externalized to the environment, the environment can take "revenge" by forcing the enterprise to re-internalize certain costs that it had formerly exter-

nalized. This phenomenon can be observed with pollution or in the evolution of social security contributions.

- *Indirectly productive time/directly productive time ratio:* This is an indicator of a loss of professionalism when the ratio declines. When a company reduces its size and cuts back its workforce, most of its time is henceforth devoted to operations, sacrificing research, preparation, methods improvement, necessary internal training, and so forth. It thus attempts to maximize the amount of time directly applied to products, reasoning that that is the best way to heighten its competitiveness. A deterioration of this ratio constitutes a warning signal that the enterprise is in the process of losing its professionalism.

Surveying these three ratios and their evolution provides a way for the enterprise to maintain the economic alert system instigated during the socio-economic intervention.

CONCLUSION

The socio-economic innovation process created and implemented by ISE-OR—in numerous enterprises since 1974, in its full-fledged version since 1979—attempts to take into account three fundamental phenomena of company operations: entropy, chronobiology and the creation of stimulating information.

This process was constructed and perfected to fight against the *entropy* of enterprises, namely their spontaneous tendency to allow their energies to disintegrate under the "disorder" entailed by daily life. This approach also attempts to avoid overly disturbing the company's *chronobiological rhythms,* i.e., the rhythms of professional life, the rhythms of the evolution of behaviors. The socio-economic innovation process constitutes a contribution of energy aimed at modifying only certain rhythms, in terms of increasing the rhythm of progress and decreasing the rhythm of entropy. It is also represents an ongoing contribution of *new information* that helps the enterprise learn to know itself better, to learn other modes of operation, and to periodically evaluate the results of actions it has undertaken. Viewed from this perspective, the four-stage action can be thought of as a learning process, which can lead the company to more effectively implement a more efficient, ongoing piloting system. This piloting system is, of course, implemented by modifying company culture, as we have seen in this volume, but it also constitutes the creation of permanent management tools, especially the periodically negotiable activity contract and the socio-economic piloting logbook.

NOTE

1. The principal results of the bank's diagnostic and project were presented in Chapter 6.

REFERENCE

Bonnet, M., (1982). *Action de formation des ouvriers par la maîtrise et expérimentation d'une nouvelle forme d'organisation du travail. Cas d'un atelier de métallurgie: évaluation socio-économique des résultats* [Worker training actions carried out by supervisors and experimentation of new forms of work organization. Case of a metallurgy workshop: Socio-economic evaluation of results]. Ecully, France: ISEOR Report.

POSTSCRIPT

Our pilot-actions in socio-economic innovation were conducted in businesses and not-for-profit organizations from the beginning of the economic crisis (1974), guided by an adherence to ISEOR's methodological framework and evaluated with scientific rigor. This experience has led to come to several conclusions, which are offered in the spirit of enhancing the debate and actions of private and public policymakers.

THE NEED FOR A HOLISTIC APPROACH TO MANAGEMENT

Improving organizational effectiveness is possible without new financial resources. Improving work life conditions is a necessary but insufficient condition for growth of economic effectiveness in organizations. In addition, improvements must be made in the overall management system of the enterprise, by developing the stimulating character of the information and decision-making system. Only a holistic approach uniting both types of action is capable of sustainably improving the enterprise's degree of socio-economic performance.

Any action to improve economic effectiveness in an organization comes under the direct responsibility of top management, given the interweavings and multiple interactions of hidden costs, their origins and the nature of solutions. Researching, designing and implementing solutions require strategic input from the highest level, synchronized with the entire enterprise. These actions also demand the development of the mid- and supervisory management ("co-pilot") function, (reflected by increased competency in

Mastering Hidden Costs and Socio-Economic Performance, pages 297–302
Copyright © 2008 by Information Age Publishing
297

management and sales at all levels of the organization, whether private or public), at every level of management. However, these performance-improvement actions—researching, designing and implementing solutions—are a function of senior management's actions.

Investments in new technologies that are not accompanied by socio-economic innovation actions introduce a high level of counter-performance risk into the enterprise, not to mention disturbances of social order. Indeed, we have observed that the introduction of new technologies, without accompanying measures addressing working conditions, work organization, time management, communication-coordination-cooperation, integrated training and strategy implementation, produces an *effect of hidden cost multiplication*. In the end, such actions paradoxically raise the cost of products. When technological investments are typically made, there is an attempt to economize on accompanying actions, undertaking an authentic organizational cleanup and restructuring of operating modes. Yet, as we have observed, these effort only add new hidden costs to the hidden costs that existed prior to the investment—hidden costs that are caused by the insertion of new equipment. Accelerated development of computer-integrated manufacturing and office automation, by itself, constitutes a risk of deteriorating profitability—unless an overall examination of company sectors affected by the change is carried out concomitantly with the material investment. Such material investment must be accompanied by an immaterial investment sufficient to rapidly, yet "calmly" (considering a learning curve effect) upgrade the competencies and behaviors of *all* organizational members. The database constructed from the multitude of change processes conducted by the ISEOR over the past 30 years shows that the rate of return on immaterial investment is very high and that it accelerates a return on material and technological investment.

As for our increasing reliance on information technology (IT), the risk of multiplying hidden costs is also very high. Organizations are rife with an overabundant amount of information that is unexploited, costly and a source of frustration to actors submerged, sometime asphyxiated, by an excessive mass of unusable data. IT-based systems, of course, can be a real asset in businesses where their introduction and development are accompanied by a careful reexamination of the organization. These systems should be developed and seen as technical instruments, designed to be part of a stimulating information and decision-making system. The latter requires development of a more didactic form of information, the goal of which is to encourage the largest possible number of data-supported decisions and actions.

In terms of personnel training and policies, our pilot actions show that in order to confront current challenges (commercial, technological, financial), businesses should schedule significantly higher training budgets than they are accustomed to: 1 to 2 percent of total wages is a ludicrous amount in relation to company needs and stakes in terms of economic efficiency. Evaluations of integrated training pilot actions that we have carried out for over thirty years show that businesses do have the necessary resources, thanks to the considerable reduction of hidden costs that can be attained in a matter of months through actions of this nature. Still, training must be designed and carried out as a fully *integrated* element of the company strategy. As needed, it should also include a certain number of external contributors, conducting training sessions for certain internal actors (e.g., key managers and technicians) and frameworks to disseminate these insights throughout the entire enterprise, enabling any externally-acquired training to be multiplied and extended to a great number of employees. Overall, this should entail only minor costs to the enterprise. An integrated training policy should be inscribed in an ambitious strategy of high qualifications and high salaries, the best guarantee for a business to be competitive (flexible, dynamic, changing) and profitable. As a general rule, the most highly competent personnel cause the least amount of hidden costs—*if* they are well piloted within the framework of an explicit, coherent company strategy.

The architecture of hierarchical powers requires, in most enterprises, restructuring and consolidation. Yet, company success (e.g., short- and long-term competitiveness, profitability) requires the participation of *all* personnel, and not just the effectiveness of a few. This widespread participation does not require the reduction of hierarchical powers. The underlying key is to ensure all possible "relays" between organizational members, creating a veritable network linking and disseminating the various activities of human-size teams (i.e., less than 10 people), which are constituted around authentic poles of competency in terms of techniques and employee stimulation. A high performance business is a strong federation of coordinated team activity, such as the team gathered around the CEO, worker teams gathered around a supervisor, or management teams gathered around the head of a department or division. Hierarchical power is an important source of effectiveness when it coincides with the power that comes from indisputable professional competency. One of the factors of a manager's legitimacy and effectiveness, from the CEO to the team leader, is his or her capacity to manage conflict (tension, latent or overt conflict, in varying degrees of gravity) with which daily life is rife, and to construct in team operational consensus, which is always fragile yet indispensable, constantly in need of reconstruction.

All of these recommendations have been tested and implemented in an array of businesses and organizations, of all sizes and every legal status, in numerous sectors of industrial activity and services, regardless of their economic and social situation (e.g., thriving, middling, distressed). Therefore, these solutions can be considered as achievable and their effectiveness has been assessed. The search for solutions to improve socio-economic effectiveness is no longer haphazard or random, as it has now become the object of solid prognostics and the operating modes for implementation are no less scientific than the procedures utilized in the physical, material domains.

TIME IS OF THE ESSENCE

The severity of economic crisis and the demand to become more competitive has spared no sector of activity. Sectors that enjoyed a protected status until recent years no longer escape this grave historical tendency. Hospitals, municipal governments, social establishments and educational institutions are subject to the restrictions of the law of finances, in the same way that small business and large industrial groups, banks and retail chains are dealt painful financial blows by market pressure, competition and conflict between customer demands and those of the organization.

Time is running out. Change-related procedures in organizations that are too slow or too limited in their scope and sphere of action are unlikely to succeed, and fall well short of responding to the need to improve social *and* economic effectiveness in businesses and organizations.

The time has come for the inevitable cleanup of company work methods, management tools and operating modes. But businesses are not alone, as our joint research with consultancy firms shows. Business methods and intervention products utilized by consultants, organizational engineers, experts, instructors and teachers must also be reexamined and renewed. The development of business competency requires innovation in the relationship between the enterprise and its consulting and training partners.

Faced with this urgency, effectiveness improvement actions cannot be content with approaches that timidly set up small groups of volunteers tucked away in a workshop corner, equipped with no more than Pareto's old diagram or Ishikawa's exotic fishbone (referred to as "quality circles") and charged with studying localized, well-circumscribed microcosmic problems in view of improving larger problems of effectiveness. There is no longer time to elude the veritable source of overall economic effectiveness and improved competitiveness. There is a dire need for an *innovative approach* to management that businesses and organizations truly need. ISEOR's ongoing conceptualization and experimentation have formulated such an approach, one that is operational, effective, and applicable to a wide range of organizational types. It is original, for its construction was based on experiences in French and European professional milieus, which are more conflictual than those in enterprises belonging to other cultures with seemingly stronger consensus about the final goal of the enterprise. In France, consensus is not a "given" of professional life; it must be constructed day after day by means of *management* practices that are personalized for individuals who are neither an indistinguishable part of the masses nor entirely independent and self-sufficient.

The conceptual and theoretical development of socio-economic analysis, carried out in numerous research-experimentations in a multitude of enterprises, has revealed numerous concrete manifestations of confidence in the enterprise, in the different domains of management sciences we are dealing with.

THE FOCUS ON SOCIO-ECONOMIC ANALYSIS AND DEVELOPMENT

Developments in ISEOR's socio-economic theory have shown the importance of creating bridgeheads between the enterprise and its environment. This bridgehead involves confidence in the capacity and practice of the enterprise's commercial actors to capture ongoing commercial information from their clients, and to transmit this information to the enterprise, providing marketing with warning signals and the organization with strategic direction (Savall & Zardet, 1995). Sales personnel are not only creators of affairs and orders—they also possess strategic information concerning market threats and opportunities. The functions of marketing and the sales force, very distant today in most enterprises, can be redesigned based on marketing "micro-functions" assumed by every vendor. In a word, a new "philosophy" of sales force management, typically seen as highly independent, highly competitive and subjected to its market, can thus be implemented.

Consultancy intervention also entails a component of confidence relations among actors. Socio-economic management control consists of mastering the enterprise's hidden costs-performance in order to develop the function of *managerial self-control*, making every individual a "mini-controller," capable of developing their own "business streak," marked by simple competency in elementary management focused on the company's economic performance. This makes it possible to move management controllers upward, toward a more active role involving more anticipative support of the hierarchy, an expert role providing advice to operational actors.

The *socio-economic organization method (SEAM)*, implemented in both industrial and service sectors, is also founded on actors' confidence. The principles of socio-economic organization require confidence, based on fully empowered groups of employees equipped with socio-economic management tools, responsible for the entire manufacturing process of a product or for the management of a client portfolio. This also requires confidence in the competency and change-energy of actors, in their interest for a more complex, more demanding social game. Last but not least, the socio-economic method requires actors' confidence that their hierarchy can be trusted to shift toward a more pedagogical role vis-à-vis the personnel and toward a more attentive, strategic piloting of product quality, team operation and human potential.

In France, the problem-solving process for improving enterprise effectiveness seems to be well underway. Constructive lessons have been drawn from the experience of a long economic crisis. Actors who were formerly insensitive to economic discipline have modified their discourse, and often their behavior as well. Among the key messages of this transformation, the notion of quality has made its way into public opinion and professional milieus. This notion should be pushed to its very roots. As our way of pushing this focus, since 1974 ISEOR has applied the notion of *integral quality* in businesses and organizations. *Our focus is on* quality in terms of products and services to clients, but also quality in terms of the worklife of the people in the enterprise—workplace quality, operational quality, quality of management tools and procedures—in a phrase, the quality of the enterprise. This topic merits a small encyclopedia devoted to the socio-economic approach to integral quality, the very foundation of the socio-economic theory of organizations.

There are numerous management methods that are *ephemerally* effective. These approaches, however, are being increasingly questioned by stakeholders in the enterprise: CEOs, executives, shareholders, management, line personnel, unions, clients, suppliers, and private and public institutions. The socio-economic theory of organizations, created more than thirty years ago, endeavors to demonstrate that innovative methods are capable of producing *sustainable overall socio-economic performance.* Our goal is to improve the satisfaction level of all stakeholders ("socio") as well as financial outcomes ("economic") over the long term, creating sustainable business practices that enhance all dimensions of organizational performance. As a start, all we ask of you is to question obsolete management and organizational theories, as well as the methods and tools they spawned, moving beyond the increasingly inefficient and ineffective approaches that have guided us for all too long. The time has come for a true socio-economic approach to management.

REFERENCE

Savall, H., & Zardet, V. (1995, 2005). *Ingénierie stratégique du roseau* [Strategic engineering of the reed]. Paris: Economica

THE RESEARCH WORK OF THE SOCIO-ECONOMIC INSTITUTE OF ENTERPRISES AND ORGANIZATIONS (ISEOR)

The Socio-Economic Institute of Enterprises and Organizations was created and is directed by Henri Savall, professor of Management Sciences at the University of Lyon. The ISEOR is an independent research center in association with the University Jean Moulin Lyon 3 and the Graduate School of Management (E.M. Lyon). Savall first began working on the socio-economic analysis of the enterprise in 1973, initially applying it to the domains of working conditions and work organization. Over the course of this ongoing work, a research team was created in 1975 and established in 1976. Today, the team represents a group of more than 125 active researchers.

The research program is oriented in two general directions: a) demonstrating, through *experimentation* inside organizations and the *conceptualization* that derives from that experimentation, the *conditions for compatibility* between *social* objectives and *economic* objectives of enterprises; and b) studying the conditions of success for socio-economic strategies that firmly associate social and personnel policy to the overall company policy. A great number of enterprises have constituted the research field for studies and experimentation over thirty three years. The socio-economic approach has been applied to social policy development, working conditions and work

Mastering Hidden Costs and Socio-Economic Performance, pages 303–322

organization improvement, management control, investment decisions and quality improvement strategy. It has been particularly developed in large industrial and financial groups, in small and medium industrial businesses, in services and liberal professions. Studies and experimentation in hospitals, public and cultural services have demonstrated that socio-economic analysis is applicable to nonprofit organizations as well. Today, this research represents more than 1,000,000 hours of investigation (half of which takes place inside enterprises themselves) and more than 90,000 published pages.

The research themes of the ISEOR have been situated for many years around the axis of public action development. Since 1976, ISEOR's work has been supported by the Ministry of Labor and the ANACT [National agency for working conditions improvement], the Ministry of Industry, the Urban Planning General Commission, the FNEGE [National foundation for the instruction of enterprise management], the DGRST [General delegation for scientific and technical research] and the Rhône-Alps Regional Mission. The experimental research carried out by ISEOR is based mainly on the *socio-economic approach,* which includes a method of analysis and problem solving, centered on a holistic approach to the operations of enterprises and organizations, articulating social and economic variables. This approach was created by Savall in 1973–1974 and developed around the concept of "hidden costs-performances." Supervision for this research is provided by a team whose research and activities have gained national and international scope, including Quebec, the United States, Mexico, Portugal, Spain, Switzerland, Belgium, Tunisia and Morocco). More than 140 doctoral theses in Management Sciences (103 of which were defended) enabled progress in the scientific construction of the socio-economic approach to organizations.

THE RESEARCH AXES

Fundamental Axes

- Systems and models of stimulating information for decision making in enterprises and organizations.
- Effectiveness of enterprises and product quality: analysis and improvement conditions.
- Strategy of technological and product innovation: consequences on human potential and on investment decision procedures.
- Socio-economic analysis of working conditions, work organization, jobs and training in relation to the overall structure of enterprises and organizations.
- Modernization of public services—public and private partnerships.

- Regional projects for sustainable development.
- Competitive challenges and dynamics of Tetra-normalization

Principal Methods

- Methods adapted to small and medium businesses and industries, large industries, nonprofit organizations and public services.
- Dysfunction diagnostic.
- Methods of hidden cost-performance calculation.
- Methods of qualitative, quantitative and financial evaluation (qQFi).
- Methods of socio-economic evaluation.

Applied Research

- Stimulating information systems (SIS), modes of management and incentive remuneration.
- Diagnostic and processes for improving the effectiveness and quality of small and medium size businesses and industries.
- Technological innovations and subsequent job restructuring: piloting and decision-aid tools. New procedures for investment choice. Conception and implementation of company and organizational strategy integrating the variables of personnel management. Applications for hospitals, banks, industries and local government.
- Job restructuring actions and the organization of integrated training. Experimentation and evaluation of socio-economic results.

RESEARCH PROGRAMS

The most outstanding research results of the ISEOR's scientific program were obtained in the following domains.

The Period from 1983–1990

Fundamental research

The work of the ISEOR has permitted constructing two fundamental concepts of the socio-economic theory of organizations by means of:

- Demonstrating through experimentation the HISOFIS effect (humanly integrated and stimulating operational and functional information system), the degree of impact on the organization's economic performances and production conditions, of propagation and reproduction over the course of time in organizations.

- Conceptualization of the socio-economic intervention as a set of HISOFISGENESIS actions, namely the creation of HISOFIS effects by contributing external energy for the transformation of organizational operations, contribution teamed up with the reactivity of organization's internal actors, according to a dialectical process of cultural shock/conformity.

Experimental Research (Applied Research)

The two principal results, in terms of methodological progress, concern two decision-aid tools. The method of *socio-economic diagnostic* of organization has been deepened and simplified to make it more easily operational. Numerous applications in small- and medium-sized industries and businesses have reinforced the method through hierarchical classification of its various components to permit less costly and more rapid applications for businesses.

The result was formalized in an agreement proposal made to the ISEOR by the Chamber of Commerce and Industry of Lille-Roubaix-Tourcoing in view of application of the socio-economic intervention method, created and perfected by the ISEOR in 50 small and medium industries and businesses in the Northern Region of France. The ISEOR took charge of *expert-intervener training*, the synthesis of pilot-action evaluation and several trial experimentations. This was the first time that a pilot-action of this scope was carried out and evaluated according to a homogeneous method. It is also the first time, it appears, that *professional fees were paid* to a CNRS [National center for scientific research] social science research team by small and medium businesses under an agreement such as the one concluded with the Chamber of Commerce and Industry of Lille-Roubaix-Tourcoing.

The method of *qQFi evaluation (qualitative, quantitative and financial)* organizes different types of company information by means of a *decentralized company piloting* instrument. This method, created by the ISEOR, was significantly consolidated through experimentation of the socio-economic *strategic piloting logbook* and applied in three company situations: socio-organizational innovation actions, economic turnaround actions and technological investment projects.

The Period from 1990–1994

Results of Fundamental Research

The following results of the ISEOR's scientific program are among the most remarkable:

1. Stabilizing the concept of *synchronized decentralization,* a much more productive and relevant approach in terms of explicative and prescriptive research, than the extremely popular concept of centralization (and its opposite, decentralization). In 1990 we discovered that the synchronization concept was an essential factor for socio-economic performance in organizations. We then refined and stabilized the concept through extensive research-experimentation.

   Another important result is the large field of application of this concept: it applies of course, to an individual organization, but it also applies to very large organizations and administrations, sometimes made up of independent entities. This was demonstrated by our research results within the framework of public programs (e.g., the fight against illiteracy) and large inter-institutional and inter-enterprise projects (e.g., construction sites).

2. Formalizing *immaterial* production (which today largely replaces material production in our developed economies). *A methodology for formalization* was designed, tested and refined, giving rise to differentiation between tertiary products and quaternary products (highly innovative services defined by interaction and negotiation between producers and consumers). Two fields of application were developed over that four-year period: a) operational entities in enterprises, not manufacturing for external clients, but for other services of the enterprise; and b) management consulting offices.

   This formalization is part of the axis of research on *immaterial, intellectual and intangible investment* and enables us to make progress in terms of management intervention phenomenology and *transfer of know-how* in the immaterial domain.

3. The conceptualization, supported by extensive research-experimentation carried out over fifteen years, of socio-economic strategy of enterprises and its articulation to macro-economic problematics of survival and development of firms and jobs. Savall and Zardet's (1995) book, published by Economica, was devoted to this research program. The ISEOR's research work was positioned in reference to contemporary economic heterodoxy, as pointed out in the work by Weiller and Carrier (1994).

4. Significant progress in a transdisciplinary research program conducted by the LISI team (Laboratory of Information Systems Engineering), directed by Professor Jacques Kouloumdjian at the INSA of Lyon (National Institute of Applied Sciences), involving the formalization of rules for obtaining and improving the economic performances of enterprises. Resorting to techniques of artificial intelligence, a first socio-organizational diagnostic expert-system was designed (1986) and tested (1987–1988). It has been used ever since in the context of the ISEOR's applied research programs. A second expert-system was designed and developed in recent years permitting to identify the protocols and actions that reduce the dysfunctions detected during diagnostic and to evaluate their economic effects. This tool is based on the knowledgebase constructed by the ISEOR thanks to more than 1,200 research-experimentations spread across more than 34 countries in Europe, North, Central and South America, Africa and Asia carried out in a wide range of enterprises.

Research-Experimentation Results (applied research)

Detailed results can be synthesized through the following results:

1. Validation of the socio-economic model and adaptation of intervention protocols to *very large organizations*. Three very large enterprises (17,000 employees, 300,000 employees and 160,000 employees) have been the object of long-term research-experimentation since 1990. This has made it possible, on one hand, to validate concepts, and on the other hand, to forge the *new conceptualizations* described above: synchronized decentralization, formalization of immaterial products and socio-economic strategy.

2. Evaluation of impacts and results of *public decision* in *loosely structured* organizations. There were two applied research programs: the first in conjunction with Urban Planning on *professional orientation-insertion* of young people in urban neighborhoods; and the second with Construction Planning in prevention on multi-enterprise construction sites in the *Housing and Public Works sector*. The latter project helped to demonstrate, using the hidden costs concept, the numerous effects of wastage engendered by desynchronization of actors, and to test tools and practices for developing synchronization.

3. Improvement of job-training adequacy at the level of employment pools. In the framework of the *European program MED Campus*, a research project was carried out in conjunction with the ONISEP, the ISEOR, the University of Barcelona (Spain) and the University of Sfax (Tunisia) in 1992–1993. Based on in-depth inquiries in enterprises and training institutions carried out in three regions (Rhone-

Alps in France, Barcelona in Spain and Sfax in Tunisia), a methodology for *training-job adequacy diagnostic* was defined, followed by the development of *training and information engineering*.

4. Evolution of the C.P.A. profession toward that of management consultant. A research program in partnership with the Council of the Order of Public Accountants began in 1992. Extensive shared work and manifestations (cf. below) have been developed. They have led to the conception of a *methodology for the transformation of classic products* in the domain of public accounting (keeping and monitoring accounts, statutory auditors) and the conception in 1993 of a training internship for public accountants in the formalization of consultancy products.

Dissemination of Research Results and Research-Enterprise Partnership

The ISEOR has a committed policy to disseminate its research results. The most significant actions of the period from 1990–1994 are:

1. Creation of three new university diplomas that are innovative both in terms of content as well as their goals:
   - Masters degree in management engineering consultancy, created in 1990 at the University of Lyon.
   - Masters degree in local government and environmental organizations at the Institut d'Etudes Politiques (IEP) of Lyon, with the support of the ISEOR for the management axis.
   - University diploma in project management for public health and welfare, created in 1994 in conjunction with University of Lyon 1, University of Lyon 2, University of Lyon 3 and in close partnership with the Public Hospital Administration Authority of Lyon.
2. Creation and development of pilot-programs of ongoing training for management consultants:
   - The ISEOR conducts every year (since 1979) eight 10-day workshops destined to external and internal company consultants on consultant professionalism (approximately 180 persons trained each year).
   - The ISEOR designed in 1992 and conducted until 1996, in partnership with public account profession, a workshop on the formalization of consultancy products.
   - Set-up of a consultancy office network applying the methods created by the ISEOR, including a methodology-support program.
   - Organization of an annual colloquium (with publication of conference proceedings) on the development of management consultancy professionalism, welcoming every year since 1987, 250 participants from universities and businesses.

– Dissemination of books and journals, in addition to the ISEOR website (www.iseor.com) in order to make known our research findings and publications.

The Fundamental Theoretical Hypothesis

An underlying objective of socio-economic analysis of organizations is to validate, through experimentation inside businesses and organizations, the following theoretical hypothesis: A productive organization (enterprise or other entity) is considered as a set of *structures* (physical, technological, organizational, demographic and psychological structures) and a set of *behaviors* (individual and collective) in constant interaction.

$$[S \rightleftarrows B]$$

The company's level of economic performance (EP) is linked to levels and structures of certain so-called *"hidden" costs-performance* (HC) because they have not been explicitly identified (and thus are uncontrolled) by the usual economic information systems of the organization (accounting, budget, economic calculation for decision aid).

$$HC \rightarrow EP$$

However, hidden costs, a particularly significant subset of hidden costs-performances, are the financial expression of certain *dysfunctions* the organization is subjected to, namely the observed gaps between actual performance of the organization and its expected or anticipated performance.

Socio-economic analysis tends to show that dysfunctions include an incompressible component that is inherent to operation, however well-run it may be, in all organizations, and a compressible component, which experience shows results from the relatively ineffective exchange (in light of the fixed objectives) between the $[S \rightleftarrows B]$ systems.

The operations of the organization, in terms of pathology, can then be schematically expressed as in Figure A.1. Observe that $[S \rightleftarrows B]$ also expresses a performance linked to the *economic performance* [EP], which can be qualified as *social performance* since it is made up of a set of *quality of company*

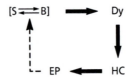

Figure A.1 Schematic relationship between Structures (S), Behaviors (B), Dysfunctions (Dy), Hidden Costs (HC), and Economic Performance (EP).

operation indicators, or in other terms, the organization's Quality of Work Life. Such a theory, to the degree that its validity is consolidated, could then provide a conceptualization of the organization's structuro-behavioral type, which is socio-economic in essence. Indeed, evaluation of economic performance is only valid when it is expressed in terms of both economic and "social" variables (physiological, psychological, sociological). Therefore, what we have here is a *formal analysis* with a multi-disciplinary and multi-dimensional objective, as an attempt to increase the demonstrative impact of economic results observed within organizations.

The Period from 1994–1998

Fundamental research

The four-year research program of the ISEOR team is aimed at developing and reinforcing the team's multi-disciplinary aspect regarding sub-domains of management science and neighboring domains in the social sciences. Increasing the size of the research team and, thus, reinforcing the competency of the teacher-researcher team in management sciences at the ISEOR (up from five teacher-researchers in 1989 to thirteen in 1994) provided the opportunity to identify and focus the team's thematic research programs.

The break-down of the analysis of interfaces between socio-economic management and each discipline of management sciences is carried out through examination of different themes:

- **Strategic and socio-economic management of the enterprise**: Henri Savall, Véronique Zardet, Olivier Voyant
- **Socio-economic management of quality and innovation**: Nathalie Krief
- **Socio-economic management, small size businesses and entrepreneurship**: Frantz Datry, Isabelle Géniaux
- **Public organization management**: Françoise Goter
- **Socio-economic marketing and prospective**: Isabelle Barth, Georges Aublé
- **Socio-economic management control**: Emmanuel Beck, Laurent Cappelletti, Djamel Khouatra, Béatrice Lallé
- **Socio-economic management of human resources**: Marc Bonnet, Vincent Cristallini
- **Intercultural management**: Michel Péron, Rickie Moore, Jeannette Rencoret
- **Computer-assisted management and decision-aid information systems**: Nouria Harbi, Michel Grivel

- **Production management**: Philippe Benollet
- **Corporate responsibility**: François Ecoto

Research-Experimentation (Applied Research)

During this period, significant progress has been made, most notably in the following domains:

- **Transfer of management engineering know-how:** In the framework of partnerships concluded and developed with enterprises, extensive intervention-research has been carried out.

  The validation of socio-economic management concepts was confirmed through several cases of research conducted inside enterprises that displayed remarkable results; it was confirmed through intervention-research carried out in new sectors of activity: public health and welfare organizations and Certified Public Accountants (CPA) professions.

- **Strategic watch:** When the strategic watch function was introduced in several partner enterprises, an in-depth experimental research program on information systems in small and medium businesses and industries was set up; it is part of the thematic research framework supported by the Rhone-Alps regional government.

- **Total quality procedure:** This research axis was also strongly developed in the framework of business partnerships, notably in a group of Walloon enterprises (Belgium). The results were presented in detail in the quantitative evaluation (valorization/business partnership). In parallel, the team strongly involved itself in the interuniversity collective tutoring network of Southeastern France. The 1998 session organized by the laboratory was focused on this theme.

- **Human resource management:** This axis consisted in demonstrating the contribution of socio-economic management to human resource management, in conjunction with company strategy: involving the entire personnel in the search for pools of strategic effectiveness.

- **Management control:** This axis was the object of major development, demonstrating the feasibility of adding, to the traditional approach of management control centered on cost reduction, a new axis focused on the creation of value-added.

- **Scaling down of HORIVERT Socio-economic change process** through a large number of experiments conducted within very small enterprises.

Since 1997, ISEOR has carried out socio-economic interventions in 350 notary public offices, small size enterprises employing from 1 to 55 people, located in nine French regions. This approach helped attaining significant results as regards the improvement of socio-economic performance. The specific-value added of this intervention-research both in terms of methodology and of the problematics dealt with, contributes to enhancing the scientific knowledge base of ISEOR. This intervention conducted on a large sale within one single activity sector spread between a number of geographical locations, enabled us to assess the transformation capacities of a government-controlled profession, in spite of the disturbances entailed by the evolution of European and international norms.

Dissemination of Research Results to the International Community

Over the course of this period, the international activity of the Research Center increased significantly, with a 40 percent increase recorded for this axis. Initiation and development of cooperation was launched in numerous countries and on several continents, including, for example Mexico, Morocco and Canada. The most significant achievements were formalized through agreements and usually included the transfer of "know-how" in Socio-Economic Management Engineering.

Mexico: ISEOR concluded an agreement of close cooperation with the Universidad Autónoma Metropolitana de Mexico (UAM) in Xochimilco and operated a transfer of Socio-Economic Management Engineering know-how, which led to the creation of a Laboratory of Socio-Economic Management in that university. The creation of this laboratory was based on a cooperation agreement signed on November 10, 1997 between the Université de Lyon and the Universidad Autónoma Metropolitana de Mexico. In addition to accomplishments in the domain of socio-economic management, the partnership pursues the objective of conducting academic activities of teaching, research and dissemination of university culture and development, corresponding to the needs of Mexican society. It led to the creation of two diplomas and a Management Sciences doctorate.

Morocco: A similar cooperative partnership agreement was concluded between the ISEOR and the RESO Group (training group with 14 training establishments throughout the Moroccan territory—Efet, Eurelec and Esig). Several training sessions made it possible to transfer socio-economic analysis and management to the directors of those entities, as well as several CEOs and executive managers of enterprises. This action was an integral part of the policy of Moroccan public powers and part of an agreement with European Community and the World Bank. This cooperation will be pursued and eventually lead to the creation of a Master's degree in Socio-Economic Management and a Doctorate in Management Sciences in collaboration with these Moroccan establishments. A second research-inquiry operation on restructuring African enterprises and its impact on human resources was conducted in partnership with the Association of Personnel Managers and Training Programs:

- **Canada (Quebec):** An agreement was signed between the HEC Montréal and the Université of Lyon in November, 1997, designating, among other things, exchange of students between the Master's Degree in Management Sciences and the Doctorate in Business Administration at the HEC, in addition to the graduate degrees piloted and organized by the team of teacher-researchers at the ISEOR (Université de Lyon).

- **United States:** The socio-economic theory has operated its first breakthrough in the United States en 1981, beginning with the publication of Henri Savall's groundbreaking study "Work and People: An Economic Evaluation of Job Enrichment", prefaced by H. I. Ansoff (founder of the concept of "strategic management"), published by the Oxford University Press, New York.

  Another axis was then launched with the constitution of a Research Group in charge of studying the specificities of Socio-Economic Management as compared to the current tendencies in management in the United States. A member of the research team, Rickie Moore, attended the University of Southern California (Center for Effective Organization) during one year for in-depth study of the themes defined by the Research Group: a) positioning the contributions of the socio-economic method with regards to American consulting practices (e.g., measuring the creation of potential, detecting pools of hidden performance/costs) and b) cooperation with American universities with methodological options similar to those of the ISEOR (i.e., experimental research in management sciences).

- **International Labor Office (ILO), Geneva:** ISEOR teacher-researchers transferred the concepts and tools of socio-economic management to the heads of the ILO's World Training Center in Turino and to train Vietnamese professors from Ho Chi Minh Ville (carried out in the framework of Pacific-Asian Programs). The plan is to continue to develop this type of cooperation in other countries. The ILO, in its book entitled Management Consulting, devoted 20 pages to the Socio-Economic method and the ISEOR Research Center.

The Period from 1998–2002

Research on the International Scale

The development of cooperation initiated over the course of the last four-year plan was intensively developed and anchored mainly in Mexico and the United States:

- **Mexico:** Following signature of agreements in 1997 and 1998 with the Universidad Autónoma Metropolitana de Mexico (UAM), the program organized an international colloquium in November 2000 in Mexico City, co-organized by the UAM, the University of Lyon and ISEOR on the theme "socio-economic models of management in Mexican organizations," setting up a Doctorate in Socio-Economic Management at the UAM and supervising cotutelle theses.

  Another cooperation agreement was signed in 2001–2002 in partnership with local small and medium businesses, professional organizations and the State Government of Yucatan.

- **United States**: Cooperation with a team of management professors at Central Michigan University (CMU), with a training program for professors of that university alternately at the ISEOR-Ecully, France and in Michigan, and participation at the annual Academy of Management Conference (6,000 participants), with a session on the work of the ISEOR team.

  An international colloquium organized by ISEOR and the Management Consulting Division of the Academy of Management (March, 2001) in Lyon, held for the first time outside of North American territory. The forum was held in collaboration with Graduate School of Business HEC Paris, the Copenhagen Business School and Central Michigan University, with publication of the conference proceedings in English (more than 700 pages) by the ISEOR team.

  Our bridgehead was then consolidated when Professor David Boje (New Mexico State University, Las Cruces, USA), director of the renowned academic review "Journal of Organizational Change Management", Emerald, 2003) devoted an entire issue (a very rare occurrence for theories not inspired by Anglo-Saxon concepts) dedicated to the socio-economic model, guest edited by Henri Savall. An entire book dedicated to the socio-economic theory of organizations was recently published in the United States, edited by Professor Anthony Buono (Bentley College) and Henri Savall entitled *Socio-Economic Interventions in Organizations* (Buono & Savall, 2007).

- **International Labor Office, Geneva**: The socio-economic model is the only theory that has been endorsed and published by the ILO (Geneva 2000), simultaneously in English, Spanish and French for the directors of small and medium-size firms. Publication of a book (2000) on the socio-economic method created and developed by ISEOR, released simultaneously in French, English and Spanish. This work has been disseminated to all member countries of the ILO (UN).

- **Southeast Asia**: Outreach development with Cambodia and Viet Nam to develop Masters and Doctoral level researchers.

- **North Africa:** Outreach development, mainly in Tunisia and Morocco, with the defense of two theses by Moroccan doctoral candidates.

Dissemination of Results and Scientific Collaboration

- **Training activities:** Creation of the University School of Innovative Management (EUGINOV) and proposition of a coordinated training program leading to university degrees. This school proposes an original and differentiated offer in the domain of management training, implementing the pedagogical option of work/study with professional management training through different syllabi in varied disciplines. The emergence of this school was accompanied by the 2000 creation of the IUP (Professionalized University Institute) Management of Teams and Quality (work/study program), a Masters degree in Management Engineering Consulting, a Masters degree in sales (work/study), and a Program of Certification (Certificate of Management Aptitude).

  ISEOR also developed the journal *Revue Sciences de Gestion—Management Sciences—Ciencias de gestión,* which, in order to guarantee its full international development, took its independence in 2001 from the *Collection Economies et Sociétés,* of which it was a part since its creation in 1978, under the auspices of the ISMEA (Paris), founded by world famous economist François Perroux, and is today edited by the ISEOR. Four editions per year, in addition to two special editions (one in English and one in Spanish) of unpublished articles since 2003.

  The editorial board is composed of 120 tenured university and graduate school professors in three distinct linguistic committees: French, English, and Spanish. Boards members come from Argentina, Belgium, Brazil, Canada, Denmark, France, Germany, Great Britain, Holland, Ireland, Mexico, Portugal, Spain, Switzerland,

United States and Venezuela. Editorial board members participate in the rigorous selection of articles proposed for publication.
- **Scientific collaboration:** ISEOR has created a partnership with the "Stratégie Grand-Sud," which networks 6 university research groups (Universities of Grenoble 2, Savoie, Montpellier 1, Aix-Marseille 2 and Toulon-Var), with the CERVEPAS (Sorbonne 3 Nouvelle), AIMS, IAS, Academy of Management (USA), IFSAM, UAM and Instituto Politécnico Nacional (México), HEC Paris and ILO (Geneva).

During this period (1998–2002) the ISEOR team also organized 14 major colloquiums.

Scientific and Academic Recognition

In November 2001, the Socio-Economic Theory of Organizations was recognized by the Academy of Moral and Political Sciences (*Institut de France*). Henri Savall and Véronique Zardet were awarded the Rossi Prize Medal for their joint work on the integration of social variables into business strategies. International recognition was also extended to Henri Savall and Marc Bonnet by the Academy of Management (USA) for their organization in Lyon of the first AOM Meeting beyond the American continent (March 2001) on consultancy theory, one of ISEOR's domains of expertise.

The Long-Term Scientific Program

In the framework of the fundamental theoretical hypothesis above, ISEOR's work has made it possible to create and perfect the following instruments of analysis:

- *Evaluation model* of organizational operation from the social and economic point of view, called the socio-economic balance sheet.
- *S.O.F. method* (Social, Organizational and Financial) of *dysfunction analysis.*
- *Experimental method of inquiry* according to which the validation of theoretical hypotheses is obtained through developing concepts and determining connections *inside the process of transforming* the organization as an economically finalized socio-technical system.

The work of the ISEOR team has continued to develop through the accumulation of elements consigned to its database from a wide diversity of organizations, in terms of their activity (industrial, commercial, banking, hospitals, local government, cultural enterprises, notary publics, chambers of commerce, liberal professions), legal status (private, public, para-public), their goals (profit and not-for-profit), size and geographical location. The multitude of analyses has enabled the creation of three typologies:

1. *A typology of organizational characteristics*, according to the sector of activity, relative to three principal evaluators derived from the basic theoretical model:

$$[S \rightleftarrows B] \rightarrow EP$$

   a) The nature of the $[S \rightleftarrows B]$ interaction;
   b) The level of hidden costs-performances;
   c) The level of economic performance.

2. *A typology of organizations* in the course of transformation, evaluated from a double point of view: a) medium- and long-term evolution of the enterprise's or organization's *strategic potential*; and b) short-term results of the *productivity-quality* couple.

3. *A typology of transformation processes* of organizations according to the evolution of such criteria as: a) professional qualification of the personnel, b) modes of organization (division of labor, functional responsibility and autonomy); c) CEO/top management styles and the role of the hierarchy; d) physical working conditions; and e) management frameworks (remuneration, communication and information systems).

Over the course of the following years, the research program became particularly oriented toward the priorities established by the General Planning Commission and the Ministry of Industry and Research, notably under the framework of the general theme "Technology and Work." Four themes were particularly developed along this axis:

1. The connection between *product quality* (goods and services), work organization, company structures and personnel qualifications. The program was part of the framework of priorities as defined by the Ministry of Industry.

2. The evolution of *qualification-training-technology*, in particular as applied to the problems of *industrial mastery* (transfer of technology).

3. The relationship between *hospital management and healthcare economy*. The application of socio-economic analysis in the context of experimentations in progress on "overall budget" and individual service budgets enabled in-depth knowledge of the "costs of production" of health, referring to the notion of hidden costs and perfecting decentralized management tools at the healthcare-unit level, in view of better mastering their costs. Experimental research was carried out by the ISEOR with the participation of the GIS "Economy of Healthcare" (National Scientific Research Center, Public Hospital Admin-

istrations of Lyon) and the Regional University Hospital Center of Saint Etienne.

4. The impact of socio-economic analysis (hidden costs-performances, qualitative and quantitative dysfunctions) on the *decision-making process* in organizations. The hypothesis to be validated in enterprises, administrations and nonprofit organizations was the following: *explicit knowledge* of information items such as dysfunctions and their financial impact is capable of influencing and even *modifying management decision*, which has been found to be associated to the ambisystem [perceived information system problematics].

The Period from 2003–2008

Scientific Policy

The research program during this period included three principal aspects: a) continuing in-depth development of the themes launched over the course of the previous four-year research program, b) launching several themes related to socio-economic management of quality and innovation, and c) developing international research cooperation actions.

- **Continuing in-depth study of permanent research themes:** ISEOR's overall scientific research program pursues the objective of constructing the socio-economic theory of organizations, which enables cross-sectional collaboration among the various disciplines of management and their synchronization in the profession of manager. This cross-sectional research includes breaking down analysis of interfaces between socio-economic management and each management science discipline. This program notably includes collaboration with university associations specialized in each domain: AIMS, AGRH, IAS, AFC, AFM, AIM, ADERSE, the Academy of Management and the American Accounting Association (USA), ACACIA (México), ACEDE (Spain), International Institute of Costs (a network of 11 national academic associations from Latinamerica, Spain, Portugal and France), EURAM, IFSAM, EGOS, as well as setting up a network of French and European universities on quality management (in collaboration with the University of Toulon and the University of Barcelona).
- **Socio-economic management of quality and innovation:** The challenge is shedding light on current organizational problematics based on innovative management research that integrates the management of quality and innovation. These research themes correspond to a social demand, expressed to the University notably by

the professional milieu. One could cite, in particular, the following themes, each one of which is the object of several doctoral theses supervised by the ISEOR team:

- **Transformation of public service organizations**, including: accreditation process management in hospitals, transforming the role of public service organizations, improving the effectiveness of local regional governments, and introducing quality problematics in public services
- **Transformation of liberal professions in the European context, in collaboration with their professional organizations**, including: certified public accountants, statutory auditors and notary publics.
- **Competitive challenges and dynamics of tetra-normalization:** Study of present developments in contradictory normalization systems which tend to complexify the strategic piloting of organizations.
- **Fight against discrimination**, including: management of underprivileged neighborhoods, management of frameworks to fight illiteracy, and positioning and managing work-placement enterprises.

Every year, the ISEOR organizes a colloquium to valorize research, dedicated to strategic change in various sectors and professions. This event also showcases enterprises and organizations in European, American, African and Asian countries, featuring the results of the ISEOR's socio-economic intervention. Such presentations at the annual colloquium enable validating the Institute's research findings.

Research

ISEOR has continued its long tradition of international collaboration, supervising researchers that become interveners in businesses in their native countries (34 different countries). Certain collaborations are the object of particular, in-depth efforts:

- **Doctoral program in cotutelle with the Universidad Autonoma Metropolitana de Mexico (UAM)**: Henri Savall, Véronique Zardet and Jeannette Rencoret
- **"Lafayette 2010" research program in the United States:** Comparative management analysis (European/American management); and research on the possible contributions of socio-economic management to American management (e.g., measurement of medium and long-term economic performance, measurement of dysfunction costs linked to the informal power of actors). The team includes Henri Savall, Véronique Zardet, Marc Bonnet, Michel Péron, Em-

manuel Beck, Vincent Cristallini, Laurent Cappelletti, François
Ecoto and Rickie Moore, professor at the Graduate School of Business, EM Lyon.

A consultant training program in English will be set up for the
first time in 2008 (3 days in June and 3 days in November).

More than 70 papers and articles have been presented in English at the Academy of Management from 1998 to 2007 and EGOS
conferences.

ISEOR has organized in partnership with the Academy of Management, 6 conferences in Lyon (France) from 2001 to 2007.

- **Competency transfer programs in Management Engineering**: This
program consists essentially in training intervener-researchers
associated with the ISEOR, who subsequently intervene in enterprises in different countries, in order to derive some information
on the modes of engineering transfer. This program is especially
concerned with the following countries: United States, Morocco,
Mexico, Belgium, Switzerland, Viet Nam and Germany.
- **Research program on international social norms** in collaboration
with the International Labor Office (ILO - Geneva): The objective
is to demonstrate hidden costs and performances, linked to the
degree of application of minimal social norms. The ISEOR team
includes Henri Savall, Véronique Zardet and Marc Bonnet.
- **Publications:** Overall, since 1980, there were 103 theses defended,
307 research reports, 136 articles, 494 communications and 58
books published. A full list of publications is available on ISEOR
website www.iseor.com

BOOKS BY ISEOR INTERVENER-RESEARCHERS

This section includes a selection of ISEOR's most significant books. The
complete and extensive list of all research work carried out since the beginning of the ISEOR, as well as the research reports themselves, are available upon request at: ISEOR/15 Chemin du Petit-Bois/69134 Ecully cedex,
France. [Telephone: + (33) 478–330–966. www.iseor.com].

Brignone, A., Lambert, J., Martinet, A-C., & Savall, H. (1978). *Encyclopédie de
l'économie: Le present en question* [Encyclopedia of economics: The present in
question]. Paris: Larousse.
Buono, A. F., & Savall, H. (2007). *Socio-Economic intervention in organizations: The intervener-researcher and the SEAM approach to organizational analysis.* Charlotte, NC:
Information Age Publishing.

Fernandez, M., & Savall, H., eds (2004). *El modelo des gestión socioeconómica en orga-nizaciones Mexicanas* [The socio-economic model in Mexican organizations], Mexico City: UAM.

Savall, H. (1974, 1975). *Enrichir le travail humain: l'évaluation économique.* [Job en-richment, an economic evaluation]. Paris: Dunod ; 4th edition 1989, Paris : Economica.

Savall, H. (1975). *Germán Bernácer: l'hétérodoxie en sciences économique* [G. Bernácer : Heterodoxy in economic sciences]. Paris: Dalloz (Great Economists Series).

Savall, H. (1979). *Reconstruire l'entreprise: Analyse socio-économique des conditions de travail* [Reconstructing the enterprise : Socio-economic analysis of working conditions]. Paris: Dunod.

Savall, H. (1981). *Work and people: An economic evaluation of job enrichment; preface by Ansoff,* New-York: Oxford University Press.

Savall, H., ed (2003). Socio-economic approach to management. *Journal of Organiza-tional change management.* Emerald.

Savall, H., & Zardet, V. (1987, 1990, 1995, 2003). *Maîtriser les coûts et les performan-ces caches: Le contrat d'activité périodiquement négociable* [Mastering hidden costs and performances: The periodically negotiable activity contract]. Paris: Eco-nomica.

Savall, H., & Zardet, V. (1992). *Le nouveau contrôle de gestion. Méthode des coûts-per-formances cachés* [New management control: The hidden cost-performance method]. Paris: Eyrolles.

Savall, H., & Zardet, V. (1995, 2005). *Ingénierie stratégique du Roseau* [Strategic engi-neering of the reed, flexible and rooted]. Paris: Economica.

Savall, H., & Zardet, V. (2004). *Recherche en sciences de gestion: Approche qualimétrique. Observer l'objet complexe* [Research in management sciences: The qualimetric approach: Observing the complex object]. Paris: Economica.

Savall, H., & Zardet, V. (2005). *Tétranormalisation: Défis et dynamiques* [Competitive challenges and dynamics of tetra-normalization]. Paris: Economica.

Savall, H., & Zardet, V., (eds.) (2007). *Evaluación del desempeño y gestión socioeconómica* [Performance evaluation and socio-economic management]. Mérida, Mexi-co: ISEOR.

Savall, H., Zardet, V., & Bonnet, M. (2000). *Releasing the untapped potential of enter-prises through socio-economic management.* Geneva: ILO.

REFERENCES

Buono, A. F., & Savall, H. (2007). *Socio-Economic Intervention in Organizations: The intervener-researcher and the SEAM approach to organizational analysis.* Charlotte, NC: Information Age Publishing.

Savall, H., & Zardet, V. (1995). *Ingénierie stratégique du roseau* [Strategic engineering of the reed, flexible and rooted]. Paris: Economica.

Weiller, J., & Carrier, B. (1994). *L'économie non-conformiste en France au 20ᵉ siècle* [Non-conformist economic in 20th Century France]. Paris: Presses Universitaires de France, Collection économie en liberté.

APPENDIX B

TABLE OF STUDIED
ENTERPRISES

Selected ISEOR's intervention-research sites: Examples of enterprises (from among 1,200 interventions)

Activity	Year	Total number of company employees	Number of employees involved in the action	Duration of intervention	Sales figure
1 Aluminum production		250	120	1 year	150 million francs
2 Magnet manufacturing		750	60	2 years	
3 Aluminum plaque treatment		260	70	1 year	
4 Chemicals: polychloride of vinyl		450	75	1 year	2 billion francs
5 Forge		230	95	3 years	90 million francs
6 Metallurgy sheet metal works	1977	350	350	5 years	150 million francs
7 Electrical parts		500	15	2 months	300 million francs
8 Manufacturing bottles forged in aluminum		170	10	2 months	64 million francs
9 Reactive metals		280	4	2 months	500 million francs
10 Uranium transformation		360	7	2 months	
11 Television tubes	1985	1,250	190	5 years	700 million francs
12 Household glassware	1981	750	150	2 years	50 million francs
13 Bank	1981	460	400	3 years	250 million francs
14 Not-for-profit clinic (medical services)	1980	3,350	60	1.5 years	500 million francs
15 Construction & management social housing	1989	350	350	2 years	140 million francs
16 Sales, installment and maintenance of telecommunication systems	1984	300	100	2 years	138 million francs
17 Health and welfare establishment		40	40	1 year	7 million francs
18 Orthopedic care establishment	1980	300	11	1 year	70 million francs
19 Hosiery	1987	130	90	2 year	25 million francs
20 Workclothes	1984	45	45	1 year	15 million francs
21 Production and sales of pastries	1991	1,200	1,200	1.5 years	1 billion francs
22 Production and sales optical glasses		109	43	1 year	53 million francs
23 Production and sales washing machines	1975	1,950	500	2 years	732 million francs
24 Credit for individuals		150	80	2 years	200 million francs

#	Enterprise	Year			Duration	Amount
25	National television corporation		1,200	200	1.5 years	1,877 million francs (budget)
26	Brickworks	1987	90	90	6 months	60 million francs
27	Shoe factory		110	110	1 year	17 million francs
28	Forge	1988	450	450	2 years	200 million francs
29	Management consultancy		130	30	6 months	42 million francs
30	Automobile and life insurance	1985	4,500	200	1.5 years	4 billion francs (premium)
31	University	1985	700	100	1.5 years	30 million francs
32	Municipal government	1988	2,500	500	3 years	648 million francs (revenue)
33	Municipal government (city council)	1988	11	50	9 months	1.4 million francs (revenue)
34	Cookie factory	1986	2,600	2,600	2.5 years	1.5 billion francs
35	Aircraft manufacturing		400	400	1 year	150 million francs
36	Supermarket distribution	1988	1,500	1,500	3 years	2 billion francs
37	Catering service	1989	150	150	6 months	43 million francs
38	Aerospace enterprise	1988	1,300	13	3 months	1.6 billion francs
39	Production of periodicals	1989	103	30	1 year	10 million francs
40	Agro-chemicals		370	40	1 year	78 billion francs
41	Training organism for local government employees	1990	40	20	10 months	16 million francs
42	Therapeutical work center		270	270	2 years	5 million francs
43	Foundry	1990	1,100	50	6 months	456 million francs
44	Shoe manufacturing		100	100	1 year	8 million francs
45	Courier and financial services to businesses	1990	270,000	26,000	4 years	66 billion francs
46	Mechanics	1989	15,000	7,000	4 years	6.8 billion francs
47	Luxury restaurants	1991	1,000	1,000	2 years	535 million francs
48	Post and Telecommunications Portugal		28,500	450	3 years	
49	Technical inspection of automobiles	1991	1,100	1,100	2 years	3 billion francs
50	Public establishment of industrial surveillance	1993	2,000	300 (one region)	1 year	53 million francs (regions)
51	Specialized coated fabrics	1995	105	105	9 months	100 million francs
52	SB group specialized in electricity and industrial computing	1995	220	146	3 months	

Every year new intervention-research is carried out in enterprises in new activity sectors, new countries and new types of organizations. For example:

- Shoe manufacturing enterprise
- Wire drawing plant
- Draw frame blending workshop
- Metallurgy enterprise
- Anodized aluminum manufacturing firm
- Hospitals
- Chemical factory
- Industrial woodworking
- Enameled metal manufacturing enterprise
- Construction work training center
- Savings and loan bank
- Certified public accountant office
- Large telecommunications enterprise
- Bookstore group
- Professional training and job promotion office of Morocco
- Notary public education
- Medical services
- University—Information systems and academic systems coordination
- University—Department of Human Sciences
- Public transport enterprise
- Social security organism
- Social housing center
- Industrial pastry enterprise
- Opera house
- Specialized steelworks enterprise
- Thermal insulation enterprise
- Audit and consultancy office
- Socio-educational foundation
- Fish processing and packaging firm
- Regional professional authorities
- Textile dying enterprise
- Surveillance company
- Belgian employment organism for occupational training and integration
- Mechanical studies and consultancy enterprise
- Rescue vehicle customizing and body shop
- National agency for the improvement of working conditions
- West African hospital establishment
- Urban community government of a major French city

RECOMMENDED READING

Adam, G., & Reynaud, J. D. (1978). *Conflits du travail et changement social* [Work conflict and social change]. Paris: Presse Universitaire de France.

AFC [French Accounting Association]. (1984). *Proceedings of the fifth AFC Congress,* Vol. 1 (April), Nice, France.

AFC-CESTA (1982). Assises pour le développement des sciences de l'organisation [Meeting for the development of organizational sciences]. *Proceeding of the AFC-CESTA colloquium,* 3 volumes (November), Paris: AFC-CESTA.

AFCET (1984). Développement des sciences et pratiques de l'organisation: Les outils de l'action collective [Development of organizational sciences and practices: The tools of collective action]. *Proceedings of the AFCET colloquium,* Paris: AFCET.

ANACT [National agency for improvement of working conditions]. (1979). *Le coût des conditions de travail* [The cost of working conditions]. Paris : ANACT.

Ansoff, H. I. (1976). *Stratégie du développement de l'entreprise: Analyse d'une politique de croissance et d'expansion* [Strategy of enterprise development: Analysis of growth and expansion policy]. Suresnes, France: Hommes et techniques.

Arrow, K. (1962). The economic implication of learning by doing. *Revue humanisme et entreprise, 29.*

Auray, J. P., Duru, G., Savall, H., & Zardet, V. (1985). La méthode socio économétrique: Contribution innovante à la gestion des entreprises [The socio-economic method: Innovative contribution to enterprise management]. *Revue humanisme et entreprise, N°* (January).

Avenier, M. J. (1984). *Pilotage d'entreprise et environnement complexe* [Enterprise piloting and complex environment]. Unpublished doctoral dissertation, University of Aix-Marseille.

De Backer, P. (1972). Négociation et conflits dans l'entreprise: Quelques indications d'application de la psychologie des conflits [Negotiation and conflict in the enterprise: Some indications of application of conflict psychology]. *Revue metra, 11* (1).

Bartoli, H. (1977). *Economie et création collective* [Economics and collective creation]. Paris: Economica.

Becker, G. (1965). Economics of discrimination: A theory of allocation of time. *Economic journal, 5.*

Berry, M. (1983). *Une technologie invisible? L'impact des instruments de gestion sur l'évolution des systèmes humains* [Invisible technology? The impact of management instruments on the evolution of human systems]. Paris: Ecole Polytechnique, Centre de recherche en gestion.

Berry, M. (1985). *Logique de la connaissance et logique de l'action* [Logic of knowledge and logic of action]. Paris : Ecole Polytechnique, Centre de recherche en gestion.

Bienaymé, A. (1971). *La croissance des entreprises* [The growth of enterprises] (2nd edition 1973), 2 volumes. Paris: Bordas.

Bienaymé, A. (1980). *Stratégies de l'entreprise compétitive* [Strategies of the competitive enterprise], *Institut de l'Entreprise Series*. Paris: Masson.

Boje, D., & Rosile, G. A. (2003). Comparison of socio-economic and other transorganizational development methods. *Journal of organizational change management, 16* (1).

Brignone, A., Lambert, J., Martinet, A., & Savall, H. (1978). *Encyclopédie de l'économie: Le présent en question* [Encyclopedia of economics: The present in question]. Paris: Larousse.

Buono, A. F. (2003). SEAM-less post-merger integration strategies: A cause for concern. *Journal of organizational change management, 16* (1).

Buono, A. F., & Savall, H. (Eds.) (2007). *Socio-Economic Intervention in Organizations: The Intervener-Researcher and the SEAM Approach to Organizational Analysis.* Charlotte, NC: Information Age Publishing.

Capet, M., & Total-Jacquot, C. (année). *Comptabilité, diagnostic et décision* [Accounting, diagnostic and decision]. Paris: Presse Universitaire de France.

Causse, G. (année). Vers une théorie organisationnelle de la gestion de la trésorerie [Toward an organizational theory of treasury management]. *Cahiers d'étude et de recherches, 82* (25). Paris: Groupe ESCP.

Cazamian, P. (1977). *Leçons d'ergonomie industrielle: Une approche globale* [Lessons of industrial ergonomics: A holistic approach]. Paris: Cujas.

CEREQ [Center for study and research on qualifications]. (1976). L'organisation du travail et ses formes nouvelles [Work organization and its new forms]. *The CEREQ library series, 10.*

CFDT [French democratic work confederation]. (1977). *Les dégâts du progrès: Les travailleurs techniques face au changement* [The casualties of progress: Technical works faced with change]. Paris: Seuil.

CFDT [French democratic work confederation]. (1978). *Analyse des conditions de travail* [Analysis of working conditions]. Paris: Montholon-Services.

CGC [General management confederation] (1976). Conditions de travail: Pour des accords globaux [Working conditions: For an overall agreement]. *Le creuset, N° 6.*

CGC [General management confederation] (1974). Les conditions du travail du personnel d'encadrement [Working conditions of management personnel] *Le creuset, N° 5* (May), special issue.

CGT [General work confederation] (1979). Des manufactures à la crise du taylorisme [From manufactories to the crisis of Taylor-style work organization]. *La voix du people, 11* (78).

Charnes, C., Cooper, G., & Kuznetsky, P. (1973). Measuring, monitoring and modeling quality of life. *Management science, 19* (10).

Cherns, A. B. (1973). Research: Can behavioral scientists help managers improve their organizations. *Organizational dynamics, N° 4.*

Chevalier, A. (1976). *Le bilan social de l'entreprise* [Social evaluation of the enterprise]. Paris: Masson.

CNPF [French national confederation of chief executives]. (1977). Patronat: Assises nationales [Chief executives: National meeting]. *CNPF, N° 11,* special issue.

Crozier, M. (1963). *Le phénomène bureaucratique: Essai sur les tendances bureaucratiques des systèmes d'organisations modernes et sur leurs relations en France avec le système social et culturel* [The bureaucratic phenomenon: Essay on the bureaucratic tendencies of modern systems of organization and their relationships in France with the social and cultural system]. Paris: Seuil.

Crozier, M. (1979). *On ne change pas la société par décret* [You don't change society by decree]. Paris: Seuil.

Cyert, R. M., & March, J. G. (1970). *Processus de décision dans l'entreprise* [Decision making process in enterprises]. Paris: Dunod.

Davis, L. E. (1966). Conception du poste de travail et productivité (Reprinted from *Personnel,* 1957). *L'étude du travail, N° 178.*

Davis L. E., & Cherns, A. B. (1975). *The quality of working life,* vol. 1: *Problems, prospects and the state of the art,* vol. 2: *Cases and commentary.* New York: Macmillan.

Degot, V., Girin, J., & Midler, C. (1982). *Chroniques muxiennes: L'utopie au service des utilisateurs de bureautique* [The Muxian chronicles: Utopia at the service of office automation users]. Paris: Editions Entente.

Delors, J. (1971). *Les indicateurs sociaux* [Social indicators] (preface by B. de Jouvenel). Paris: Sedeis.

Delors, J. (1975). *Changer* [Change]. Paris: Stock.

De Montmollin, M. (1984). *L'intelligence de la tâche: Eléments d'ergonomie cognitive* [Task intelligence: Elements of cognitive ergonomics]. Bern, Switzerland: Peter Lang.

Dubreuil, H. (1935). *A chacun sa chance: L'organisation du travail fondée sur la liberté* [Equal opportunity: Work organization based on liberty] (2nd edition 1939). Paris: Grasset.

Dubreuil, H. (1963). *Promotion* [Promotion] (Preface by L. Armand). Paris: Editions de l'Entreprise Moderne.

Dupuy, Y. (1984). Réflexions sur la modélisation des processus organisationnels liés à l'informatisation [Thoughts on modelizing the organizational processes related to computerization]. *Revue sciences de gestion* (Economies et sociétés series), N° *4.*

Eicher, J. C., & Levy-Garboua, L. (1979). *Economique de l'éducation* [Economics of education]. Paris: Economica.

Emery, F. E. (1969). *Systems thinking.* Harmondsworth, Middlesex: Penguin modern management reading.

Fayol, H. (1970). *Administration industrielle et générale* [General and industrial administration]. Paris: Dunod.

Freyssenet, M. (1974). *Le processus de déqualification-surqualification de la force de travail: Eléments pour une problématique de l'évolution des rapports sociaux* [The workforce underqualification-overqualification process: Elements for the problematics of social relationship evolution]. Paris: Centre de Sociologie Urbaine.

Friedmann, G. (1956). *Le travail en miettes* [Fragmented work]. Paris: Gallimard.

Friedmann, G. (1974). Comme un brin de paille [Like a hay straw]. *Le Monde,* March 21–25.

Galbraith, J. K. (1968). *Le nouvel état industriel* [The new industrial state]. Paris: Gallimard.

Gelinier, O. (1979). *Stratégie sociale de l'entreprise* [The enterprise's social strategy]. Paris: Hommes et techniques.

Girin, J. (1982). Langage en actes et organisations [Language in action and organizations]. *Revue sciences de gestion, 3* (December), *(Economies et sociétés series).*

Godet, M. (1977). *Crise de la prévision: Essor de la prospective* [The decline of forecasting: The rise of long-term strategy]. Paris: Presse universitaire de France.

Grote, R. C. (1972). Implementing job enrichment. *California management review, vol. 15* (1).

Hatchuel, A., & Molet, H. (1983). *Recherche opérationnelle et théorie des organisations: L'utilisation des modèles rationnels dans la compréhension et la transformation des mécanismes organisationnels* [Operational research and organizational theory: The utilization of rational models in understanding and transforming organizational mechanisms]. Unpublished doctoral dissertation in Management science engineering. Paris: Ecole Nationale Supérieure des Mines de Paris.

Herrick, N. (1975). *La qualité du travail et ses résultats: Gains de productivité potentiels* [The quality of work and its results: Potential gains in productivity]. Columbus, OH: Academy for Contemporary Problems.

Herzberg, F. (1971). *Le travail et la nature de l'homme* [Originally published in 1966, *Work and the nature of man,* Cleveland, OH: World publishing]. Paris: Entreprise moderne d'édition.

Institut de l'Entreprise [Institute of the Enterprise] (1978). *Pour une nouvelle approche de l'emploi* [For a new approach to employment]. Paris: Entreprise moderne d'édition.

Joffre, P., & Koenig, G. (1985). *Stratégie d'entreprise - Antimanuel* [Enterprise strategy - Antimanual]. Paris: Economica.

Johansen, L. (1979). The bargaining society and the inefficiency of bargaining. *Kyklos, 32* (3).

Kolb, D. (1974). On management and the learning process. *Organizational psychology,* (March-April).

Laville, A. (1976). *L'ergonomie* [Ergonomics]. Paris: Presse Universitaire de France.

Lebraty, J. (1974). Evolution de la théorie de l'entreprise: Sa signification, ses implications [Evolution of business theory: Its significance, its implications]. *Revue Economique,* (January).

Lebraty, J. (1976). Gestion des ressources humaines dans l'entreprise [Human resource management in the enterprise]. *Revue de l'IAE de Nice,* (January).

Lebraty, J. (1984). *Comptabilité et décision* [Accounting and decision-making]. *Cahiers de l'IAE de Nice, 16* (April).

Le Moigne, J. L. (1979). Informer la décision ou décider de l'information [Informing decision-making or deciding about information]. *Revue sciences de gestion,* N° 1 (April-June), *(Economies et sociétés series).*

Le Moigne, J. L. (1977). *La théorie du système général: Théorie de la modélisation* [The theory of the general system: Theory of modelization]. Paris: Presses Universitaires de France.

Leplat, J., & Cuny, X. (1977). *Introduction à la psychologie du travail* [Introduction to work psychology]. Paris: Presses Universitaires de France.

Lesca, H. (1982). *Structure et système d'information: Facteurs de compétitivité de l'entreprise* [Structure and information system: Factors of business competitiveness]. Paris: Masson.

Lesourne, J. (1974). La pensée de Crozier [The theory of systems and economic theory]. *L'Expansion.* Paris: Seuil.

Lesourne, J. (1976). *Le système du destin* [The system of destiny]. Paris: Dalloz.

Lesourne, J. (1978). La théorie des systèmes et la théorie économique [The theory of systems and economic theory]. *Economie appliqué, 3–4.*

Likert, R. (1967). *The human organization: Its Management and value.* New York: McGraw-Hill.

Linhart, R. (1978). *L'établi* [The workbench]. Paris: Editions de Minuit.

Lussato, B. (1972). *Introduction critique aux théories d'organisation* [Critical introduction to organizational theories] (2nd edition 1977). Paris: Dunod.

Mahaux, R. (1974). *Le gaspillage du capital humain dans l'entreprise: Une enquête auprès de mille deux cents cadres et trois cents dirigeants* [Wasting human capital in enterprises: Inquiry conducted with one thousand two hundred managers and three hundred executives]. Verviers, France: Editons Marabout - Monde contemporain.

Malm, T., Pigors, P., & Myers, A. (1977). *La gestion des ressources humains: Choix de textes* [Human resource management: Selected reading] (Translated from the American, originally published in 1964). Paris: Hommes et techniques.

March, J. G., & Simon, H. A. (1974). *Les organisations* [Organizations]. Paris: Dunod.

Marchesnay, M., & Morvan, Y. (1979). *Economie de la firme et de l'industrie* [Economy of firms and industries]. Paris: Sirey.

Melese, J. (1979). *Approche systémique des organisations* [Systemic approach to organizations]. Paris: Hommes et techniques.

Mintzberg, H. (1982). *Structure et dynamique des organisations* [Structure and dynamics of organizations]. Paris: Editions d'organisation.

Moisdon, J. C. (1977). Théorie de la décision en quête d'une pratique [Decision theory in search of practical application]. *Annales des Mines de Paris,* (January).

Moisdon, J. C., & Hatchuel, A. (1984). Théorie de la décision et pratiques organi-
sationnelles: Le cas des investissements pétroliers [Decision theory and organizational practices: The case of petroleum investments]. *Revue sciences de
gestion*, 4 (January), (*Economies et sociétés series*).

Moscarola, J. (1980). *La contribution des travaux empiriques allemands à la théorie du
processus de décision dans les organisations* [The contribution of German empi-
rical research work to decision-process theory in organizations]. University
Dauphine Paris 9: LAMSADE research report, 10.

Myers, M. S. (1978). *Gestion participative et enrichissement des tâches à la Texas Instruments* [Participative management and job enrichment at Texas Instruments].
Paris: Dalloz.

OCDE [Organization for Economic Cooperation and Development]. (1977). *Vers
une politique sociale intégrée au Japon* [Towards an integrated social policy in
Japan]. Paris: OCED.

Ordre des Experts-Comptables et Comptables Agrées [Order of certified public
accountants and affiliated accountants] (1984). *Comptabilité et prospective: Ré-
ponses comptables aux nouveaux besoins d'information* [Accounting and long-term
strategic planning: Accounting responses to new information needs]. Proceedings of the 39th OECCA Conference in Nice, France, 2 volumes.

Perroux, F. (1973). *Pouvoir et économie* [Power and economy], 2nd edition 1977.
Paris: Dunod.

Perroux, F. (1974). L'entreprise, l'équilibre rénové et les coûts «cachées» [The
enterprise, renewed equilibrium and «hidden» costs] preface to H. Savall
(1979), *Reconstruire l'entreprise* [Reconstructing the enterprise]. Paris: Dunod.

Perroux, F. (1974). Economie de la ressource humaine [Economy of the human
resource]. *Revue mondes en développement, 7.*

Perroux, F. (1975). *Unités actives et mathématiques nouvelles: Révision de la théorie de
l'équilibre économique général* [Active units and new mathematics: Revision of
the general economic equilibrium theory]. Paris: Dunod.

Perroux, F. (1979). La notion de dépense stratégique et l'unité active [The notion
of strategic expenditure and the active unit]. *Cahiers de l'AFEDE*, (April), *special issue.*

Piaget, J. (1975). *L'équilibration de structures cognitives: Problème central du développement*
[Balancing cognitive structures: Central problem of development]. Paris:
Presses universitaires de France.

Pras, B. (1981). Approche qualitative ou approche quantitative? [Qualitative approach or quantitative approach?]. *Revue science de gestion*, 2 (October-December), pp. 1975–1978.

Reinberg, A. (1974). *Des rythmes biologiques à la chronobiologie* [From biological
rhythms to chronobiology]. Paris: Gauthier-Villars.

Reix, R. (1985). *Conception de système d'information ou conception d'organisation* [In-
formation systems design or organizational design]. Research report IAE of
Montpellier: Centre de recherche en gestion des organisations.

Rémond, R. (1979). *La règle et le consentement: Gouverner une société* [Rules and consent:
Governing a firm]. Paris: Fayard.

Riveline, C. (1985). Essai sur le dur et le mou [Essay on tough and soft]. *La jaune et la rouge, 406* (June-July).

Roustang, G., Guelaud, F., Beauchesne, M. N., & Gautrat, J. (1975). *Pour une analyse des conditions du travail ouvrier dans l'entreprise* [For the analysis of working conditions of company workers] (preface by Y. Delamotte). Paris: Armand Colin.

Roy, R. (1983). *La décision: Ses disciplines, ses acteurs* [The decision: Its discipline, its actors], proceedings of the Cerisy Colloquium. Lyon, France: Presses Universitaires de Lyon.

Sainsaulieu, R. (1977). *L'identité au travail: Les effets culturels de l'organisation* [Work identity: The cultural effects of the organization]. Paris: Presses de la fondation nationale de sciences politiques.

Salzman, C. (1982). Coûts et efficacité des systèmes d'information [Cost and effectiveness of information systems]. *Revue informatique et gestion, 136* (October).

Savall, H., & Martinet, A. (1978). Dysfonctionnements, coûts et performances cachés dans l'entreprise [Hidden dysfunctions, costs and performances in the enterprise]. *Revue d'économie industrielle, 5*

Savall, H., Zardet, V., Bonnet, M. & Peron, M. (2008, in press). Implicit criteria for quality in qualitative management research. *Organizational Research Methods, Academy of Management*. Thousand Oaks, CA: Sage Publications.

Sfez, L. (1973). *Critique de la décision* [Critical analysis of decision-making] (2nd edition 1976). Paris: Presses de la fondation nationale de sciences politiques.

Simon, H. A. (1974). *La science des systèmes: Sciences de l'artificiel* [French translation of *The sciences of the artificial*]. Paris: Edition de l'épi.

Sperandio, J.C. (1984). *L'ergonomie du travail mental* [The ergonomics of mental work]. Paris: Masson.

Tabatoni, P., & Jarniou, P. (1975). *Les systèmes de gestion: Politiques et structures* [Systems of management: Policies and structures]. Paris: Presses universitaires de France.

Taylor, F. W. (1911). *Scientific management*. New York: Harpers and Brothers.

Teller, R. (1984). Evolution et insuffisance des analyses "profit-coût-volume" pour le contrôle de gestion [Evolution and inadequacy of "profit-cost-volume" analysis for management control]. *Revue sciences de gestion, 5, Economies et sociétés* series, pp 293–324.

Tézenas du Moncel, H. (1973). *Les performances sociales des organisations* [Social performances of organizations]. Doctoral dissertation in economic sciences. Paris: University Dauphine.

Thépot, J. (coord.) (1998). *Gestion et théorie des jeux: L'interaction stratégique dans la décision* [Management and game theory: Strategic interaction during decision-making], FNEGE series. Paris: Vuibert.

Vaté, M. (1976). *Le temps de la décision* [Decision-time]. Lyon, France: Presses Universitaires Lyonnaises.

Watzlawick, P., Bea Vin, J. H., & Jackson, D. D. (1972). *Une logique de la communication* [Translation from the American, originally published in 1967]. Paris: Seuil.

Weiss, D. (1978). *La démocratie industrielle: Co-gestion ou contrôle ouvrier. Expériences et projets* [Industrial democracy: Co-management or worker control. Experiments and projects] Paris: Editions d'organisation.

Weiss, D. (1979). *Politique, partis et syndicats dans l'entreprise* [Politics, political parties and unions in the enterprise]. Paris: Editions d'organisation.

Wisner, A., & Laville, A. (1974). Contenu des tâches et charge de travail [Work content and workload]. *Sociologie du travail,* (October-December).

Wolfelsperger, A. (1973). La détermination des conditions de travail dans l'entreprise [Determining working conditions in the enterprise]. *Revue d'économie politique,* (March-April).

ABOUT THE AUTHORS

Anthony F. Buono, series editor, has a joint appointment as Professor of Management and Sociology at Bentley College, and is Coordinator of the Bentley Alliance for Ethics and Social Responsibility. He holds a Ph.D. with a concentration in Industrial and Organizational Sociology from Boston College. His current research and consulting interests focus on the management-consulting industry, organizational change, and interorganizational alliances, with an emphasis on mergers, acquisitions, strategic partnerships, and firm-stakeholder relationships.

Henri Savall is a Professor at the Institut d'Administration des Entreprises, University Jean Moulin Lyon 3, where he is the Director of the Centre EU-GINOV (Ecole Universitaire de Gestion Innovante) and of the Socio-Economic Management Master's program. He is the Founder and Director of the ISEOR Research Center. He holds a Ph. D. in Economic Sciences and in Management Sciences from the University of Paris. His current research interests are socio-economic theory, strategic management, qualimetric methodology (hybrid of qualitative and quantitative approaches) and tetra-normalization new program. He received the famous Rossi Award from the Academy of Moral and Political Sciences (*Institut de France*) for his work on the integration of social variables into business strategy.

Véronique Zardet is a Professor at the Institut d'Administration des Entreprises, University Jean Moulin Lyon 3 and Co-Director of the ISEOR Research Center. She heads the Research in Socio-Economic Management Master's program. She holds a Ph. D. in Management Sciences from the University of Lyon. Her research is centered on the conduct of strategic

Mastering Hidden Costs and Socio-Economic Performance, pages 335–336
Copyright © 2008 by Information Age Publishing
All rights of reproduction in any form reserved.

change and the improvement of socio-economic performance in private enterprises and public services. She received the famous Rossi Award from the Academy of Moral and Political Sciences (*Institut de France*) for her work on the integration of social variables into business strategy.

INDEX

A

Absenteeism
    as a hidden cost indicator, xxi
    hidden costs evaluation examples,
        43–50
Accounting information systems,
        inadequate measuring tools for
        hidden costs, 2–3
Activity group (business departments)
        logic/behavior type in enter-
        prises, xxi, 13
Affinity group logic/behavior type in
        enterprises, xxi, 14
Assessment, 77–78
Attitude, vs. behavior, 13
Axes of socio-economic intervention,
        94, 97f
    policy axis, 96, 98
    process axis, 95
    tools axis, 95–96

B

Behavior types in enterprises, xxi,
        13–14
    and boundary with structure, 14–16

evolution into structures/transfor-
        mation cycle, 15–16
    underlying factors, 14
    vs. attitude, 13
Behavioral algorithms, 15
Behavioralist current, 8
Business departments. *See* Activity
        group (business departments)
        logic/behavior type in enter-
        prises

C

Categorical (socio-professional) logic/
        behavior type in enterprises, xxi,
        13–14
Change management issues, 75–77
    assessment, 77–78
    See also Socio-economic manage-
        ment tools
Chronobiology, 25, 295
Collaborative-training by clusters, 114,
        115t
Collective (organization as a whole)
        logic/behavior type in enter-
        prises, xxi, 14

Mastering Hidden Costs and Socio-Economic Performance, pages 337–346
Copyright © 2008 by Information Age Publishing
All rights of reproduction in any form reserved.   **337**

LaVergne, TN USA
15 December 2010

208845LV00001B/85/P